# A PASSION
# FOR PURPOSE

# A PASSION
# FOR PURPOSE

KIMBERLY SOWELL • EDNA ELLISON • JOY BROWN
TRICIA SCRIBNER • MARIE ALSTON

NEW HOPE
PUBLISHERS
Birmingham, Alabama

## ❀ *About the Authors* ❀

Kimberly Sowell, Edna Ellison, Joy Brown, Tricia Scribner, and Marie Alston are frequently invited to host women's retreats and conferences. While each has an individual ministry, their combined purpose is to share a message of wisdom seasoned with humor, boldness with mercy, and truth with joy. These women meet together regularly to relate the new and exciting ways God is working in their lives and to pray. *A Passion for Purpose* is a product of their praying and sharing times and their desire to encourage women to live a life inspired by the glory of God. Each author has published individual works; however, they collaborated to publish the devotional *A Month of Miracles* (New Hope Publishers, 2008).

New Hope® Publishers
P. O. Box 12065
Birmingham, AL 35202–2065
www.newhopepublishers.com
New Hope Publishers is a division of WMU®.
Cover design: Left Coast Design, www.lcoast.com

Library of Congress Cataloging-in-Publication Data

A passion for purpose : 365 daily devotions for missional living / Kimberly Sowell ... [et al.].
    p. cm.
  ISBN 978-1-59669-242-8 (sc)
  1. Devotional calendars.  I. Sowell, Kimberly.
  BV4810.P38 2009
  242'.2--dc22

                    2009029744

ISBN–10: 1-59669-242-1
ISBN–13: 978-1-59669-242-8

N094137 • 1109 • 6M1

# ❀ *Dedication* ❀

Kimberly Sowell—To my precious babies, Julia, Jay, and John Mark: every day we are learning together to walk in the Lord as a family. Your precious ways and love for Jesus make it special to be a part of this missional family. I love you! It is my joy to watch you grow into the mighty men and the dynamic woman of God that He has created you to be.

Edna Ellison—To Snow Ellison; Jack, Wendy, and Blakely Ellison; and Patsy and Tim Farmer: a family of dedicated, missions-hearted Christians.

Joy Brown—I dedicate this book to our two grandbabies, Ty (Thomas Wesley Howard IV) and Mazi Grace Howard. God has opened my heart to a new understanding of love through them.

Tricia Scribner—To our precious children, all grown up: Neli, Sara and son-in-law Andrew, and Emily:

You each know the Lord and have become missional believers. Neli, what a missions field in your home with Noah, May, and Nathan. Sara and Andrew; I love your passion for ministering in the Dominican Republic. Emily, Wow. We share a passion for Africa, and you have already traveled on two missions trips to Senegal. I can't wait to see what adventure the Lord will call us to next!

Marie Alston—To my earthly God-sent angels—my children . . . Jennifer, Emanuel, Joshua, and Elizabeth "Liz" Alston. May you always put God first in your life and seek His face, just as Matthew 6:33 states: *"But seek ye first the kingdom of God, and his righteousness; and all these things shall be added unto you"* (KJV); and 2 Timothy 2:15: *Study to show thyself approved unto God, a workman that needeth not to be ashamed, rightly dividing the word of truth* (KJV).

# ❀ *Acknowledgments* ❀

God has enriched our journeys with godly people who have taught us to walk in the ways of our Lord. We acknowledge with grateful hearts these special individuals who have been God's instruments, helping to set our hearts to the rhythm of God's mission.

Kimberly Sowell:

Mama and Dad, I love you. I could never thank you enough for the selfless way you have poured yourself into my life. From my early days of childhood, teaching me to be thankful, to share, to do my very best, and never to be afraid to try new adventures, you placed all of these and so many other life principles into an unshakable framework that is Jesus Christ our Lord. For time spent on your knees laboring in prayer over me, I will forever be grateful. Dad, you have taught me a lifetime of truth about leadership, and about upholding the truth of God's Word. Mama, your compassionate heart for others, your selfless attitude in all things, and your stalwart commitment to holiness have inspired me to be more like Jesus. Thank you.

Kevin, you are such an incredible husband, and I love you. As you and I have grown in the Lord together over the years, I thank you for inspiring me to walk through every door of missional growth God has placed before me, and for being the loving and equipping leader in my life who has allowed me to fulfill God's call to missional living. Thank you for your many sacrifices as we serve the Lord together.

Edna Ellison:

How grateful I am to spiritual mentors who taught me the importance of an evangelistic spirit and a missions heart for every Christian: Rosalyn Martin, Sarah Cason, Helen Dean, Alice Corley, Ida King, and other godly women at First Baptist Church, Clinton, South Carolina.

I also want to thank Joy and Wayne Brown for their long hours of extra work on organizing these devotionals. I am especially grateful to God for Lynn Millwood, who spent untold hours collating and editing this manuscript. We also thank the staff at New Hope Publishers for all their hard work: Andrea Mullins, publisher; Joyce Dinkins, managing editor; Randy Bishop, editor; Kathryne Solomon, copy editor; Sherry Hunt and Bruce Watford, graphic designers; Jonathan Howe, marketing manager; Ashley Stephens, publicity and advertising specialist; and Kathy Caltabelotta, administrative assistant.

Joy Brown:

I thank my father, James Clary, deceased in 2001, who instilled missional living in me both by what he taught and lived, and my mother, Mary Clary, who continues to be my role model of a missions-hearted Proverbs 31 woman.

I thank my precious husband, Wayne, for being an everyday example of a missional heart that beats to spread the gospel to the ends of the earth. I thank our daughters, Meri Beth and Molly, and their husbands, Thomas and Christman, who continually bless me through the way they love and serve others.

Tricia Scribner:

Mama and Daddy, my whole life you showed me what it means to love Jesus by sharing Him with other folks. Daddy, in your "milkshake ministry" you made milkshakes for the shut-ins to nourish and love on them. Mama, as teens we teased you when you made a cake, saying, "Who is sick this time?" because you loved people in such practical ways. You both also took me to GA and told me at age 12 when I walked the aisle to surrender my life to the Lord in vocational mission service—probably in Africa—that you would support me wherever the Lord called me. I now know how hard it must have been for you to say those words.

Randy, through your hard work and love for me, you have made possible more than 20 missions trips for us as a couple or individually over the past 33 years. Without you, my passion for carrying the gospel to the ends of the earth would have been just a pipe dream. While life is sometimes tough, with you it is never boring! I love you.

Marie Alston:

To my parents who have already completed their journey here on earth, who taught me at an earlier age to love God and His people, and who showed by example to read and study God's Word. Their warm, "open-door hospitality" attitude to all they encountered was truly a blessing in my life. They taught my seven sisters and me that everybody is somebody, especially in God's eyes.

# ❀ Foreword ❀

Every woman is on a journey; a few along the way discover the passion of living for God's purpose. They are transformed from ordinary women to exceptional women, crafted by God Himself to see His divine purpose in every aspect of their lives. They awaken each day ready to discover and live the truths of God's plan as He reveals it to them. I believe that you are one of these women, unwilling to settle for anything less than a passionate commitment to God's plan for you.

Edna, Kimberly, Tricia, Joy, and Marie are five women you need to know. Whether you find them at home, in their workplaces, at their churches, in the community, or somewhere in the world where they are serving, you will discover that the stories they tell in *A Passion for Purpose* are only a few examples of the overflowing abundant lives they each are living.

Of course, these aren't ordinary women. They are gifted and sought-after speakers. And they are authors of many books. They are singers and comedians. On the other hand, they are mothers, grandmothers, wives, widows, working women, sisters, and friends, just like you and me. They have overcome adversity and they have faced loss. Regardless of all of this, they are exceptional for one reason. They made their decisions to live passionately for God's purpose long ago, and their decisions shaped who they are today and what they have done with the lives they have lived.

You have 365 days ahead of you in this book to discover for yourself what it means to be passionate for a purpose beyond yourself. You'll explore spirituality, Scripture, worldview, relationships, communication, ministry, and leadership in light of God's purposes. Your hunger for a passionate spirituality will increase as you draw close to God and choose to obey His commands. Scripture will come alive with meaning as you see God's purposes written on every page. God's love for the world will become your love. Relationships will be more precious as you respond to God's requests—that you risk leaving the comfortable to receive God's blessings. You'll overflow with the good news of Jesus, and discover gifts for service beyond your imagining. And above all else, your passion for God's purpose will have immeasurable influence on those whose lives you touch each day.

*"God can do anything, you know—far more than you could ever imagine or guess or request in your wildest dreams! He does it not by pushing us around but by working within us, his Spirit deeply and gently within us" (Ephesians 3:20* The Message*).*

Dr. Andrea Mullins

# ❀ Using *A Passion for Purpose* ❀

We pray you will use this devotional to experience a deep relationship with God—and to carry out His mission for your life. These pages encourage you weekly to reflect on seven aspects for passionate, missional living:

- SPIRITUALITY
- SCRIPTURE STUDY
- WORLDVIEW
- RELATIONSHIPS
- COMMUNICATION
- MINISTRY
- LEADERSHIP

Touching on one aspect each day, a devotional Scripture, story, prayer prompt, and more help to inspire you to live fully and to follow God's will for your life.

We pray these daily times enrich you, lead you ever closer in relationship with the Lord Jesus Christ, and overflow into God's world.

This book can be helpful for group fellowship sessions too. Here is an easy guide for using this book with others:

➤ **Pray.** Starting each session with prayer opens hearts to truth from God's Word.

➤ **Discuss daily quiet times.** Group members can describe both the joys and challenges they experienced in the previous week(s) through consistent quiet time with the Lord.

➤ **Review Scripture memory verses.** Ask members each to select, memorize, and be prepared to quote a verse memorized from a devotional choice, and to tell why they selected their verses.

➤ **Guide discussion of previous week devotionals.** Ask group members to review the devotionals from the previous week(s). Some suggested questions:

1. What had the greatest impact on you?
2. What new truth did you learn or find confirmed in your heart?
3. Is there an illustration you want to remember and share?
4. Is there a promise or a truth that comforts and encourages you?
5. Is there wisdom—even a correction offered—that is leading to a change in an action or attitude?
6. Discuss how the devotionals affected you in one (or more) of the following areas of missional living:
   a. Missional Spirituality: becoming more like Christ, to meet others' needs, rather than living for self
   b. Missional Scripture Study: seeing God's mission to humanity
   c. Missional Worldview: thinking and living out the biblical view of life and the world
   d. Missional Relationships: building relationships that cross barriers to love and reach people for Christ
   e. Missional Communication: explaining and confidently proclaiming the truth of salvation through Jesus Christ
   f. Missional Ministry: using personal spiritual gifts to serve Christ and others, including the church and the lost
   g. Missional Leadership: seeking to influence others toward God and His purposes.

➤ **Close in prayer.** Pray with and for group members to follow God's leading.

# ❀ *Little Orange Puppies* ❀

*Be thankful to Him, and bless His name* (Psalm 100:4 NKJV).

"Remember, Mama, I want a new Barbie and a Barbie car for my birthday." I tailed my mother around the house, pestering her about what I just had to have for my seventh birthday. Growing up, we received presents on our birthdays and at Christmas, and rarely in between; therefore, I wanted to be clear about what I wanted for my birthday! True, I already had several Barbies, but every little girl knows that there's no such thing as too many Barbies, and furthermore, my Barbies were tired of hopping into Kleenex boxes and pretending they were convertibles!

My mother was usually patient, but on this particular morning, I recall she offered a "you'll-be-thankful-for-what-you-get" comment and sent me away. Feeling mischievous, I then snooped around my parents' closet for my gift, and found a brown paper bag. The contents were two children's books and a stuffed animal, an orange puppy dog. No Barbie, and no motorized vehicles for rich and beautiful ten-inched people.

My first reaction was deep disappointment. *Gifts twice a year, and I'm getting an orange puppy?!* But then I began to think about my mother. I wanted a Barbie, but not at the expense of my mother's feelings. I walked straight into the den and said, "Mama, I've changed my mind. What I really want for my birthday are some books and an orange puppy." (Side note: my mother is a genius; somehow she figured out I had sneaked a peek into the bag!)

We often walk around with a big wish list of what we feel we must have in order to be satisfied. Instead, what a delightful act of worship it would be if we were to look carefully at what God has given us—His gifts for today as well as His assurances for all of eternity—and then go promptly to Him to announce with a truthful heart, "God, what I really want is what You've selected for me. You pick out the best gifts– thank You with all of my heart!" Consider every gift God has hand-picked just for you, and give Him thanks.

Father, I want to exchange all of my selfish dissatisfaction
for a heart of gratitude. Help me to see Your blessings in my life. Amen.

# ❀ More About Jesus ❀

*I want to know Christ and the power of his resurrection*
(Philippians 3:10).

A woman at a Christian conference carried an unusual Bible covered with a quilted jacket with wild ruffles. I asked, "What a creative Bible! Do you enjoy reading it?"

She smiled. "I love reading this book. I love Jesus." She said. Then she paused, looking away. "But I haven't picked it up since last summer."

"Nine months ago? That's a long time."

"Yes. I'm pretty busy...."

She and I talked a long time about children, husbands, recipes for quick meals. Changing the subject, she said, "You have to actually read the Bible, I guess, to get any good out of it."

"Yes," I said, looking into her tender brown eyes.

In a few moments we entered the church sanctuary, where a worship leader led us in a song:

More about Jesus I would know,

More of His grace to others show;

More of His saving fullness see,

More of His love who died for me." ❃ *Baptist Hymnal, 1991 edition.*

"I want more," she said in a stage whisper.

"Me, too."

Most Christians claim to love God's words, but sometimes forget the number-one basic principle about the Bible: we must *read* it. When we pour over every word, it comes alive! God's power can burst through every verse, exploding in our hearts. We become more than the sum of our parts: more able, more energetic, more powerful, and more influential.

More.

We know more about Christ only as we pray and study His Word with the Holy Spirit's help. We'll never know what might have been if we don't get back to basics: know Him; read His Word; communicate with our personal Savior; find hope in the power of His resurrection. Paul said, "What is more, I consider everything a loss compared to the surpassing greatness of knowing Christ Jesus my Lord" (Philippians 3:8). How could Paul be such an optimistic evangelist, even in prison? He *knew*.

O Christ, teach us to know the power of Your resurrection in Your Word.
Send Your Spirit to help us live it out in the world. We want more. Amen.

# ❦ In Name Only ❦

*"Come out from among them and be separate," says the Lord*
(2 Corinthians 6:17 NKJV).

Many individuals call themselves Christians solely because they live in a particular nation or belong to a church. They've never confessed their sinfulness to God. They have never turned away from being the boss of their own lives to humble themselves in faith before Jesus. How could people so completely miss the point of Christianity? Perhaps they misunderstand because they see virtually no difference between the way they think, talk, and act and the way many who claim to know Jesus as Savior think, talk, and act.

Ask yourself, *Do I live differently than unbelievers? Is it clear to those around me that while I sin at times, my first priority is to please the Lord Jesus Christ?*

Christians are not to be different for the sake of being different. We know people whose belief systems are *different*, and not necessarily in a good way. It's popular in our culture for people to boast about their personal version of spirituality—the more bizarre the better. Believe in the power of crystals, in reincarnation, in communication with the dead, in paranormal activity, or in unlimited inner power, and you'll earn the respect of many. The desire to be different grows from pride: the longing to be center stage.

As believers, though, the essence of our being different has nothing to do with our desire for personal uniqueness. Instead, we are different because our relationship with Jesus Christ brings us peace with God and sets us apart from those who are in rebellion against the Creator.

Today is a good day to confirm we are in the faith and then to come out from among the world and be distinct in the way we live. We can begin by asking ourselves, *Am I a Christian in name only? Is Christianity merely a label I wear, my heritage; or have I believed in Jesus, casting my lot with Him for eternity?*

Christianity is more than a label. It's a relationship with the one true God who loved us and gave Himself for us. Make sure you know Him today.

> Lord, I don't want simply to wear the label of Christian.
> I affirm You as my Savior. Amen.

# ❀ Dealing with Anger ❀

*Fathers, do not exasperate your children; instead, bring them up in the
training and instruction of the Lord* (Ephesians 6:4).

Have you ever seen two young children trying to resolve a conflict? The
wronged child usually tries a push, and if the other child doesn't run, the
first falls, kicking and screaming on the floor. Sometimes they use physical force: slapping or hitting their way to victory. My job as a teacher is
teaching preschoolers how to deal with anger. If they don't learn how to
handle it early, they may grow up to be angry adults. Bitterness can settle
in, causing greater conflict in older years.

Children look to us for examples of handling conflict. What do children
see *us* do when we're at odds with one another?

Paul says, *"'In your anger do not sin'; Do not let the sun go down while you are
still angry"* (Ephesians 4:26), quoting Psalm 4:4, an adage hundreds of years
old that gives good advice even today. We can go to the person with whom
we have a conflict—no matter who is right—and resolve it before sundown
with patience and love.

We tell children to say, "I'm sorry," but it's obvious some don't mean
those words. Are *we* able to say "I'm sorry"? Do we mean it?

Here are ten things I've learned about anger from helping preschoolers
deal with it.

1. Talk it out. Practice saying how you feel; let others express
   their feelings.
2. Avoid using mean words that hurt others.
3. Pushing and hitting don't help.
4. Cool down (count to ten if you have to) before reacting.
5. It's OK to say you are sorry.
6. Walk away, if you must, to avoid more conflict.
7. For the future, role play possible conflicts and resolve them
   peaceably.
8. Treat others the way you want to be treated.
9. Teach cooperation.
10. Be good examples of anger management.

Remember, sometimes we all disagree. It's how we handle the anger that
matters. Whether we teach children or not, we can be role models in all we
do. As Christians, our relationships are important to the kingdom of God.

Dear God, thank You for being the perfect role model
on how to resolve conflict in the right way. Amen.

# ❀ Walking and Jumping, ❀ and Praising God

*Now, Lord.....enable your servants to speak your word
with great boldness* (Acts 4:29).

Peter and John healed a lame beggar and preached about Jesus to the crowd that witnessed him *"walking and jumping, and praising God"* (Acts 3:8). The religious leaders had them arrested and, after much deliberation, released them.

Peter and John returned to the believers who had gathered in prayer. As they prayed together (Acts 4:24–30), they concluded by asking God to make them bold witnesses.

When I think of a bold witness, I think of Tommy whom I met when I was a teenager working at the LifeWay Conference Center. He was a patient at the North Carolina Tuberculosis Sanatorium.

One of my friends who had been visiting patients discovered Tommy on the basement floor. He took me into the ward filled with beds and led me to Tommy in the middle of the room. He was a small man who was deaf, blind, and crippled (a double amputee) in addition to having tuberculosis. His sightless eyes were fixated as though he were staring straight up into heaven.

My friend touched Tommy to let him know we were there. He took a hearing device that looked like part of an old phonograph with a pointed end and placed it into Tommy's ear. He then instructed me to put my face into the round part and loudly ask, "Tommy, do you love Jesus?"

When Tommy heard my question, he raised his gnarled, chapped hands in the air and loudly proclaimed, "Jesus, I love You, Jesus. Oh, Jesus, I love You." He started singing, "Oh, How I Love Jesus." We started singing with him, and before we realized it, the hospital room had become a sanctuary of praise. All of this happened because a man in a deaf, blind, crippled, and diseased body chose to be a bold witness. Today in God's presence, Tommy, like the lame man Peter and John encountered, is walking and leaping and praising God!

Dear Lord, to quote the believers in chapter four of Acts,
*"'Enable Your servants to speak Your word with great boldness.'"* Amen.

# ❀ African Ponytails ❀

*"Ask, and it will be given to you; seek, and you will find;*
*knock, and it will be opened to you"* (Luke 11:9–10 NKJV).

A friend and I once visited a South African school in an "informal settlement," the polite term for hillsides covered with tiny cardboard and tin dwellings with dirt floors. We had gathered mounds of pencils, hair products, and toiletries to give away, but when we arrived and saw the unimaginable destitution of the children, we felt woefully empty-handed. We had hoped to give every child one item.

Our last visit was to share the gospel with a classroom filled with lovely girls with hollow eyes. Afterward, the girls thronged us. One by one, the girls stuck out their hands for the treasure of a 5-cent ponytail holder. My supply was depleting quickly, until finally the last girl stood before us, undoubtedly the most gracious to have not pushed her way in front of her classmates. As she stuck out her hand with expectation in her eyes, I felt sick as I reached into the bag and found nothing. My partner and I scanned the ground for the potential of one lonely ponytail holder that might have dropped in the fray. Nothing.

Another student standing near walked over to her classmate and made one of the most amazing sacrifices—this young girl who lived on a dirt floor, with no running water, no electricity, likely no toothbrush or hairbrush—walked over to her classmate and gave up her ponytail holder. Then my teammate reached down into her bag one more time, and there in the corner of the sack was one lonely ponytail holder.

Maybe God dropped one extra ponytail holder in the bag at just the right moment, or maybe He hid that last holder from our sight until the student had been provided the opportunity to give generously to her classmate. No matter, God proved His point. At that moment when the young girl stood looking at me hopefully with outstretched hand, I became fully aware that I was completely unable to supply her needs. However, God is able to meet every need she could ever have for all of eternity. Jesus can fill every outstretched hand.

Father, help me to point others to You, the supplier of all needs. Amen.

# ❀ *Nurses on the Delta* ❀

*"Do not think of yourself more highly than you ought"* (Romans 12:3).

We set up a medical clinic in a church parking lot. A state fellowship of Christian nurses and two doctors volunteered in a poor area on the Mississippi River delta. They took blood pressure readings; taught people about good nutrition; tested for diabetes, deafness, and vision problems. As exit counselor, I referred them to a free clinic for follow-up and told them about Jesus.

For cholesterol checks, the nurses began drawing blood in vials, which we planned to save in the church's empty refrigerator, transport to a nearby hospital, and mail results to clients the next day.

When I took a box of vials inside the church, a woman in the hallway asked who had contributed the blood. "The church neighbors," I explained, thanking her for their hospitality. She turned pale and ran out of the room.

I found the hysterical woman down the hall leaning over her pastor's desk.

"Have we caused a problem?" I asked.

"Those people may have AIDS!" she said. "Who knows what they may have!"

The pastor apologized. When he tried to quiet her, she stood nose-to-nose with him, refusing to budge. "Not in *our* refrigerator!" she shouted. "*Those people* will have to go somewhere else." Rather than cause a quarrel, I took the vials back outside where a volunteer stored them in a cooler.

Overall, we had a good ministry. We referred many people without any form of health care to a free clinic. Six people accepted Jesus as their Savior. A wealthy man came in out of curiosity, asked to be tested, and discovered a big health problem.

On the way out, he said, "I've always thought the Christians in this town were do-gooders without love for God or anyone else. Today this opened my eyes. I really felt Jesus talking to me! I'm joining the church Sunday morning."

I pray he'll make a difference in that church, that *all* church members will love others in their needy community—and that one day "those people" will join that church.

Lord, help us to love all people, never feeling we're better than *those people*.
May we show Your love to everyone, in Jesus's name, amen.

# ❀ I Can Do It ❀

*I do believe; help me overcome my unbelief!* (Mark 9:24).

One of the loveliest Christians I know is a manicurist, Heather Loftis. Her blue eyes sparkle as she talks about God!

During the economic crunch in 2008, Heather and I celebrated our peace of mind because God has promised to provide. As January 2009 approached, Heather prayed about an amount to pledge through her church's missions-focused budget—thrilled when she arrived at a generous figure. *God, I'm so proud I can give this amount to You for church and world ministries.* She felt good about her pledge card that Sunday.

At work, others talked about hard times. Television and radio covered lost jobs and tightened belts. An inner voice said, *Heather, you're foolish to pledge so much. It's likely you won't even meet a smaller pledge this year!*

She prayed, *Lord, am I about to lose my business? I know with all my heart that I want all people to know Jesus. Am I way off base? Am I foolish to think I can do this?*

The next moment was unforgettable. Heather said, "I heard God. I *knew* it was Him! He spoke with a clear, certain voice to her heart and mind: *'I will give through you when I won't give to you.'* Heather had God's promise. He would bless her generously for ministries and evangelism, but not for personal profit. She says, "I had tears in my eyes. He was definite. I wouldn't get rich in this secular world, but I am already rich spiritually."

Mark gives us a good example of a man of uncertain faith whose son had convulsions. The man said to Jesus, *"If you can do anything"* (Mark 9:22).

*"'If you can?' said Jesus. 'Everything is possible for him who believes'"* (v. 23). Jesus healed the man's son immediately.

I'm sure that man changed his worldview that day. And listening to the world, Heather hesitated, but she was on solid ground when she put her church pledge in God's hands. In a world saying "fear," we can trust Him. We dare to believe in blessings beyond our highest dreams.

Lord, we want to join You in what You are doing in the world.
Give us high dreams and help us keep our focus on You. Amen.

# ❀ *Fire!* ❀

*And whosoever was not found written in the book of life*
*was cast into the lake of fire* (Revelation 20:15 KJV).

During October, schools usually observe Fire Prevention Week. We share fire safety with children, teaching what even small children can do to be safe at home and at play. In my preschool classes I teach these rules: Don't play with matches. Don't touch a hot stove. Don't stick anything into electrical outlets. We also teach them the terminology: "fire in the hole," "build a fire," "fire away," and "forest fire."

Fire can be positive. When we camp, we need a campfire. We need fire in a coal or wood stove—and what could be more romantic than a soft-glowing fire as we snuggle to keep warm when it's snowing outside?

Yet God warns us about total destruction in fire if we fail to acknowledge Him. Pastors tell us, as believers, we're accountable for the way we behave. They warn that we're not promised tomorrow, so we should remain obedient to God today. We sometimes play with fire in a spiritual sense. In spite of warnings, we still "fool around" with dangerous sins: we don't speak to one another; we hold grudges, use bad language, and don't help when we know we should. God says, *"Watch therefore, for ye know neither the day nor the hour wherein the Son of man cometh"* (Matthew 25:13 KJV).

I hope God won't come and catch us with our work undone. We don't want to be caught playing on Satan's turf. Yet it's so easy to bow to peer pressure the way children do. We sometimes slip over into godlessness and become a disgrace to our Savior! We need to stay close to Him daily, obeying what His Word teaches. May each of us be found loyal to our Lord, staying away from places and things we know are not pleasing to God, reading our Bibles, working for Him as His Word leads us.

We can't say we weren't warned. His Word is clear. Don't play with fire!

O God, thank You for Your Scripture that encourages us, but also warns us.
Lead us, Lord, through Your Word. Help us to obey Your laws
and act within Your commandments. Amen.

# ❀ The Old Back Days ❀

*So we Your people and the sheep of Your pasture will give thanks to You
forever; to all generations we will tell of Your praise*
(Psalm 79:13 NASB).

Our oldest daughter, now in her 20s, used to say to me things such as, "Mom, did you have cars in the old back days?" I have no idea where she got the phrase, but it stuck. At first I was offended; her words made me sound ancient! *My* mom lived in the old, back days! Each generation honestly believes they are the cutting-edge renegades, only to realize one day that they also have been relegated to "the old back days."

Though we may balk at the idea that our habits, attitudes, and preferences hint at our generational ties, we must admit there's some truth in that charge. And since each of us has firsthand information of only one generation—our own—we evaluate all others in light of the best of our own era. In order to understand, love, and collaborate with all women for Jesus and His kingdom's sake we need to identify our personal misconceptions of other generations. Reflect on the following comments you may have heard.

"*They* just don't understand us."

Translation: "Our goal in life is to be understood."

"*They* just want to take over and run things."

Translation: "We want to keep control and run things."

"It was good enough for *my* generation; it should be good enough for *them*."

Translation: "They deserve to have it as hard as we did."

We find it easy to notice the frailties of others, and we are quick to label an entire generation by a single descriptive sentence. Let's change that.

First, let's get to know those generations of women we perceive as "they." Second, let's learn how generations can work together collaboratively in God's mission. The Scriptures hold forth stellar examples—such as Ruth and Naomi—to teach us that servants of different generations working together for God are not the exception but the norm for God's people. We can follow their lead so that future generations will praise Him as well.

Lord, forgive my critical spirit. Help me learn to love and appreciate
women from other generations. Amen.

---

# ❀ *Build a Snowman* ❀

*Yes, and if I am being poured out as a drink offering on the sacrifice*
*and service of your faith, I am glad and rejoice with you all*
(Philippians 2:17 NKJV).

My husband probably doesn't realize it, but he gave the most wonderful gift to our family the last time it snowed. We awoke to sparkling pockets of white fluff nestled on the branches of every tree. He spontaneously decided to take the day off from work to play in the snow with the children.

It seemed like a perfect day. Although my husband knew the children wouldn't behave perfectly all day, he made the decision to stay home because he loves them. Several snow angels and snowmen later, my children had a collection of joyful memories made possible by their daddy. As for my husband, he took great pleasure in a day with the children, and I fell in love with him all over again.

Time spent with others is a worthwhile investment. Paul invested himself in the spiritual lives of young believers in Philippi. Celebrating their spiritual milestones and personal victories made him glad and caused rejoicing in his heart. He had such a strong bond with them that he felt a sense of ownership in their spiritual growth. He took seriously his role as a discipler. Interesting, however, Paul described his role in the relationship as a sacrificial pouring-out of himself.

Investing in the life of a babe in Christ who will go through the growing pains of spiritually maturing is indeed a journey of ups and downs, trials and triumphs, delights and disappointments—much like parenting. The journey of sacrifice is worth it, though, for the joy of seeing that new believer experience Christ in new and exciting ways.

Do you know a new or young believer who needs encouragement in her faith walk? Begin sharing your life with her, starting with something as simple as getting coffee together, attending a conference, or even building a snowman!

Father, teach me to make wise investments in the lives of others.
In Jesus's name, amen.

# ❀ *Like Sheep Among Wolves* ❀

*"I am sending you out like sheep among wolves. Therefore be as shrewd as snakes and as innocent as doves"*
(Matthew 10:16).

Jesus sent His followers as forerunners to announce His coming to the villages along the way before His final journey to Jerusalem. He first instructed them to pray for more laborers. Praying for laborers is an obvious answer to spreading the gospel around the world, yet one that is often ignored. Many believers feel they are overworked and over-burdened, but they fail to pray for more laborers.

Second, he warned them that they would face persecution. He told them He was sending them forth *"like lambs among wolves"* (Luke 10:3).

Wolves are predators. They are flesh-eating animals that often travel in packs and are enemies of livestock farmers. A pack of wolves can attack an entire herd of cows or sheep. Jesus's followers well understood this metaphor. Like lambs among wolves, their lives would be in danger. Yet, they were to remain faithful to the mission.

They returned with great joy, amazed at the power they had experienced (Luke 10:17). Even demons were subject to them. Jesus saw the danger in their astonishment. He quickly turned their attention from what they had done to what God had done for them. He moved the emphasis away from their authority over the demons to the fact that their names were written in heaven. Jesus knew that pride was one of the "wolves" that devour His sheep.

This Scripture concludes with a verse that warms my heart: *"in that hour Jesus rejoiced in spirit"* (Luke 10:21 KJV). We might transfer the word "rejoices" to our setting as meaning "to jump for joy." Can you visualize this? Our Savior was so proud of His students, you might say that He literally jumped for joy!

I often hear people say they want to please God, but they don't know how. The key to pleasing God (as step one) is found in making sure your name is written in heaven.

Dear Lord, thank You for Your provision. Help us to remain faithful to You even when we are in the midst of persecution. In Jesus's name, amen.

# ❀ Blessed Are They ❀ That Mourn

*Blessed are they that mourn: for they shall be comforted*
(Matthew 5:4 KJV).

What does it mean to mourn? After a loss, mourning—the grieving process—helps heal the hurts.

My church has taught me that grief is similar to a freezing process. At first, after a deep loss like a death in the family, we feel frozen in time. We place ourselves in isolation, wanting to be left alone—but not forgotten. During the isolation stage, we may spend extended hours sleeping. We hope rest will heal the body, mind, and soul. Next we feel frustration and anger. We're mad at God and the one who has died and left us behind. Finally, in the thawing stage, our hearts thaw out; normal feelings return. In time we're ready to laugh and hope again.

People ask their pastors, "Shouldn't Christian grief be better—easier?" My husband and other pastors answer something like: "Even with Christians, grief can sap the life out of you." Some Christians feel Satan is making them feel guilty—that they have no right to be happy—but we can and will move on. We may continue to experience sudden moments of grief, but it's best to just let them wash over us. Pause, take a deep breath, and then let them go.

Wrestling with God during a period of grieving will make positive differences in a Christian's life. The depths of mourning helps renew faith. Despite heartache, God sustains His children with humor and hope.

Life is a choice. The hardest choice for those who mourn is to get up when every bone in their body wants to quit. We must keep on breathing… stepping…healing. With practice, we learn to dance with God during the hardest times. We cannot let Satan steal our joy.

When others are grieving, be there for them. Simply say, "I'm sorry." Don't overwhelm them with Scriptures, though you may share a pretty card with a verse like: *Restore unto me the joy of my salvation; and uphold me with thy generous Spirit* (Psalm 51:12 KJV). When they're ready, let them know you care.

Lord, thank You for walking me through a period of grief.
Help me to minister to others and show them I care. Amen.

# ❀ *Facing the Mountain* ❀

*But may the God of all grace, who called us to His eternal glory by*
*Christ Jesus, after you have suffered awhile, perfect, establish, strengthen*
*and settle you* (1 Peter 5:10 NKJV).

As we pursue God's will for our lives, the journey could be compared to climbing a steep mountain. When we reach a stretch of difficulty in the journey, we are challenged by our inability to see what lies ahead; we are face to face with the mountain, and all we can see before our eyes is rock, rock, rock. We do not dare to look back from where we have ascended, or we may be paralyzed by fear and anxiety. So we trudge on, clawing inch by inch, and the scenery does not change for what seems to be miles.

We occasionally occupy our minds by dwelling on the destination of this climb, and other times we cannot think past the pain in our joints and the intense grip we have on the mountain, trying to hold on, trying not to fall, trying to be certain the struggle of the climb does not end in vain. And when we finally reach the top of that rugged, steep mountain, we take the final step onto sure footing, praising the Maker of that solid rock. We breathe in the fresh air found only at such an exhilarating height, and we feel settled in our spirits. Yes, the journey brought strength to our souls.

We gaze in wonder at the spectacular view before us, a panoramic view of God's will. We rejoice as we feel the warm sunshine on our faces, and we know the journey was surely worth the struggle. Then we look before us and realize we cannot tarry on this mountaintop for long, for other mountains remain yet to be climbed.

> Dear Lord, grant me patience as I climb these mountains
> You've set before me, pursuing Your will for my life.
> Thank You for Your promise never to leave me or forsake me.
> Teach me perseverance, and may I trust You
> not only for the final destination where You're taking me,
> but also for the journey to get there. Amen.

# ❁ *Spiritual Housecleaning* ❁

*Let us draw near to God with a sincere heart in full assurance of faith,*
*having our hearts sprinkled to cleanse us from a guilty conscience and*
*having our bodies washed with pure water* (Hebrews 10: 22).

Last January I hosted my book club in my home. I spent hours checking baseboards for grime, taking a toothbrush to the corners, and getting the last stubborn dots of dust, so the rooms sparkled. Since we have a dog, Eliza, I used a dog-hair roller on each sofa and chair. I checked the dining room chandelier for last-minute spider webs and polished the front hallway to remove every dull spot on the hardwood floors.

On the meeting day, my son-in-law, Tim, took Eliza for a long afternoon's walk, and I swept off the walkway, picking up dead leaves near the door. Then, fluffing up a few pillows, I mused, "This house looks great!"

The event went well: the members enjoyed each other's company, talking, sampling food, and listening to a wonderful speaker. As they left, I noticed one error in my cleaning. The glass storm door was filthy—covered with little puppy marks—nasty-nose smudges and muddy paw prints! I had spent so much time on the tiny specks in the baseboard corners that I hadn't noticed the large doggie streaks from mid-door to the bottom.

No matter how hard we try, we'll always face dirt in life. Though we do everything we can to live a clean life, we'll never be perfect spiritual housecleaners. Just as physical dust builds up daily, dogs track in dirt, and families generate trash, our imperfect world generates sin daily. Spiritual dirt is as invasive as physical dirt all over the earth.

As today's verse above highlights, God sprinkles our hearts to cleanse us from guilty consciences and washes our bodies clean. Though we face a daily dusting of sin, His grace allows us to draw near Him in full assurance of faith and soak in the pure Living Water within.

> Lord, thank You for helping us see dirt and sin in our lives.
> Come cleanse our hearts from guilty consciences
> and help us serve You with pure bodies. Amen.

# ❃ *How About a Poem?* ❃

*"For in him we live and move and have our being. As some of your
own poets have said, 'We are his offspring'"* (Acts 17: 28).

I love poetry! Since the third grade, I loved listening to poetry. That year
we learned how to write rhymed poetry. Later I learned to write unrhymed
poetry, adding rhyming words or alliteration to key stanzas. Through the
years poetry classes (sometimes called "poesy") have helped me. I have
taught poetry for more than 20 years. The Bible doesn't mention the word
*poetry* or *poems*, but it *contains* the poetry of David and others in the Psalms,
Job, Proverbs, Ecclesiastes, and Song of Songs—the wisdom passages.
Paul used a significant reference to poets as a witness to the Greeks,
who, as a people, loved poetry. Have you ever thought of following Paul's
lead in Athens, using references to a poem as a witness to those who are
not Christians but may love poetry? It worked that day. (Read more in
Acts 17: 29–34.)

Decorate and frame Scripture or simple poems such as this testimony
based on John 3:16 and give to an unchurched friend.

### God Loves

One day someone told me true:
"God must have a plan for you."
"Oh, not me, for as a rule,
I'm the meanest girl in school."

"God so loved the world," He said,
"I died for you. No longer dead,
May I come, live in your heart?"
"Yes," I said. "We'll never part."

Knocked Ray's teeth out with a ball;
Wasn't sorry then at all.
Yet God spoke to me that night,
Shared His grace and love and light.

Dear One, if the wrong seems right,
Or—when frightened in the night,
Just ask Jesus to come in;
He will give you peace within.

© Edna Ellison, 2009

Thank You for loving us, Lord. Help us show others Your Word
through poetry or prose. Amen.

# ❀ Can't We All ❀ Just Get Along?

*We should no longer be children, tossed to and fro and carried about*
*with every wind of doctrine, by the trickery of men, in the cunning*
*craftiness of deceitful plotting, but, speaking the truth in love . . . grow*
*up in all things into Him who is the head—Christ*
(Ephesians 4:14–15 NKJV).

In our culture today, personal opinion reigns supreme, and we are faced with a menagerie of divergent views. Ours is a pluralistic society filled with cultural diversity and characterized by a demand for sub-cultural identity and recognition.

Tolerance has taken on new meaning, no longer calling for us to respect other *persons* but also requiring us to accept their *beliefs* as another facet of truth. Tolerance for every belief system and its "god," no matter how irrational, is now expected.

This popular mind-set was reflected recently by a lost friend who asked me, "Don't you think you should respect other persons' beliefs?" I explained that I respect other persons' right to choose their beliefs, but to say I accept all beliefs as true is illogical since many are contradictory. And if all beliefs were true, why bother to choose?

Unfortunately, many Christians seem to embrace the postmodern definition of *tolerance*. Seeking to avoid the accusation of being judgmental, they have abandoned Christ's admonition to discern right from wrong and good from evil (Hebrews 5:14). Thinking they are taking the high road, they, too, proclaim tolerance as a worthy goal, instead of loving sacrificially as Christ did.

As on-mission women of Jesus Christ the condition of our world should deeply burden us. Our responses to the world should reflect our sure hope in Jesus Christ, not a bowing to popular thinking. We can take advantage of the cultural push toward tolerance and pluralism by confidently voicing the message of Jesus Christ. Instead of accepting the tolerance mantra, we can teach and mirror Christ's attitude. Not just tolerating people, but loving them.

Lord, forgive me for wearing the garb of the society in which I live
and mistaking the good for the best. Teach me to love.
In Jesus's name, amen.

# ❀ Don't Let Your Past ❀ Hold You Hostage

*One thing I do: Forgetting what is behind…I press on toward the goal to win the prize for which God has called me heavenward in Christ Jesus* (Philippians 3:13–14).

All Christians come into the church family with a past, positive or negative. Often, after being in the church for a while, becoming active—not just a bench warmer, Satan starts to attack us through memories of our past. We're grateful for our relationships with other good Christians, but we often face an unexpected relationship with Satan, the Evil One.

Satan talks a lot, using the "remember when" syndrome: "Remember when you used to drink? You'll always be an alcoholic." "Remember when you partied all night? What would good Christians think if they knew?" "Remember when you smoked pot? You *can't* be a Christian!" "Remember when you were an adulteress? No one wants *you* as an on-mission church member."

But God has a stronger voice. He says: "I know you did drugs, or were promiscuous, but I've cleaned you up! You're now a part of *My* family. You belong to Me!"

Christians must resolve to listen to the strongest voice—God—the best friend anyone ever had.

Satan tries to make us feel guilty about our past and fearful of our future so that we can't function well in the present. But when we listen to the strong voice of God, we remember that He *will* and *always does* forgive and forget our sins. We know Jesus's shed blood covers a multitude of sins.

I once heard a story called "No Fishing Allowed." It goes like this: God has a fishing dock on the Sea of Forgetfulness. He gathers all our sins and throws them into the sea. Then He puts up a sign, "No Fishing Allowed," inviting us simply to stay there and enjoy the beautiful sea. Soon along comes Satan, ready to establish a warped relationship with us. He makes us feel guilty, telling us we have no right to be happy. He hangs around and tries to fish in our pond. But we have a choice—we can stand strong and tell him: "Look at that sign. No Fishing Allowed!"

Lord, thank You for Your loving relationship with us.
Don't let our past hold us hostage in the present.
Help us tell Satan loudly: "No Fishing Allowed." Amen.

# ❀ He Is Glorified ❀

*On their part He is blasphemed, but on your part He is glorified*
(1 Peter 4:14 NKJV).

Isaiah was a mighty prophet of God, communicating powerful messages to the people of his day as well as issuing prophecy that you and I now study centuries later. But would Isaiah have called himself a success?

When Isaiah first offered his life completely to God, saying, *"Here am I! Send me"* (Isaiah 6:8 NKJV), God then gave him a glimpse of what he'd signed up to do. God described a dullness of heart and a weakening of the senses in the lives of people that would cause Isaiah's message to fall on deaf ears (Isaiah 6:9–10). God forewarned Isaiah that people would refuse to heed his messages, the very words that would come directly from the heart of God! Surely Isaiah felt discouraged many days of his life, enjoying the nearness of God yet being forced to watch the destructive ways of a people whose hearts had turned like flint.

We can learn a lesson from Isaiah's experiences as a messenger of God. Are we tempted to measure our success by the response of the listener, whether it's teaching the Bible, sharing Scripture with a friend, or presenting the gospel message? Just as in Isaiah's day, many people's hearts are hardened today toward the message of the Lord. God will judge our ministry of words, not based on how well people responded to the message, but on our faithfulness to deliver those words. In 1 Peter 4:14, Peter explains that the spiritual accountability of the listener is separate from the accountability of the one giving the message.

Almighty God affirmed Isaiah's ministry, for thousands of years later, you and I are reading his prophetic messages as Scripture. If you are feeling discouraged as a messenger of God's Word, ask God to reveal to you any areas of weakness He will refine in you. Then, trust God with the results of your ministry. On your part, may He be glorified.

Heavenly Father above, I come to You desiring to be Your faithful messenger. I want to glorify You through my obedience. Instead of looking to others for affirmation, I am looking to You. In Jesus's name, amen.

# ❀ Keep On Keeping On ❀

*Let us hold unswervingly to the hope we profess,*
*for he who promised is faithful* (Hebrews 10:23).

An ancient Chinese proverb says the journey of a thousand miles begins with one step. No matter how weary Christians get, we can, through the eyes of faith, "keep on keeping on."

In Hebrews 10, Christians are urged not to lose faith, but to persevere. There are two reasons to continue walking by faith: (1) *"since we have confidence to enter the Most Holy Place by the blood of Jesus by a new and living way opened for us through the curtain, that is, his body" (vv. 19–20),* and (2) *"since we have a great priest over the house of God"* (v. 21). Because Jesus died on the Cross to open the way for us to go to heaven, and because Jesus is the greatest priest ever, far surpassing all human priests, then we're able to confidently grow close to God—without any barrier or curtain.

*"Let us draw near to God with a sincere heart in full assurance of faith, having our hearts sprinkled to cleanse us from a guilty conscience and having our bodies washed with pure water"* (v. 22). Notice two parts of our cleansing: internal and external. God can take a sinful life and wash away psychological and spiritual hang-ups; He can also heal physical addictions or bondage to evil things.

Hebrews 10 also says to encourage others: *"And let us consider how we may spur one another on toward love and good deeds. Let us not give up meeting together, as some are in the habit of doing, but let us encourage one another—and all the more as you see the Day approaching"* (v. 25). What can we do? We can love others and unselfishly do good deeds as an example *before* them and as a gift *to* them.

One important principle is that we *be there.* As Christians with *"sincere hearts in full assurance of faith"* (v. 22), we exercise the ministry of presence. Filling a pew, attending a revival, helping with projects, praying with troubled people—with patience, we just keep on keeping on.

Faithful God, help us to hold unswervingly to the hope we profess
and to encourage others. Amen.

# ❀ *Cradle to Cross* ❀

*You were not redeemed with corruptible things, like silver or gold …,*
*but with the precious blood of Christ, as of a lamb without blemish*
*and without spot. He was foreordained before the foundation of the*
*world* (1 Peter 1:18–20 NKJV).

"The most wretched of deaths" is the way the Jewish historian Josephus described crucifixion. Though the Jews rarely crucified people, the Romans had refined the technique to maximize pain, prolong agony, and magnify humiliation, sometimes using crucifixions as a macabre form of entertainment.

Victims were prepared by laying them on the ground and then tying or nailing their hands or wrists to a wooden crossbar, which was then lifted onto one of the vertical posts permanently set up outside the city. For nailing victims, soldiers hammered hand-forged metal spikes, about five-to-seven inches long, through the hands and feet. After the victims' deaths, the nails were confiscated and worn as healing charms or were removed and reused by the soldiers.

Morbid. Depressing. Sad. Why focus on the gory details of Jesus's death? Shouldn't we just think about what His sacrifice accomplished for us: the wonder of salvation and the sure hope of heaven? Or, why not focus on rejoicing over His coming in the manger rather than the pitiful death scene?

Our joy comes not only from remembering the manger. Jesus didn't come just to decorate the cradle in the nativity scene. He was born to die. Before His first cry as a newborn, the Father had already marked the road to Calvary. Rather, the manger compels us to also look at the hammer in our hands driving the nails into His hands. That's when anguish provokes repentance, and faith gives way to boundless joy. For, as Isaiah said, "He was pierced through for our transgressions,…by His scourging we are healed" (Isaiah 53:5 NASB).

Precious Savior, I don't want to think about Your suffering. I'd prefer to freeze in time the image of You as the tender child in the manger. It hurts me to think my sins caused You such excruciating pain on that Cross. Yet, without the Cross, without the shedding of Your blood, I would be utterly without hope. So, thank You, Lord, for not abandoning that bloody, exquisitely beautiful Cross. Amen.

# ❀ *Pipes* ❀

*If I regard iniquity in my heart, the Lord will not hear*
(Psalm 66:18 NKJV).

My husband Kevin likes long hair on a woman. Unfortunately, it's affecting our plumbing. For weeks we've battled a bad shower drain clog. Drano might've tackled it at the first signs of trouble, but I got busy folding laundry, Kevin was busy blogging, and the problem worsened over time. Yesterday Kevin had to pull out a plumber's snake. He announced after ten minutes of backbreaking labor, "You know we wouldn't have this problem if it weren't for your long hair."

Oh, my. Did he mean the long hair that I endure for his sake during long, hot summer months? Yeah, I think he was talking about me.

A clogged drain is bad news. Can you conjure up a visual image of the yucky, gunky, black stuff that clogs a drain? Those things don't seem so bad going down—things like hair and soapsuds and shampoo—but when they collect over time, they become disgusting.

As born-again believers, we have direct access to the Heavenly Father (Hebrews 10:19). It's like a pipeline directly into the throne room of God, where you honor God with your love and praise, and make your petitions known. Unconfessed sin clogs up this communication.

Just like the drain-clogging things in your pipes, your "little" sins may not seem so bad when they first appear in your life. An unkind thought, a selfish motive, five minutes of time stolen at work...but God hates sin, period, and as unconfessed sin builds up over time, it's a disgusting gunky mess, interfering with your ability to communicate clearly with God. Kevin jokingly blamed the clog on me, just as we Christians sometimes blame our sins on others with phrases like, "I know I shouldn't say this but...", or, "I know it's wrong, but...."

Consistent "pipe-cleaning" through confessing sin will keep your communication with God flowing smoothly. If Kevin and I had addressed the clog early on, we would have never had to deal with a major build-up; how long has it been since you've had a quality conversation with the heavenly Father about your sin?

Father, convict me of my sins today
that I might confess them to You. Amen.

# ❀ *Stop in the Name of the Law!* ❀

*Therefore no one will be declared righteous in his sight by observing the*
*law; rather, through the law we become conscious of sin*
(Romans 3:20).

One day my young teenaged son, Jack, said, "I don't have to obey the law. I can do anything I want!"

"What?" I said, stunned.

"I read it in the Bible. We don't have to obey the law: the police or sheriffs."

"That sounds a little dangerous to me. Let's look that up in the Bible."

He showed me verses about people living by faith, not by law. We talked a long time, off and on, that day, looking at passages that explained "the law of Moses." Despite his childhood years in Sunday School, Jack hadn't fully understood what the word *law* meant in the Bible. (Not the local law enforcement, "the law" refers to the Old Testament law God gave Moses on Mt. Sinai, beginning with the Ten Commandments, and explained primarily in Exodus, Leviticus, and Deuteronomy.)

Then Jack asked a good question: "If God intended us to live by faith, then why did He create the law in the first place?"

Paul answered that question in Galatians 3: God used the Old Testament law to show people their sin. Nobody could possibly live up to the letter of God's law. Especially with Jesus's definition—if we think of sin in our hearts, we're guilty of that sin (Matthew 5:28). If that idea is true—and it is—then we sin often. We can't keep even *one* of the Ten Commandments, since we break each of them in our hearts, if not outwardly!

God's law is a mirror in which we see our own sin. Once we see ourselves as we really are—imperfect sinners—then we recognize the need for a Savior. *"So the law was put in charge to lead us to Christ that we might be justified by faith. Now that faith has come, we are no longer under the supervision of the law"* (Galatians 3:24–25).

May we study God's law often so we become conscious of sin, accept salvation, and live the Christian life.

O God, thank You for giving us Your Word to show us our sin
and help us rely on Your grace. Amen.

# ❀ *How You See It* ❀

*Beware lest anyone cheat you through philosophy and empty deceit,*
*according to the tradition of men, according to the basic principles of*
*the world, and not according to Christ* (Colossians 2:8 NKJV).

It guides decisions as trivial as what you eat and as monumental as whom you marry: it's your *worldview*. Your beliefs about humankind's purpose on earth, about God, and what happens at death all comprise your worldview. When an acquaintance asked me why I believed in Christ, I shared my testimony and evidence that Christianity was true, giving a glimpse of my worldview.

Why do we need to discuss esoteric subjects such as worldviews? Shouldn't we focus on more practical issues in winning the lost world to Jesus Christ and leave the philosophical discussions to academia? I don't think so. In fact, the significance of understanding your biblical worldview, as well as familiarizing yourself with predominant thought systems of the culture in which you live and witness, cannot be overestimated. When you share the gospel with a friend, for instance, she filters your message through the grid of her own belief system.

Imagine trying to explain to a Muslim woman how God came as a man and died on the Cross for our sins. To a Muslim, this view of God is blasphemous because it diminishes God. Understanding the way a person thinks helps you address specific issues intrinsic to her worldview.

Now imagine yourself talking with someone who believes in millions of gods. You mention Jesus is God, meaning the One and Only God, and you are thrilled when she wants to believe in Christ as Savior. What you don't realize is that she wants to add Jesus to her pantheon of gods so she doesn't miss any!

So, study not only the truths of the Christian faith but also the good reasons for believing in Christ, as well as the competing worldviews in our culture. You will strengthen your own faith and become equipped to help others make genuine commitments to Jesus Christ.

Lord, strengthen my own faith and help me listen carefully
to what people believe so that I can meet them
where they are and introduce them to the truth of Your love. Amen.

# ❀ *Memory Prompts* ❀

*Wash me thoroughly from my iniquity, and cleanse me from my sin.*
*For I acknowledge my transgressions, and my sin is always before me*
(Psalm 51:2–3 NKJV).

Every time I attempt to make macaroni and cheese in a crock pot, I think of a friend who brought the most fabulous crock pot macaroni and cheese to my family after my youngest son was born. The iron filigree over my television reminds me of my father-in-law who hung those pieces for me, and eighties music brings up instant memories of my middle sister. A stain on the carpet in my office makes me think about my friend who spilled her plate of food on that very spot; nevertheless, it was a fun-filled dinner party!

Memory prompts abound throughout my day, some pleasant and some painful. My worst memories are of the times when I have sinned against God. If I indulge the thought for even an instant, floods of shame and guilt overtake my heart. We all have those unpleasant memories stored in our brains that we cannot erase. We can relate to the sorrow of the Psalmist, who felt the burden of his sins always flashing before his eyes.

Followers of Christ have the truth of God's forgiveness that quickly replaces those feelings of shame with feelings of victory. However, the person who does not know Christ does not know the relief of forgiveness. Imagine the heaping storehouse of shame that unbelievers have to deal with on a daily basis, with reminders all around them of their transgressions and sin. As you pray for the lost, seeking God's guidance, ask Him to help you convey the promise of forgiveness of sins He's given us through Jesus Christ. What words will you use to describe the peace of knowing that your sins are forgiven?

Heavenly Father, thank You from the depths of my soul for Your forgiveness! You have cleansed me from my sins! I desire to communicate to the lost around me that forgiveness is available through Jesus Christ. Please reveal anyone who is feeling heavy laden with the weight of her sin, and give me the words to say. In Jesus's name, amen.

# ❀ *Shine On!* ❀

*But now that you have been set free from sin and have become
slaves to God, the benefit you reap leads to holiness,
and the result is eternal life* (Romans 6:22).

*Holiness* is an interesting word. It is derived from the Hebrew word *qadash* meaning "to be clean ceremonially or morally; consecrate, dedicate, sanctify wholly" and/or the Greek word *hagios* meaning "sacred, physically pure, morally blameless or religious, consecrated." In other words, it means to be "set apart" or "different" from other things.

However, the most profound aspect of holiness is God's holiness. Holiness is a predominant attribute of God in both the Old and New Testaments. *Holy* is used as a prefix for His name more than any other word.

Scientists say combining all the colors of the spectrum creates pure, white light. Similarly, all the attributes of God combined are the essence of His holiness.

Paul teaches in Romans 6:22 that once God sets us free from sin we become partakers of His holiness. He dedicates us as different and consecrates us. However, it is our responsibility to live differently from the world, for truly we are set apart for Him.

Recently I met a fine young man wearing a beautiful ring. He explained it's his promise ring. He wears it as a commitment to God that he will refrain from any sexual relationship until marriage.

He's a handsome young man, and I'm sure many temptations will come his way. Nevertheless, he has vowed to live his life differently from the world—"consecrated, physically pure and morally blameless." In other words, he has chosen holiness.

I've noticed that those who live holy lives seem to radiate a light. Their eyes sparkle when speaking of their love for Jesus, and they glow when sharing their experiences in God's presence. It seems the closer we move to the holiness of God, the more brightly His light shines through us.

Dear Lord, please help us desire to live a consecrated life of holiness
so we may shine more brightly for You. In Jesus's name, amen.

# ❀ *Dusty Feet* ❀

*"If I then, your Lord and Teacher, have washed your feet, you also*
*ought to wash one another's feet"* (John 13:14 NKJV).

I never felt closer to Bible times than on the dusty roads of Niger. As we walked through the villages, dirt and sand covered our sandaled feet. With the river a long walk away and no running water, grit clung to our skin.

On the last day of a week of discipling a small group of women believers, we studied the story of Jesus washing the disciples' feet. As my friend completed the study, she picked up a basin of water and a towel, asking Nigerian women permission to wash their feet. Each woman looked curiously at her, pulling her feet as far as possible beneath the bench where they sat. After some discussion, they explained their feet were too dirty to allow her to wash them. How ironic. Clean feet don't need to be washed. Nevertheless, the shame of their dirtiness prohibited them from getting cleansed.

However, one brave little boy sat in the circle that afternoon. I called him F1 because he daily wore a tattered Formula One T-shirt, and he was my friend. He eagerly watched the scene as we discussed the foot washing. I asked him, "Would you allow me to wash your feet?" Little F1 had no concept of what this experience would be like. The American woman who loved Jesus, his friend since a handful of days, wanted to wash his feet. How odd it must've seemed to him. F1 nodded yes. As I washed his feet, the water quickly turned brown as I rubbed dirt off what felt like old-man's feet. I wondered what ran through his young mind. I prayed that the memory he would carry the rest of his life is that Christians serve others.

Have you realized lately your need for the cleansing touch of Jesus Christ? Have you knelt at the feet of another to minister to her as a humble servant, following the example of your Savior?

My Lord, how great is Your love! I'm Your humble servant,
and I'll be a servant to others. May I kneel with a grateful heart
to minister to others. Amen.

# ❀ *Learn from the Past* ❀

*Then God said to Jacob, "Go up to Bethel and settle there,
and build an altar there to God, who appeared to you
when you were fleeing from your brother Esau"* (Genesis 35:1).

Recently I visited the home I had lived in for 20 years. My children grew up there; we lived there when their father died. I saw the play area where a sandbox sat years ago. I could almost see Jack and Patsy digging in the sand. I looked near the garage at an oily spot of ground. Though it had been many years, I recognized that place where Patsy set the grass on fire with a Christmas sparkler she had lit without permission. She cried as Jack sprayed water from the garden hose, putting out the fire. (They didn't tell me until ten years later.) Then I walked on the porch, where my husband sat an hour before his death. The place held bittersweet memories.

Jacob visited such a place: Bethel, where God had appeared as he ran from Esau, his twin. He recalled the fear, but also the comfort of God's presence. He built an altar to God, *"who answered me in the day of my distress"* (Genesis 35:3).

Looking at the past, most great leaders can see failure and mistakes and, like Jacob, recall some fear. The mark of great leaders is that they move beyond past mistakes and try again. Jacob gave God thanks for His love and forgiveness. God had allowed him to be a great leader of men, the father of nations.

When we look back at the past, how do we scan the horizon? With bittersweet memories? With regret over past mistakes? With joy because God loves and forgives?

Nothing we can ever do will make Him stop loving us. We can thank God for everything we learned from past errors and sin. As leaders, we can believe in His power to restore us to serve Him as He directs, without wavering. We hope in the future, since we know Who holds the key to it.

O God, thank You for Your love and comfort during times of distress. You've taught us leadership principles through failures as well as successes. Because of Your faithfulness, we have hope for the future. Amen.

# ❀ *Holding On* ❀

*Let us hold fast the confession of our hope without wavering,*
*for He who promised is faithful* (Hebrews 10:23 NKJV).

The lights were low as I sang softly in my newborn's ear. John Mark's hand brushed mine, and he grabbed my finger tightly. *How precious,* I thought. *My son is clinging to me for comfort and security.* But then, a realistic thought occurred to me. Had John Mark's fingers brushed up against a blanket or even a crayon, he would've clung to these things. He was willing to grab onto anything offered to him, whether good or bad.

What about you? When moments of loneliness or depressed feelings creep into your heart, what will you cling to for comfort and security? When you feel down or desperate, will you grab the first thing that comes along?

The writer of Hebrews encourages us: *"Let us hold fast the confession of our hope without wavering, for He who promised is faithful"* (10:23 NKJV). The Greek word for *confession* means "acknowledging the truth," stemming from the verb that literally means "to speak the same thing." Whatever God has said in His Word, we can say the same thing and know that it's true. We can cling to the truth, declaring without wavering that we believe all things are just as God has said.

Holding fast to our confession is vital to our witness, whether we're testifying about God as our Sustainer, Defender, or Savior. When circumstances look bleak, we may feel tempted to search for a person to help or protect us, but Psalm 108:12 says, *"Give us help from trouble, for the help of man is useless"* (NKJV). Instead of settling for a false sense of security, we can lean on God's promises. Our reliance on God instead of fretful behavior offers a resounding witness to those around us. When we feel down on ourselves and need affirmation, the world encourages us to turn to a person, a lifestyle, a credit card, or even good works to help us feel good about ourselves. Instead, we cling to God's terms of endearment toward us: *"I have loved you with an everlasting love"* (Jeremiah 31:3 NKJV).

Father, what am I holding onto for security? If You find anything
in my hands other than Your precious Hand,
please teach me to cling only to You and Your Word. Amen.

# ❊ *Walking Blind on the Path* ❊

*Open my eyes, that I may see wonderful things in your law*
(Psalm 119:18).

I once told 1,200 women in a Bible study to turn to Isaiah 42:19. With assurance I flipped over to the passage, grateful that God had given me something instructive to say. When I looked, I saw only 11 verses in chapter 42. I scanned the page. I *was* in chapter 42, so I said, "Uh…chapter 42 doesn't have 19 verses." Embarrassed, I thought how ignorant I must seem to these women.

I looked again. I'd opened my Bible to *Psalm* 42 instead of *Isaiah* 42. Immediately I felt God's presence beside me. I had been braggadocios about what *I* knew about the Bible, and God was teaching me humility.

"Thank You, Lord," I said aloud, "for humiliating me right here in front of everyone!" The group laughed. Then they looked with me at Isaiah 42:19, as I read: *"Who is blind like the one committed to me, blind like the servant of the LORD?"* They giggled. I then read the next words: *"You have seen many things, but have paid no attention."* God was speaking, *not* to the group, as I had thought earlier, but to *me*. By then, everyone was laughing.

I got it. God had taught me a good lesson. Sometimes when we think we know everything about Scripture, we are just scratching the surface. I began to study Isaiah 42, and here's what I learned. The word for *blind* is used several times in Isaiah. For instance, God says in Isaiah 42:16, *"I will lead the blind by ways they have not known, along unfamiliar paths I will guide them."* In Isaiah 32, He says when the King of Righteousness will reign, *"Then the eyes of those who see will no longer be closed, and the ears of those who hear will listen"* (v. 3). As God makes His Word clearer before us, some phrases almost jump off the page! His Word convicts and refines our hearts as we pay attention. Give a closer look at His Word today as you follow His path.

King of Righteousness, thank You for Your living words that convict us,
refine us, and open our eyes to truth. Amen.

# ❊ The Key to Heaven ❊

*These things says He who is holy, He who is true, "He who has the key*
*of David, He who opens and no one shuts, and shuts and no one opens"*
(Revelation 3:7 NKJV).

How many keys do you have on your key ring? Keys exist for only one
purpose—to open and shut things. God's Word says Jesus holds the key
to heaven. Because Jesus alone has authority over the key, He decides not
only *who* enters heaven, but also the *requirements* for entering heaven. Christ,
after describing heaven as His "Father's house," made an astounding claim:
*"I am the way, and the truth, and the life; no one comes to the Father, but through*
*Me"* (John 14:6 NASB). Imagine, He asserted that anyone who wanted
to enter had to be willing to swallow his pride and acknowledge there was
absolutely nothing he could do to gain entry on his own.

Perhaps you've designed your own keys, or beliefs, for entering heaven.
You may believe the key is crossing your fingers and hoping that God will
overlook sin and in the end usher everyone into heaven. Or, you think the
key is sincerity—no matter what you believe, as long as you are sincere
in that belief, God will open heaven's door. Maybe you think the key that
opens heaven's door is doing more good things than bad. Or maybe that
you'll gain entry because you confess to a priest, were christened as a baby,
give money to a charity, or sponsored a child in a third-world country.

But God never granted you authority to design your own key. After all,
He owns the house and has the right to design the entry key however He
wishes. But in His grace, He has gone to great effort to share His key with
you. So, you must decide, when standing at the precipice of eternity, whose
key will you trust to open heaven's door—yours or His?

Lord Jesus, You not only hold the key to heaven, You are the key.
In You abides all my hope for heaven. How gracious of the Father to have You,
His Son, to open the door for me! Thank You. Amen.

# ❀ Dreams Do Come True ❀

*Quench not the Spirit* (1 Thessalonians 5:19).

We all have dreams to hold onto and think about when we're discouraged. Women love to dream they are Cinderella—that one day their prince will come and sweep them away to a lifetime of happiness. Some dream of taking a tour of the world, of being a famous opera star, or winning a million dollars and living happily ever after.

Then along come the dream-killers. You know them. They may work with you or live in your house. At least one of them belongs to every church. They sarcastically destroy all your dreams. They bluntly tell you your optimism about success can never come true. They quench your enthusiasm, collapse your faith, and weaken your resolve to hope.

Though the dream-killers try to destroy your faith in Jesus, He's the ultimate Prince Charming who will redeem His bride, the church. The bride will be perfect, without spot or blemish, and will live with Him in heaven eternally. What a feeling of security!

Have you ever been a dream-killer? Do you think some others could never be worthy of heaven? When we look at the poor, the lost, or the hungry, do we help fulfill their dreams, or does our apathy lead us to look the other way? Sometimes we discourage people who want to become Christians; we spread gossip, prejudice, or discouragement.

Since God is Love, we say we are godly, filled with love for all, yet our relationship of love with Jesus sometimes does not carry over to our relationships with society's outcasts. We say we love all people, but we just can't fall in love with the poor, the lost, or the hungry. It's hard to love a dirty person, a prostitute, or a drug addict.

May we reignite our love for God's people, continuing to dream, to encourage downcast people to dream, to share their dreams, and to help them to find their Prince, the One who is their way to eternal happiness.

Dear Lord, help us to dream, to share the dreams of others,
and to lead all of them to the Bridegroom, our Savior. Amen.

# ❀ I Just Assumed ❀

*So from now on we regard no one from a worldly point of view....*
*He has committed to us the message of reconciliation*
(2 Corinthians 5:16–19).

I was a pastor's daughter, and often during my teen years my family was invited to a member's home to eat lunch after Sunday services. Meals invariably offered a smorgasbord of great southern cooking, with fried chicken, mashed potatoes, corn bread, and sweet iced tea, not to mention homemade pies for dessert.

On one particular day, Miss Marie, a sweet, faithful member of our rural church, invited us to her home. After filling our plates, we joined hands, and Miss Marie asked my dad to lead the customary blessing. When he finished praying, I could hardly wait to take the first bite.

Just as we lifted our forks, Miss Marie announced matter-of-factly, "Brother Sargent, I don't think I'm saved."

My dad didn't miss a beat. "Well, Miss Marie," he said, "we can take care of that right now. Would you like to do that?"

"Yes, sir, I believe I would." Daddy escorted Miss Marie to her living room, where she confessed to the Lord she was a sinner and invited Him to be her personal Savior.

When they returned, we praised God for His salvation and Miss Marie's courage. The experience taught me never to assume that someone I know and love, and who is a faithful church member, has trusted Christ as personal Savior.

Do you ever become so comfortable in relationships with friends that you sometimes fail to ask the important questions? I confess I do. After all, I reason, they've been in church longer than I have, and they've prayed and ministered alongside me. I don't want to offend.

But can I truly say that I love my friends if I am not willing to risk my relationship with them to make sure they have embraced the most important relationship of all eternity?

Lord Jesus, make me the kind of friend who risks a friendship
to make sure someone I care about knows You personally. Amen.

# ❀ *The Invisible Umbilical* ❀

*This is my command: Love each other* (John 15:17).

Our older daughter, Meri Beth, excitedly handed me an official letter stating that she was a perfect match as a bone marrow donor. The letter requested that she come for a preliminary meeting.

We sat in rapt attention as the facts were presented. A thirty-eight-year old woman was dying with leukemia. It appeared that her only hope was the marrow transplant. Due to confidentiality laws, that was all they could tell us about her. They carefully explained the painful surgery that Meri Beth would endure if she chose to provide the needed marrow. Meri Beth agreed.

Our family and an entourage of friends traveled to the hospital where the surgery was performed. A Red Cross representative, cooler in hand, boarded a plane to transport the marrow. We received a call around 9:00 P.M. that the marrow had been delivered and the transfusion had begun.

We prayed for this unknown woman daily. Meri Beth told us that the name "Linda" had come to her as she prayed and we agreed that we would call her "Linda" in our prayers.

Almost a year later, "Linda" relapsed and needed more marrow. Our remarkable daughter willingly underwent the painful surgery again for a person she did not know.

The head of the Red Cross Bone Marrow program stayed with us during that surgery. She explained that the woman was very sick and she wanted to prepare us to help Meri Beth if "Linda" didn't survive. "No one can explain it," she said, "but a strong emotional tie forms between the donor and the recipient, even though they do not know each other. It's called the 'invisible umbilical.'"

Several months later we received the dreaded call. Tearfully, I told the caller how the name "Linda" had come to Meri Beth in praying for the recipient and I wondered if we could at least find out her first name. There was stunned silence on the other end.

"Mrs. Brown," she replied, "you have no idea how close you are."
The invisible umbilical…what a powerful bond between two strangers!

Dear Lord, please keep us attached to You and to others
through the invisible umbilical, the Holy Spirit. In Jesus's name, amen.

# ❊ Stand Down ❊

*But Jesus said to him, "Put your sword in its place, for all who take the*
*sword will perish by the sword" (Matthew 26:52 NKJV).*

It had been a trying evening for Peter. Jesus had informed him, and not in private, that He would deny the Lord three times before the rooster's crow (Matthew 26:31–35). He had disappointed Jesus in the Garden of Gethsemane by falling asleep when he should've been praying for his friend (Matthew 26:36–43). Then, when armed soldiers arrived, Peter impetuously cut off the high priest's servant's ear (John 18:10). Was Peter an expert swordsman with incredible aim to hit the ear, or was he wildly flailing his sword as nervousness caused him to strike a mere servant in the head? Only Jesus knew. The Lord refused for others' blood to be shed during His time to give His life sacrificially. Jesus told Peter to stand down with his sword (Luke 22:51).

In John's account, Jesus explained to Peter not to fight because the time had come for His death. However, note that Matthew's account gives emphasis to Jesus telling Peter not to fight because of the way fighting affects followers of Christ: those who wield a sword will eventually be pierced themselves.

Peter was a leader. He was in the inner circle of Christ's followers, a man desperately wanting to live up to the love He had for His Savior. However, he hadn't yet learned the ways of Jesus; in the face of violent opposition, he responded with violent opposition.

How do you respond to opposition? Do you "fight fire with fire"? Do you play the game of "tit for tat"? It's often hardest to remain on higher ground when your enemies begin telling lies and slinging mud, but Jesus warns that fighting leads to personal loss.

Jesus restored the servant's ear (Luke 22:51). Jesus is a Healer. As a follower of Christ, imagine the Lord standing beside you as you look into the face of your enemies. What would Jesus ask you to do?

Lord, be my Defense and Protector! Please give me strength
to fight the temptation to do harm to my enemies.
In Jesus's name I pray, amen.

# ❀ When Why Won't Do ❀

*He poured out His soul unto death, and He was numbered with the transgressors, and He bore the sin of many, and made intercession for the transgressors* (Isaiah 53:12 NKJV).

She had lost her only child to leukemia. "If I could just know why..." her voice trailed off. Perhaps you, too, have wondered why. *Why* questions come on the heels of life's worst tragedies. *Why* did my child leave behind his faith when he left for college? *Why* did the relationship I poured my life into fail? *Why* did I get fired from my job? *Why* the terrifying diagnosis, the lost dream, the betrayal that cut so deep I can barely remember to breathe, much less forgive?

*Why* is the most-often voiced question of the hurting. Yet, seldom does its answer provide the solace that its anticipation promises. Are we left then without help or hope with the *why* just sitting in the middle of our thoughts and days like an unwelcome but stubborn squatter, laying claim to territory it doesn't really own but nevertheless seems to control?

When the answers to why don't come, or *do* come and are not enough, knowing *who* can give us the safe haven we long for. The One who has foreseen and permitted our pain is also the One who took on Himself the sorrow we most fear and the sin we most hate. He set His face like flint to embrace the Cross, becoming the shield that absorbed the Father's holy anger toward our sin. Surely He carried all our grief on His very own heart.

Knowing *who*—knowing *Him*—assures that beyond all the maybe-I-should-have's and anxious if-only's there stands One Who endured the greatest grief—*our* grief—and wears the scars caused by our sins. We can rest in Him and trust that He has already been through the darkest moments of despair and has gained the other side where light shines again and the day is filled with hopes and dreams.

Thank You, Lord, for promising that I will make it through, but until then,
You will stay near, speaking gentle words of strength and peace,
for You know well the place I walk. Amen.

# ❊ *Signs of the Times* ❊

*Immediately after the distress of those days 'the sun will be darkened,
and the moon will not give its light; the stars will fall from the sky,
and the heavenly bodies will be shaken.' At that time the sign of the
Son of Man will appear in the sky, and all the nations of the earth
will mourn* (Matthew 24:29,30).

Songs, poems, paintings, books, and dramas all try to depict the Second
Coming of Jesus. Yet, as imaginative and descriptive as artists, authors,
and actors are, no mere human can comprehend how awesome and awe-
inspiring that day will be.

Biblical prophecies foretell more about the Second Coming of Jesus
than about His First Advent. Just as a great star accompanied His birth in
Bethlehem (Matthew 2:2), today's verse relates that signs and wonders in
the heavens will also accompany His Second Advent. The sun and moon
will be darkened and the stars will fall from the heavens. Can we even begin
to imagine what that will be like?

The events in Matthew 24 describe a time of great tribulation preceding Jesus's return to earth. In sequential order, Jesus explained to His disciples what would transpire on the earth prior to His appearance.

As we look at the detailed list, we certainly see that the stage is being
set for many of these events to take place. Jesus said, *"Therefore keep watch,
because you do not know on what day your Lord will come"* (Matthew 24:42).

For what are we to watch? We are to watch for the fulfillment of the
events He described in Matthew 24. The question of eternal significance in
life is "are you ready?" If the earth as we know it should end today, what
will happen to you? When all is said and done, that is what really matters.

Dear Lord, please give us the wisdom and the courage
to do what is necessary to prepare for Your return.
In Jesus's name, amen.

# ❋ One Goat ❋

*For you know the grace of our Lord Jesus Christ, that though He was*
*rich, yet for your sakes He became poor, that you through His poverty*
*might become rich* (2 Corinthians 8:9 NKJV).

The story is told that the famous nineteenth-century missionary, David Livingstone, once met with a tribal chief in Africa. The chief told Livingstone he couldn't proceed into the territory without first abiding by their trading custom: the chief could choose to keep any of Livingstone's possessions, and the chief would in turn give Livingstone something of worth. The chief looked over Livingstone's items, and then seized his goat.

The missionary was distressed to lose his goat, which was his source of milk, his only liquid nourishment in a land of impure water. However, a tribesman explained that what the chief had given him in return—a carved stick—was his royal scepter, which would serve as an entry pass into every community in the territory. Livingstone was upset about the loss of his needed goat until he realized the exchange provided a gateway for his greater cause: the gospel.

Livingstone had a passion to reach Africans with the gospel. Who are you passionate about reaching for Christ? What are you willing to sacrifice to share Jesus with them? Livingstone was upset about the loss of his needed goat until he realized the exchange provided a gateway for his greater cause: the gospel.

Perhaps God is calling you to give up something—a habit, a sense of security, or a possession—to break down a barrier to share the gospel with someone. If the people of God are going to reach the world for Jesus, we must be willing to sacrifice for His cause. Our great example, Jesus, laid down His very life that others might be saved. Lay out your possessions before the great "Chief," Holy God above. Are you willing to say to the Lord who gives and takes away, "Take anything I have if it will help me reach someone for Jesus Christ"?

Father in heaven, how I long to give my life to You completely!
What possession can I give away to further Your kingdom?
Give me greater passion for the souls of the lost
than for my personal comfort and pleasure. Amen.

# ❀ Joy-Moment Memories ❀

*Do not be anxious about anything, but in everything, by prayer and*
*petition, with thanksgiving, present your requests to God*
(Philippians 4:6).

From late January until April 2007, I was sick in the hospital with pneumonia. In the worst stages of health, I could hardly breathe. My congested lungs caused nausea, and I couldn't even keep water down. With infection and a raging fever, I became groggy. To say *my chest hurt* is an understatement; the pressure was unbearable. I went home, feeling as if I had a cement block on my chest. Anxious about my job, family, and church, all went lacking as I stayed in bed, taking my antibiotic medicine, hoping for recovery.

My doctor threatened to put me back in the hospital if I didn't begin eating. I asked God to help me keep the food down so I could regain my strength. I thanked God for His grace and mercy; He'd been good to me in spite of the pneumonia. Because my husband had died of a heart attack just a few years before, I knew God had carried me over rough times; He would carry me through this lingering pneumonia. I wanted to be able to go tell my lost friends about Him and His grace and mercy.

From personal experience I know God answers prayers, maybe not overnight, but He always comes through.

And He did in the spring.

Every day in April, I kept down solid food for the first time in weeks. Then I was able to get out of bed a few minutes at a time, and then later for extended periods. God brought me out, without a doubt.

I tell others about how good God was during that dark time. It feels good to minister to others rather than to depend on others ministering to me. I believe God creates us with a heart for ministry.

Paul was grateful for ministering friends: "I rejoice greatly in the Lord that at last you have renewed your concern for me, but you had no opportunity to show it." After we've had no opportunity, it feels great to be able to minister, bringing joy to the giver and receiver.

Dear Lord, thank You for the strength to minister in Your name, amen.

# ❊ Taking Giant Steps ❊

*"I am God, the God of your father," he said. "Do not be afraid to go
down to Egypt, for I will make you into a great nation there"*
(Genesis 46:3).

Jacob was a trickster, a worrier, and a selfish, dishonest father who caused jealousy among his children. A fly-by-the-seat-of-his-pants planner, he was not consistently an example of righteous living! Yet God chose him as the vessel to carry the message of His love. He took giant steps in God's will.

Like us, Jacob didn't deserve God's mercy. He was often afraid, yet God called him as a man of courage. Like us, after God touched him, Jacob's spirit revived and he moved out, as God led him on a journey of faith.

When God called Jacob (Genesis 46:2), he answered, *"Here I am."* God responded with the comforting words above: *"Do not be afraid"* (Genesis 46:3).

How about our courage today? Are we eager to move out on new ventures with our Lord? Some Christians confess that they have secretly prayed no one would ever ask them about Jesus. Others want to move out for God, but are uncomfortable around Christ-seekers. Perhaps they're afraid they'll stumble over their words. As God empowers us, we can relax and share His love with others.

Sometimes Christians think they must be perfect before they say, "Send me." Even the most capable ones may fear they have little to offer. When God leads, we can witness, mentor, and take giant steps we've never taken before; we can sail out on a successful missions trip. We *do* have great things to offer.

Take heart. God is always ready to quell our fears. Today, rejoice that He's always near—and sufficient to help us do *the impossible*. We just ask. As we approach opportunities, may we answer as Jacob did when God called him: *"Here I am."*

> God of Courage, thank You for dissolving our fears.
> Help us take giant steps to follow You wherever You lead.
> Open doors and move us out! In Jesus's name, amen.

# ❀ A Walk in the Park ❀

*Righteousness goes before him and prepares the way for his steps*
(Psalm 85:13).

Have you ever known for sure that you were in the right place at the right time? A few years ago I had such an experience.

I accompanied the youth from our church to what's known as MissionFuge, in Philadelphia. Our team had the task of working in a neighborhood park. A gang had taken it over and the citizens banded together to reclaim it for the children to have a place to play. Every night the gang trashed it and painted graffiti on the buildings and playground equipment. Every morning, a group of citizens cleaned up the debris and repainted the damaged items. Eventually, the gang moved on to another location.

On our last day, I met a woman walking her dogs. I began playing with her dogs. As we talked, we found out that we both had similar work backgrounds. We each had been itinerant teachers with a degree in reading.

Our conversation then moved to spiritual matters. She admitted she needed a relationship with the Lord. I shared with her about Christ's atoning love. She bowed her head to pray to receive Christ when a large dog ran across the park. Her dogs broke loose and chased him.

We ran as fast as we could to catch her beloved pets. Some of the youth joined in the chase and brought them back to her. The bus arrived for us to return to the college where we were staying, and I knew our time was short.

"Getting back to where we were," I continued, half afraid she would change the subject. However, she joyfully followed through with her commitment.

We prayed; we rejoiced; and we cried. We hugged each other just before I boarded the bus, and we affirmed that now we were sisters.

I thank God that a walk in the park became a walk into a relationship with Him. I praise Him for placing my new sister and me in the right place at the right time!

> Dear Lord, thank You for all the ways You work to have us
> where You want us to be. In Jesus's name, amen.

# ❀ *Red Rover* ❀

*God has chosen the weak things of the world*
*to put to shame the things which are mighty*
(1 Corinthians 1:27 NKJV).

The kids huddled in the schoolyard, sun beaming down on sweaty faces. Two teams faced off for battle. The goal: break through the other team's chain-link of gripped arms and gritted teeth.

But first, teams had to be chosen. Team captains reviewed potential recruits with the glaring eyes of marine sergeants. Finally, as I stood staring at my feet, I was selected by a disenchanted captain who called my name with a sigh. Then the game was on. My heart thumped hard. The call rang out. "Red Rover, Red Rover, let Tricia come over!"

My mouth went dry, my stomach turned to lead, and my knees buckled beneath me. I couldn't have run through a wet noodle on a warm day, and everyone knew it. I ran, eyes scanning for the weakest link, two wimpy girls whose eyes showed fear like mine. I raced forward with the renewed confidence of a marathon runner. I hurled my body against the entwined pair of skinny arms.

They were stronger than they looked. My body rebounded through the air, and I landed like a rag doll in a poof of dust. I stood slowly and limped away, pondering the depressing prospect of countless future games in which this scene would repeat itself. It was going to be a long school career.

When I think that God Almighty chose me for His team, I'm flabbergasted. *Me?* And He was smiling when He called my name! No annoyed resignation in His tone: "OK, I *guess* I'll take Tricia."

No! He said, "Look, Tricia, I've made the greatest sacrifice for you to be on my team."

"But, Jesus, don't You know my story? Remember, I'm 'Can't-run-through-a-wet-noodle-on-a-warm-day' Tricia!" He just opened His arms and said I was the perfect candidate for showing how gracious and how strong and how loving our God is. For if God chose me, then there's hope for any willing heart.

Thank You, Lord, for using me to reveal Your magnificent love.
Let every person reading this today know that success is not determined
by how strong we are but how strong our God is! Amen.

# ❀ Boxed In or Coming Out ❀

*But you will receive power when the Holy Spirit comes on you;*
*and you will be my witnesses in Jerusalem, and in all Judea and*
*Samaria, and to the ends of the earth* (Acts 1:8).

This year I'm compiling a local history of Woman's Missionary Union (WMU). For fodder, former leaders for this association (the "Network") have given me stacks of reports, prayer retreat schedules, and meeting agendas. Betty Jo Littlefield, the former WMU director for the Network, gave me a large plastic box for these precious items. When I pull one item out, I can hardly squeeze it back in; the items are compressed under tremendous pressure. Several times the papers have exploded like prisoners trying to escape.

These items are useless as they lie idle in this box, but one day they'll come alive in a beautiful history book of God's work. Then others may reminisce about working in tandem with God in our area. It will be stored electronically as well as on a hard copy saved as a keepsake in the archives of an office of record.

Imagine a young woman centuries from now dusting off the old book and reading. Her eyes may light up as it comes alive in her heart. She may grow closer to her Savior as she reads about His salvation of lost persons in the Network. Each person who reads it may experience a personal, living reaction.

How many times have people picked up the Bible and have it come alive in their hands as they read the written Word? Luke says they'll receive power from the Holy Spirit so they may be witnesses in Jerusalem, Judea, Samaria, and the ends of the earth. God waits for us to ask for His power, and then to explode out of the box and *be* the message of God, molding the world with our Christian worldview. We can start now, asking for a vision to represent Him to lost, troubled people.

O Savior, come alive in the hearts of people in our day and in the future.
Give us a vision for getting out of our boxes and exploding with the gospel
from our own towns to the ends of the earth. Amen.

# ❀ *It's All Gone, Mama?* ❀

*But to you who fear My name the Sun of Righteousness shall arise with*
*healing in His wings* (Malachi 4:2 NKJV).

Recently my husband, Randy, was diagnosed with a cancerous lung tumor. Before we knew the diagnosis, Randy went through numerous tests, including a biopsy, during which the growth was removed for testing. Days passed as we waited for the results. We asked the Lord to help us trust in Him, not in the probability of a good outcome, and He granted us an undergirding peace.

Finally, Randy called me while I was teaching at our Christian high school. He said, "Tricia, I just talked with the doctor, and he said the tumor is gone. I don't need surgery because there's nothing to remove."

I ran to the kindergarten classroom where our daughter Sara works. "Sara, the doctor called and Dad's tumor is gone. The biopsy got it all," I said. Huge tears welled, and as though she hadn't heard right she said, "It's all gone, mama?"

"It's gone. No surgery, no chemo, no radiation, no nothing. We hugged, and that night we all went out for a celebration supper.

Randy is monitored closely. We realize these things can sneak back. We also know that sometimes God says no to our requests for reasons we don't understand but trust are best. Yet, we can confidently affirm that every healing and peace that occurs in this life comes from the Healer alone.

Throughout history God has repeatedly shown compassion for our physical ills brought on by the curse of sin. He particularly seems to enjoy healing on the heels of exercised faith.

In the Old Testament, the Great Physician's healing in response to faith is demonstrated in stories such as Naaman's, a pompous man with leprosy, who finally humbled himself to God by dunking himself seven times in the dirty Jordan River, only to find his oozing sores replaced by baby-soft skin as he came up from the water the seventh time. In the New Testament, the Gospel writers often recorded the Lord healing sick people. Every one of these healings hints at the ultimate restoring of our physical bodies at His return for those who fear His name.

Lord, we anticipate with great joy
the future healing to come for those who fear Your name. Amen.

# ❀ A Whale of a Revival ❀

*But the LORD provided a great fish to swallow Jonah, and Jonah was*
*inside the fish three days and three nights* (Jonah 1:17).

God told Jonah, a Jewish prophet, to go to Nineveh to preach the message of repentance. Jonah did not want to go to this well-known city in Assyria. The cruelty of the Assyrians was unparalleled in ancient history. Some of their torturous practices included pulling out the tongues of their victims by the roots, flaying the skin of war prisoners inch by inch to stretch their skins on the city walls, and impaling people on long poles and raising them into the air, leaving them until they died. It has been said that large piles of human heads marked the path of these brutal conquerors. Can you imagine how difficult it must have been for Jonah to consider taking a message of repentance to such people? However, the real heart of the matter is mentioned twice in this same verse. Jonah tried to flee from God.

The real miracle of this story is not that Jonah lived after being swallowed by a great fish. Several documented accounts confirm the same thing happening to other people. The real miracle is that God did not give up on the people of Nineveh or on Jonah. When the fish deposited Jonah onto dry land, *"the word of the Lord came to Jonah a second time: 'Go to the great city of Nineveh and proclaim to it the message I give you'"* (Jonah 3:1–2).

This time Jonah went where God told him to go and did what God told him to do. The Ninevites believed God. They declared a fast, and all of them, from the greatest to the least, put on sackcloth. God not only had provided a great fish to accomplish His purpose, but He also had prepared a great prophet for one of the greatest revivals recorded in Scripture!

Dear God, please forgive us for our disobedience.
Help us to go willingly and do all You call us to do.
Please use us to help bring revival wherever we go.
In Jesus's name, amen.

# ❀ *What's to Love?* ❀

*When Jesus reached the spot, he looked up and said to him, "Zacchaeus,
come down immediately. I must stay at your house today." So he came
down at once and welcomed him gladly* (Luke 19:5–6).

When our youngest daughter Emily was little, her daddy and her sister,
Sara, brought home a stuffed animal—a wombat—from their trip to
Australia. He wasn't a hi-tech toy, just a stuffed "burrowing marsupial,"
according to Webster. At first, I couldn't see anything endearing about
the rodent-like toy. But "Wombattie," as Emily called him, had found a
place in her heart. She kissed him good-bye when she left for school
each morning, and at bedtime, he was her favorite snuggle friend. After
a few years, most of Wombattie's hair had been loved off, but still nearly-
hairless Wombattie remained a faithful friend, sitting in the honored place
atop her bed pillow. Interestingly, over time, *I* started to notice Wombattie's
endearing qualities!

Perhaps you've come across a rather unlovable person. In fact, you
might say, she's rather wombat-like. Maybe she's lived a life you find repul-
sive. Or maybe her mannerisms rub you the wrong way. Yet, God has called
you to love her and you know it. What will you do? Will you find ways to
get to know her or will you keep her at arms-length?

In Luke 19, we read that Jesus met an unlovable tax collector,
Zacchaeus. Zach's own people hated him, since he worked for the Roman
government and demanded exorbitant sums for taxes, pocketing some for
himself.

Yet, Jesus went to Zacchaeus' home, and reclining at the supper table
(as was customary), fellowshipped with him.

So, when your "Zacchaeus" shows up at the door or starts chatting
in the coffee room at work, will you push her away, or will you see her as
Jesus does?

Lord, I realize I'm rather wombat-like myself, yet You have loved me
with an everlasting love. Help me see this woman as You see her
and love her in Your name. Amen.

*°Wombat's story first appeared in* Woman to Woman: Preparing Yourself to Mentor *by Edna Ellison and
Tricia Scribner (New Hope Publishers, 2005).*

# ❀ *Valentine Love* ❀

*No one has ever seen God; but if we love one another, God lives in us*
*and his love is made complete in us* (1 John 4:12).

"I've met the perfect man, Drew," Sharon said. "No one's ever loved me as much as Drew. I've been searching for him all my life." Shortly afterward, Sharon and Drew married.

I moved out of town, but spoke with Sharon three years later. "How are you and Drew?" I asked. Looking down, she told me of a shallow love that diminished a few months after their wedding. Two years later, they divorced. As we talked over lunch, she explained her discovery of the true meaning of love.

"We had Valentine love," she said. "You know, *eros*, romantic love. We had a little *philos*, brotherly love. We liked watching television together and going to football games with friends, but I'm sure we didn't have *agape*, the unselfish love of Christ."

"Sounds like you've been to a Bible study!"

"Yes, just finished studying about what love really means. I figured I needed it, since I've been confused for years. Our teacher called them: Valentine love—the *eros* kind; Buddy love—the philos kind; and Jesus love—the *agape* kind.

Sharon suffered from the same kind of confusion many of us have. With only one English word for love, we say: "I love practical jokes; I love chocolate; I love my dog to death; and I love revenge."

Of course, Jesus is the best example of *agape*, the highest form of love, since He sacrificed Himself on the Cross for our salvation. "Jesus love" is unselfish love that lasts. Sharon finally understood that great marriages need all three: Valentine love, Buddy love, and Jesus love. May each single Christian wait for that balanced combination, settling for nothing less in a spouse.

And what about our loving relationship with the rest of the world? May each of us reflect on *agape*, study it in action, and strive to show the depth of His compassion and endurance every day.

Loving Lord, keep us ever in Your agape love. May we show it constantly
to others. Help us to understand the difference between
the three kinds of love, and lead others in agape.

*The real names of persons in this story have been changed.*

# ❀ A Minis-tree in Your Yard ❀

*Do not forget the things your eyes have seen… Teach them to your*
*children and to their children after them* (Deuteronomy 4:9).

One Sunday morning, Sara sat in church enjoying the organ music her sister, Carole, played. Carole's daughters sang with the praise team, along with Sara's daughter, Elizabeth. Her mother was serving in child care and her brother, Alex, helped as an usher, along with her husband, Dave. Each had special talent for ministry.

"Where's my ministry, God?" Sara whispered. "I have no musical talent." She remembered the humiliation of trying to sing in a children's choir. Later, she had flopped at playing the guitar. Her shyness had held her back from teaching a Sunday School class or witnessing to unsaved people. *Lord, show me my ministry. What could it be?*

Sara waked from her daydreaming to hear her pastor say, "You're looking in the wrong place. Have you looked at your family lately? Usually my message focuses on outreach, thinking beyond these walls, helping unchurched people, but your ministry may center around those in your immediate or extended family who don't know God or have drifted apart from Him."

The pastor read the verse above from Deuteronomy. "We need to remember what we've seen, too. In one generation we can lose our Christian heritage if we don't pass it along. Think of your family tree: parents, children, siblings, nieces, nephews, and cousins. What about your in-laws?" Laughter followed as he joked about loving their in-laws. "And," he said, "You may have a minis-tree, as well as a family tree, in your own backyard!"

Sara had always loved genealogy, visiting family cemeteries to fill out family-tree charts. She thought of her cousins, Heather and Sam, who seldom came to church. Suddenly, she had her answer: she could visit them, asking about others in their family tree whose full names were missing from her chart. Sharing her faith, she could encourage them to come to church. Her ministry would be a minis-tree in her own backyard.

O God, help us not to forget what our eyes have seen
and pass Your love along to our children and others in the family tree. Amen.

# ❀ Not-So-Precious Memories ❀

*For we have spent enough of our past lifetime*
*in doing the will of the Gentiles* (1 Peter 4:3 NKJV).

A few times a year, I open every closet, search under beds, pull out drawers, examine the shelves, and bag up every unwanted item in the house. Oh, it's sheer pleasure to rid the house of clutter! Last year, I tackled a neglected spot filled with forgotten collectibles: my hope chest.

When I got married, my grandfather made a beautiful cedar chest for me to store my precious memories, but as a young woman, my then-precious memories were softball trophies, academic plaques, newspaper clippings, and yearbooks. As I opened the chest, my eyes met with memory after memory, many of which were unpleasant. I tried to hurry through the process, but finally gave into the temptation to settle on the carpet and thumb through my high school yearbooks. I saw names I had forgotten and faces I hadn't seen in years, including my own young face, smiling in the photos to mask the confusion within my heart. I caught myself reliving old feelings of hopelessness and regret, and I closed the yearbook.

I then deposited six years' worth of yearbooks in the trash. How could I throw away my records of the past? I hadn't looked back in years, and when I sat down for a brief moment and began to revisit who I used to be, all that came to mind were days wasted on worldly living.

When you look back into your past, do you recall dark moments of time when you were out of the will of God? I won't allow those memories in my heart to discourage me in my present walk with Christ, but I will use them as a reminder that I have wasted far too much time living for myself, pleasing the world; I must press on for Jesus. I must be committed to live for Him. I must be surrendered to His calling. I must do the will of God.

Heavenly Father, I can say with certainty that I've spent enough time
in my past doing the will of the world. My heart's desire is
to spend the rest of my life doing Your will!
Teach me to make my days count. Amen.

# ❋ *Noteworthy* ❋

*Then those who feared the LORD spoke to one another, and the LORD
listened and heard them; so a book of remembrance was written before
Him for those who fear the LORD and who meditate on His name*
(Malachi 3:16 NKJV).

What an amazing glimpse this verse gives us into the interactions of heaven
and earth, between God on His throne and people who walk dusty roads.
Believers gathered together and shared testimonies of God's goodness with
each other. None of their dialogue is disclosed to us, not even a hint of a
single story. Did a mother talk about her healthy children? Did a father
mention God's provision of food? Perhaps they were thankful just to be alive
and credited the Giver of Life for His hand of mercy. Whatever testimonials
those mortal tongues spoke, divine ears were listening. Almighty God had
"eavesdropped" from on high, and He found their words noteworthy.

The events of Malachi 3:16 happened after God told the people they
had spoken harshly against their God (Malachi 3:13–15). This small faithful remnant of believers had risen above the murmuring and complaining
of their people. When people around you begin to grumble, do you catch a
case of the grumbles yourself? Or, do you speak words to build up others
and praise God, allowing God, not outside circumstances, to direct your
thoughts?

Your words matter to God. He is not only *able* to hear you, but He
is in tune to every syllable that rolls off your tongue. Is God pleased with
your conversations with others lately? Let Malachi 3:16 motivate you to
choose your words carefully today. Ask God to help you get into a habit of
speaking words that are pleasing to Him at all times, always praising His
name and acknowledging His goodness as you talk with people throughout
the day.

Heavenly Father, help me be aware of Your listening ears today.
I want to please You with my words, and I want to give You praise
no matter what situation I have to face today. When others begin
to complain, guard my heart to remain pure in thought, word, and deed.
In the name of Jesus I pray, amen.

# ❀ No Excuse ❀

*For the wrath of God is revealed from heaven against all ungodliness and unrighteousness of men, who suppress the truth in unrighteousness, because what may be known of God is manifest in them, for God has shown it to them (Romans 1:18–20 NKJV).*

"Why would God send people to hell who have never heard of Jesus?" asked a student in my Bible class at the Christian high school where I teach. This question has left a few of us staring at our toes during conversations with unbelievers.

Paul addressed the issue in the first two chapters of Romans by asserting that God has made Himself known to *all* people through *creation* and *conscience*. Humans are accountable for how they respond to God's general revelation. First, Romans 1:18–20 says every person has been shown evidence of God's existence through creation. When a person looks at the sky, he knows that Someone far bigger, more powerful, and supremely intelligent exists.

Second, Romans 2:14–15 says every person has been given *conscience*—an innate awareness of right and wrong. God Himself instilled this universal sense of morality as *"the work of the law written in their hearts, their conscience also bearing witness"* (Romans 2:15 NKJV). Conscience cannot merely be a socially learned concept because even isolated tribes develop their own code of conduct—right and wrong—showing that conscience comes from a morally perfect external Source.

Instead of humbly responding to God's revelation, Paul said many *"suppress the truth in unrighteousness"* (Romans 1:18), and make their own gods. You probably know people who believe that nature is all there is, or that they themselves possess inner godness, or that one must live morally to go to heaven: all evidences that people choose their own gods. Those who reject the truth revealed through creation and conscience close the door to receiving further truth about Jesus Christ's provision for every person's salvation. The Scripture says their hearts *"are darkened."*

While God is loving, He does not force anyone to believe. He reveals Himself, lets the person choose, then honors the choice made, even the choice to separate one's self from God.

God, You took the initiative to reveal Yourself to us.
Please open the eyes of lost friends so that they turn to You
and are given more light to know Jesus. Amen.

# ❧ *The Cattle on a Thousand Hills* ❧

*For every animal of the forest is mine,*
*and the cattle on a thousand hills* (Psalm 50:10).

When I was a child, my family traveled often to the mountains of North Carolina. I was fascinated by the large herds of cattle we saw grazing in mountain pastures.

Today's verse gives me great comfort. It helps me realize that just as God owns everything in this world, including the cattle on a thousand hills, certainly He has the resources to take care of all my needs. He also has the desire to do so.

We are assured in Philippians 4:19, *"my God will meet all your needs according to his glorious riches in Christ Jesus."* The first part of that verse is thrilling. Just knowing that God will supply all my needs is wonderful. But, the verse does not end there. God not only promises to supply all my needs, He promises to do so according to His riches in glory.

Therefore, whenever we have a need, we can rest assured that God will fill that need from His treasure of unlimited supplies. His Word promises us so.

The most wonderful awareness of all is the way in which He chooses to supply our needs—through Christ Jesus. Those who have come into a relationship with Jesus Christ never have to worry about anything. Every need will be met—abundantly, sometimes miraculously, and lovingly.

I once heard the story of a seminary that needed a large sum of money in order to remain open. The president prayed in faith that, since God owned the cattle on a thousand hills, He would provide what the school needed. Unknowingly, a wealthy cattle rancher felt led to make a large donation in the exact amount the school needed. As a member of the Board of Trustees handed the cattleman's check to the seminary president, he smiled and said, "I think God just sold some of those cows."

Dear God, we thank You in advance for the way(s) You will choose
to answer our prayers. In Jesus's name, amen.

# ❀ *Wi-Fi Woes* ❀

*For He made Him who knew no sin to be sin for us, that we might
become the righteousness of God in Him* (2 Corinthians 5:21 NKJV).

I bought a new computer six months ago, only to learn that a newer version with more RAM hit the market two months later. I'm not sure what RAM is, but I suspect it will cost me several hundred dollars to get more of it. Not only am I pushed to my intellectual limit when working on a computer, but also the complexity of my remote-control run TV has forced me to consult my 18-year-old daughter just to watch a DVD movie.

I admit I'm a little intimidated by the millennial generation and their high-tech appetites and abilities. Yet, they are fast becoming the bulk of the population. Since I've housed three teens, I'm looking forward in my aged years to rubbing shoulders with a million or two more all-knowing youngsters who honestly believe they invented flare jeans.

Jesus must have felt similarly when He came to earth. Imagine, one day He heard the perpetual angelic rendition, "Holy, holy, holy!" The next day He awakened to a rough-hewn manger and donkeys braying.

He could have said, "No, way. I'm going home." Instead, He stayed. And He didn't just tolerate us. He *loved* us. He lived with, walked with, and ate with us. He healed us. He even learned our language.

It's true I'm going to have to work pretty hard to get to know the millennial generation. Their "wi-fi" and "bluetooth" language is foreign, and some of their ways are rough around the edges. But even if I can't fully appreciate their dialect, I can listen to the cry of their hearts just as Jesus listened to mine, and respond to them as Jesus did to me when He *"made Himself of no reputation,"* took on the form of a servant, and came *"in the likeness of men"* (Philippians 2:8 NKJV).

Instead of treating me as different, Lord, You became like me,
wearing clothes like me and even talking in ways I could understand.
How gracious is Your love. Amen.

# ❀ A Faithful Servant ❀

*I have fought the good fight. I have finished my course,*
*I have kept the faith* (2 Timothy 4:7 KJV).

If we want to be faithful servants, we can turn to our Bibles for good examples. Paul is one of the best examples of a faithful servant. He writes to the young evangelist he had mentored, Timothy, to assure the younger Christian that he hadn't given up hope. Earlier, he had left a life of influence as a Roman citizen, a respected Jewish rabbi, and became a humble servant to the small band of Christians who believed in Jesus. Unlike some of us who burn hot with fervor and then burnout and lose our enthusiasm for Christian service, Paul was faithful to death, becoming one of many first-century martyrs.

Jesus advised early Christians, *"And as you go, preach, saying, the kingdom of heaven is at hand"* (Matthew 10:7 NKJV). Following these words that earlier Christians handed down to Paul, he had become an evangelist and missionary who traveled the known world at that time, preaching and telling the world about Jesus, the Messiah, who had come to bring salvation to everyone. Paul had also become a church planter, establishing churches across Asia Minor. He was the first missionary to what's now Europe and led many people to know the Lord.

As remarkable as that record is, Paul had done more. He had persevered. He had finished the course. His faith had never wavered. He could have rejected Christ and probably have avoided death, but He was faithful to the end, regardless of persecution or punishment.

Paul knew how to communicate the gospel. He did it through active evangelism across his own country, missions trips to faraway lands, preaching in various areas, and establishing thriving churches. Perhaps his best missional communication, however, was not through his courageous activity, but simply through his long-lasting, unwavering, serene living-out of his faith till the end.

As zealous Christians, we talk about preaching and teaching and traveling great distances for God, but perhaps our greatest method for communicating the gospel is simply being faithful.

Dear Lord, help us to be found faithful to the end. In Jesus's name, amen.

# ❦ *How Long Is Ministry?* ❦

*And as for you, brothers, never tire of doing what is right*
(2 Thessalonians 3:13).

"We shouldn't just give a token ministry of compassion to a poor family at Christmas," one of the young women in our missions group said, "or give food to the homeless on Thanksgiving. Let's do something that is ongoing…lasting."

I missed the next meeting, but one member told me they had decided to take food to a paralyzed woman with multiple sclerosis, whose husband had just divorced her. Her two teenaged sons bathed, dressed, and fed her every morning before school and took care of her after school, but she had no one to care for her during the day. Our group decided to spend an hour or two each day, bringing lunch with enough leftovers for their family's dinner.

That sounded like a worthwhile ministry. "How long will we do it?" I asked.

"For the duration," she answered. "Until the end of her life."

"What?" I asked.

"We decided to help her until she dies."

"I never thought of that."

"Our group is large enough that we shouldn't have to prepare lunch more than once or twice a month. Some people will get off work for an extended lunch hour, so they can take lunch to her and have time to feed her. Their employers have already said they could. It's going to work great!"

We fulfilled our promise to the paralyzed woman and her sons. Instead of being tired in the ministry, it became an incredible blessing the longer we did it. The precious mother grew closer to God daily. Her sons became close to all of us over the years, and we followed up with them after their mother died.

Have you ever wondered how long ministry lasts? Forever! No Christian retires from service. As long as we live, God will give us opportunities to share His love. And He loved the verse above so much that He repeated the thought in another place in the Bible. *"Let us not become weary in doing good"* (Galatians 6:9).

Lord, thank You for trusting us to minister to Your children.
Help us not grow weary in doing good.
Give us energy and enthusiasm for each day's ministry. Amen.

---

# ❧ The "Wow" Factor ❧

*"He must increase, but I must decrease"* (John 3:30 NKJV).

As you seek to root out pride in your heart, do you usually approach it from the angle of not considering yourself better than others? Be aware: pride can manifest itself in many different forms. Any time you focus on yourself instead of God, whether it's exalting yourself because of your abilities or belittling yourself because of your inabilities, it's a form of pride. Focus on self fails to consider the most important factor to spiritual success, which is the power of God.

The words of John the Baptist are quoted above in John 3:30. John the Baptist had what you might call the "wow" factor; a man who eats locusts and honey, preaching powerful words of repentance in the wilderness, tends to get a reaction of "wow" from the crowd. However, John knew what he had to offer people was of no consequence in comparison to what Jesus was coming to offer—eternal life.

Likewise, when people come in contact with you, the memory of you once you've gone away will dwindle over time no matter how charming, how intelligent—no matter how much "wow" factor you possess—but if people meet Jesus as a result of interacting with you, then your effect on them will be eternal. Give no further thought to your personal inadequacies, or trying to build up your "wow" factor. God working in you and through you is the matchless power that can turn your world toward Jesus.

As you step out for Christ in faith each day, you must decrease—in the way you see yourself as well as how you present yourself to others—that Christ may increase. In your prayertime today, be mindful of making Christ the center of your focus. For all aspects of your life, ask God to give you the desire to magnify Christ instead of yourself.

> Heavenly Father, I want to adjust my prayers today
> to reflect a desire for Jesus Christ to increase in my life.
> I want Jesus Christ to be magnified in my life
> that others might turn to Him. Amen.

# ❀ *Show Me the Stairway* ❀

*Be anxious for nothing, but in everything by prayer and supplication,*
*with thanksgiving, let your requests be made known to God*
(Philippians 4:6 NKJV).

The first solo I ever sang in church was "One Day at a Time." I was seven, and there were quite a few snickers when I belted out, "I'm only human; I'm just a woman." I remember memorizing those song lyrics, having no concept of what most of them meant. I was a child living in a nurturing, godly home, and I had been sheltered from the world's depravity. I had never known hardship, tragedy, disappointment, or weariness, and my heart had never ached.

As I sang the words, "Show me the stairway I have to climb," I was deeply perplexed by what climbing stairs had to do with God, and why God would make me go up those stairs. My best guess was that these stairs would take me to heaven some day, and I had to keep living my life and walking up those stairs until I reached the top, where God would be waiting to invite me into heaven. But why, I wondered, did the song make going up those stairs sound so dreadful?

Now that I've experienced adulthood, I know more than I ever cared to learn about that staircase I have to climb. My journey's hardships are different from the next woman's, but I collect bruises and battle scars as I ascend each step by the grace of God. Some steps are easier than others, and sometimes I find myself pulling my body up only with a tight grip on the rails, but now I understand the beauty of the song. I need daily strength to face each trial, to do what I've been called to do as I move upward toward the day when Jesus calls me home.

Before your eyes meet the next step facing you today, take all of your worries and concerns to Jesus. Then climb that stair in the strength of God.

Heavenly Father, how kind You are to listen for my tiny voice.
You care about my problems. I'm giving them to You today.
I've much to do for Your glory. Amen.

# ❀ *Not an Afterthought* ❀

*"And I will put enmity between you and the woman,*
*and between your seed and her Seed; He shall bruise your head,*
*and you shall bruise His heel"* (Genesis 3:15 NKJV).

Growing up as a kid in the 1960s, I dreamed of traveling to Africa—it might as well have been Mars. During my childhood and teen years career foreign missionaries comprised an elite group, and volunteering for short-term missions trips overseas was virtually unheard of. Now almost anyone can serve as a volunteer on a missions trip, abroad as well as in this country.

All three of our daughters have volunteered on missions trips in foreign countries prior to their high school graduations. Understandably, young adults, for whom the uttermost part of the earth lay virtually within the reach of a day's travel, view the call to missions as a call to go and do. In contrast, in earlier generations when travel was more difficult, mission-mindedness meant studying about missions work in foreign countries, then praying and giving to make sure that the gospel reached all nations through missionaries who spent their careers on the missions field.

However God leads us to get involved in His mission, we can be assured that His passion has always been to redeem all peoples of the earth. Redemption through Christ was not an afterthought provision tacked onto God's plan once He realized humankind would crash and burn when it came to obeying His Ten Commandments.

Even Genesis records that God had already made provision for man's sin when Adam and Eve fell. God promised that the woman's Seed would ultimately win a decisive victory over Satan by "bruising" Satan's head. God has invited us to join Him in His redemptive mission. If we ponder His passion and provision, then, as a grateful act of worship, we will listen, and He will show us how we can do our part.

Lord God, You shared Your plan to take care of our sin problem
in the early chapters of Your written Word. Multiply in our own hearts
the same love toward the lost that You showed to us. Amen.

# ❀ The Living Water ❀

*Indeed, the water I give him will become in him a spring of water
welling up to eternal life* (John 4:14).

One busy Saturday afternoon, I bought a piece of fried chicken at a market and devoured it in the car between errands. In my haste, I swallowed a rib bone of the chicken breast and it lodged in my esophagus. I drove myself to the hospital emergency room where attendants performed the necessary x-rays and examinations. Then, I called my husband and, as only a woman would do, asked him to vacuum the floor and clean the bathroom instead of coming to the hospital. (We were expecting guests for supper.)

I didn't realize the seriousness of the situation. They suddenly whisked me to surgery, after giving me a medication to dry my mouth and throat. I was admitted to the hospital and the doctor warned I could not eat or drink anything until the next day. I begged the nurses for even a chip of ice to quench the thirst. They, of course, could not give me any liquids.

Jesus was tired from traveling so He sat beside Jacob's well. He encountered a person who was the opposite gender (a woman), of another culture (a Samaritan), poor (she was drawing her own water), and an outcast (she was an adulteress). Jesus had mercy on her. Using the common substance of water as the basis for teaching, He explained to the Samaritan woman the way to eternal life. He revealed that it is a gift from God (v. 10), obtained by asking for it from the Savior (v. 10). He showed that the water He offered would well up into eternal life (v. 14).

The next day when I awoke in the hospital, the nurses brought me a drink of water. However, as wonderful as it was, it in no way compared to the Living Water I received when I bowed on my knees as an eight-year-old child and drank from the well of eternal life—the same well from which the Samaritan woman drank many years before.

Dear God, how I thank You for Your free gift which leads to eternal life!
In Jesus's name, amen.

# ❊ Scattered to Serve ❊

*When the crowds heard Philip and saw the miraculous signs
he did, they all paid close attention to what he said*
(Acts 8:6).

The early Christians experienced an amazing unity. God kept them together
in Jerusalem experiencing this unity long enough to strengthen and prepare
them for persecution they were about to endure.

Jesus's last words on earth had been uttered right before He ascended
back to heaven: *But you will receive power when the Holy Spirit comes on you; and
you will be my witnesses in **Jerusalem**, and in all **Judea** and **Samaria**, and to the
ends of the earth"* (Acts 1:8, author's emphasis). No doubt the early believers
cherished these words, often repeating them to each other.

The persecution in Jerusalem became so great that it was dangerous for the believers to continue to meet together: *On that day* (Stephen's
martyrdom) *a great persecution broke out against the church at **Jerusalem**, and
all except the apostles were scattered throughout **Judea** and **Samaria*** (Acts 8:1).
Then, through Philip, the evangelist, and the Ethiopian eunuch, the gospel
began to spread *to the ends of the earth.*

Many years ago a group of us met together on Tuesday nights to pray.
Our group had little in common except that we love the Lord passionately
and we love to pray. God's presence through the Holy Spirit was electrifying.
We heard answers to prayer each time we met. Praise flowed as freely as
water in a brook.

Then it happened. One by one we moved to different towns. The good-
byes were painful. However, it didn't take us long to realize that God meant
for us to take what we had experienced together to the new places. We
were being scattered to serve and to share.

I can only imagine how painful it was for the early Christians to leave
each other. But, as a result, the gospel was taken to *Judea, Samaria,* and
to *the ends of the earth.* Aren't we glad? That's how the good news came
to us!

Dear Lord, help us to realize that no matter where we are,
we are there to serve, in Jesus's name, amen.

# ❀ Anxious for Nothing ❀

*Rejoice in the Lord always....Do not be anxious about anything*
(Philippians 4:4, 6).

When I was in the third grade, our teacher explained why fingers and toes get cold during a crisis—blood rushes to the torso to protect and nourish vital organs. To highlight the explanation, she showed a film that demonstrated the intestines turning bright red when a person becomes angry. We learned that the stress of anger may damage our immune system, allowing disease or pain to attack us.

I listened intently. I decided at age eight never to allow any anger to bother me (or my vulnerable viscera!). I'd protect my intestines at all cost! This resolve has served me well over the years. I don't fret over most things and can face a crisis calmly because of the long-standing habit of ignoring irritating situations that might cause me to become angry.

Paul taught us how to control our attitudes as we approach conflict or the resulting anger. Writing from prison, he appears to ask for unrealistic attitudes from the early Christians, who were running from persecution in the streets, hiding in the catacombs underground, and facing lions in the coliseum. He simply says we shouldn't be anxious about anything. What an understatement. But there's a logical progression of reason behind his simple words.

First, if we believe in Jesus as Savior, He gives us eternal life in heaven.

If we know we have eternal life in heaven, then we don't fear death.

If we don't fear death, then violence can't intimidate us; we've already won!

If violence can't intimidate us, then we have no fear of the future.

If we have no fear of the future, then we can absorb the joy of the present.

If we absorb the joy of the present, then we're able to love others with joy.

If we love others with joy, then we can change the world.

If we can grasp the truth of the vast dimensions of changing the whole world, then we won't be anxious about anything. Besides, we'll be too busy telling others about Jesus.

> Lord, what a joy-giving God You are! We praise You for helping us
> control our attitudes, taking away worry, and giving us incredible peace
> to share with the world. Amen.

# ❀ A Good Night's Sleep ❀

*And the peace of God, which transcends all understanding, will guard
your hearts and your minds in Christ Jesus* (Philippians 4:7).

Granny Queen had a jolly giggle and eyes that sparkled. My good friend,
Rita, and I took the senior adults in our church on various outings. One
group of ladies was always *sitting on go*. If the church van moved out of the
parking lot, they wanted to be on it. Rita and I nicknamed them the "go-go-
girls." Granny Queen was one of the go-go girls.

Life was not always easy for her, but she made it enjoyable. She had
been a widow for years and, as her health declined, she moved to a nursing
home. While there, she met a widower and they got married. My husband,
Wayne, stood before them as they were seated in their wheelchairs and
united them as husband and wife.

One evening I got a call that Granny Queen's husband was dying.
Wayne was out of town, so I went to the hospital.

The end of his life came quickly, and the family had to tend to the
details of his funeral. I volunteered to take Granny back to the nursing
home. When we walked into their room, Granny cried as she looked around
at her husband's belongings. My heart broke as I tucked her into bed and
observed the vacant bed beside her.

I told Granny I would stay with her until she went to sleep. As I lay
where her husband had slept, I could hear her whimpering. One of my
prayers for her that night was that she would be able to sleep in spite of her
grief.

The next day, I could tell by Granny's expression that, even though she
was sorrowful, she had the *peace that transcends all understanding*. I also found
out that Granny had a good night's sleep.

Dear Lord, thank You for providing comfort through the Holy Spirit.
Thank you for Granny Queen's example that even when life is difficult,
it can still be enjoyable. In Jesus's name, amen.

# ❀ We're Counting on You! ❀

*"Be of good courage, and let us be strong for our people and for the cities of our God. And may the LORD do what is good in His sight"*
(1 Chronicles 19:13 NKJV).

With my hand over my heart, I joined 86,000 fans standing in silence, honoring the families assembled on the football field. They had recently lost loved ones on a very different field—a battlefield—protecting American freedoms. For a moment or two we were united with a common bond—our love for America.

Christians are facing a growing distrust and intolerance of Christian beliefs in America, and our brothers and sisters in Christ suffer persecution in dark corners of the world. We are outnumbered and misunderstood, but the very people who would harm us are the ones whom God has commissioned us to reach out to in Christian love.

In our modern-day context, what does it mean to be strong "for our people"? Our brothers and sisters in Christ count on us to stand for the Word of God and believe in the power of the Cross. They count on us to remain strong, modeling a Christ-like life. We are the people of God, unified by our love for one another and for the Lord. That same love compels us to be strong and of good courage in the face of growing opposition to our faith.

Paul's words are as meaningful today as they were in biblical times. We need to remain strong and courageous to defend our people and cities, and trust the outcome to God. Let us be faithful in these trying days, honoring God above all, and trusting Him to move mightily among us. Be strong—your brothers and sisters in Christ are counting on you.

> Father, I don't want to do what is easy; I want to do what is right.
> Please remind me throughout the day that other Christians
> are counting on me to be courageous, growing my influence
> today as well as my legacy tomorrow. In Jesus's name, amen.

# ❀ *Balanced Living* ❀

*And Jesus grew in wisdom and stature,*
*and in favor with God and men* (Luke 2:52).

Jesus has been and always will be the perfect role model. Today's verse gives the formula for patterning our lives after His. Luke informs us that Jesus led a balanced life. Jesus grew mentally (in wisdom), physically (in stature), spiritually (in favor with God), and emotionally (in favor with men). In other words, He grew in Spirit (spiritually), soul (mentally and emotionally), and body (physically). As His followers, we are to endeavor to do the same.

Often we put emphasis on one of these areas to the neglect of the others. A life out of balance is the result. For example, people who are obsessed with physical fitness may neglect the expansion of their minds through continual learning. Others may be so studious or work-oriented that they become recluses, avoiding people. However, the greatest tragedy is when any emphasis leads to the neglect of developing a personal relationship with God.

Once while driving my car on a routine errand, the steering wheel suddenly began to shake. At first it shook only a little, but it continued to worsen until it was difficult to keep the car on the road. I stopped by a service station and the mechanic discovered that the front tires were out of balance. Just one part of the car out of balance had affected the entire car, making it almost impossible to drive.

The same is true of our lives. One unbalanced area can affect the other parts of our lives causing us to lose sight of our reasons for living. As with Jesus, we find our purposes in life as we develop a balance among Spirit, soul, and body.

Dear Lord, please help us follow Your example to maintain
balance in our lives. In Jesus's name, amen.

# ❀ Consider the Word ❀

*Consider what I say, and may the Lord give you understanding in all things* (2 Timothy 2:7 NKJV).

One of my most challenging college courses was advanced statistics. I'd never been exposed to statistics in high school. I took careful notes of the professor's lectures, but his teaching made no sense to me as I wrote down the facts and figures in class. It was only after I returned to my dorm room and began to study the examples that the pieces of information began to lock into place. I could see patterns developing on the pages of my notes, which helped me know how to work new problems when I took the tests. The statistics course required me to work harder than I ever had before, but the studying paid off in test scores.

We are called not merely to be *readers* of the Word, but *students* of the Word. The Word of God can present a challenge. The Holy Spirit is our Teacher as we read the Scriptures carefully, but we still must study to grasp the great truths of the Bible. We wrestle with the words, sometimes reading a passage over and over, and we look for the patterns of truth that God has woven into His holy and perfect Word. As the Holy Spirit guides us to principles for living, we reap the rewards of our studies when we can apply God's truths to life's daily tests.

Perhaps it's time to take a fresh approach to your study of Scripture. Have you been reading long portions of the Bible at each sitting? Consider reading smaller portions several times over, asking God to reveal His wisdom. Or, if you've been in the habit of reading short passages repetitively, consider investing your time in reading larger passages at a time, asking the Lord to open your mind to the patterns developing from chapter to chapter. However you study the Bible, consider each word carefully. May the Lord give you understanding in all things!

Father, help me wrap my whole mind around Your Word today as I study the Scripture. I desire the understanding and wisdom that can only come from You. Amen.

# ❀ Not Your Own ❀

*Or do you not know that your body is the temple of the Holy Spirit
who is in you, whom you have from God, and you are not your own?
For you were bought at a price; therefore glorify God in your
body and in your spirit, which are God's*
(1 Corinthians 6:19–20 NKJV).

In 1878, convinced the Lord had called her to missions work, Charlotte Digges Moon (Lottie) boarded a ship in San Francisco for a five-week journey to China, one-way ticket in hand. When she arrived, green with seasickness, she traveled 60 more miles by *shentze*—a tiny covered hut supported by two long poles attached to mules—to her new home, Tengchow.

Lottie spent more than 30 years sharing the gospel in Chinese villages, discipling converts; and during the murderous Boxer Rebellion, she disguised herself as a Chinese official to reach Pingtu, where she consoled tortured Chinese believers. When she wrote home to beg for missionaries, she did not paint a glorious picture to entice them. Instead, she said, "They are coming to a life of hardship, responsibility, and constant self-denial....They will be alone...and will need to be strong and courageous."

When, in 1912, famine became severe, Lottie was burdened with the plight of her people and could not eat. Recognizing her failing health, friends put her on a ship headed for medical treatment in America. She died before reaching America. Years later, her denomination named their yearly offering for international missions after her.

Lottie's devotion to Christ teaches us that once we belong to Christ, our lives are not our own. We have been bought with the price of Jesus's sacrifice, and He has the right to do with us whatever will bring Him glory, whether He chooses us to shine for Him on foreign soil, in catastrophic illness, or in our own pagan homeland. The question is, when called to our missions field, will we flinch, or will we walk forward into the place He calls us, trusting Him as Lottie did?

Lord, when I cling to desires for a "normal" life,
remind me that my life belongs to You and give me courage
to gladly abandon the good for the best—Your glory. Amen.

# ❀ Ever Think of God's Wrath? ❀

*So I will pour out my wrath on them and consume them with my fiery*
*anger, bringing down on their own heads all they have done, declares*
*the Sovereign Lord* (Ezekiel 22:31).

As most mothers know, sometimes children don't move until a parent speaks in a stern voice. Some children don't even move when their parents speak sternly, and at that point a yell or a scream becomes the signal that parents mean business! Without meaning to, parents have conditioned children that parents aren't serious until they yell or pull the children up so they finally come to do what the parents have requested. Parents' consistent behavior (with rewards and punishment) and their high expectations pay off in children's good behavior. Parents should mean what they say—the first time.

Over the last century, most discipline has become more lenient. We seldom think of *negative* punishment, focusing on *positive* reinforcement. Society's focus on the positive carries over into our thoughts about God. Present-day pastors seldom preach sermons like "Sinners in the Hands of an Angry God" as their ancestors did.

The Old Testament contains many references to the wrath of God. Prophets like Ezekiel prophesied dire consequences for sin and disobedience. One truth is sure: God means what He says. We're accountable to Him; He follows through with punishment.

In today's world, we need to consider our relationship with God. Do we really believe He is the Ultimate God of Justice who punishes wrong doers? Do we believe He punishes sin, as He says in His Word? Do we believe in a day of reckoning? Do we live as if we do? These are questions we should consider as we pray.

As Christians, we can make a difference. Through an obedient relationship with Almighty God, we can influence others to establish a better relationship with Him. The choice is ours.

Lord, forgive us when we drift away from a close relationship with You.
Help us not to act like children, failing to listen to You,
but to be obedient the first time You call. May we show our love
by taking a courageous stand for You. In Jesus's name, amen.

# ❀ The Hungry ❀

*"Man shall not live bread alone"* (Deuteronomy 8:3 NKJV).

A man with matted hair and ragged clothes entered the fast-food restaurant and made his way to the clerk with eyes cast low. Quiet, he humbly begged for food. The clerk nervously rejected his pleas. Tears filled my eyes as God reminded me that the Son of Man had no place to lay His head. I stepped up to the counter to pay for whatever he wanted. He kept his eyes to the floor, except for one powerful moment; he turned his face, locking eyes with me, and said, "Thank you." Taking his tray, he quietly slipped into a dark corner to eat in silence.

I sat with my friend at a booth, but my eyes refused to stop gazing over at the homeless man's table. I nearly choked as I ate and thought about what I *hadn't* done.

Cold nights on the street would overwhelm his body, much like the confusion and lostness that seemed to overwhelm his heart. He needed a friend, but I never even asked his name. He needed compassion, but I never asked him his story. He needed encouragement, but I never told him my story. He needed Jesus, but I never spoke of His name.

I met a man who was lonely, desperate, and hurting, and I bought him a sandwich and sent him on his way. I daily feast at the banquet table my Lord provides, yet walked away from a spiritually starving man and never told him about God's provision for him.

Do we desire to be the hands and feet of Christ? We are most like Jesus when we reach out to meet the spiritual needs as well as the physical needs of the people we meet who stand in need.

Dear Father, help me be an effective minister in your name!
Flood my heart with compassion for the lost and hurting,
and may I never lose sight of their greatest need:
their need for a Savior. Amen.

*Adapted from* Journey to Significance *by Kimberly Sowell (New Hope Publishers, 2008), and the June 2007 article "Compassion Has a Voice" from womenonmission.com.*

# ❀ Will You Remember ❀ My Name?

*See, I have engraved you on the palms of my hands* (Isaiah 49:16).

Our *Women by Design* conference was coming to an end. All day we, as team members, had been aware of God's Holy Spirit working in a special way.

In our team prayertime prior to the conference, we recommitted ourselves to being used as God's vessels. The day had been a true day of joy in ministry. The congregation was responsive and we sensed God's presence at every turn.

Many people responded during the invitation. A woman named Jackie came forward with a special prayer concern. After I had prayed with her, she looked into my eyes and asked, "Will you remember my name, and will you keep praying for me?"

I wanted to say yes but I thought, *What if I forget her name, or what if I forget to pray for her?* If I promised to pray, I wanted to be accountable to that promise.

I looked at Jackie and said, "I will ask God to keep reminding me of your name, and when He does, I will pray for you." She smiled and returned to her seat.

We, as *Women by Design* team members, started toward the back of the church to greet people as they left. I took a step when I noticed something stuck to the bottom of my shoe. I bent down to get it and could hardly believe my eyes. It was Jackie's name tag! Without our awareness, it had come off her jacket while we prayed.

I quickly placed it in my Bible. Now each time I open my Bible, I see Jackie's name and remember to pray for her.

God will never forget us, and He reminds us of this in the most beautiful ways. Today's verse assures us that we are engraved on the palms of His hands. I wonder if those engraved marks are in the shape of nail prints, don't you?

Dear Lord, thank You for not only remembering our names,
but also for knowing everything about us and loving us anyway.
In Jesus's name, amen.

# ❀ *Marching in Step* ❀

*And in this one body to reconcile both of them to God through the*
*Cross, by which he put to death their hostility* (Ephesians 2:16).

Paul writes about the difference between Jewish Christians, who followed the ancient law of circumcision, and the Gentiles, uncircumcised Christians. He says they're one body and, as the incarnate church of Christ, can reconcile both Jews and Gentiles to God. How is that possible? Through the Cross by which He destroyed their hostility.

Is the hostility between Jews and non-Jews in your community destroyed? How about other friction among races or groups of people? Most of us still find pockets of hostility. It's been more than 2,000 years, and still ignorant prejudice and suspicion exists among clashing cultures!

Our questions today are: How can we Christians unite as one body to reconcile everyone to God? How can we present the Cross to every person and *put to death* these persistent hostilities?

All Christians can lead in their own area of expertise. What do you have—a spiritual gift, a natural talent, or a learned skill—that can help someone accept Jesus as their Savior? Do you live in an opportune place, perhaps a spot where different faiths and cultures come together? Are you interested in a sport or hobby that bridges a gap between two groups? We're reconciled in three ways: first to God, then to fellow Christians, and finally to non-Christians. How can we use our interests to march in step in these three areas?

Compare your Christian leadership to marching soldiers. It takes focused attention and cooperation to march in step, whether on a military field or in a church. As soldiers of the Cross, we may have to apologize for being out of step. We may have to admit someone else is better suited for a certain position. As we're willing to work as a part of the cooperative body, we can serve as a point person to help others walk in sync. Reflect today on how God might lead you to use your gifts, skills, or talents to help your church keep in step.

Lord, I love You and my fellow Christians.
Help us march together in sync as one body
to share Your love and destroy hostility. Amen.

# ❀ *The Goal of Our Faith* ❀

*Though you have not seen him, you love him; and even though you do not see him now, you believe in him and are filled with an inexpressible and glorious joy, for you are receiving the goal of your faith, the salvation of your souls* (1 Peter 1:8–9).

Life is wonderful! However, life is filled with trials, tribulations, and temptations. In this world everyone—including Christians—will experience these obstacles.

In 1 Peter 1:7 we read that like gold we must be refined by fire to be genuine. When gold is heated by fire, the impurities float to the surface and can be skimmed off and removed. The product that is left is pure and unadulterated.

The same is true of us as we are put through the fires of trials, tribulations, and temptations. They are purposeful. God uses them to make us pure and to draw us closer to Him.

How can we know we are genuine? The answer is found in 1 Peter 1:8–9.

1. Love Jesus, even though we cannot see Him.
2. Believe in Him.
3. Rejoice through the Holy Spirit.
4. Keep our eyes focused on the salvation of our souls.

Several years ago I was hiking with a group in the mountains. On the way down to the waterfall, I fell and twisted my knee. I felt I could not make it back up the mountain. As I looked at the vertical trail ahead, it seemed insurmountable. The pain in my knee was intense, but I knew I had to keep climbing. Even though I couldn't see the summit of the mountain, I knew it was there. So, I chose a rock ahead and stayed focused on climbing to that point. Then I chose another landmark toward which to climb. Finally, I reached the mountaintop and descended the trail to level ground.

In much the same way, we must believe in Jesus although we cannot see Him. Staying focused on the goal of our faith helps even when the way may seem difficult and painful.

Dear Lord, thank You for letting us receive the goal of our faith, salvation of our souls. In Jesus's name, amen.

# ❋ The New Testament— ❋ Truth or Myth?

*That which we have seen and heard we declare to you*
(1 John 1:3 NKJV).

Were the writings of the New Testament cleverly constructed myths of the early church written not by real men living during the time of Jesus but by well-intentioned church leaders during the following centuries after Jesus died? What does historical evidence say?

Before we can decide whether real first-century believers wrote the New Testament, we must determine whether these men and the Savior they proclaim ever existed. At least 17 ancient non-Christian sources, including historians and government officials, corroborate many facts recorded in the New Testament, including the fact that Jesus Christ lived during the time of Tiberius Caesar. No one questions that the early Christian Polycarp actually lived, and Polycarp, says ancient church writer Irenaeus knew John the apostle personally. John knew Jesus Christ and Peter. Peter knew John Mark and Paul personally, who knew Titus, Timothy, and Luke personally.

If these men were not fictitious figures but real people, then the question is whether these historical persons wrote books of the Bible. One fantastic piece of evidence is called the John Ryland's fragment, a first-century fragment of a verse copied from John's gospel. Its existence shows that copies of John's gospel were transcribed around the end of the first century A.D. Originals must have been written before that time, *during the years that Jesus and the eyewitnesses lived*, not hundreds of years later.

The apostles and other disciples really believed the things about which they wrote. Historians say many died as martyrs, claiming until their final breath that the body of Jesus Christ rose alive from the grave. They also claimed to be writing historically accurate documents of events they and their contemporaries personally witnessed.

These and other evidences affirm that the New Testament books were written, indeed, by the apostles and their contemporaries. We can choose to believe their record is true or false, but we must contend with the writers themselves, real men who lived during a real time, and wrote real documents about real events concerning the real person of Jesus Christ.

Thank You, Father, for assuring us through the holy writings
that we who believe in Jesus may know that we have eternal life (1 John 5:13).

# ❀ *Loving the World* ❀

*Therefore I want you to know that God's salvation has been sent to the*
*Gentiles, and they will listen!* (Acts 28:28).

"Don't these people eat burgers and fries?" said Jan, one of 16 people on a
missions trip to Germany.

"Shh," someone whispered. "We don't want anyone to see the 'Ugly
American.'"

"Right," she whispered, eating her plate of *schnitzel*.

All of us were road-weary, having drunk too many bottles of warm
Coca Cola and eaten one-too-many plates of *schnitzel*. From the southern United States, we longed for an ice-filled glass of sweet tea with
southern-fried chicken, black-eyed peas, and sweet potato pie. European
buttermilk and raw oatmeal just didn't have the appeal of a down-home
breakfast—with bacon, eggs, and homemade biscuits (and I do *not* mean
British cookies!). In short, we had lost our focus on worldwide evangelism and looked toward home.

Weary though we were, we wanted to be good witnesses to our faith. We
remembered the words above in Acts, and talked about Jewish Christians,
like Paul, Barnabas, and Peter, who went on missionary trips much like
ours, to share the gospel with Gentiles in the first century. Crossing the
English Channel on a hovercraft and arriving near the white cliffs of Dover,
England, we prayed we'd be able to witness to people there, where people
spoke English.

A few miles later, we met the cutest tour guide of our trip. When asked
about her church, she proudly said, "Actually, I'm an atheist!" That night
we planned a prayertime before we flew home, hoping she would hear our
sincere prayers and see our faith in a living Jesus.

The moment came and went, but she didn't appear. Disappointed, we
joined hands and prayed for her, that somehow our witness would intrigue
her to inquire about Christ in the future. Occasionally I still pray for this
friendly woman, asking God to bring someone into her life to *share salvation*
*with the Gentiles*, and that they (including me)—and all the world's people—
will listen to His voice.

O Savior, call all Jews and Gentiles to You.
We know no one is saved except through Your Holy Spirit.
Help us continue to share the message of Your salvation. Amen.

# ❁ Storms Are Coming ❁

*And he arose, and rebuked the wind, and said unto the sea, "Peace, be
still." And the wind ceased, and there was a great calm. And he said
unto them, "Why are ye so fearful? How is it that ye have no faith?"*
(Mark 4:39–40 KJV).

My late husband, Charles, used to say. "We're always in a storm." Some
say storms are always brewing, and others say life is one big storm! In
most families, we're either going into a storm, in the middle of a storm, or
coming out of a storm. Examples of storms in the family—besides a hurried
daily schedule—are financial problems, divorce, wayward children, illness
or death of a loved one, or job loss. As a pastor, Charles counseled and
encouraged others going though stormy times. Sometimes he helped them
establish a relationship with God as they went through a stormy situation
together.

How do you handle your stormy situations? Some people lash out at
the ones they love the most. Some swear or kick the car tires. Some rely on
the Holy Spirit to encourage and calm them during and after the storm. The
Christian response to the storms of life is to rely on Jesus to give us peace in
the midst of every storm, strength to endure them, and a sense of calm after
they go away.

As missions-hearted Christians, we can't spread fear or lack of faith.
Jesus calls us to peace and courage: *"Why are ye so fearful?"* (v. 40, above).
If the men in the storm hadn't called Jesus from the ship's hull, the ship
may have gone down, but they did call on Him, just as we do today when
tempted to fear. He calms our fear, and then we share the story of how He
rescued the perishing. In storms, people huddle together for comfort. As
you go through storms, look around for hurting people. Use the storm as a
time of healing hurts and calming fears. Remember, storms are coming. Are
you ready?

Dear Lord, thank You for being with us, guiding us through the storms of life
unafraid. Help us to hold fast to You, to deepen our relationship,
and to encourage others as they experience fear. Amen.

# ❀ Stuck in the Parking Lot ❀

*"But from there you will seek the LORD your God, and you will find
Him if you seek Him with all your heart and with all your soul"*
(Deuteronomy 4:29 NKJV).

Aren't we funny creatures? I took my boys to their pre-school class at church one morning, learned the electricity was off in the building when we arrived, and moments later, school was cancelled for the day. As I was about to drive away, a man in a truck pulled beside me. I rolled down my window and told him the situation. He thanked me.

I then noticed as I looked out the car window that several moms were standing in the parking lot, backseat doors open, sort of paralyzed in place. Someone had also told them that school was canceled, trying to spare them from having to unbuckle and then refasten their children in their seats, but I could tell the moms were struggling to believe the news enough to get back in their cars and drive home.

They could see the church building was dark, and they witnessed several other parents streaming out the doors with their children, but the temptation was strong to go inside and see for themselves. I drove away, amused by human nature.

As you attempt to reach others with the gospel, you may encounter skeptics. They can see that Christ has changed your life, they see evidence of God in nature and through God's self-revelation, but they feel compelled to seek the truth for themselves. How can you respond? Your best choice is to trust God.

You can point people to the truth and then boldly live it before them, but ultimately they must seek the Lord for themselves. God's hand must guide them to that door of hope, where they'll choose to walk through it in faith or not. What seems so obvious to us is veiled to unbelievers who are blinded to the truth, until that moment when they open their lives to God. Be bold, be faithful, be patient, and be praying. If they seek God, they will find Him.

Heavenly Father, I pray for people seeking truth.
May they seek You with all their hearts. Reveal Yourself to them.
Help me be an authentic witness. Amen.

# ❀ Everything I Need ❀

*Then he… chose five smooth stones…, put them in the pouch
of his shepherd's bag and, with his sling in his hand,
approached the Philistine* (1 Samuel 17:40).

My husband, Randy, and I were sleeping soundly when we were startled by the sound of cracking glass. Someone had broken into our small-engine repair shop that sat 50 yards in front of our home. Snow, our Siberian-husky-wannabe, barked and gyrated in the front yard.

Randy grabbed his 38-special and GI Joe'd out the back door. Crouched on the floor in the dark, I dialed the sheriff.

After settling into the ditch near the building's front door, Randy waited for the perpetrator to exit. There was just one problem. Snow pounced, she bounced, she slurped. Randy, in a firm whisper, commanded her to stop. She ignored him. Randy whacked her and pinned her to the ground in a full Nelson hold to her neck.

Back in the trailer, I listened and waited in the eerie silence. Finally, I panicked, grabbed my red velour housecoat, and then crawled to the closet where I took the first pair of shoes I touched. Just before I slipped out the door, I realized I had nothing for protection. I grabbed the nearby fire extinguisher.

When I arrived at the front of the building, Randy stood holding a gun over the would-be thief. About that time, the sheriff screeched onto the scene, lights and sirens blaring. There Randy stood, guarding the perpetrator, who lay face down, spread-eagle on the ground. And where was I? Backing him up, dressed in my red velour housecoat, wedge stacked-heel shoes, and holding a fire extinguisher.

I looked pretty stupid, but I used the resources I had at hand. How about you? Maybe the Lord has called you to a task, but you think there's no way He would ask you to attempt this endeavor lacking adequate resources. On the other hand, God used young David, equipped with five stones and a sling, to bring down a giant.

Father, I can trust that I have everything I need
to accomplish whatever You have called me to do, by Your power. Amen.

*Tricia's story first appeared in* Seeking Wisdom: Preparing Yourself to Be Mentored *by Edna Ellison and Tricia Scribner (New Hope Publishers, 2001).*

# ❀ A Field of Dreams ❀

*And without faith it is impossible to please God,*
*because anyone who comes to him must believe that he exists*
*and that he rewards those who earnestly seek him* (Hebrews 11:6).

Last night the air in our beautiful mountain town was electric with excitement. Our local college, Appalachian State University, won the national conference semi-final football game and next weekend will play for their third consecutive national championship. They're making college football history!

Many reasons can explain the football team's success. However, I feel that the most significant one is the faithfulness of the head coach, Jerry Moore. Jerry uses the game of football as a microcosm of life. He is more concerned about the future of the players than their ability to play. He has mentored them on how to be young men of integrity, character, and he is bold in his witness as a Christian.

A strong core of believers exists within the team. They willingly and openly share their faith. I love to watch them kneel and pray at the end of each game. Last night with the onslaught of fans converging on the field to tear down the goal post after the game, the players were swept up in the crowd. However, even in the midst of the chaos, I saw several players look up to heaven and thank God for the victory.

A football commentator on national television said, "Jerry Moore's legacy is not taking these kids to three back-to-back national championship games. It's what he has invested in their lives. He's been like a father to many of them."

I realize that many Christian coaches work year after year without outstanding success in the eyes of the world. However, the faith-impact they make on the lives of their players is the greatest reward of all. And God loves to reward *"those who earnestly seek him"* (Hebrews 11:6).

Will Appalachian win next week? We hope so. However, we realize they've already won what really counts—their faith. As we say around here, "Go Apps!"

Dear God, help us go through life recognizing the many ways You reward us
when we earnestly seek You. In Jesus's name, amen.

*PS: They won!*

# ❀ *Our Sinful Best* ❀

*Without faith it is impossible to please God* (Hebrews 11:6 NKJV).

Apart from experiencing the saving power of Jesus Christ in our lives, even our best efforts at doing good and moral things are still dirty in God's eyes. Perhaps you are thinking, *But Tricia, I know good people who do good things, and who live much better lives than believers in Jesus Christ do.* That's true—at least by our standards. Many unbelievers live morally upright lives, and in fact, many non-believers perform benevolent actions. They see children in need and adopt them, giving them loving homes. They donate large sums of money to people in need. They may even give their lives as martyrs for causes in which they believe.

But do these actions, however benevolent, produce holiness and a right relationship with God? If it is impossible to please God without faith in Him, then can any behavior initiated by humans, no matter how seemingly honorable and even helpful in the temporal world, be anything less than falling short of God's glory?

God cannot be bought. He doesn't want our sacrifices, our penance will not please Him, and our self-proclaimed efforts to make the world a better place fail to win His favor. Why? Because our works don't change the ugly fact that deep down inside, whether we do good deeds, speak good words, or give away all of our earthly possessions to help others, we want to be the boss of ourselves. We want to decide what is good and kind and what earns us the right to heaven.

It's true that adopted children may be better off, and hungry people will appreciate food purchased with donated money. But, when the adopted child goes to bed at night, will she thank God in heaven for providing her new family? Or, will the one whose stomach is filled because of a kind benefactor thank the Provider for the meal? How many works will burn as straw in light of the truth that only what is done in Christ and for His honor will accomplish God's eternal purposes?

Lord, You remind us that our good deeds don't do anything
about our rebellious, self-willed heart, a heart that wants to call the shots
and rears its head against the rightful authority of God over our lives.
Forgive us. Amen.

# ❀ The Razor's Edge ❀

*For the word of God is living and powerful, and sharper than any two-edged sword, piercing even to the division of soul and spirit, and of joints and marrow, and is a discerner of the thoughts and intents of the heart* (Hebrews 4:12 NKJV).

After standing in the shower one night, using my razor on both legs, I realized that all my efforts would have to be repeated; I had failed to remove the see-through plastic cover on my razor!

I had mistakenly thought I was being productive. The cover wasn't easily seen, and the process felt normal; it wasn't until I looked carefully at my legs and saw what remained that I realized I hadn't accomplished a thing. Similarly, sometimes we allow an attitude to surface that comes between our hearts and the cutting power of the Word of God.

The attitude can be subtle and not easily detected, but it's there nonetheless, and it blocks the work of Scripture from removing those things that don't belong in our hearts. We go through the motions of reading the Word, and we feel like we're doing something spiritually productive, but with the barrier between our hearts and the Word, lasting change won't occur.

Think about what mind sets we could potentially allow to act as a subtle barrier between our hearts and God's two-edged sword. What about pride? *I would never commit such a sin as described in that verse.* What about being judgmental? *I need to point this passage out to Sally—this describes her to a "T"!* How about distractedness? *How much do I have to read to please God today? Let me find a short chapter and get this over with quickly.* And laziness? *This passage is too difficult to understand. I'm going to skip to something simpler to read.*

As you approach your Bible study time, pray about how God will use the Scriptures to change your life. Ask God to remove even the slightest hindrance to the piercing power of His Word.

Dear Lord, I desire to receive Your powerful Word into my life.
What attitudes do I need to change before I open up the Bible today?
Please remove those barriers, Lord. In Jesus's name, amen.

# ❃ Spirituality in a Toy Store ❃

*For they being ignorant of God's righteousness,*
*and seeking to establish their own righteousness,*
*have not submitted to the righteousness of God*
(Romans 10:3 NKJV).

As I stood in the toy store of that quaint little vacation town, I tried to share my daughter's enthusiasm for the sparkly plastic shoes labeled "Wizard of Oz" displayed on the wall. "The pink ones, Mama!"

"Your daughter would love my house," claimed a fellow customer, smiling with admiration at my daughter's selection. "I have a room filled with Wizard of Oz stuff, and I just love it. You know, it's such a spiritual movie when you think about it." Yes, I knew that, but what did she mean by "spiritual"?

"Yes, I've read some about that, how Dorothy and the others coming to the Wizard symbolizes how we all must come to God through Jesus Christ, and God meets our needs and makes us whole," I replied. Now it was her turn to try to conceal a puzzled look. Were she and I talking about the same thing?

All that is "spiritual" is not holy. Ephesians 6 describes our battle as believers against "spiritual hosts of wickedness" (v. 12). Many Americans claim to be spiritual; what can we glean from the heightened "spirituality" in America? As Christians, where do we begin?

1. Praise God that people around you are seeking a "higher power." We're often unaware of the spiritual seeking of others, who search for God behind closed doors. Ask God to help you trust Him as He opens opportunities to interject your Christian faith into everyday conversations.

2. Intercede for those who are currently seeking God through means other than a relationship with Jesus. Ask God to tear down their strongholds, and for them to sense the emptiness of false spiritual experiences Satan has provided to confuse them.

Dear Father, give me awareness of the seekers around me;
grant me courage to share Christ with those who desperately
need truthful answers. Amen.

# ❁ A Near Miss ❁

*With God all things are possible* (Matthew 19:26 NKJV).

I traveled to a small, country health clinic to gather survey information for a research project. All day long I explained to clients how to complete the 110 questions on the survey. The hours passed quickly while the respondents seemed to complete the surveys in slow motion. I became concerned I wouldn't meet my deadline. Late in the afternoon I approached Myra, a woman about my age, asking her to complete the survey. She hesitated then said, "I can't read." The looming deadline faded from my thoughts as I pondered her dilemma.

This woman was well spoken and engaging. How could it be that she had never learned to read?

I asked, "How did it happen, Myra?"

She said, "When I was little my parents thought I was retarded, so they never cared about my schooling. So, later I never thought I could. Now, I'm too old to learn." Myra then shared how she wished she could help her children with their homework or read simple instructions.

I read the questionnaire aloud to her so she could complete the survey then talked with her about taking a reading course offered by the local adult education program. Myra wasn't sure she could do it. Besides, she felt embarrassed. I promised to get the information and share with her.

With lots of encouragement and assurance that other adults would be learning along with her, Myra began to believe perhaps she *could* learn to read and signed up for the course. After her first few weeks of study, I stopped by her house to see how things were going. She greeted me with a smile and said, "Tricia, I can actually read my son's school book to him."

I thought about my mind set the day I had come to the clinic. I was so concerned about my project, my deadline, and my goals that I almost missed the opportunity the Lord placed in my path for His purposes.

Lord, forgive me for becoming consumed with my own priorities
that I forget Your kingdom priorities. Amen.

# ❀ *Paris in the Spring* ❀

*That is why [this place] was called Babel—because there
the Lord confused the language of the whole world*
(Genesis 11:9).

I stood in a field with the beautiful silhouette of Chartres Cathedral in the distance. Fellow travelers Joe and Lalla McDaniel stood with our pastor, Dr. Russell Dean. His wife, Helen, stood against the blue-grey sky with her mother, "Grannie" Phillips, their dresses rustling in the wind.

Our group had seen the Passion Play in Oberammergau, Germany, and talked with people who spoke little English. Some babbled fast as they scurried down a crooked sidewalk! Here in the French farmlands, Joe requested I ask a farmer about the price of hay and milk. I knew the French word for *milk*, but while teaching French to high school students, I'd never heard the word for *hay*. Chatting with the farmer, I found the price of a double-gill (gill is a common European unit of measure) of milk. I figured an approximate amount in cups and told Joe. When I attempted to describe the haystack, the French farmer shrugged and went back to loading the sweet-smelling spring hay on a cart with his pitchfork. When I asked the price for haystacks again, he looked as if I'd asked the price of the moon (which I may have actually asked)! My mind went blank.

*What was that third word the farmer used? I should have understood. I want to help Joe, but I've let him down.*

Imagine how people in Genesis 11, who tried to build a tower to heaven, must have felt when they couldn't communicate in the same language. Of course they scratched their lofty plans for a tower! Have you ever spoken in another language? If so, you know the frustration of surprising a stranger (and yourself) with something you hadn't meant to say.

As I left the field, Joe was talking to the farmer in part-sign-language, part-primal grunts. With no training in French, this master farmer showed his love for farming and for all humanity. The two men "talked," finally shaking hands as a knowing look passed between them. Getting back on the bus toward Paris, Joe grinned at me. "That man's a Christian. The love of Christ makes all people family."

Lord, help us love all people as sisters and brothers in Christ. Amen.

# ❀ *Heavenly* ❀

*"Rejoice because your names are written in heaven"*
(Luke 10:20 NKJV).

As I walked out the door, I felt refreshed by the beauty of a new day and the perfect temperature against my skin. *God, thank You for days like these, not too hot and not too cold.* I thought about how wonderful it will be in heaven, when the temperature will be perfectly pleasant to our bodies all the time. I caught a sob in my throat before it could escape as I contrasted the wonders of heaven with my recent days; I felt so tired, mentally and physically, and all morning my mind had been racing to decide what I would try to accomplish and what would remain on my to-do list. I was struggling to talk to God in complete sentences that morning.

Sometimes no matter how intentional I try to be, unexpected problems and obligations crop up in this imperfect world that bring chaos to my attempts to keep order in my life. I love my family and the way God has shaped my life, but sometimes I dream a little of going home. I don't get too caught up in streets of gold or walls of jasper, though I'm sure both will be lovely and pleasing as God has designed them. But I tend to agree with what Tricia has said about heaven. "What's so great about heaven? Jesus will be there!" I'll be with my Savior. I'll be welcomed to sit at His feet for eternity. I'll feel the warmth of His glory all about me in a new, perfect way. And what's too amazing for me to imagine is that somehow, *we'll* be made like Him. That thought thrills my soul, because I know anything good within me now is what Jesus has created while He dwells in my heart. I'll continue to be privileged to serve the Lord in heaven, but in perfect order and with no resistance from a fatigued body, a weary mind, or a resistant flesh. Doesn't that sound heavenly? Sometimes I just want to go home.

Heavenly Father, thank You for glimpses into heaven
found in Your Word. Please bring peace into my life today. Amen.

# ❧ *A Word of Caution* ❧

*The whole assembly grumbled against the leaders, but all the leaders
answered, "We have given them our oath by the Lord, the God of Israel,
and we cannot touch them now"* (Joshua 9:18–19).

Scripture teaches that we should treat people with love and respect: *So in
everything, do to others what you would have them do to you, for this sums up the Law
and Prophets* (Matthew 7:12).

However, Scripture teaches that we are not to form alliances with those
whose beliefs might lead us astray: *I urge you, brothers, to watch out for those who
cause divisions and put obstacles in your way that are contrary to the teaching you have
learned. Keep away from them* (Romans 16:17).

Today's verse puts these principles in a clear light. God warned Israel
that when they entered the Promised Land they were not to associate with
certain peoples (Deuteronomy 20:17, 18). The reason: these people had
defiled the land through polytheism, idolatry, and sexual immorality. God
knew they would entice the Israelites to do the same.

After Joshua led in several major military victories, the inhabitants
of the land became frightened. The Gibeonites (Hivites) came to Joshua
and the Israeli leaders under false pretenses. Even though they were from
nearby, they claimed to be from a foreign land. In their deception they
brought worn-out camel sacks (indicating they had traveled for a long time),
molded bread (saying it was fresh and warm when they left), old, patched
wineskins (saying the wineskins were new when they left), and worn-out
sandals and clothes (saying the materials were in good shape when they
left home.) They begged for a covenant, or alliance, with the children of
Israel.

Joshua sought answers from them, but he did not seek answers from
God. So, the Israelites formed a covenant with the Gibeonites and promised them protection. As a result, Joshua and the leaders of Israel unknowingly disobeyed God's commands and put themselves in harm's way.

The people around us can either strengthen or weaken us. We need
caution concerning those with whom we choose to partner.

Dear Lord, please guide us in our decisions concerning others.
We pray in Jesus's name. Amen.

# ❀ *Enter with Confidence* ❀

*Therefore, brethren, having boldness to enter the Holiest by the blood
of Jesus, by a new and living way which He consecrated for us, through
the veil, that is, His flesh* (Hebrews 10:19–20 NKJV).

In the musical, *The King and I*, the king demanded strict reverence from
his subjects. People entered his presence cowering, face to the floor, not
speaking until spoken to, except for the king's children. The king had scores
of children. They respected him as king, but they were able to love him
as daddy. They had special privileges to enjoy his presence, hugging him,
talking with him, all without fear because of their special relationship with
the king.

We Christians have the greatest status ever offered to humankind:
we're adopted children of the Lord. We who are covered under the blood
of Jesus can enjoy being in the presence of almighty God because of our
special relationship with the King of kings.

To the Jews who read this passage in Hebrews several hundred years
ago, the idea of entering into the presence of God through the Holy of
Holies would have been an unheard-of privilege. This was the holiest place
in the temple, for it was the inner chamber where God's glory rested. It was
off-limits to everyone except the chief priest, who himself entered only once
a year. The veil hanging in the temple was thicker than a rug. It separated
the Holy of Holies from the outer sanctum, a curtain symbolically separat-
ing God and man, through which sinful man couldn't pass.

When Jesus breathed his last breath on the Cross, Matthew 27:51
records, the veil was ripped in two, from top to bottom. What used to separate man from God has been replaced by the flesh of Jesus Christ, providing a way for us to enter into God's presence. Instead of separation, there is
now a bridge of reconciliation through Jesus Christ.

Exercise your privileges as a daughter of the Lord today, and spend
quality time in prayer before God. Jesus died to offer us that privilege.

Heavenly Father, I come before You now with confidence
because Jesus my Savior has eliminated our separation.
Thank You for the awesome privilege to approach Your throne room,
for You are a Holy God. Amen.

# ❀ *Be Ready* ❀

*For the Lord himself shall descend from heaven… and the dead in*
*Christ shall rise first. After that, we who are still alive and are left will*
*be caught up together with them in the clouds to meet the Lord in the*
*air. And so we will be with the Lord forever*
(1 Thessalonians 4:16–17).

Paul calls the event in today's verse a mystery because it is difficult to comprehend. Not everyone will die. Someday, Jesus will give the command, the archangel will shout, and a trumpet will sound. Jesus will descend from heaven to take His followers with Him. It will happen as quickly as the blinking of an eye. The Bible calls this "the blessed hope" (Titus 2:13).

In Matthew 24, Jesus warned we must always remain ready because His return could happen at any time. He said not even the angels in heaven know the day nor hour, but the signs (fulfillment of Bible prophecies) hint of when the time is near.

With great emotion a friend shared the following dream: She was at an outdoor family gathering. Suddenly she heard the sound of a trumpet. She could tell by the expressions on the faces of family members that only she and her children heard it. Frantically, she ran from one to another screaming, "Did you hear that? Surely you heard that."

The response from each one was, "Did we hear what?"

As she and her small children began rising into the air, she saw the bewildered look on the faces of the relatives still standing on the ground. She and her children continued to rise as those on the ground appeared smaller and smaller. Then the dream ended.

This vivid dream reminds us of Jesus's warning that we be ready. Are you?

> Lord, please fill me with the power of Your Holy Spirit
> so that I can be ready for Your return and help others
> come into Your kingdom. In Jesus's name I pray. Amen.

# ❧ A Little "Truth" ❧ Can Hurt You

*And if Christ has not been raised, our preaching is useless
and so is your faith. More than that, we are then found to be false
witnesses about God, for we have testified about God that he raised
Christ from the dead* (1 Corinthians 15:14–15).

Many argue that all religions have a little "truth" in them. The question is, whether diverse religions have the truth—period—or, in fact, have a lot of fallacy.

A religion could say snow is cold, and people from virtually every religion in the world would agree. Is believing snow is cold essential to salvation? No. Further, to say a religion has a *bit* of truth actually means it has untruth.

Three major world religions—Judaism, Islam, and Christianity—agree to the existence of the one, personal, Creator God. Yet we find mutually exclusive claims about the *nature* of this God. Islam asserts that Jesus was not God, as also does Judaism. Christianity holds that Jesus *is* God who took on human flesh, coming to earth to absorb the punishment that humans deserved for sin, dying and rising to life again.

Can all three religions be true in their view of God? No, because a foundational principle of all thought called the law of non-contradiction is always in operation. It says, "Something cannot be both true and false at the same time and in the same sense." In today's passage, Paul points out the intrinsic difference between truth and fallacy. Applied to our example, Jesus Christ cannot both be "God in the flesh" and also *not* God in the flesh, at the same time.

Principles of logic such as the law of non-contradiction are used by everyone, even those who claim not to live by them. These principles form the basis on which we make sense of life. They reveal God's intelligence and rationality.

So, when someone insists that contradictory religions can be true at the same time, we can use logic to show them their reasoning is flawed. It is not whether snow is cold that matters, but whether the divine truth is upheld.

Lord, help me respond wisely to those
who believe contradictory beliefs can be true. Amen.

# ❀ This Little Light of Mine ❀

*Let your light shine before men, that they may see your good deeds and*
*praise your Father in heaven* (Matthew 5:16).

When my children were young, I kept night lights in their rooms to comfort them. During their preteen years, they didn't have them in their rooms, but I kept one on in the hall so they could see their way to the bathroom in the middle of the night without bumping into anything. Even the corners of the hall seemed illuminated from that tiny night light.

Have you ever noticed a small light in the distance seems to light up the whole world? If you walk down a dark street, one dim light flickering on someone's porch seems to multiply light for the neighborhood. The darker the night, the brighter the light.

We live in a dark world. Negativity, incivility, and sin shroud us in dark thoughts and feelings. Just one negative-minded person can ruin our day. People who aren't civil can hurt our feelings, even when we don't know them. Negative people who are dear loved ones can bring us even greater darkness. They shatter our expectations of the light of comfort when they turn off our hope.

Sin is the worst light-extinguisher of all. It closes down the positive light in each person's life and can doom each of us to utter darkness. However, God shines light in the dark, negative corners of our hearts so we can deal with whatever darkness we must face. Jesus, the Light of the world, bursts forth as the Light of truth, bringing positive hope—even in our dark corners.

Jesus says we shouldn't hide our light under a basket, but shine in every way possible. As a reflection of His light, we then pass it to others. Bring your light out this day. Show the power of Light! Let it shine as you smile, think positively, and set a good example before others. You never know who's watching you, waiting for your smile or kind word. As we relate to others, we have the best opportunity to let our light shine!

Dear Lord, may Your light of love continue to shine through me. Amen.

# ❀ Thoughts of Me ❀

*"My strength is made perfect in weakness"*
(2 Corinthians 12:9 NKJV).

Everyone said a missions trip would change my life. I had never been on one before, so I signed up to go to Mexico. What's more, I was traveling with fellow seminary students and professors, which made for a great deal of self-inflicted stress and pressure to "measure up."

The reality of what I was about to do profoundly hit me as I sat on the plane beside a teammate, listening to her talk about the Lord in between her witnessing to everyone seated around us. I felt inadequate, was sure I would quickly be exposed as the only nervous team member, the weakest link. My other flight buddy wasn't witnessing to everyone, but he had memorized the entire Book of John, *in two languages*, and he was taking the opportunity to review while in flight.

As panic and dread swept over me, I finally admitted to myself and God that I was fully aware of my plight: I just couldn't cut it. I wasn't capable of effectively ministering for Christ in Mexico. My first instinct in the flesh was to criticize my teammates for being religious nuts, but I had already seen within them a genuine passion for Christ, so criticizing was not going to make me feel better about myself. I began to pray. I told God how lonely I felt. I desired to bring a blaze of glory to God, but I could only muster a weak flicker.

Suddenly I realized my prayer focus was all about *me*. Was this missions trip about me proving something to myself or to others? Did it really matter to God if I was the weakest link in everyone else's eyes? I gave my fears and concerns to God. I asked Him to give me great boldness for His glory, that I might focus on *Him*.

We can do nothing in our own strength, but amazing things with God's power flowing through us. Let God use you today!

Father, be my strength to witness for Christ.
Overcome my weakness with Your power and might. Amen.

# ❀ *Invisible Children* ❀

*When he had placed his hands on them, he went on from there*
(Matthew 19:15).

When Jesus left Galilee and went into Judea, a crowd gathered. Soon people asked Jesus to pray for their children (Matthew 19:13). The disciples tried to turn them away, but Jesus took time to talk with them, saying "the kingdom of heaven belongs to such as these" (v. 14).

What an affirmation for children! Busy clarifying the law to Pharisees, Jesus took time to treat children kindly, placing His hands on them for a blessing! Surely parents must have realized a new respect for children. Even the disciples must have been amazed!

All of us need a renewed respect for children. Once a friend, I'll call her Ginger, dropped by my house to talk with me about children: "God's given me a burden for children in your neighborhood."

"There are no children in my neighborhood," I said. "When mine were small, our neighborhood was filled, but they're in college or in other cities now. Three elderly ladies live on my block...but no children."

"If I find any, will you let me have a Bible school on your carport? I'll bring a big quilt for them to sit on."

"Sure, but I doubt if you'll find any."

In three days she called again. She had found 12 children within three blocks of my house! I offered to provide juice and cookies. Obviously God was working here.

I still marvel over God's grace that week. Three visiting grandchildren nearby asked to participate. A newcomer sent four children. The list grew daily as Ginger lovingly led in games, a Bible study, and music.

That week changed Ginger, the children, and me. I realized I needed to pay more attention to children. Many *invisible* children needed my care. I recalled many times ignoring children in the grocery store or at church. How many times had I overlooked those who were precious in His sight?

As Christians, one important ministry is everywhere: simply *seeing* the invisible children. We can do as Jesus did: reach out to them, care about them, and pray for them.

Lord, thank You for little children.
Help us to minister to them in love. Amen.

# ❀ Dare to Be a Daniel ❀

*Be sure of this: The wicked will not go unpunished,*
*but those who are righteous will go free* (Proverbs 11:21).

When I was a child, I loved the song, "Dare to be a Daniel." The more I learned about Daniel, the more I admired him and enjoyed singing about him.

As a teenager, Daniel was among the brightest and best of the Jewish people taken captive into Babylon. He was righteous (Ezekiel 14:14) and wise (Ezekiel 28:3). However, his most outstanding characteristic is that he was committed to God. He stood for his convictions.

By the time of the events in the story of the lion's den (Daniel 6:1–28), Daniel was more than 80 years old. During his time in Babylon, he had served in a position of authority under three rulers, the last being the Persian ruler Darius. Darius planned to reorganize his newly conquered Babylon into 129 provinces with three presidents. Daniel was appointed as a president because of his wisdom and integrity.

King Darius considered placing Daniel above the other two presidents. They became so jealous that they tricked him into signing a 30-day decree stating that all prayer during that time period had to be directed to him as king. The other two presidents felt sure Daniel would break the decree. He did.

Daniel continued to face Jerusalem and pray to God three times a day. King Darius sorrowfully had to adhere to his edict, so he cast Daniel into a pit with hungry lions.

The next morning he rushed to the pit and had the capstone removed. Daniel was alive! God had sent an angel to shut the mouths of the lions. The king then issued a new decree ordering all the citizens in his kingdom to consider worshipping Daniel's God.

It's not always easy to stand up for our commitment to God, but it is always rewarding. Most of our situations cause us more "alarm" than "harm." Daniel was willing to stand for his convictions no matter the cost. In the words of the old song, are we willing to "Dare to be a Daniel?"

Dear God, please help us develop courage to stand up
for our convictions like Daniel. In Jesus's name, amen.

# ❀ I Think Myself Happy ❀

*I think myself happy, king Agrippa, because I shall answer
for myself this day* (Acts 26:2 KJV).

We are as happy as we think we are. When Paul said, "I think myself
happy," he used a powerful choice of words. We can either think ourselves
happy or unhappy.

We alone control the thoughts we dwell on daily. Our thoughts
evoke the emotions that lead to our behaviors, which eventually become
our habits. Solomon said, "For as a man thinketh in his heart, so is he"
(Proverbs 23:7 KJV).

How can we think ourselves happy in the midst of troubling circumstances? The answer lies in Psalm 146:5: "Happy is he that hath the God
of Jacob for his help, whose hope is in the LORD his God" (KJV). What
more could we ever need than the assurance of God's help no matter what
we are facing? That assurance is our hope. That assurance is our happiness.
Dwelling on God's love and seeking His will keeps our thoughts where they
should be—on Him.

Imagine that your thoughts were graded based on 100 percent as a
perfect score. What would be your grade? Can you think of steps you need
to take to cultivate the habit of happiness?

The story is told about two construction workers who sat down to eat
lunch. One opened his lunch box and began eating. The other pulled a sandwich out of his lunch bag and began complaining. He grumbled because he
had another bologna sandwich. For five straight days he had eaten a bologna sandwich. Now here was another one! His co-worker suggested he tell
his wife that he was tired of bologna. He looked at his friend and exclaimed,
"My wife? I fix my own lunches!"

We are the ones who allow destructively negative thoughts into our
minds. We, like Paul, can change our thought patterns by "thinking ourselves happy."

> Dear Lord, You have given me so many wonderful things to make
> me happy. Please forgive me when I choose to dwell on thoughts
> that are negative and steal my happiness. I want to live each day
> basking in the goodness of Your love. In Jesus's name, amen.

# ❧ *Seeing Is Believing* ❧

*Your words were found, and I ate them, and Your word was to me the
joy and rejoicing of my heart; for I am called by Your name, O LORD
God of hosts* (Jeremiah 15:16 NKJV).

As I looked across the audience that night, a handful of women had
especially eager eyes and devoted ears, absorbing the message God had
given me to share. I could see the Holy Spirit making personal applications
in their lives as they received His Word. They came hungry, and God satisfied their longing for Him.

These precious women were members of Christian Women's Job
Corps, a ministry providing a Christian context for women to be equipped
for life and employment. One particular participant touched my heart as
she shared her life story with me. She had struggled with alcohol and drug
abuse in her past, but she was walking in victory with a new life in Christ.
Her hunger for God was inspiring. She thanked God for the way He had
increased her daily free time little by little over the past few years, giving
her more time to pray and study Scripture. As she shared with me what she
had learned from her personal study of Scripture that morning, the glory of
the Lord lit up her countenance.

These precious women reminded me of the never-ending cycle God
creates in our lives. The more we see God's power, the closer we draw near
to Him; the closer we draw near to God, the more we see God's power
in our lives. These women had learned that God truly is the answer to all
of life's problems. They had witnessed in their own circumstances God's
ability to transform any situation by bringing new life and hope where there
had been spiritual death and hopelessness. God was a dear companion to
them, and they could not get enough of His company.

Do you need a renewed passion for the Word of God? Reflect on God's
powerful transformation of your life. Think about the many ways He has
made Himself known to you. Yes, God can make all things new.

> Father, I need more of You. Awaken my passion for Your Word.
> I desire for You to be my greatest daily yearning. Amen.

# ❦ *True or False?* ❦

*There will be false teachers among you, who will secretly bring in destructive heresies, even denying the Lord who bought them, and bring on themselves swift destruction* (2 Peter 2:1 NKJV).

I was in high school when I first encountered false teaching in the church. My Sunday School teacher's comment seemed innocent, yet subtly off base. "God doesn't care what we believe as long as we are sincere in our worship," she said. *That's not true,* I thought. *The Bible says God cares very much what we believe. It's possible to be sincerely wrong.* Even then I recognized the lie, as sweetly as it was purported by someone in authority, someone I should have been able to trust.

Second Peter chapter two provides a helpful description of those false teachers, their techniques, and the heresies they commonly taught. Reviewing this list will enable us to distinguish truth from deception. False teachers are secretive and often distort the truth about Christ (2:1). Greed motivates their exploitation of weak persons who gullibly believe their self-styled fables (2:3). Their actions are motivated by sinful desires and they want to be answerable to no one. They brazenly disparage and misrepresent God's angels (2:10).

False teachers are like animals who are directed by base instinct, and they criticize others regarding truths about which they themselves know nothing (2:12). They may blatantly practice immorality, enticing immature victims to join them in their revelry (2:13–14). They can be guided by their own stupidity and belligerence, as was Balaam, the Old Testament prophet whom God corrected through the miraculous speaking of a donkey (2:15–16). They are as barren as "springs without water" and as unstable as "mists driven by the storm" (2:17). They arrogantly seek out weak ones to entice into evil, promising freedom, when in reality they are enslaved to sin (2:18–19).

They suffer the gravest condemnation reserved for people who know the truth and then choose to entangle themselves once again in sin (2:20–21). They wallow in their sin and are filthy through and through (2:22).

Review this helpful list from time to time in order to discern the truth from false teaching.

Holy Spirit, by Your power I can know truth and distinguish truth from error.
May I love Your truth so much that I quickly recognize anything
that departs from it. Amen.

# ❀ Born to Be the Ultimate Me ❀

*All the days ordained for me were written in your book before one of
them came to be* (Psalm 139:16).

A baby's birth is one of the most remarkable occurrences in the world.
Just think of it: your great-grandparents found each other and your grandparents were born. Your grandparents found each other and your parents
were born. Your parents found each other and you were born. From thousands of possibilities of dormant and dominant traits, they possessed just
the right DNA to form a baby that was uniquely YOU.

Every fingerprint, footprint, and ear print in the world is different. How
could that happen outside Intelligent Design? Unless you were created by
the Creator of the universe, it would be impossible. He created the one-and-
only you!

Though Christians know we're created as unique, we sometimes
complain about our characteristics. I complain about my short height
and propensity for cholesterol (which my doctor says I inherited from my
father) and the diabetes factor I inherited from my mother. I wish I'd inherited her tall height and my father's no-diabetes gene!

God makes no mistakes, no accidents. He creates whom He plans to
create, and He created you just the way you are, born into your unique
family—so you could be who you are in Christ. Each of us has a unique
way we can relate to the world. If you have almond eyes and your ancestors
came from Asia, you have a special touch to reach Asians for Christ. If you
have wavy hair or straight, you can walk up to someone with like texture
and immediately talk about ways to comb, brush, and design hairdos with
that texture.

I can be a missionary to short, round individuals, called "endomorphs."
I can cross barriers a beautiful tall, thin woman can't cross because I can
relate to other endomorphs. You also are uniquely equipped, rich or poor,
tall or short, to reach certain segments of His creation.

Born to be the ultimate witness, you were ordained by God to be
exactly as you are for His purpose and glory.

O Creator, I give you my family characteristics, my personality, and my gifts.
Help me be Your witness in my own unique way. Amen.

# ❊ *Wear Red* ❊

*Now when they saw the boldness of Peter and John, and perceived that*
*they were uneducated and untrained men, they marveled. And they*
*realized that they had been with Jesus* (Acts 4:13 NKJV).

Do you like to wear red? I used to, and I still occasionally will muster up
the courage to wear red, but I have to really be in the right frame of mind.
When I wear red, I feel as if I've invited the world to look at me. Thus,
I never wear red on a bad hair day!

To be bold is neither good nor bad. The subject of your stance determines the merit of your boldness. If you're being bold and daring for
adventure, perhaps you're in for a fabulous experience, or maybe your fool-
hardiness will land you in a sticky predicament. If you're standing strong to
get your way, that's not nearly as admirable as standing for a cause, but it's
often when we feel threatened or oppressed that we muster up the courage
to be bold.

What about being bold for Jesus? Peter and John were uneducated
men, by their hearers' standards. Based on Acts 4:13, they might've broken grammar rules when they spoke, or perhaps they presented their arguments with nervous pacing, but their words were nonetheless compelling.
The Sanhedrin didn't know Jesus as Lord, but they could tell that Jesus
made a profound impact on Peter and John. These two men spoke with
such boldness that surely they had been with Jesus. Only those who had
walked alongside the Savior would speak such strong words about Jesus,
unashamedly and fully convinced of the truth.

Are you fully convinced that Jesus is the Way, the Truth, and the Life?
If you've been with Jesus, if you've sensed His presence along your life's
journey, if He has lifted your burdens of sin and despair, you can testify
with great boldness and confidence that Jesus is alive, and He is Savior and
Lord. Tell it out, and just for fun, maybe wear red when you say it!

Precious Father, I never want to lose the bold assurance of my faith in Your Son.
I want to lead others to You. I want to speak about Jesus in such a way that
people know that I have been in His presence. Amen.

# ❧ *Loading the Dishwasher* ❧

*"But you shall receive power when the Holy Spirit has come upon you;
and you shall be witnesses to Me in Jerusalem, and in all Judea and
Samaria, and to the end of the earth"* (Acts 1:8 NKJV).

My older brother's single contribution to kitchen cleanup duty was to lick
the bowls clean. My two older sisters spent countless hours washing and
drying dishes by hand after family meals for six, and they're still grumbling
about their dishpan hands. As the youngest, my responsibility was to help
bring the dishes to the sink, and place the ketchup and butter back in the
refrigerator. By the time my oldest sister moved out of the house and I had
to assume her chores, the world had changed; instead of washing dishes by
hand, I loaded the dishwasher.

My family moved often because my father was in the army, and
I remember the first house we owned that had a dishwasher. We lived there
for three years, and we never once opened the door of the dishwasher.
Mother was skeptical the machine could sanitize the dishes to her satisfaction, so my sisters stood at the sink, directly beside the dishwasher, and
scrubbed each pot and pan by hand.

Any time I bring up that first dishwasher to my sisters, they groan in
unison. How could our mother have done such a thing to them? We owned
a perfectly good piece of machinery that would've saved my sisters hours of
scrubbing, but because our mother wasn't sure about the dishwasher, they
had to deal with the chores the hard way.

Similarly, do you find yourself doing ministry the hard way? If you're
a follower of Jesus, you have the power of the Holy Spirit dwelling within,
but do you rely upon His power to tackle the challenges of ministry? Ask
God to apply Holy Spirit power to your challenges, and then by faith, trust
God to do His great work in your ministry.

Powerful and sovereign Lord, too often I am weary from trying to do ministry
the hard way, apart from Your power. I pray for the Holy Spirit's power
to intervene in the challenges I'm currently facing. Amen.

# ❀ *Take a Rest* ❀

*Peace to the brothers, and love with faith from God the Father and the
LORD Jesus Christ* (Ephesians 6:23).

In the most luxurious hotel in Panama City, I taught a leadership retreat
for missionary wives who lived throughout Panama. They'd saved funds
several years for this renewal—for body and soul. Some served in a remote
Panama jungle, with few books, needles, sewing thread, or other essentials
for work among indigenous women in malaria-ridden areas. Everyone was
overjoyed to stay in a first-class hotel for one night—including me! What
a treat this retreat was! That night they enjoyed fluffy beds in gorgeous
rooms with a beautiful view of the Panama Canal, with ships lining up to
go through the locks.

"Don't get used to this. You won't be staying here after tonight," said
the leader, smiling. "We've dreamed of this day, but we're "getting real"
tomorrow. You'll be staying at the church house."

"OK," I replied, thinking, *That won't be hard*. I made the mistake many
novices do when they agree to lead: misunderstanding the context in which
they lead. We drove to an average urban church service, where women
with muddy shoes wore beautiful white dresses. I learned they lived in
homes with dirt floors, though their donated clothes hung on nails above
the mud.

People sat in hard chairs to hear the enthusiastic pastor. They listened
for two hours with amazing focus. My sweat-soaked cotton dress was
wilted, my hair plastered to my head. After a reception, I spoke about the
importance of mentoring with a few women in a small conference room.
I needed rest, and longed for a cool bed.

Alone, I didn't sleep much that night. Gunshots and sirens kept me
awake. I had two bathrooms in the apartment at the rear of the church,
but the rooms were rustic. As I lay in the warm bed, I kept remembering
one Panamanian woman's words, "Thank You for giving us refreshing rest
tonight." I thought about her words for a long time. What *I* saw as miserable circumstances, *she* saw as rest for her body and soul.

Lord, forgive us for our prideful ways. Help us understand the sacrifices
of others and find rest in You as we lead. Amen.

# ❀ *In Deep Water* ❀

*Put out into deep water, and let down the nets for a catch*
(Luke 5:4).

They had worked all night and had caught no fish. They were tired. In fact, they were already washing their nets, ready to quit for a while. Can you imagine how exasperated Peter must have been when Jesus told him to put out into deep water again? I must admit that I am proud of Peter and crew. Although they probably thought it was useless, they went back out to sea and let down their nets in complete obedience to the words of Jesus.

Notice that as soon as they fully obeyed, they were blessed beyond their wildest imagination. When they had followed Jesus's command (Luke 5:6a), the nets became so full they began to break and back-up help had to be summoned. Then, both boats almost sank because they were so full of fish.

It all began with obedience to the command, "Put out into deep water." In order to receive the blessings, we must be willing to get back in the boat. No matter how tired we may be. No matter how many times we have tried and failed. No matter how badly we want to quit. As long as He summons us to a task, we must climb back on board and move forward.

The obedience of the disciples resulted in:
• A spiritual renewal occurred (v. 8).
• Everyone around was astonished by what happened (v. 9).
• They were promised even greater miracles (v. 10).
• They left everything and followed Him (v. 11).

These hard-working fishermen had learned one of the greatest lessons of life: Blessings come through obedience. In order to experience the blessings of obedience we must be willing to put out into deep water. When we do, our blessings will be more than we ourselves can contain. We will have to share them with others!

Dear Lord, help us develop a willingness to be obedient,
even if it means leaving the security of the shore and
putting out into deep water. In Jesus's name, amen.

# ❀ Two Little Jellybeans ❀

*Every word of God is pure* (Proverbs 30:5 NKJV).

The immunizations nurse was giving final instructions about how to take the oral vaccinations. "Be sure you take these on an empty stomach."

"OK," I said. "I would like to take the first dose now. I only ate two jellybeans. Is that OK?"

"No," the nurse replied. "Your stomach has to be *completely* empty—nothing in there at all."

Two jellybeans. Now that's about as empty as a stomach can get without being truly empty. How could two tiny tablets of sugar make that much of a difference? The nurse's reaction to my trivialization of two jellybeans reminded me that words really do matter—*empty* means *empty*.

God's Word is pure. How pure is pure? How many flaws are allowed before something is no longer perfect? If two jellybeans can make a stomach *not empty*, even one error in the Word of God makes it impure.

Skeptics have spent countless hours trying to discredit the Word of God. Unfortunately, their efforts have slowly begun to impact the thoughts and beliefs of Christians. Did God create the heavens and earth? Are any of the characters of the Bible merely fictional and not historical figures? Can modern science explain the miracles in Scripture? Did Jesus really claim to be God? And is He the only way?

The next time you feel tempted to doubt the Word of God, think about the two jelly beans. If a stomach isn't completely empty, it's not empty at all. Similarly, if you concede only two jellybeans' worth of what someone perceives to be impurity in the Bible, your decision is conceding the Word of God is not fully pure.

Stand strong on the truth of God's Word. The God who holds the universe in its place is big enough and powerful enough to maintain His Word given to us.

God, Your words are the only wisdom and truth.
How can I help others to believe in the truth of Scripture?
Show me the way, Lord. In the name of Jesus I pray, amen.

# ❀ *Moving On Out* ❀

*Then the family heads of Judah and Benjamin, and the priests and*
*Levites—everyone whose heart God had moved—prepared to go up*
*and build the house of the LORD in Jerusalem* (Ezra 1:5).

King Cyrus, the ruler of Persia, allowed exiled Israelites to return to Jerusalem to rebuild the temple. God moved like a catalyst in the hearts of His people. Yearning to serve Him, their hearts changed first; then they acted. (For the whole story, read Ezra 1:1–8, 68–70.)

In this passage, notice the following truths:

• *Not everyone went on the missions trip.*
Only those "whose hearts God has moved" prepared to go to Jerusalem. Though many were comfortable and apathetic in exile, those with a relationship with God listened to Him, willed to follow Him, and then moved!

• *Heads of households became leaders.*
Those with influence took leadership roles. Captives for years, they took the risk of a wider worldview. Parents led children; family units moved together. (For family ministry opportunities in the US and overseas, contact FamilyFEST at (205) 991–4097 or www.wmu.com/ministry/volunteer.) Consider *your* family; you're a powerful influence—with responsibility for instilling a Christian worldview in them.

• *Family units did construction projects.* Have you ever wished your family could do something to grow closer? Nothing brings cohesiveness more than common work. In a current movie, *Evan Almighty*, a modern Noah near Washington, D.C., found building an ark with his three sons brought loyalty and love within the family. It could happen to you! Encouraging pre-teens and teenagers to move out with Christian motives will instill a lifetime of world-focused service.

• *Others contributed to the project.* Maybe we're not apathetic, as some Israelites were, about moving out, but circumstances—or God's will—may prevent our going on a ministry trip. Ezra 1:6 tells what happened in Persia: "All their neighbors assisted them with articles of silver and gold . . . with valuable gifts, in addition to all the freewill offerings." Look around. Reflect on what we can give to those who are going on a missions trip. Each of us can be a part of moving on out!

Lord, help us take responsibility for instilling a Christian worldview
in our children, our church, and our circle of influence. Amen.

# ❀ Can't Do It on My Own ❀

*If one falls down, his friend can help him up* (Ecclesiastes 4:10).

Have you ever wished for a farther-along-friend who would help you grow spiritually? We all need help to accomplish goals, even though we often have difficulty asking for help.

I recall one day when Edna and I worked on our second book manuscript together at her daughter Patsy's home, "holed up" in the upstairs room where we clicked away on two computers. Edna decided to move a pile of her belongings downstairs. With clothes and other junk piled high in her arms, I could barely see the top of her head.

"May I help?" I asked.

"Oh, no. I think I've got it," she said, turning sideways so she could see the stairs.

"Don't break your neck," I warned. Two steps down, a hairspray bottle tumbled from her arms. Giggling, I retrieved the hairspray bottle.

"Just drop it on top of the pile," said Edna, lifting up her chin to make room.

By this time *she* had started chuckling, too. She gingerly groped for the next step, and the next. I still stood at the top of the stairs, observing her effort at independence and laughing so hard I was hunkered over.

"Are you sure I can't help?"

"No thanks," came her muffled reply. "I think I've got it."

Why is it so hard for us to ask for help? Sometimes we wait until the problems are piled so high we fear sharing *one* will upset the delicate balance and cause an avalanche! A wise woman asks for help *before* desperation sets in!

Whether you simply want friendship or someone in whom to confide, or you want someone to teach you how to use a computer, ask God for a farther-along-friend to come alongside. Then, open your eyes to see what the Lord provides.

> Lord, please humble my heart and open my eyes to the women
> who could help me along in my spiritual walk. Amen.

*Adapted from* Seeking Wisdom: Preparing Yourself to Be Mentored *by Edna Ellison and Tricia Scribner (New Hope Publishers, 2001).*

# ❀ Imagine No Heaven ❀

*We are not of those who shrink back and are destroyed,*
*but of those who believe and are saved* (Hebrews 10:39).

The poem below was written on September 9, 2008, at the Logos Writers' meeting at Morningside Baptist Church, Spartanburg, South Carolina, after a discussion of John Lennon's song "Imagine" ("There Is No Heaven"). The poem represents the thoughts of a Christian with strong beliefs who can neither understand atheists' denial of God's existence nor bear to face the future without hope of heaven.

I'm in a spin, a dream, a play,
A quandary, and a mess;
John Lennon's held all heav'n at
bay—
An atheist like the rest:

Voltaire and Marx, Kurt Vonnegut
And those that You call heathen....
How can they live their lives on earth
Without the hope of heaven?

No streets of gold? No crystal sea?
No angels, lake, or throne?
No cherubim or seraphim,
No place of heav'nly home?

When I've got troubles and my head
Is hanging really low,
I'll give up hope of all my peace?
I've got nowhere to go.

In life, then death! Is that just all
There is to us? Just this?
Dear Christian Friend, this is
deranged.
It is a shame! It is!

You know, without a chance to see
My Savior face to face;
To be interred beneath the grass,
In sin and dirt—disgrace!

Why, what's the use of trying hard
Or smiling in this place?
You're telling me it's all for naught?
I float in endless space?

There is no joy in Mudville, Friend;
No silver lining, Dear,
Behind the dark black cloud of rain?
That's it! I'm outa here!
© *Edna Ellison, 2009*

O God, may we always be repulsed by atheism and—when we face it—
hold even stronger to our faith in You. Help us to praise You for the everlasting
life You freely give us. May we always be ready to communicate Your love and
solid promises that encourage faith and hope for the future. Amen.

# ❦ Out of Her Poverty ❦

*"Assuredly, I say to you that this poor widow has put in more than all those who have given to the treasury; for they all put in out of their abundance, but she out of her poverty put in all that she had, her whole livelihood"* (Mark 12:43–44 NKJV).

God has instructed His people to care for the needs of the widow. However, this widow didn't consider herself excused from helping the needy while she herself waited for the charity of others. She desired to bless and honor God with what little means she had to contribute. She didn't give her money with fanfare; we read nothing to indicate that she delivered a scornful, resentful look to the hypocritical rich, nor that she acted mournfully to elicit pity from bystanders. The widow didn't even realize that the Son of God had His eyes fixed upon her.

The widow was at a distinct disadvantage in her ability to give, but she was not deterred by her limitations. Did you notice how many coins the widow dropped into the treasury? Two. She had only two coins in her possession, yet she didn't withhold even one for her own sense of security. She gave the entire amount, an amazing expression of genuine faith.

Have you made excuses lately about why you cannot serve or minister due to circumstances or limitations in your life? Consider Christ's high regard for the widow's great sacrifice; He was fully aware of every detail of her personal plight, and He was touched by her deep devotion to the work of God expressed through her gift. Give what you have to offer, give of yourself joyfully, and know that God will honor your efforts when made with a willing heart.

I often have wondered what thoughts and emotions filled the widow's heart as she dropped her coins and then walked away, heading toward her home with no money inside her robe. My guess is she was overflowing with joy.

Father, please forgive me for excusing myself from kingdom work
because of my personal limitations. Teach me to honor You with my tithes
and gifts, giving materially as well as of my time, to bless and honor You. Amen.

# ❁ *Stand Firm* ❁

*Do not be afraid. Stand firm and you will see the deliverance the LORD*
*will bring you today* (Exodus 14:13).

The Book of Exodus records that God did not lead the children of Israel in the way they expected. Instead of the shorter path, through Philistine country, He led them into what seemed like an impossible situation. The mass of people followed Moses out of slavery in Egypt into the desert wilderness. Suddenly, everything seemed hopeless. A sea lay to the east, hills to the north and south, and an open valley to the west. The sophisticated Egyptian army easily could overcome the unorganized crowd of wanderers through this valley.

They panicked. Sarcastically, they asked if Moses brought them there to die as though he felt there were not enough graves in Egypt to bury them all. They begged to retreat and return to a life of bondage in Egypt. Moses's response was not what they had anticipated. "Stand firm." He assured them God would fight for them.

Then, in a miracle unparalleled in Old Testament history, God parted the Red Sea and allowed His children to pass over on dry land. Once they were safely across, He allowed the waters to flow back over the Egyptians who pursued them.

When you follow God's leading, the enemy will pursue you. Satan will try to lure you into returning to a life of bondage. If you've accepted Jesus Christ as Savior, you've been set free. You've walked across on dry land. You no longer have to fear the enemy. Stand firm and see God's deliverance. We don't have to fight the battle. It belongs to the Lord and it was won at Calvary!

Dear God, I pray for the faith to trust You in all circumstances.
Please give me the courage to stand firm even when it looks as though
the victory is impossible. In Jesus's name I pray. Amen.

# ❀ *The Right Prayer* ❀

*Pray … words may be given me so that I will fearlessly make known
the mystery of the gospel, for which I am an ambassador in chains. Pray
that I may declare it fearlessly, as I should* (Ephesians 6:19–20).

Have you been in a miserable situation lately? Perhaps someone has betrayed you at work, accusing you of a wrong you didn't commit or slandering your reputation. Maybe you're in a circumstance in which you must decide between two bad choices. Perhaps you walk through a valley in which you awaken every day to the same dismal scene without a ray of sunshine in your remote future.

How are you praying? If you're like me, your prayers cry out to the Lord for deliverance, resolution, or maybe even vindication. Paul found himself in such a situation. It seemed that every time he opened his mouth he got beat up, stoned, mocked, or ended up in jail. His enemies claimed he was a troublemaker, and his list of friends dwindled during his many crises. Now he found himself incarcerated in Rome.

I suspect in a similar situation I would have complained, "Lord, here I am serving You and end up in jail. I know You want me to be happy, and I'm sure not happy locked up. So, this can't be Your will. Please get me out of here so I can get back to doing Your work."

In our shortsightedness we seldom see the grand purpose of God. Yet Paul had the Spirit-led insight to see God's purposes in every situation and pray in accordance with those purposes. Notice how he asks his readers to pray. No complaints about the poor prison food. No comment about the unfairness of his plight. Instead, not once but twice he asked them to pray that he would fearlessly declare the gospel. Moreover, during his imprisonment in Rome, he wrote four surviving letters: Ephesians, Philippians, Colossians, and Philemon. Paul didn't waste time and he never doubted that God would use every situation to further His kingdom purposes.

Father, change my heart so that my prayers echo Your heart and purposes
rather than merely my self-centered concerns. Amen.

# ❀ Be-Our-Attitudes ❀

*Now that you know these things, you will be blessed if you do them*
(John 13:17).

Have you ever noticed that in the Declaration of Independence, Thomas Jefferson does not list happiness as an inalienable right? He lists the pursuit of happiness. Perhaps our wise forefather knew that people must pursue happiness to obtain it.

In Matthew 5:1–12, Jesus shows us how to both pursue and obtain it. He has given us the perfect prescription for happiness in the Beatitudes. Even the word *blessed* might be thought of as "happy." These verses should, indeed, be-our-attitudes.

- Have a repentant heart.
- Admit sorrow for your sins.
- Pursue meekness.
- Protect righteousness.
- Initiate mercy.
- Nurture a pure heart.
- Exemplify peacemaking.
- Suffer persecution for godly living.
- Sing and praise when falsely accused for the kingdom's sake.

Are these the things we seek in our pursuit of happiness? They are the only ways we will ever find it. In our world today, we confuse happiness with pleasure. In this prescription for happiness many of the things on the list would not be considered pleasurable, would they? Yet, they lead to God's version of happiness.

Decades ago, an article in the Miami *Herald* expressed this same sentiment. The article stated that happiness is not a commodity, but a condition. It is not freedom from pain, but the ability to turn pain into power. It comes neither from owning, nor from the lack of owning possessions. It comes not from without, but from within the heart.

Jesus gave the blueprint for happiness: "You will be blessed if you do them" (John 13:17).

Dear Lord, please help me live discerning the difference between pleasure and true happiness. In Jesus's name I pray. Amen.

# ❀ A Worthy Pursuit ❀

*"If you will not hear, and if you will not take it to heart, to give glory to
My name," says the LORD of hosts, "I will send a curse upon you,
And I will curse your blessings. Yes, I have cursed them already,
because you do not take it to heart"* (Malachi 2:2 NKJV).

Consider the laws, the customs, the entertainment, and what is glorified in
this "Christian nation" in which we live. For whom do we roll out the red
carpet? And what do we Christians pursue? Have the Christians of this
generation taken it to heart to give glory to God's name?

Jesus has defined what our pursuit should be, what our resolve of the
heart is all about. He said, *"Seek first the kingdom of God and His righteousness"*
(Matthew 6:33 NKJV). The Christians of the early church knew what it
meant to seek first the kingdom of God. In Acts 2:41, we read that on the
Day of Pentecost, some 3,000 souls were added to the kingdom, and later,
new souls were added daily.

But pursuing the kingdom of God didn't come without a price for the
early believers. Many were ostracized by family and friends, persecuted in
their communities, or died a martyr's death. And though we know only a
few early Christians by name, like Peter and Barnabas and later Paul, if the
early church believers could stand before us today, each one would testify
that his or her life was significant, because it was a worthy pursuit. They
had received Jesus's instructions to seek the kingdom of God, and they
obeyed. The resolve of their hearts was satisfying to their souls because
they brought glory to God's name.

Let your actions, your words, and even your attitudes glorify your Lord
and Savior today. Approach God's Word with a desire to obey, and reject
a lifestyle to pursue your own gain. Take it to heart to bring glory to God's
name. Your choice to put God first will be in stark contrast to society's
pursuits, earning you opportunities to tell others about Jesus the Savior.

Heavenly Father, I am taking it to heart to glorify Your name.
I want to live for You. Teach me Your ways, God. Amen.

# ❀ A Person of Peace ❀

*When you enter a house, first say, "Peace to this house." If a man of*
*peace is there, your peace will rest on him"* (Luke 10:5–6).

I went by a mobile home park often, observing a dozen small children
playing hide-and-seek in the bedraggled bushes or splashing in mud
puddles on rainy days. I often prayed for them, not knowing if they had
spiritual or physical needs. Discussing this burden on my heart, two other
women offered to help with a ministry there, and we printed a leaflet ready
to distribute.

That week we stopped at the park and prayed for a "person of peace" to
welcome us and suggest a good time for a children's Vacation Bible School.
Near a shady tree, we knocked on the door and told our concerns to a
young woman I will call Tanya.

"You're an answer to prayer," said Tanya. "I've wanted to do something
for these children. You can use the shade of my tree! How about using my
porch for Bible study? It'll be completely shady every morning. I can provide refreshments."

Tanya helped us share the leaflets. At every door, women wanted their
children to participate.

"Can I come, too?" asked a young woman with three children.

"Me, too?" asked a second.

I asked more friends to help. For five days, one volunteer helped Tanya
with games and served refreshments, one led the children in singing, one
led small children while others helped with older ones, and another taught
a mothers' Bible study. One 12-year-old boy accepted Christ as his Savior,
and several moms rededicated their lives to Him.

At the end of the week, we held a celebration. Since the weatherman
predicted rain, we asked a nearby church to host the party. (They cheerfully followed up with families later.) We enjoyed the exuberant celebration with cookies, lemonade, and balloons! Tanya thanked everyone for
attending, and passed out crafts the children had made.

Tired, but happy, a few lingering volunteers agreed we'd never forget
this special week with the person of peace God had provided.

Lord, thank You for providing persons of peace
to help us reach neighborhoods and for Your Presence,
which goes before us to open doors for the gospel. Amen.

# ❀ And They Crucified Him ❀

*They brought Jesus to the place called Golgotha (which means
"the place of the skull"). Then they offered him wine mixed with myrrh,
but he did not take it. And they crucified him. Dividing up his clothes,
they cast lots to see what each would get* (Mark 15:22–24).

"And they crucified him." Never have so few words said so much. *And*
alludes to all that Jesus had already endured: the beating, the mockery, the
spitting, the crown of thorns. *They* refers to Roman soldiers in the immediate
context. But the Jews, both the too religious leaders and also some common
people, had already condemned Christ to death. Lest we become arrogant
or blame the people on that day for being fickle and evil, we should remember. In the larger context, our own sins created the need for His intercession
on our behalf, making us personally culpable.

*Crucified* describes the most heinous form of capital punishment known.
Soldiers nailed the victim's hands or wrists with spikes to a crossbeam,
which they then hoisted and affixed to an upright stake. The victim died a
slow, agonizing death. *Him* refers to Jesus, the Holy One, Beloved of the
Father, the Prince of Peace.

Old Testament prophets had forecasted the event hundreds of years
prior, down to the piercing of His body and the dividing of His garments
for which soldiers would gamble (Psalm 22:16–18). Jesus made sure every
portion of the prophecies was fulfilled in Him, leaving nothing undone, all
for our sakes.

Now, say those four words, replacing *Him* with your own name. If
God's righteous wrath against man's sin had prevailed, your name would
have finished the sentence. Instead, mercy reigned "and they crucified *Him*"
(author's emphasis).

> Precious Lord, the crucifixion did not catch You unaware or in any way
> surprise You. From all eternity You planned to die for us, even granting
> glimpses of the event hundreds of years before it occurred. Yet knowing
> that coming here meant suffering and death, You abdicated Your rights as
> heavenly King, donned the flesh of humans, and persevered in doing the
> Father's will until Your job was finished. Thank You. Amen.

*Adapted from Tricia's Prayer Patterns devotionals in* Missions Mosaic (Woman's Missionary Union),
*January 2005.*

# ❀ *Wrapped in a Fajita Was Love* ❀

*For you, brethren, have been called to liberty; only do not use liberty*
*as an opportunity for the flesh, but through love serve one another*
(Galatians 5:13 NKJV).

We climbed up a dusty hillside peppered with metal and cinderblock dwellings. A mangy dog with bulging ribs crossed my path, and dirty children sat in doorways. We entered the home of a man and his wife, two people I will have only met once in my life. I'd never done anything for them personally, nor did I have anything to offer them except a kind word in a language they couldn't understand.

As we sat at their table, the couple and their children stood surrounding us, watching us as we awkwardly filled our glasses with Coke and our plates with fajitas. On my plate was meat I was uncertain about and lettuce I was sure I shouldn't eat, but behind me were a man and his wife who were joyfully and eagerly watching me partake of their hospitality. The missionary leaned over and whispered, "Eat enough to be polite, but let's leave most of the food on the table. What they'll have to eat today will be only what we leave on our plates." Humbled, I thankfully consumed my meal while the couple beamed with the joy of the Lord.

We as Christians will likely never fully grasp how blessed we are that God doesn't base our salvation on our good works. How fearful we would be as we daily wrestle with our flesh. Our joy of serving others would be tainted by the burden we would feel to earn God's favor. But praise be to God, we live in the liberty of Christ! We can serve others out of a heart of love instead of the chains of compulsion.

As we serve others today, let love compel us, making our gifts to others a beautiful reminder of the love of Christ so freely given.

Oh, God! I thank You for my freedom in Christ! I want to serve others today
more freely and generously than ever before, motivated by the love
You've planted in my heart. Please allow me the joy of serving others
in Your name this day. Amen.

# ❀ Follow the Leader ❀

*We all, like sheep, have gone astray, each of us has turned to his own way; and the LORD has laid on him the iniquity of us all*
(Isaiah 53:6).

Throughout the Bible, we are compared to sheep and God to our Shepherd. The following are characteristics of sheep verified through familiar verses taken from the King James Version of Psalm 23:

Sheep are considered unintelligent. All their needs have to be met by the shepherd or they will die: *"The LORD is my Shepherd; I shall not want"* (v. 1).

Sheep have a tendency to keep moving to the point of exhaustion. The shepherd plans times of rest: *"He maketh me to lie down in green pastures"* (v. 2).

Sheep sink rather than swim when their wet fleece weighs them down. They must be kept away from swift water: *"He leadeth me beside the still waters"* (v. 2).

Sheep are lost easily if they stray from the shepherd. *"He leadeth me in the paths of righteousness for His name's sake"* (v. 3).

Sheep are defenseless. Without the shepherd's protection, they are easy prey for predators: *"Yea, though I walk through the valley of the shadow of death, I will fear no evil for thou art with me; thy rod and thy staff they comfort me"* (v. 4).

Sheep do not know the difference between what is good and what is harmful. They will eat poisonous herbs if the shepherd does not lead them to safe pastures: *"Thou preparest a table before me in the presence of mine enemies"* (v. 5).

Sheep are almost blind and often run into things that hurt them. The shepherd applies healing oils and balms to their wounds: *"Thou anointest my head with oil"* (v. 5).

*Sheep are thirsty after a long day and depend on a cup of cool water straight from the Shepherd's hand: "my cup runneth over"* (v. 5).

Sheep form a strong attachment to their shepherd, knowing he cares for their needs: *"Surely goodness and mercy shall follow me all the days of my life: and I will dwell in the house of the LORD forever"* (v. 6).

Oh, Good Shepherd, help us to follow as You lead. In Jesus's name, amen.

# ❀ For the First Time ❀ in a Long Time

*I will instruct you and teach you in the way you should go*
(Psalm 32:8 NKJV).

I was a teen with an identity crisis. A wild lifestyle eventually drained me emotionally and spiritually. With God's help, I was starting over. I struggled to make peace with my past. "You need to get your mind off yourself and onto somebody else," my mom suggested. "Find a way to help others." My oldest sister arranged for me to volunteer at a rehabilitation center where she worked.

For the first time in a long time, I was doing something good. I felt safe in the center's environment; I had no reputation to live down, or up to, among the patients or staff.

The director kept me busy: I swept walkways, cleaned the recreation room, and wheeled patients through the corridors. Then the director gave me a project: planting flowers in the cement pot by the pool.

After nervously purchasing flowers and a bag of potting soil, I sat totally perplexed. The pot was large, and I saw I hadn't purchased enough soil, but my budget was spent.

Suddenly I turned to see a man in a wheelchair nearby. A stroke patient unable to talk, he was trying desperately to make a suggestion. I tried to put him courteously, off without success. He pointed and grunted, and finally I figured out he wanted me to layer the bottom of the pot with rocks. Then he directed me to scoop dirt from the yard into the pot. The container was now nearly full. Next, he motioned me through the process of planting the flowers in the potting soil. As I watered the beautiful arrangement, he sat back, exhausted, but satisfied at the accomplishment.

God assured my heart. Emotionally and spiritually, I was much like that man. I was undergoing major life changes and struggled to express myself. My old familiar ways of life were no longer an option, and I had to learn how to function all over again. Yet, I still had something to offer the world. The man who couldn't walk or talk reached out to me in my need. Helping me exhausted him, but it gave his day purpose. And with patience, I had chosen to receive help from someone who could steer me in doing something the *right* way. The right way felt good—for the first time in a long time.

Father, teach me to follow Your ways, filling my days with fulfillment, purpose, and your goodness. Amen.

# ❀ Mary Had a Little Lamb ❀

*For you know that it was not with perishable things such as silver or gold that you were redeemed… but with the precious blood of Christ, a lamb without blemish or defect* (1 Peter 1:18–19).

What is your earliest childhood memory? My earliest memory is a decal of a little lamb that was on my crib. When I was five years old, my sister was born, and the crib became hers.

My sister was born with serious physical problems. Many times, I stood and watched her sleep. I loved her so much, and whenever I felt worried about her illness, looking at the little lamb on the crib comforted me. I somehow felt the lamb was watching over my baby sister.

Three years later, when I was eight years old, I opened my heart to the only Lamb who could truly offer security. Even at that young age, I understood that I was a sinner and that God had provided the answer for my salvation.

In John 1:19–39, John was questioned about being the promised Messiah. He declared that he was not, but his mission was to prepare the way for the Promised One. The next day, John saw Jesus coming toward him and exclaimed, "Look, the Lamb of God, who takes away the sin of the world!" (John 1:29).

On this earth, we may never comprehend fully the depth of God's love. He loved each of us so much that He died in our place so we can live. His death fulfilled the sacrificial system given by God in the Torah. His death is the means by which we can enter into covenant with God. His death provides direct access into the spiritual Holy of Holies where we can experience the presence of God. His death gives us life.

In time, my baby sister recovered from her illness and the crib was given away. However, I will never forget standing and looking at the lamb on the crib. And—praise God—I will never forget standing and looking through Scripture at the Lamb on the Cross.

> Dear God, thank You for being the Lamb through whom
> we can be saved from our sins. In Jesus's name, amen.

# ❀ The Eyes Have It ❀

*Turn my eyes away from worthless things* (Psalm 119:37).

A woman at our church read Psalm 119:37 and said, "If we spent as much time praying for missions as we do making our faces look good, we'd change the world." Several members gathered afterwards to consider her words. Our group, including teens, estimated a large amount spent on makeup. We were surprised to find out how much they spent *just to highlight their eyes*.

Try thinking of the above verse all day today, focusing on the word *eyes*. At work or at home, if you catch a glimpse of your eyes in a mirror, let that brief glimpse remind you to turn your eyes away from worthless things, concentrating on things of eternal value that make an eternal difference.

As you apply eye shadow, curl your lashes, or brush on mascara, ask God to open them to new missions adventures. What could He show you? A hungry man on the streets outside your grocery store? An empty lot where gang members hang out? A home that needs repair? Poor children playing in the streets? Our speaker was right. We *could* change the world by changing our focus, but are we willing to make lifestyle changes? Ask God to show you something specific He wants you to *be* or *do* today.

Jesus said, "I tell you, open your eyes and look at the fields! They are ripe for harvest" (John 4:35). Pray God will help you see the harvest of people who need to know Him personally.

Can't we just do missions with our eyes closed? Sure! More can be done through prayer than most of us imagine! Accept this three-fold challenge:

1. Pray for every situation you see that needs God's presence.
2. Keep your eyes busy, looking for mission situations for which you can pray.
3. As God leads, move out and change your world, starting with those situations.

Don't forget, *the eyes have it!* Once you've *seen* the situation through God's eyes, keep yours open!

God, protect my eyes from worthless things. Lead me to see the world through Your eyes and follow Your path with open eyes. Amen.

# ❀ What is J-O-Y? ❀

*Rejoice in the LORD, you who are righteous, and praise his Holy name*
(Psalm 97:12).

You probably would not be reading this book unless you are seeking righteousness. Jesus gives all Christians righteousness when they confess Him as their Savior. Our reaction to salvation is to praise Him forever. A personal relationship with our living Lord then encourages righteous relationships with others.

I love sharing verses of joy from the Psalms with others, reaching out as a bridge to them, connecting them with Almighty God. Here are some favorite verses:

- *"Sing to the LORD a new song, for he has done marvelous things"* (Psalm 98:1).
- *"Shout for joy to the LORD, all the earth, burst into jubilant song with music; make music to the LORD with the harp, with the harp and the sound of singing, with trumpets and the blast of the ram's horn — shout before the LORD, the King"* (Psalm 98:4–6).
- *"Let the sea resound and everything in it, the world, and all who live in it"* (Psalm 98:7).
- *"Let the rivers clap their hands, let the mountains sing together for joy; let them sing before the LORD"* (Psalm 98:8–9).
- *"Shout for joy to the LORD, all the earth. Worship the LORD with gladness; come before him with joyful songs"* (Psalm 100:1).
- *"I will sing of your love and justice; to you, O LORD, I will sing praise"* (Psalm 101:1).

Will you join me today in reading each of these in holy relationship with the Lord? Then will you decide how you can share these verses with others? Use your imagination and creativity. Think electronic networks. Think family networks. Think professional networks. Which methods might be attractive to share these words?

Dear Lord, help us think of ways we can use these beautiful praise words to share the joy with others in our circles of influence. In Jesus's name, amen.

# ❀ *Making a Nest* ❀

*And everyone who has left houses or brothers or sisters or father or*
*mother or wife or children or lands, for My name's sake, shall receive a*
*hundredfold, and inherit eternal life* (Matthew 19:29 NKJV).

As I traveled the perimeter of my house sweeping up leaves and debris, I stumbled across two bird nests in odd locations. One was nestled deeply within a piece of pottery on my front porch, and the other was loosely fitted in the opening of my husband's golf bag. I mused at the creativity of the mother birds that sought out these foreign containers to host their homes. Though the locations might've been unconventional, these mother birds made familiar homes in which to raise their young—soft, rounded beds of straw and small twigs. It was the mother bird's nesting abilities that brought comfort to the baby chicks, not the containers that housed the nests.

Have you ever given much thought to the life of a missionary family? Perhaps you've heard people make comments like, "How could any responsible parent uproot their children and drag them halfway across the world to India?" Missionaries who serve in faraway places are single men and women who traverse foreign lands with only the Lord as a traveling companion, retired couples learning to keep pace in a world filled with ever-changing conditions, or mommies and daddies who find themselves answering God's call to "make their nests" and raise their children in dots across the planet.

Give careful attention to praying for missionary families today. Pray for singles to find sweet companionship in the Lord. Pray for senior adults to run swiftly each day for the cause of Christ. Pray for children on mission for God in exciting yet challenging ways in their young lives. Pray for parents of these children as they build safe, welcoming homes for their children in the exceptional environment of a distant land. Then pray for yourself to be open to God's leading, willing to go wherever God would have you build your nest.

Dear God, please bless the missionary families serving around the world
for the sake of the gospel. I want to be available to go wherever You want me.
In Jesus's name, amen.

# ❀ Wait for the Power ❀

*Stay in the city until you have been clothed with power from on high*
(Luke 24:49).

The Bible records many stories of people who acted before they had a good direction or plan. Take Moses, for example: he tried to rescue one mistreated Hebrew slave by killing the Egyptian taskmaster (Exodus 2:11–12). Then he fled and spent 40 years in the desert before God called him to save *all* the Hebrew slaves. Once God empowered him through the burning bush experience (Exodus 3), he was able to lead them fearlessly and successfully.

Also take Peter, for example: the New Testament records the account of Christ's most impetuous disciple, who proclaimed his loyalty to the Lord and yet soon denied knowing Him three times (John 18:15–27). However, after Jesus's resurrection and ascension to heaven, Peter received the power of the Holy Spirit (Acts 2). Then he grew in maturity and steadfast ministry, boldly becoming a foundational apostle upon which Christ built the early church. Like Moses, he now had direction for his life.

Another disciple, Luke, records several visits from the risen Christ *after* his resurrection. As the 11 disciples discussed these encounters, Christ appeared. He explained how they would preach in His name all over the world, beginning in Jerusalem, but He warns them about beginning without Him. To us, Christ's words in Luke 24:49 above seem to say, "How about you? Have you already received the power from on high? If you are unsure of what God wants you to do, stay where you are until you are clothed with His assurance and power. Once you have received His direction, you can minister fearlessly and successfully in the power of His Spirit."

O, God of all power, help me stay calm as I wait on You.
Send your power, Lord, in Your timing. Amen.

# ❈ *Daily Resolve* ❈

*And daily in the temple, and in every house, they did not cease teaching
and preaching Jesus as the Christ* (Acts 5:42 NKJV).

Can you imagine having such an incredible resolve to tell the good news
of Jesus Christ? Each day, Peter and the apostles were focused on their
mission: reaching their corner of the world with the gospel. They had been
arrested; they were constantly under threat, yet they remained committed to the task. What was their explanation for staying true to the cause?
Peter and John once said, "'For we cannot but speak the things which
we have seen and heard'" (Acts 4:20 NKJV). They had experienced the
love of Jesus and the power of the Cross, and their lives would never be
the same. Unwilling to keep such blessed news to themselves, these early
Christians had an unquenched longing for the souls of their neighbors to
know Christ.

You, too, have seen and heard from Jesus, yet perhaps you sometimes
struggle with distractions and falter in your resolve. Have you grown weary
in doing good, taking a mini-vacation from the Great Commission of Christ
to go into the world to make disciples? Does the daily commitment to live
for Christ with such zeal seem a bit "over the top" to you? Retrace your
steps on your journey with Jesus, and allow Him once again to ignite a holy
fire within you. Or, maybe you are "teaching and preaching" to the people
whom God places in your path, but your message has veered from what
people most need to hear: Jesus is Lord of all. Ask God to give you words of
wisdom to share the news of Jesus as Christ with a purity of message that
will penetrate the hearts of those who need to make Jesus their Savior.

Daily they went to the temple and from house to house. What a legacy!
May you and I follow in those footsteps, leading others to do the same.

Heavenly Father, ignite within me a passion to proclaim that Jesus is the
Savior of the world! Please give me sweet reminders of who You are in my life,
prompting me to be faithful in my witness with a heart of gratitude. Amen.

# ❀ The Bible as Counselor ❀

*Your statutes are my delight; they are my counselors* (Psalm 119:24).

Have you ever been to a counselor? God tells us we need counselors: "Plans fail for lack of counsel, but with many advisers they succeed" (Proverbs 15:22). When I was experiencing a hard time in my life, I sought good advice. I went not to one counselor, but two! My pastor, a wonderful counselor, gave me wise advice, but I also went across town to a pastor who had a degree in counseling. Each of them approached my situation from a different perspective; both helped my family get back on track.

There's no doubt families need counselors to make it through life: for parenting advice—especially with preschool and teenaged children—marital counseling, financial consultation, and spiritual direction. Today many CEOs of big companies—and their managers—have spiritual as well as business advisors to teach them ethical business practices. We also need good counselors for legal matters and everyday project management.

When we plan projects at church, we usually gather a planning committee, engage in brainstorming, ask for discussion, set priorities, form a to-do list, and then move forward. From the beginning through the end, we *need* counsel from godly Christians.

Notice what the psalmist says in Psalm 119:24 above. Who are *his* counselors? "God's statutes," or laws. He takes *delight* from his interaction with the counselors. What do you do when you experience delight? Dance? Sing? Smile a big silly grin? Laugh out loud? Jump up and down?

The psalmist gives us a good rule for life: read the Bible and celebrate God's laws. His statutes give us cause for joyful festivity. We communicate outwardly our inner joy over His comforting words. Spend time now reflecting on your joy in God's Word. How can you relax and release the joy? Think how you usually express happiness. How about letting it explode all around you, covering your family and friends!

Lord, thank You for Your words of wisdom that bring us inner joy. Help us not to keep Your words just to ponder in our hearts. May we show our happiness to others through a hug, a song, a grin, or a belly laugh today. Amen.

# ❀ The Best Day of Your Life ❀

*Which of you, if his son asks for bread, will give him a stone?*
*Or if he asks for a fish, will give him a snake?*
(Matthew 7:9–10).

In Hebrew thought, Deuteronomy 5:4–9 is known as the *Shema*. The word *Shema* means "hear." God longs that we hear the important message that He is the one true God. He commands that this truth be passed down from father to child throughout all generations.

In Matthew 7:9–10, Jesus used a form of exaggeration to show that fathers (and mothers) desire to meet the needs of their children. The greatest need that any child has, or will ever have, is for someone to take the time to teach him or her about God. *Shema*!

A young boy longed for his father to take him fishing, but the father was a busy man. Each time he asked the answer was always the same, "Not today, son; I have to work."

Finally, one beautiful morning his father awakened him and instructed him to hurry and dress. They were going fishing. It was the happiest day of the boy's childhood.

Years later, his father died. He and his mother were sorting through his father's belongings when he discovered that his father had kept daily journals. With shaky hands, he nervously searched to find the journal entry for the day he and his dad had gone fishing. He was anxious to see how his father had described what he himself considered the happiest day of his life.

He found the year, the month, and eagerly thumbed to the day. There it was! His heart pounded as he began to read. That day's entry was short stating, "Did not go to the office today. Did not get any work done. I went fishing. Day wasted."

The old saying, "The best things in life are free" is true. A day fishing and talking about the things of God would cost nothing except time. And it could end up being the happiest day of someone's life...maybe yours!

Dear God, help us set proper priorities of time for ourselves and those we love.
In Jesus's name, amen.

# ❀ My Lucky Earrings ❀

*"She calls her friends and neighbors together and says, 'Rejoice with me;*
*I have found my lost coin'"* (Luke 15:9).

At a wedding reception, someone noticed I had only one earring. Feeling my naked ear, I wandered through the large reception hall, out on the porch, and finally in the yard searching for the lost jewelry.

After a few minutes searching the wide, graveled parking lot—an impossible task—I spied something gleaming in the sun. There it was, smashed flat, with a tire mark on the back! I picked up the earring, pulled on the piercing-stem, and watched it pop back! I washed it off and proudly wore it the rest of the day.

A few months later, I dropped the same earring at church, but someone found it, returned it, and dubbed it my "lucky earring." Still loving my lucky earring, I enjoy telling others how lucky it is.

Only one problem remains: how can I, a Christian, who believe everything in my life has purpose—that God directs every detail of life for His glory—believe in luck? I don't. Then if I don't believe in luck, why do I talk about luck casually in my everyday life? Because I have allowed the culture of the world to overcome the culture of my Christianity, and that mistake can destroy my effectiveness as a Christian.

I'm not alone. Many other Christians accept ideas about good luck, lucky charms, and horoscopes. We may hum the song, "Luck, Be a Lady Tonight," treat Chinese fortune cookies too seriously, and listen to conversations in the media about "getting lucky" without thinking.

Today's times require a reality check. Do we take a stand against anything in our culture that is anti-Christian? If God were to ask me to account for the way I spend my time, money, and energy, would He be pleased with my talk about a "lucky earring"? In these days, I often remind myself to be careful, since the world is watching my flippant use of words and the casual things I do every day.

Holy God, may we live so others may see only You in every song we sing,
every joke we tell, and every trinket we cherish. Amen.

# ❀ *Contented Misery* ❀

*Not that I speak from want, for I have learned to be content in whatever circumstances I am* (Philippians 4:11 NASB).

The night had dipped below freezing as we jostled along in the old bus that carried our volunteer team to a rural church somewhere in South Korea to lead a worship service. On arrival, I realized that being cold was the norm. A pot-bellied woodstove sat in the center of the room, and I suspected even a shipload of burning wood wouldn't stop my teeth chattering. I consoled myself that at least I was wrapped in multiple layers from head to toe. Not that my cumbersome clothes would provide complete protection. The missionary couple we worked with shared how Judy, the wife, had gotten frostbite *inside* the church during a worship service.

As we sang songs, I tried to concentrate, mentally clicking off the minutes until I could head back to the hotel for a two-hour steaming hot bath. Then an uncomfortable sensation hit. I needed a restroom.

"Where's the bathroom?" I asked the missionary. He pointed outside, where I found a cubicle with a hole cut in the cement floor. I slowly unswathed myself and perched gingerly above the opening. This was what I called misery.

I wondered how the Korean Christians managed to worship regularly in rooms so cold they could see the smoke of their breath. Yet they seemed contented. They reminded me of the apostle Paul, often beaten and bloody, shipwrecked, chained in filthy prisons, or stoned and left for dead.

In 1 Corinthians 5:9 Paul said, though, that one driving passion helped him learn how to be content in every circumstance. "We make it our goal to please him." How simple but daunting these few words. Paul awoke each morning, praying, *"Lord, help me please You."* Through Paul's example, I learn that if I lift my eyes from the circumstance and pursue the goal of pleasing Him, I, too, can be content, even in miserable situation.

God, help us to make it my goal to please You. Refocus my attention to Your concerns. Amen.

*This story first appeared in* Missions Mosaic, *(Woman's Missionary Union) September 2002.*

# ❀ Language of Your Environment ❀

*Solomon also made all the furnishings that were in the LORD's temple;*
*the golden altar; the golden table on which was the bread of the*
*Presence; the lampstands of pure gold* (1 Kings 7:48–49).

When Solomon built the Jewish temple in Jerusalem, he commissioned craftsmen to build wooden, silver, and gold items. Wood, the basic material, was often overlaid with a precious metal. As it is today, gold was worth more than silver. Israeli leaders honored God by placing the most expensive things near His altar. The golden ark, or mercy seat, was a major focus inside the holiest place (Holy of Holies, or Most Holy Place) where the Spirit of God dwelled. In the outer holy room sat the table (holding the sacred bread for worship) and the lampstands (providing light for worship).

Outside that inner sanctum, workmen prioritized as they placed more expensive golden items at the front and silver items near the back of the main room, each according to its importance in worship. Plain wooden items sat at the extreme rear and outside in the courtyard. As a general rule, gold symbolized the most precious items and communicated this value to the priests. (See 1 Chronicles 28:14–18.)

Today we also communicate the worth of our possessions according to their monetary value. Most economists say our homes and clothes reflect a silent communication of what we designate as "valuable." For which of the following would you pay the higher price: a cup of ice with no nutrition; or a delicious steak, salad, and bread for a well-balanced meal? A Lexus or a Volkswagen? Tickets to a bowl game or to a local junior-high game? A four-story brick mansion or a single-wide mobile home? Most of us prefer the more expensive in each set, if we can afford it.

How do we communicate? Can people tell we're Christians by our furniture or jewelry? What do we possess that tells them we're His people? Can they tell we're generous by the things we give to others? Can they tell we're His people by the way we care?

Lord, help us to set priorities as we communicate our love for You—
and others—by the way we place value on items in our lives. Amen.

# ❋ Do You Despise ❋ the Small Things?

*"For who has despised the day of small things?"*
(Zechariah 4:10 NKJV).

Load the dishwasher. Unload the dishwasher. Wash the clothes. Dry the clothes. Fold the clothes. Pick up dirty clothes off the floor. Boil the eggs. Wash more clothes. Scrape the eggs off the ceiling because you forgot to watch the pot while washing the clothes. Sigh….

Are you in a daily cycle of an endless list of small stuff that just has to be done? Where is God in the small stuff? We keep pace with the small stuff because we have to—who else is going to make the bed? But what about the small stuff of ministry?

Ministry burnout is a Christian's enemy. Tasks of ministry can be thankless and sometimes tedious. We get tired; we get our feelings hurt; we feel overworked and underappreciated; we start comparing our lifestyle to that of others in the body of Christ who seem so blissful and peaceful as they sit on the stool of do-nothing, and we begin to wonder: *don't I deserve a break?* Couldn't we let someone else have a turn at churning the wheel, grinding the wheat, or however we view our list of "small" things God has assigned to us?

There's nothing small about our labor of service if God is in it. Thousands of words describe God, but *small* is not one of them. We are God's servants in His bountiful harvest field. Very few of us are Billy Grahams, and many others are not well known. Some of us are foremen in the field, while others are laborers. But no matter what our place of service in extending the kingdom of God, remember that God measures our significance with a much different measuring stick, and He reminds us today: *Do not despise the small things.*

Dear Father, today I recommit to do every "small" thing, whether at home, at work, or at church, with a thankful heart and to Your glory. Grant me eyes to see You in every detail of my life. Grant me a sense of the pleasure You receive from my labors of love today. Amen.

# ❀ Mighty Men of Valor ❀

*I was thirsty and you gave me something to drink* (Matthew 25:35).

King Saul persecuted David for at least 10 years. Saul was insanely jealous of David's popularity with the people of Israel. On many occasions Saul tried either to kill David or have him killed. Saul exiled David from his beloved country, and he tried to turn the people against David. King Saul sought David on a daily basis (1 Samuel 18–26).

David seemed to have lost everything. Then, in the midst of his exile, David's father and brothers found him and helped him form a rag-tag army. In 1 Samuel 22:2 a description is given of the 400 men who became David's soldiers. They were a stressed-out, debt-laden, discontented army. Yet, David, whose name may mean "beloved," transformed this motley crew of soldiers.

Notice the description of those same men in 2 Samuel 23:8–23. They had become men who were mighty (v. 8), leaders (v. 8), committed and diligent (v. 10), victorious defenders (v. 12), loyal and courageous (v. 16), famous (v. 18), honorable (v. 19), and valiant fighters (v. 20). David believed in them. He looked beyond what they were to what they could become.

The story in 2 Samuel 23:14–17 paints a beautiful picture of faithfulness, commitment, and bravery. David had been away from his hometown for some time, and he longed to drink water from the well near the gate of Bethlehem. This craving came in the middle of a battle against some of his most fierce enemies, the Philistines. When three of his soldiers heard of his desire, they broke through enemy lines, went to Bethlehem, and brought water back to him.

Could the same be said of our commitment? Our Commander, Jesus, takes us just as we are—stressed-out, debt-laden, discontented, or whatever our stance in life may be—and believes in us. He sees beyond what we are to what we can become. Are we willing to risk breaking through enemy lines to give a cup of cold water in His name?

> Thank You, God, for choosing me to be one of Your followers.
> Please develop in me the same traits exemplified in the lives of
> David's mighty men. In Jesus's name, amen.

# ❀ All Tangled Up ❀

*No one engaged in warfare entangles himself with the affairs of this life,*
*that he may please him who enlisted him as a soldier*
(2 Timothy 2:4 NKJV).

Can you imagine a soldier on the battlefield, stooping behind a blockade in the heat of battle, daydreaming about some trite event in his life? Soldiers for the Lord have no time for distractions. Do you find yourself tangled up in the goings-on of life, holding you back from effectively engaging the enemy in battle?

The word *entangle* may mean to weave in, creating a word picture steeped in meaning. It's as if your life is a beautiful tapestry that God is creating as the days of your life are fulfilled. God has a perfect design in mind, and He carefully selects each color and strand as He sits at the loom. The tapestry is strong and beautiful by His design. Day by day, the design takes shape as you bring glory to God as His masterpiece.

When you become entangled in the world's wrong affairs, it's like picking up a wad of tacky threads and throwing them into the loom, trying to weave something amiss into God's plan and thus interfering with God's perfectly ordered design for your life. What was a masterpiece in the making then becomes a less-than-prefect picture of God's best for your life. As a soldier in the army of God, you simply don't have time to pursue worldly whims, weakening the fabric of your life when you most need to stand firm against the enemy. Worldly threads thrown in with God's threads makes only a tangled mess.

Do you want to please God? The Lord is the one who enlisted you to be a soldier in His army, and He is calling you to stay alert, focused on the godly pursuits He's planned for you.

Father, I want to be an effective soldier for the army of God. Reveal to me what
I am trying to force wrongly into Your great weaving loom, and teach me
to trust You with all the days of my life. In the name of Jesus I pray, amen.

*Adapted from Kimberly Sowell's* Journey to Confidence: Becoming Women Who Witness *(New Hope Publishers, 1999).*

# ❀ God's Song ❀

*The LORD your God is with you, he is mighty to save. He will take
great delight in you, he will quiet you with his love, he will rejoice over
you with singing* (Zephaniah 3:17).

Zephaniah is a prophetic book in the Bible that pictorially weaves the threat
of judgment with the admonition of repentance and the promise of salvation. Zephaniah's exhortation was intended not only for Judah, but also for
us and for the entire world: *"I have decided to assemble the nations, to gather the
kingdoms and to pour out my wrath on them—all my fierce anger. The whole world
will be consumed by the fire of my jealous anger"* (Zephaniah 3:8) on *"the great day
of the LORD"* (Zephaniah 1:14).

The prophet warned that this time of judgment would be dark and
frightening but the end result would be wonderful. As with most prophetic
books of the Bible, Zephaniah presents a two-fold prophecy—a "near fulfillment" and a "future fulfillment."

The "near fulfillment" occurred when Judah was led into captivity—
then returned from dispersion a purified and humbled people. The "future
fulfillment" will occur when all the nations of the earth praise God in one
accord during the final times.

Nighttime is often a time of fright for young children. As darkness
deepens, so do their fears. Nothing quiets the fears of frightened children
more than when their parents hold them closely and sing lullabies to them.
This special time also blesses the parents as they rejoice over their treasured
children.

*"The great day of the LORD"* promises to be a frightful day of darkness
and gloom (Zephaniah 1:15). But, like a parent stealing into the room of
a frightened child at night, God also promises in Zephaniah 3:17 to quiet
our fears ("he will quiet you with his love"), hold us closely ("The Lord
your God is with you"), and, yes, sing to us ("he will rejoice over you with
singing").

Many times God quiets me with His love. Often I feel Him with me.
But I hardly can wait for the time I hear Him sing!

Dear God, my song to You is a song of thankfulness. In Jesus's name, amen.

# ❀ Spaghetti Ice Cream ❀

*Taste and see that the* LORD *is good* (Psalm 34:8).

Have you ever eaten spaghetti ice cream? I have, once in Frankfurt, Germany. A group from the United States and England went on a missions trip to Dorfeil, Germany, centered high in the mountains near Frankfurt. The night before I flew home, a local pastor, Horace ("Race") Lariscy and his wife, Linda, took us out to eat spaghetti ice cream in a beautiful plaza near a majestic bridge over the Rhine River. An ice cream shop provided vanilla ice cream, which their staff had pushed through a grinder with spaghetti-sized round holes, covering the bottom of a large ice cream dish with spaghetti-looking ice cream. Chunky dark raspberry preserves looked just like a meat sauce on the "spaghetti," and shredded coconut looked like parmesan cheese sprinkled on top!

Race, Linda, and I lingered over the spaghetti ice cream, savoring the moment of Christian friendship. Stars sparkled overhead, as people milled across the plaza, laughing and talking. Then a beautiful young woman in a peasant costume with laced-up vest stood near a large green-bronze fountain and sang several arias from familiar operas. Without orchestra or musical instrument, her clear voice rang out over the plaza.

I've eaten peanut soup cooked by African men, buttermilk and raw oatmeal for a Danish breakfast, a Honduran chopped goat-meat lunch wrapped in leaves, blood pudding in England, fried fish with its eyes open in Panama, and southern-fried alligator in Louisiana, but nothing was as good the German spaghetti ice cream!

Many people dress in colorful national costumes and stir their foods with curry, jalapenos, papaya, or mint — not flavors with which some of us grew up. All those people begin life with a common condition: they're lost, separated from God, needing the knowledge of the love and sacrifice of Jesus as Savior. God has chosen to let His Church carry the message. As we travel from our doorsteps to the farthest area on Earth, we can share His love. May each of us be found faithful — sampling the flavor of other cultures as we go, sharing Christ in a contextual way in each people group around the world!

Lord, thank You for diversity in our world. Help us to taste the "flavors" of other cultures and to savor each person as one who needs You. Amen

# ❀ *The Shepherd I Know* ❀

*The LORD is my shepherd, I shall not want* (Psalm 23:1 KJV).

One of my favorite Scriptures is the Twenty-third Psalm, which I learned as a child. Most little children hear at least some of the words in this familiar Psalm. Later they memorize it, sometimes for a prize their church gives to children who learn selected passages. As years pass, old familiar verses get stale, and we forget the most important parts of a verse like this one. Today, let's look at the first two words: *The Lord*. God can be our Shepherd only if we ask Him to be our Giver of eternal life. Our relationship with Him is the most important relationship in life. Take a minute now and praise Him as the Lord of your life. Thank Him for daily blessings and for Who He is in the world.

What does God do as *your shepherd*? He owns you. You are His. He calls you by name. He nurtures you in the family of God. He teaches you to know Him better. He knows your every move. He keeps you out of trouble. He protects you from your enemies. He leads you with His staff. He guides you to green pastures, seeking resources for you: food, water, shade from the heat, and a place of rest. You *don't lack* for anything you need. If you're lost, He seeks you until He finds you. If you're anxious and worried, He takes you back beside still waters for peace and quiet. If you're in danger, He pulls you out of that danger, takes you in His arms, and leads you home.

Jesus says in John 10:11: *"I am the good shepherd. The good shepherd lays down his life for the sheep."* The greatest fulfillment of God's love for you happened at the Cross of Calvary, where His Son died so you might have eternal life. Praise the Good Shepherd today for His lasting relationship, and tell others about it.

O Jesus, thank You for being my Shepherd. Help me follow Your every step on the path toward home as I tell other people about our relationship.

# ❀ The Inconvenient Jesus ❀

*As they traveled along the road, they came to some water and the
eunuch said, "Look, here is water. Why shouldn't I be baptized?"*
(Acts 8:36).

Have you noticed when God gives an opportunity to witness, it's usually at
an inconvenient time? I once led a woman to accept Jesus as Savior at a
fast-food drive-through. I didn't want to be late for church, but since we'd
become friends, she asked me about Jesus, right there in line! Another
time, in an airplane, I needed to study before I arrived in the next city. An
eavesdropping flight attendant interrupted me and accepted Christ as her
Savior. It's always a surprise to find the people God nudges toward us.

Today's Scripture is part of the story of Philip and the Ethiopian
eunuch: the high-ranking eunuch had gone to Jerusalem to worship, but
was probably disappointed as he returned, reading from Isaiah without
understanding it. God nudged Philip, on his way to Gaza, to go to the
eunuch. He did, explaining the passage as a foretelling of Jesus. Then an
unusual turn of event happened: they "came to some water." An accident?
Hardly! This eunuch was a new born-again believer with a Savior, and he
wanted to follow up with baptism!

Have you ever "come to some water" as God leads you into a witnessing
situation on the busiest day of your life? On busy days, you may have to
stop what you're doing and welcome a *parenthesis* in your life. You pause,
communicate the gospel, and then continue. You may call these moments
"holy coincidences"—those coincidences that can't quite be *just coincidences*.
You sense God is at work.

Jesus's Spirit isn't on our timed schedule. In the world's eye, He appears
at unusual moments—usually when we least expect it. The *inconvenient Jesus*
speaks in a still, small voice, but He cannot be ignored. We listen expec-
tantly on those over-busy days, knowing a holy coincidence may insert a
parenthesis in our day, and a God-moment is near.

Lord, open our hearts to Your Spirit. May we never see Jesus as inconvenient;
may we always be open to communicating Your love to those
You lead into our lives. Amen.

# ❀ Gracias, Senora ❀

*"But go and learn what this means: 'I desire mercy, not sacrifice.'*
*For I have not come to call the righteous, but sinners"*
(Matthew 9:13).

It's exciting to join a growing church. Godly Christians there stayed busy starting innovative programs, welcoming the influx of people, and adding new wings to the building. One fellow church member, I'll call her Margie, was full of new ideas.

As Jesus did in Matthew 9, Margie made friends with those who were different from the neighborhood crowd. Our church was "plain vanilla," she said, and she wanted to add a worldwide flavor. One night she asked, "Have you noticed the new Chinese and Mexican restaurants in this neighborhood?"

"Yes, I have noticed."

"And have you noticed the water-servers don't speak English?"

"Yes, only the greeters seem to speak English."

"Edna, shouldn't we teach them English?"

Frankly, I'd never thought about it. I saw confusing service in restaurants as an irritation, not a ministry opportunity. Margie asked me to pray if God wanted us to reach out, not focused on our comfort with new buildings and discipleship activities, but on outreach to those with needs, especially the need for a Savior.

In a few weeks Margie had our women trained and ready! In two months, we began an exciting ministry of Conversation English. I fell in love with my beginners from Mexico, Guatemala, China, and Thailand.

As usual, Margie had greater ideas. That summer a Mexican child accepted Jesus as Savior, so she asked if I'd go with her to follow up with the parents. Once I agreed, she said, "Good! You witness. I'll hold the baby!"

After I gave a simple presentation of the plan of salvation, the son said, "I know what that lady's talking about! Papa, if Jesus speaks to you, just say, 'Yes.'" The mother and father, both in my class, said "Yes," accepting Jesus into their hearts. She hugged me and said, "Gracias, senora—uh, I mean 'Thank you, ma'am.'" Her beaming smile was thanks enough!

Lord, help us remember You care about Your children all over the world.
May we never be complacent with our regular activities (or "sacrifices") inside the
church, but always ready to "go and learn" about ministering to others. Amen.

# ❀ Don't Take It to Heart ❀

*Also do not take to heart everything people say, lest you hear your
servant cursing you. For many times, also, your own heart has known
that even you have cursed others* (Ecclesiastes 7:21–22 NKJV).

Every time I smiled, I felt the people around me could detect what a fake
I was. I didn't feel the least bit jolly; in fact, I was downtrodden and wanted
to mope. Someone dear to me had said words that hurt my feelings, and
I couldn't shake the sadness. As I talked with a salesclerk later that day, I
wanted to say, "Hi. My name is Kimberly, and nobody likes me." How silly!
I began to pray. *God, how can I shake this hurt in my heart?*

God didn't hesitate in His response: I simply had to forgive her. How
could I ever doubt her love for me? She had poured her life into mine time
and time again, and she had endured my weak moments of unkind words
in the past as well. Yes, I would forgive her.

Words have the power to destroy, but the verses above remind us to
keep perspective about what we hear from others. How many times do we
find ourselves saying words that are hurtful and abrupt? Likewise, even the
loving people around us will sometimes say hurtful words in haste. We then
choose how we'll respond. We can be leaders of faith in our relationships
by guarding our hearts, not allowing hurtful words to penetrate deeply like
seeds of bitterness that take root and destroy our ability to love, help, support, and encourage others.

Others' words can never undo the truth of who we are in Christ. We
are loved and of great worth, because we belong to Jesus. When we hear
those unkind words directed our way today, let's not take them to heart!

Heavenly Father, I'm sometimes frail, giving in to the hurtful words of others.
Please teach me not to let unkind words destroy my relationships, or even affect
the manner in which I carry myself. Help me not to take unkind words to heart,
and guard my mouth against speaking unkindly today. Amen.

# ❀ *Getting Real* ❀

*Is anyone among you sick? Let him call for the elders of the church, and*
*let them pray over him.… Confess your trespasses to one another, and*
*pray for one another, that you may be healed* (James 5:14, 16 NKJV).

I grew up in the world of paper plates and napkins. I never realized my
lack of refinement until I met some dear southern belles of yesteryear. For
instance, I've learned it's acceptable to serve a store-bought dessert, but
I must present it on a proper dessert platter and hide the evidence of the
store packaging from guests! Talk about going to great lengths to conceal
our weaknesses!

James 5:13–16 instructs Christians how to interact with one another,
beginning with prayer for the sick. Society promotes self-sufficiency, but
James instructs the sick to contact the elders for prayer. Is that asking too
much of them to come all the way over to your house to minister to you personally? And they'll see you at your worst, sporting pajamas and bed hair!

Do you have difficulty allowing others to help you when you are weak?
Ask yourself, is it because of pride? Not only does accepting the prayer and
help of others allow you to rest and heal, but it also provides an outlet for
others to enjoy the great pleasure of serving. Relationships are strengthened among Christian friends, and joy flows.

Next, James instructs Christians to confess their sins to one another.
What?! Talk about asking for trouble! Or so we imagine. When we follow
God's principle to confess our sins to one another—when we get real with
one another—we can get to the spiritual root of our problems. It's often in
our trials that God is rooting out our sins of fear, anger, and selfishness. If
we willingly discuss our failures with friends, they can pray with us that our
sins may be forgiven and Christ glorified.

Getting real with one another…confessing sins, seeking support and
prayer from Christian friends, getting serious about holiness…will we
follow society's rules or the Lord's instruction?

Lord, help me open my life to my brothers and sisters in Christ to be real.
In the name of Jesus, amen.

# ❧ Running from Temptation ❧

*As for you, you were dead in your transgressions and sins,*
*in which you used to live when you followed the ways of this world*
*and of the ruler of the kingdom of the air, the spirit who is now*
*at work in those who are disobedient* (Ephesians 2:1–2).

Paul calls Satan the ruler of the kingdom of the air. Not only does this refer to his control of the fallen angels, but also it alludes to his evil influence upon the world.

Consider the ways Satan appears today through the air. Think of the temptations that come through television, radio, and the Internet—all which depend on signals through the air.

Satan repeatedly uses the same tactics. Once we become aware of his tactics, we can learn to avoid them. Temptation comes through the "lust of the flesh, the lust of the eyes and the pride of life" warns 1 John 2:16 (KJV). Satan used this pattern with Eve. In Genesis 3:6, Satan convinced Eve that the tree was good for food (lust of the flesh), pleasing to the eye (lust of the eyes), and desirable for gaining wisdom (pride of life).

Likewise, Satan used this same pattern when tempting Jesus. In Matthew 4:3, Satan instructed Jesus to "tell these stones to become bread" (lust of the flesh); in Matthew 4:6 to "throw yourself down" from the temple to prove that the angels would catch Him (pride of life); and in Matthew 4:8, Satan showed Him all the kingdoms of the world and their splendor (lust of the eyes).

Have you ever considered which tactic(s) Satan uses most often to tempt you? Through God's Word we can combat His attacks in each area.

Whether or not we are able to control what comes our way in the form of temptation, we can control what we do about it. A country preacher warned his congregation that when he looks at his neighbor's watermelon patch, he cannot keep his mouth from watering, but he can run. And so can we!

Dear God, please strengthen me so that I will not fall prey to the ruler of the
kingdom of the air. In Jesus's name I pray. Amen.

# ❦ Rambling in the Garden ❦

*The vineyard of the LORD Almighty is the house of Israel, and the men
of Judah are the garden of his delight* (Isaiah 5:7).

Rambling is a hobby for many people. They travel all over the world for
business and pleasure, seeking new sights and searching for adventure in
exotic places. I've been overseas eight times, but I wouldn't consider myself
one of the jet set. I can sit at home and ramble vicariously through books.
How about trying the Bible? You always find business *and* pleasure there.
Both the Old and New Testaments offer comfort, wisdom, and hope for the
future. God's Word also helps us see the world through His eyes.

I love to ramble in Isaiah. Isaiah 5:7 points us to the people of Judah,
who learned about God's call for them to bless to all nations. Just as a vineyard contains fruit that blesses all those who visit it, today we grow in the
Lord and bless all nations. We can be the "garden of His delight."

Here's a reality check to test ourselves on being the garden of God's
delight: Have we grown in knowledge of God? Have we read the Bible
and found spiritual adventures and learning opportunities there? Do we
know for sure we're going to heaven because we've accepted Jesus into our
hearts? Do we belong to Bible-believing churches, where we study Scriptures consistently as our pastors preach from the Word? As the garden of
God's delight, do we dare reach out to others, offering them the spiritual
fruit God has given us, such as patience, kindness, faithfulness, gentleness,
and self-control? (Read Galatians 5:22–23 for a varied list of spiritual fruit.)
Such spiritual growth reflects God's nature. Do we travel to places where
Christians are not likely to live, so we can share fruit with nonbelievers? Do
we see the world through God's eyes? God takes delight in us as we grow,
bear fruit, and share it.

Lord, help us to be the garden of Your delight,
sharing the varied fruit You have given us with others in the world. Amen.

# ❦ *Lean on Me* ❦

*Ruth said, "Do not urge me to leave you or turn back from following you; for where you go, I will go"* (Ruth 1:16 NASB).

Have you ever considered investing in a friendship with a woman of another generation? You may be thinking it's too much trouble, you are too busy, or women from other generations are just too hard to understand.

When Edna Ellison and I led a women's mentoring conference in Indiana, we divided the women into three groups: older-, middle-, and younger-aged. We asked each group what they wished the other groups knew about women of their age. We learned that mature women longed for relationships with younger women, but didn't think younger women wanted relationships with them. Younger women wanted relationships with mature Christian women who had survived the stages they were now going through. But younger women thought that the mature women didn't want to be around them and their boisterous children.

When the groups shared with each other, the women were stunned. As realization dawned on them that they desperately needed *and wanted* friendships with each other, many tears fell, as did the walls that silently separated them. One younger woman said, "I had no idea that a mature Christian woman wanted a relationship with someone like me."

Why do women need women, particularly women of other generations, in their lives? As a young mom frantically runs ahead to catch the falling lamp her toddler just toppled, the older woman, who has already seen her children grow and go, knows that the toddler years will be outlived. She can provide the assurance of God's presence and wisdom. The younger woman can enrich an older woman's life by sharing her energy and family experiences.

Ruth and Naomi exemplified the joy of building friendships with women across generations. Ruth brought the determination and energy of young adulthood to the relationship, and Naomi shared wisdom and discernment earned through her years of walking with God. Both women learned to lean on each other.

Think about how God may call you to develop a friendship that will bless you and another person and strengthen God's kingdom.

Lord Jesus, help me see new opportunities for friendship with women of other generations that bring honor to You. Amen.

# ❀ What's Your Golden Calf? ❀

*So all the people took off their earrings and brought them to Aaron. He took what they handed him and made it into an idol cast in the shape of a calf* (Exodus 32: 3–4).

I just bought a beautiful pair of chandelier earrings: four inches of dangling rhinestones that swing from side to side when I walk! I understand how Egyptians and Hebrews alike treasured their earrings in Old Testament times.

However, today's woman doesn't melt down her earrings for an *idol,* the way Israelites did in Moses's day. While he was on the mountain getting the Ten Commandments, they begged his brother Aaron to make them an idol to worship. Aaron acquiesced, melting the earrings to make the golden calf.

Today we have other golden calves: new cars with prestigious brand names, giant houses with professional interior decorations, substantial bank accounts, cherished family heirlooms, certain drugs, handy electronic indulgences—or dogs, children, and other loved ones.

Moses asked God to forgive the Israelites for their sin (Exodus 32:31–32), but God made it clear He would punish His beloved children (v. 34). God had set them apart as His *chosen people* to bless all nations, but their sin defiled their purity and influence. One highly desirable trait of a Christian is a pure heart, unfettered by wrong habits, words, or thoughts.

*Yeah, right! Like we could have a pure heart with all the movies and television shows shouting obscenities at us! Get real!*

It breaks His heart when Christians get involved in materialistic, secular values, or forgetting they're chosen, set apart as His servants, to communicate Christ's love with everyone.

*Yeah, right! But does He know how many responsibilities we have? We want to share Christ, but we have too many things to do: work, family, school....*

Sometimes even strong Christians are trapped by the golden calves of this world—anything that keeps us from focusing properly on Him, living as pure-hearted, mercy giving servants.

O God, forgive us when we take our eyes off You and begin to worship
our own idols. Help us recognize golden calves in disguise,
turn off electronic invasions into our homes as needed,
and toss all distractions so we can communicate Your love. Amen.

# ❀ For the Least of These ❀

*"I tell you the truth, whatever you did for one of the least of these*
*brothers of mine, you did for me"* (Matthew 25:40).

I live in Charlotte, North Carolina, where thousands of race fans live and breathe racing. I can even hear the faint roar of race car engines from my home. Though racing is not close to my heart, I do care for the folks who come to the races because Jesus loves them. For this reason I volunteered to help the Victory Racing Outreach ministry at Lowe's Motor Speedway on a Sunday morning during a race week. I learned that racing fans are a stalwart bunch, and before major races, many live in campers for weeks at a time in the campgrounds surrounding the speedway, awaiting the big event.

My job was simple: help set up the sound system for the Sunday morning worship service we held under a massive tent our church provided on one of the campgrounds. Not only did volunteers lead a worship service, but also they prepared a hearty breakfast of bacon, eggs, pancakes, and coffee. The smell of brewing coffee wooed many fans from their campers, even at a relatively early hour. My husband and I unloaded equipment, set up the system, and enjoyed a good breakfast while visiting with folks. We then joined in the worship service, and when done, packed up the equipment and went home.

The ministry wasn't a huge sacrifice. I only got a little chilly in the crisp morning air. But I wondered what had been accomplished. As far as I knew, most people left just as they had come, except with full stomachs. If I were to measure success by the number of salvations, I would say we made little impact. But then, our Lord never used temporal measuring tools. He said that anything I did to show His love to others, He received personally as a gift unto Himself. That one truth is enough to keep me going back.

Lord, when I picture You taking my tiny gift of service, treasuring it,
and smiling with delight, I just want to respond, "What can I do next, Lord?"
Amen.

# ❀ Every Day Is Urgent ❀

*Then Moses returned to the LORD and said, "Oh, these people have
committed a great sin, and have made for themselves a god of gold!
Yet now, if You will forgive their sin—but if not, I pray, blot me out of
Your book which You have written"* (Exodus 32:31–32 NKJV).

As I sorted through my emails, an urgent prayer request flashed across
my screen. Missionaries were requesting prayer for the thousands in Asia
who were about to experience a major natural disaster. If the storms hit as
anticipated, many thousands would perish.

I dropped to my knees to intercede for the Asian people, and the
gravity of the moment hit me: this is real. At that moment, thousands upon
thousands of people were weeping and panicked. The weakest and most
helpless were especially vulnerable, but even men and women with great
physical strength were in great danger. I began to ask God to have mercy
on this multitude of people who worship false gods, asking Him to spare
them for another opportunity to receive Jesus. My mind raced as I considered these masses of false worshippers slipping into eternity without Christ,
entering hell. God whispered to me, *Kimberly, this happens every day.*

As Moses interceded for the people, he acknowledged their sins before
God, but he loved them so fervently that he couldn't imagine them going
unforgiven. Today, more than 6 billion people belong to unreached people groups across the globe, and many die each day without the atoning
blood of Christ covering their sins. Are you moved with compassion for
the many souls in need of the Savior? Ask God to burden your heart for
the lost in the world who are worshipping false gods, and intercede on
their behalf. Encourage others to join you in praying for unreached people
groups. Open your heart to find ways to bring the gospel to them. Every
day is urgent. (For more information on unreached people groups, visit
www.joshuaproject.net.)

Heavenly Father, whom can I pray for today? Give me a global-minded heart
and a deep compassion for peoples of foreign lands who are worshipping gods
made of wood and stone. How they need You! In the name of Jesus I pray, amen.

# ❀ A Time for Everything ❀

*There is a time for everything, and a season for every activity under heaven* (Ecclesiastes 3:1).

*He has made everything beautiful in its time. He has also set eternity in the hearts of men; yet they cannot fathom what God has done from beginning to end* (Ecclesiastes 3:11).

*Back to the Future* was a box office hit produced in the 1980s. One thing that made the movie so popular with audiences was that every event in the beginning of the movie was somehow repeated later in the movie and then resolved at the end. It was a fascinating journey from present life to future life then back to a somewhat altered present life.

How many times have we wished we could see into the future and know how things turn out in the end? In a real sense, we can! Although our future vision is limited because of the reality of the present, we do have certain promises and assurances in God's Word that allow us to glimpse into the future.

Today's Scripture passages are examples of this. The Bible is very clear that the things that happen in our lives are for a purpose: "There is a time for everything" (Ecclesiastes 3:1).

Some situations may seem undesirable. When given to God they are used to bring about beauty in a person's life: "He has made everything beautiful in its time" (Ecclesiastes 3:11). God does the work. Our part is to remain patient while He is working and let Him take the time He needs to accomplish His purposes.

Regrets from our past and worry about our future can cause us to miss the joy of the present season. On our refrigerator we display a clip from the comic strip "Family Circus" by Bill Keane. In it, the older sister is explaining to her little brother that "Yesterday's the past, tomorrow's the future, but today is a GIFT. That's why it's called the PRESENT."

Yes, each season is indeed a gift. Each season has its own beautiful purpose in life...*Back to the Future* and beyond!

Dear God, please give us the wisdom and desire to accomplish
Your beautiful purposes in our lives. In Jesus's name, amen.

# ❧ *Giving that Makes God Smile* ❧

*So let each one give as he purposes in his heart, not grudgingly or of*
*necessity; for God loves a cheerful giver* (2 Corinthians 9:7 NKJV).

Paul's prompting the church in 2 Corinthians 8:1–9:15, to complete their
fund-raising project for the needy Jerusalem church, provides us with
principles that transform giving from mere habit to an act of worship that
honors God.

The kind of giving Paul called for comes from a heart dedicated to God
(8:5). It is the product of a want-to, not a have-to attitude (8:3). It is viewed
by the giver as a privilege—a high calling (8:4). It is produced in proportion
to the joy *within* the giver, rather than in proportion to the wealth owned *by*
the giver (8:2).

Worship-driven giving begins with the heart (desire), but moves to
the hands (completed with action) (8:6, 10–11). It bears witness to God's
working in His church as much as does the exercising of faith, knowledge,
sincerity, teaching, and love (8:7). It is borne of a deep awareness of the Savior's example, who *"though He was rich, yet for [our] sakes He became poor"* (8:9).

Worship-led giving believes it is wrong for a Christian to sit down to a
table of plenty while disregarding a hungry brother (8:14). It opens its hand
with the same generosity that it prays a brother would show if the shoe
were on the other foot (8:13–15). It does not contribute in order to line the
coffers of those who are not truly in need but so that all Christians may have
enough to meet their basic needs (8:14–15).

How can we apply these biblical principles? First, follow-through
with what our heart has determined to do: give the offering (9:1–2). Not to
follow-through brings dishonor to God and impugns our integrity (9:3–4).
Second, don't be tight-fisted when it comes to giving God an offering (9:5).
Third, remember that our reward will be in proportion to our generosity
(9:6) and that God delights in the one whose heart enjoys giving to Him
(9:7). Fourth, we always have enough in God; give in recognition of the
abundance He has given (9:8–9). Fifth, God provided everything in our
possession to give to another; don't forget it (9:10). Sixth, remember that
giving does not only meet the physical needs of our sisters and brothers; it
also generates thanksgiving that rises to God! (9:11–13)

Lord, in You I am fully satisfied. Teach me to give with the openness and
generosity You have shown to me. Amen.

# ❀ The Cost of a Christian Worldview ❀

*"Because you are not of the world, but I chose you out of the world,
therefore the world hates you"* (John 15:19 NKJV).

Jesus never minimized the cost of living as a Christian in a pagan world. In fact, while Jesus assured His disciples that they were God's chosen and cherished children, He also assured them that they would live as outcasts on earth.

When Jesus comes into our lives, the transformation puts us at odds with the unbelieving world. The implications of this truth:

1. All humans start life as beings *of* the world—fleshly, with a self-orientation.
2. Worldly, self-oriented, unregenerate people love and accept those who look and think like themselves.
3. Since we've trusted Christ, we are no longer *of* the world; we no longer think in many ways as the unregenerate person does.
4. For the rest of our sojourn *in* the world, if we live out our faith, we will be alienated from and hated by the world, even by those whom we've previously loved and who loved us.

This hatred may not be expressed in overt acts of malice. Instead, we sense disconnection, awkwardness, and lost intimacy with those we once viewed as soul mates. We find ourselves essentially different from those who still live according to the worldly goals and values, which we, too, once cherished.

We can take heart knowing that our Savior also faced alienation from those who loved Him only as long as He healed their sick and raised their dead. But when He pointed out their sin and offered a spiritual remedy through faith, they abandoned Him.

How do we respond to undeserved animosity? We focus on Christ's love for us, certain and eternal, and the promise that His love is enough— enough to fill us up and help us love others, even our enemies.

Lord, I admit that I long to be well-liked and respected. Please help me not to
flinch or to be ashamed when I'm misunderstood or hated
because of my faith in You. Amen.

# ❀ How Do I Love Thee? ❀ Let Me Count the Ways

*On coming to the house, they saw the child with his mother Mary, and*
*they bowed down and worshiped him. Then they opened their treasures*
*and presented him with gifts of gold and of incense and of myrrh*
(Matthew 2:11–12).

As we approach the Christmas season, we see decorations going up every-where we go: in neighborhoods, shopping malls, and churchyards. Shoppers hustle and bustle about, getting last-minute presents and stocking stuffers. People scurry everywhere, buying presents for loved ones. Later they will hide them in out-of-the-way places till Christmas Eve, pulling them out to put under the tree. This year when my children asked me, "Mom, what do you want for Christmas?" I said, "Nothing," since they're college students without a job or money. I shared with them my thoughts on the real meaning of Christmas.

When my four children were little, they focused on themselves at Christmas. They asked constantly, "What am I going to get?" Now as young adults, they've learned Christmas isn't about *getting*; it's about *giving*.

Though I said I wanted no gifts for Christmas, my precious Jennifer is so conscientious she made me something special. On Christmas morning, she presented a devotional box with 52 weeks of "Why I Love You" slips to be opened each Monday. Others gave me a variety of gifts this Christmas, and without taking anything away from the beauty and appropriateness of the others, I felt hers was the best gift I received. No, it didn't have a mon-etary value, but it was priceless to me.

The greatest present of all is God's gift of His precious Son, Jesus Christ, who came into this world to die for our sins. As the wise men pre-sented Jesus with gifts, *we* can present Him a special gift. Ours may have no monetary value, but it can show our love for Him in the best way: passing on the gift of His love to those who don't know Him. We cherish His priceless gift, wrap it up in our own personalities, and give it to others. You might even say we are re-gifting!

Lord, help us to accept Your gift of salvation
and cheerfully give it to others. Amen.

# ❀ *That's Faith* ❀

*For by grace you have been saved through faith, and that not of your-selves; it is the gift of God* (Ephesians 2:8 NKJV).

On the back row of the plane, a noticeably tall man in a grey suit squeezed himself into the seat beside me with an embarrassing bit of awkwardness. As I pulled out my Bible and began scribbling notes on a pad, I noticed the man peeking at my work. *Go ahead, be nosy,* I thought. A few polite conversational topics later, the tall man from Amsterdam and I were talking about heaven.

Nick's openness to talk about Christianity was encouraging, but his beliefs about Jesus fell short of glorifying the Lord. As I shared about our need for a Savior who would pay for our sins, my traveling companion asked: "How can Jesus do that?" I described Jesus as the sacrificial lamb, told of His sinless life, and tried to explain the power of the Cross. Then Nick asked, "But how could Jesus pay the price for sins committed past, present, and future?"

For a fraction of a second, I considered attempting a deeply theological answer, but what the Holy Spirit brought out of my mouth instead was, "He's God."

My friend laughed. "Oh, that's easy!"

"No," I replied. "That's faith."

God's plan of salvation is beautifully explained in Scripture. God never contradicts Himself; no flaws or gaping holes appear in His redemptive plan. We study Scripture to learn how to explain the gospel, but at some point we must address faith because God requires faith from us.

Nick was willing to go only as far with Christianity as logic would take him. Nick's personal religious beliefs were completely devoid of logic, but somehow he was blind to it. Later I asked God to help me understand what was going on in Nick's mind, and I was reminded—Nick had no faith that Jesus was the Savior because he refused to accept that Jesus is God. It's essential: by God's grace we are saved—through faith in Christ.

As you engage people with the gospel, pray for God to impart to them that faith the size of a mustard seed. Take the unbeliever down the path of understanding because the God of all wisdom makes perfect "sense," but then usher them to the door they must ultimately walk through—the door of faith.

Heavenly Father, allow me to be an effective witness for You, ready to give an answer to those who are seeking You. I also pray that as I tell others about You, they will receive You in faith. In Jesus's name, amen.

# ❀ *Stir Up Your Gifts* ❀
## *and Fan the Flames*

*For this reason I remind you to fan into flame the gift of God,*
*which is in you* (2 Timothy 1:6).

Do you ever feel that you don't have any spiritual gifts? According to Scripture, we all are given a spiritual gift when we come into a relationship with Jesus Christ. Most people have many more gifts than they realize.

Two delightful ladies (I'll call them Lucy and Ethel) are members of the church my husband used to pastor. Each has told me she doesn't feel she has any gifts. Yet they are two of the greatest encouragers I've ever known.

Everyone who knows them is blessed and uplifted by their written and spoken words and their deeds of kindness. Their humor adds a spark to our church that would be sorely missed were they not there.

A classic Lucy/Ethel story is the time Ethel decided to pre-arrange her funeral. Lucy accompanied her to the funeral home. When they got into the casket room, Ethel couldn't decide between a lavender one and a pink one. After a long time of indecision, Lucy finally told her, "I'll help you climb up in them and I'll step back and tell you which one you look better in."

Of course, Ethel did not agree. However, a few weeks later while attending someone's funeral, she mournfully looked over at her friend and said, "Lucy, I think she's in my casket."

A few years ago our church was going through a difficult period concerning "theological diversity." Time after time I saw these two ladies bless and encourage my husband as their pastor for his stand on the deity of Christ. I saw them continue to love and reach out to people on both sides of the controversial issue. To this day, I'm sure they have no idea how God used them as agents of His mercy and love. These two ladies "fan into flame the gift of God" (2 Timothy 1:6) without even realizing it.

Dear Lord, thank You for the gifts You give us through Your love.
Help us to keep them burning brightly to show others the way to You.
In Jesus's name, amen.

# ❀ Failing Successfully ❀

*For I know my transgressions, and my sin is always before me*
(Psalm 51:3).

"I was a Christian, but I failed big time. I left my husband for another man. Now, years later, even though I've come back to the Lord and I know God has forgiven me, I'm not sure He could use me. Still ...I want to serve Him." Her story wasn't unusual. In fact, I could have confessed a multitude of my own disqualifying failures.

King David failed big time, and he failed publicly. He committed adultery and murder, two sins that brought devastating consequences that impacted the course of his life and the lives of his children, and even his nation. But David knew how to fail successfully. When confronted with his sin, he offered no excuses. Instead, he fully confessed his sin, agreeing wholeheartedly with every judgment God raised against him. "Against you, you only, have I sinned and done what is evil in your sight, so that you are proved right when you speak and justified when you judge" (Psalm 51:4). After confessing, David threw himself on the mercy of his loving God. God was faithful and helped David once again become the humble servant-leader God had first called from the shepherd's field.

I'm not advocating big failure as the best road to righteousness. Further, I must acknowledge that some of our failures produce consequences that delay or even detour God's preferred path for our lives. But David's story gives us hope. He teaches us that big failures can be used in big ways to glorify God. David recounts the eternally significant ministry for the repentant, cleansed servant: "Then I will teach transgressors your ways, and sinners will turn back to you" (Psalm 51:13).

Lord God, I confess my sin to You, acknowledging that Your account
of my sin is completely accurate and justified. Forgive me and
restore my heart so that I may once again experience the joy
of Your salvation. Then use me to teach others that You are more than
able to forgive the worst sinner, for You have forgiven me. Amen.

# ❀ *Come Clean* ❀

*Cleanse me with hyssop, and I will be clean; wash me, and I will be
whiter than snow* (Psalm 51:7).

"I want you to clean this room right now," I said to my then eight-year-old
daughter, Neli. Her floor had become so cluttered that I couldn't tell the
carpet color. A pungent aroma confirmed many of the scattered clothes had
been worn, probably several days before.

"Hang up the clean clothes, put the dirty ones in the laundry, and put
away your toys. I'll be back to check when you've finished."

"OK, Mom," she replied. No big deal.

I walked to the kitchen to start supper. Five minutes later she shouted,
"You can come check my room, Mom. It's all clean."

The call had come a little too quickly, I thought, for the gargantuan
task to have been completed, but I decided to check anyway. Arriving at the
doorway of her room, I was impressed by the view of a spotless floor—no
toys or clothes in sight.

Suspicious, I walked to her bed and lifted the dust ruffle. There, beneath
the perfectly made bed, were stuffed all the clothes and toys I had asked her
to clean up. Needless to say, Neli needed a little clarification of the words
*clean up*.

Do we have any "dirty clothes" stashed under the bed, or perhaps,
tucked away in the recesses of our hearts? Even when we do our best to
hide them or forget them, the stench still pervades our lives.

Could it be that before we intercede for others that God would have us
speak to Him about the more pressing need for forgiveness and cleansing
in our own lives? The psalmist said it like this: *"If I regard iniquity in my heart,
The LORD will not hear"* (Psalm 66:18 NKJV).

Lord of my life, I come to share with You many needs of others that burden my
heart. But first, there are a few things I need to talk with You about…. Amen.

# ❀ *Words of Comfort* ❀

*Comfort, comfort my people, says your God* (Isaiah 40:1).

Some people feel the Holy Bible is so holy they never touch it. It gathers dust on a shelf in their homes. Even when terrifying circumstances surround them, they don't pick up the Bible and gain nourishment from it for their hungry hearts.

In Isaiah 40–43, we can find more than 14 verses to encourage us. The very first word in Isaiah 40 is *Comfort*. God told Isaiah to comfort His people, to tell those in Jerusalem their hard service was complete; their sin had been paid for. Isn't it amazing that God inspired Isaiah to write these words long before Jesus was born? Hundreds of years later, the Messiah came to earth and died for the sins of all humankind. More than 2,000 years after His resurrection, we still find comfort in God's actions; He remembers *our* hard work in life, pointing to a better future in heaven because of Jesus's unselfish sacrifice.

God also promises these things:

- *"The grass withers and the flowers fall, but the word of our God stands forever"* (40:8).
- *"The Sovereign LORD comes with power"* (40:10).
- *"He tends his flock [you and me] like a shepherd; He gathers the lambs [including your children and teens] in his arms and carries them close to his heart"* (40:11).
- *"Do you not know? Have you not heard? The LORD is the everlasting God, the Creator of the ends of the earth. He will not grow tired or weary"* (40:28).
- *"He gives strength to the weary and increases the power of the weak"* (40:29).
- *"I have chosen you and have not rejected you, so do not fear, for I am with you; …I will strengthen you and help you; I will uphold you with my righteous right hand"* (41:9–10).

May the God of everlasting comfort encourage all who read these verses in Isaiah and depend on His promises.

Heavenly Father, thank You for comforting us like a shepherd through Your Word. Help us rest in Your arms and depend on You to make our rough places level and smooth. Amen.

# ❀ Where All Roads Lead ❀

*"Small is the gate and narrow the road that leads to life,*
*and only a few find it"* (Matthew 7:13–14).

We have entered an era still somewhat unfamiliar to those of us who grew up when many Americans (generally speaking) believed in the God of the Bible and right and wrong. As youngsters we got disciplined at school if we misbehaved, and once home, we got it again when Mom and Dad found out. Sharing a Christian witness was hard, but even as kids we knew that what we believed was important because there could only be one right way.

I distinctly recall at age ten getting in a rather heated debate with another wise and world-savvy ten-year-old about whether baptism was a prerequisite for salvation. She loudly insisted yes; I more loudly insisted no. Finally, my mom came on the scene and asked what all the yelling was about. I told her; after all, the truth claims of Christianity were worth fighting over.

But now, instead of comparing truth assertions of religions, people argue that there is no "right" way. One day recently, for instance, after telling a family member of my faith in Christ, my relative, a guy who claimed no particular belief system, responded, "Well, that's good if it works for you."

Do we get to pick and choose which belief system works for us like we try on clothes to see which best fit? Thankfully, God has provided evidence that only one belief system is true, and He has shown how we can recognize it. The belief system that is true is the one that best explains everything in existence—that corresponds to reality. As Christians, we can learn and share the abundant evidences that Christianity is the belief system that tells it like it really is.

Lord, I surrender to You and will seek to learn the evidences
that Christianity is true. Teach me so that I may teach others,
so that they, too, may enter in the narrow gate.

# ❋ Another Day in Paradise ❋

*We conducted ourselves in the world in simplicity and godly sincerity,*
*not with fleshly wisdom but by the grace of God*
(2 Corinthians 1:12 NKJV).

I sat deep in thought, staring at the computer screen, when *pop!* Sounds of a small explosion traveled from the kitchen. My husband casually called from the den, "Did you blow up an egg on the stove again?"

"No," I replied. "That was a can of diet pop in the freezer."

"Oh. Well… Good luck cleaning that up."

Just another day in paradise! I strolled into the kitchen, opened the freezer door, and started wiping. My mind traveled back to ten hours earlier when I first placed the canned drink in the freezer to cool it down quickly. *If I had brought that pack of drinks in the house earlier instead of leaving them in the car, none of this would have happened.* Should I feel guilty that I had been lazy?

Then my mind went back to four hours ago. I told myself I was coming to get the drink, but got busy and forgot it again. *If my mind wasn't preoccupied, I wouldn't be wiping up slush.* Should I feel guilty about getting distracted?

Then God reminded me of a simple truth: I'm living in a fallen world. Things break, rain showers spoil parades, and yes, sometimes canned drinks explode in the freezer, much like the egg that recently burned on my stove and landed in tiny shreds all over my ceiling. Sometimes there's no need to blame anyone else, beat myself up for not being perfect, or fear that Satan is in my freezer—the world is currently in imperfect condition, and I am an imperfect person.

We're right to be sensitive to the sin in our lives, compelling us to repent. However, God will love us no less when we burn the biscuits, trip onstage, or forget to set the alarm. Today, can we try as women of God *not* to beat ourselves up over personal imperfections? With God's grace calming our hearts, can we extend that grace to another imperfect person who didn't keep your glass filled at the restaurant, cut in front of you at the copy machine, or neglected to use a turn signal? It's an imperfect world with imperfect people, but holy and perfect almighty God is on His throne. His grace encourages us to keep trying to be more like Jesus. Perhaps our grace extended to others will allow them to see Jesus in us and compel them to seek the Lord.

Father, thank You for Your grace in my life. Help me extend mercy, grace, and kindness to others today in honor of You. Amen.

# ❀ Just a Noisy Gong ❀

*If I speak with the tongues of men and of angels, but do not have love,*
*I have become a noisy gong* (1 Corinthians 13:1 NASB).

He amassed billions and gave away almost as much. The philanthropist took every opportunity to help others. Never one for publicity, he avoided public interviews and photo ops. On his deathbed, he bequeathed a fortune to charitable organizations, wanting to fuel his vision to make the world a better place. He also signed a statement to donate his body to scientific research. Yet, when he died, he went to hell.

How could that be? Surely a moral person, a kind person who really cared about people such as this guy, would deserve heaven. Not so. A man's goodness can no more get him into heaven than his badness can cause him to go to hell. But we *do* go to hell because we're bad, don't we? Actually, God says we are *all* sinners—we *all* have done bad—yet some of us sinners will go to heaven, because we have put our trust in Jesus Christ, recognizing His sacrificial death paid for all of our sins. In the end, then, our badness doesn't send us to hell; rejecting Christ does.

Our focal verse tells us that we can't get to heaven by giving all our possessions to feed the poor, or by sacrificing our bodies. In truth, only love counts for anything, but not man's tainted love. *Agape* love gives not what the receiver wants, but what he needs. Ultimately man needs only one thing: Jesus Christ. So unless you know Christ and accept Him as the only hope for eternal life, giving away your money, your talents, even your life, will count for nothing eternal. Your life will be no more than a noisy gong: starting with a bang, quickly fading, and soon forgotten.

Jesus, forgive me for mocking Your death and resurrection by thinking I could earn my way into Your heaven. Amen.

# ❧ The Blessed Holy Spirit ❧

*When the day of Pentecost came, they were all together in one place*
(Acts 2:1).

Can you imagine what it would have been like to be present in the upper room praying? Suddenly a sound like a violent wind filled the room; tongues like fire rested on each believer; and everyone was filled with the Holy Spirit and began speaking in other tongues. Wow!

Back in the 1970s, we took the youth from our church on a retreat. We arrived on Friday night and during our campfire service, God's Spirit began to move among the youth. Unbelievers were coming to salvation and believers were experiencing renewal of their faith and passion. The campfire became "holy ground" and no one wanted to leave. We stayed around the fire until two in the morning.

The next day I noticed that there was a visible change in the youth. They spontaneously clustered into little groups to pray. We offered various activities throughout the day, but most just wanted to pray. They climbed hills and prayed. They sat on the porch and prayed. They walked on the paths and prayed.

Just before lunch another chaperone and I were finishing our teaching session. We placed a cross at the front of the room and asked the youth to write down and bring to the cross anything they felt was keeping them from a closer walk with God. As they scattered and began writing on slips of paper, they started humming "Amazing Grace."

Suddenly, a breeze blew through the room. I turned and looked at the windows. To my amazement, all the windows were closed! Not even a leaf was moving on the trees outside the windows. The Holy Spirit had filled the room.

That was more than 30 years ago. Parents still tell us, "We don't know what happened on that retreat, but our children have never been the same." Many went into full-time ministry and most of the others became active lay leaders in churches. The blessed Holy Spirit of Almighty God!

Dear Lord, we are desperate for an outpouring of Your Holy Spirit.
Have Your way, Lord, and we will be careful to give You all the honor
and glory. In Jesus's name, amen.

# ❀ When Difficult Decisions Come ❀

*"Fear thou not; for I am with thee: be not dismayed; for I am thy God:
I will strengthen thee; yea, I will help thee; yea, I will uphold thee with
the right hand of my righteousness"* (Isaiah 41:10 KJV).

The morning had brought nothing but gloomy news, and my heart was burdened from having to make difficult decisions. Questions raced through my mind. What should I do? And when should I do it—should I wait to act, just in case God wanted to intervene before I had to? I started thinking through my own personal biases and opinions, trying to make sure I was ready to make fair and God-led decisions. Suddenly none of my options seemed like good ones.

I dropped to my knees and read Isaiah 41:10. God's Word comforted me, and the Holy Spirit ministered to my heart with each phrase:

- *Fear thou not, for I am with thee:* I don't have to be afraid to make decisions, because God's presence is always with me.
- *Be not dismayed; for I am thy God:* I belong to the sovereign, all-knowing, all-powerful God; why be troubled when God is on my side?
- *I will strengthen thee:* I feel weak and drained when conflict and problems overshadow me, but God will supply all the strength I need.
- *I will help thee:* Not only is God with me and for me, but He is also going to help me.
- *I will uphold thee with the right hand of my righteousness:* As a woman of God longing to do what is right and pleasing to God, I can be sure that God's righteousness will sustain me, and the Holy Spirit will teach me what is right in the midst of each situation.

I claimed every phrase of Isaiah 41:10 in prayer, thanking God for His faithfulness. With God's promises encouraging me, the difficult decisions didn't seem so large and looming anymore.

How can you apply this powerful verse to the decisions facing you today? If you feel their shadows consuming you, look to God for comfort and strength.

Father, I want to rely on You totally as I make decisions. Thank You for Your great help and encouragement that nourishes my spirit. In Jesus's name, amen.

# ❀ The Danger of Anger ❀

*"In your anger do not sin." Do not let the sun go down*
*while you are still angry* (Ephesians 4:26).

In the fourth chapter of Ephesians, Paul lists the characteristics that follow a life-changing experience with the Lord. As we allow our minds to be transformed through His Spirit, we find that we will possess the following characteristics:

v. 25 Will not lie, but will tell the truth
v. 26 Will deal with anger in an appropriate and timely manner
v. 27 Will not give Satan any place in our lives
v. 28 Will not steal, but will work hard so we can assist others
v. 29 Will speak only what benefits others
v. 30 Will not grieve the Holy Spirit
v. 31 Will not have an attitude of ill-will toward anyone
v. 32 Will love, seek to understand, and forgive others.

God knows that there are times in life when circumstances anger us. Thus, He teaches in Ephesians 4:26, "In your anger do not sin." So the question arises: when does anger become sin?

The answer is found in the latter part of the same verse. Anger becomes sin when we choose to hold onto it and refuse to deal with it. If one does not deal with anger, it turns to unforgiveness and ultimately into bitterness. The Bible is specific that we "Do not let the sun go down while you are still angry" (v. 26). We may experience some long nights as we deal with situations that anger us, but it is vitally necessary to our spiritual well-being that we do not "sleep on our anger."

Solomon admonishes in Proverbs 16:32, "Better a patient man than a warrior, a man who controls his temper than one who takes a city." With 700 wives and 300 concubines, he must have been speaking from experience!

Remember, *anger* is only one letter short of *danger*." Do not let the sun go down with "danger" in your heart.

Dear God, renew my mind through Your Spirit so I can release my anger to You. Thank You for longing to free me from any binding influence anger might have on my life! In Jesus's name, amen.

# ❦ Life on the Altar ❦

*I beseech you therefore, brethren, by the mercies of God, that you present
your bodies a living sacrifice, holy, acceptable to God, which is your
reasonable service* (Romans 12:1 NKJV).

What does Romans 12:1–2 mean when it says a Christian's premier
service is offering her life as a living sacrifice to God? In common usage,
a sacrifice, by definition, is dead. It does not exert its will. To be a living
sacrifice, then, requires that a woman of God relinquishes all of her desires
in order to obey God's will. She asks the Spirit to align her thinking to His
perspective. The Spirit enables and empowers her to discern and do the will
of God (12:1–2).

The remainder of chapter 12 shows how the believer's abandoning of
self to God expresses itself in daily life. A woman of God honestly appraises
herself—for example, not thinking too highly of herself (12:3). She values
others' giftedness and increasingly uses her spiritual gifts (12:4–8).

She loves, not pretentiously, but sincerely; she hates evil and holds
on to good (12:9). She is devoted to fellow believers (12:10). She serves
wholeheartedly—passionately—as unto the Lord (12:11). She rejoices in
the surety of Christ's hope, is faithful and steadfast in difficult times, and
commits herself to prayer (12:12). She contributes to the needs of other
believers, opening her heart to them in times of need (12:13). She seeks no
revenge when wronged; instead, she prays continually (12:14). She moves
alongside fellow-believers in the ups-and-downs of life (12:15).

She shows no favoritism and considers no act of service too menial
(v. 16). She is not prideful, thinking she knows more than others (12:16).
When making decisions, she asks, "What is right?" and ponders how her
decision will affect others' faith (12:17). Though she does not strive for
peace at all costs, she tries to live peacefully with others as much as possible
(12:18). When wronged she heaps blessings, becoming a purveyor of God's
goodness within bad situations (12:20–21).

Given the description of the altar-lived life, we each should evaluate
our life to see how we measure up to the Scripture's requirements.

Lord Jesus, when I look at my "self" in light of this passage, I see more of "me,"
"my," and "I" than You. Remove every remnant of self-centeredness that
obscures my vision of Your will. Amen.

# ❀ I'm Headed ❀ in a Different Direction

*One of them, when he saw he was healed, came back, praising God in a loud voice. He threw himself at Jesus' feet and thanked him—and he was a Samaritan* (Luke 17:15–16).

When Jack was 13, he called me "Kettle" after watching a movie featuring Ma Kettle, a bossy shrew. At 16, he started calling me the latest *cool* name, "Doll," which he still calls me today. I remember one day in particular, when he rushed in the back door:

"Hey, Doll, you won't believe this: Garth became a Christian."

"Garth? I never thought...."

"It's true. I just saw him at *church*! He told me how God spoke to him; he stopped drinking and doing drugs—he changed directions. If Garth can do it, anybody can."

The Bible gives a dynamic example of changed lives: lepers who met Jesus. "They stood at a distance, calling aloud, 'Jesus, Master, have pity on us!'" (Luke 17:12–13). Ten of the lepers left healed; one turned around and came back to Jesus. It was evident he had changed spiritual directions when he praised God, threw himself at Jesus's feet, and thanked Him (vv. 15–16).

The Book of Acts is filled with an amazing record of the disciples' enemies, whom the Holy Spirit changed. Some were heading in a direction of despair and deception, which grew out of their evil hearts. However, the Spirit of God changed their worldview completely, as they turned from evil and began to walk with Christ. Have you ever wondered what happened to the other nine lepers? The thankful leper was probably an example as he lived a renewed life of hope and health.

Contemplate the living examples in your life. Who set a moral or spiritual example before you? How did their changed worldview demonstrate a switch to another direction? May God help us to make a 180-degree turn in all the areas of our lives that need reversal.

Forgiving God, thank You for reversing the thankful leper's direction, setting him on a new path. Unchanging God, thank You for still turning people around as You did Garth. Turn us in new directions, Lord, when we need a heart change.
Amen.

*The real name of Jack's friend in this story has been changed.*

# ❀ I Never Promised You ❀ a Rose Garden

*The grass withers and the flowers fall,*
*but the word of our God stands forever* (Isaiah 40:8).

You may have heard someone sing, "I Never Promised You a Rose Garden." Since I'm allergic to flowers, their smell causes me breathlessness and watery eyes. All the years I was married, my husband, Charles, never had to worry about giving me flowers. However, on my birthday or anniversary, he often bought me silk arrangements so he could tell our friends he'd given me flowers. In his upbringing, giving a woman flowers was the proper thing to show he was thinking of her. As a minister, he set a good example before others by bringing me silk flowers.

Down through the years, I've compared my life to a favorite flower, a rose, which comes with prickly thorns. Life is beautiful and has a sweet fragrance, but it also has a thorny side, too. While we have wonderful opportunities to relate to others, even the best life has sadness and hard days. Some relationships seem lasting; others are fleeting.

On March 15, 2005, I woke up to find my husband gasping for breath. At first I just thought his snoring was worse than usual. Then I realized he was struggling for life itself. I called 911 and began to administer CPR. How many breaths do I give? Two? How many pumps on his chest? I began counting: 1…2…3….

Though help came soon, God took my husband home to be with Him that night. At first, it seemed he left me too early in life, but God always knows what He is doing. I was prepared: as a Christian, I could lean on the Lord for comfort, joy, and life itself. God never promised me a rose garden, but I have hope. I know Charles is in heaven with God today. Through a personal relationship with Jesus, I'm assured of a reunion with Charles and other saints in glory. Relationships on earth are wonderful, but our relationship with Jesus Christ is worth sharing. It's everlasting!

Dear Lord, You've guided me through rough times. Thank You for eternal relationships. Help me share eternal hope with others. Amen.

# ❈ On a Plane Bound for Nowhere ❈

*"Nor is there salvation in any other, for there is no other name*
*under heaven given among men by which we must be saved"*
(Acts 4:12 NKJV).

As I sat on a plane, talking spiritual matters with a Californian over a soda and pretzels, I inadvertently poked my spiritual finger in an area he felt it didn't belong. "So, what do you believe is the way a person can get to heaven?"

He stared out over the sea of fluffy clouds, then replied, "You have to basically be a good person and live by the teachings of Jesus."

"I see," was my answer. "Would you say, based on your beliefs, that a personal relationship with Jesus is the *only* way to salvation?"

"Now, you see? These conversations always get political." He felt I had dragged him into territory where he must choose his allegiance. And he was right. But not for the sake of politics—*"my God is bigger than your God"*—but for the sake of eternity.

When a growing number of people are questioning if Jesus could be the *only* way, some who seek "peace" believe pluralism is the answer. Pluralism is the concept that God has created many ways to get into heaven. It's not a new notion created by the postmodern mind; an ancient Hindu saying is, "Heaven is a palace with many doors, and each may enter in his own way."

Paul wrote to Timothy: "For there is one God and one Mediator between God and men, the Man Christ Jesus" (1 Timothy 2:5 NKJV). The Mediator is our advocate before the Father. Only Jesus has the authority to speak before the Father on our behalf. Paul wrote again, "For no other foundation can anyone lay than that which is laid, which is Jesus Christ" (1 Corinthians 3:11 NKJV). No counterfeit doctrine built upon any other "prophet" who claims to be the foundation of faith will stand.

No other name. Not one through whom we may be saved, except for Jesus.

Father, let me stand on this foundation of Jesus Christ without wavering, telling others of the One and Only Savior, Your Son. Amen.

# ❀ Expect the Unexpected ❀

*Amos answered Amaziah, "I was neither a prophet nor a prophet's son,*
*but I was a shepherd, and I also took care of sycamore fig trees.*
*But the LORD took me from tending the flock and said to me,*
*'Go, prophesy to my people Israel"* (Amos 7:14–15).

Gretchin is a three-year-old student in the preschool program at the church where my husband, Wayne, pastors. She is the stereotypical picture of a cherub, replete with golden ringlets of hair, big blue eyes that sparkle, and rosy, chubby cheeks. My husband knows she melts my heart, so he kept me supplied me with "Gretchin stories."

Gretchin's older sister, Allison (who is equally wonderful and beautiful), informed Wayne that she was going to be the queen in this year's play. Gretchin woefully said, "I don't know what I'm going to be."

Like Gretchin, Amos didn't know what he was going to be. His task seemed greater than his perceived abilities. How could one who was neither a prophet nor the son of a prophet end up being the voice of God to His people in Israel? However, God took him as he was and used him to deliver a mighty message.

When I found out that Gretchin was going to be the head angel, I could hardly wait for the night of the play. As the angels entered, I noticed that Gretchin had a special gold and white headband signifying that she was not only an angel but that she was the head angel. Each time she had a part, she ran from "heaven," delivered her message, and ran back. During the announcement of Jesus's birth, the headband fell from around her head across her eyes. However, she remained with her arms spread wide (as all good angels in plays do) and waited until she got back to "heaven" to make the needed adjustments.

From a shepherd-farmer to one of the greatest prophets of the past, or from a regular angel to the head angel, we should always expect the unexpected. Embrace God's calling and enjoy the journey!

Now may the God of peace Himself sanctify you entirely; and may your spirit and soul and body be preserved complete, without blame at the coming of our Lord Jesus Christ.

Dear Lord, help us learn to expect the unexpected. You are in control and life
with You is an exciting adventure. In Jesus's name, amen.

# ❀ *In the Mean Time* ❀

*"May the God of peace Himself sanctify you entirely"*
(1 Thessalonians 5:23 NASB).

Christ has come, died for our sins, risen again, and we as believers eagerly await His return. What do we do while we wait—in the meantime? Do we just busy ourselves with the demands of daily schedules? What about God's bigger purposes? Where do they fit into our lives?

It's difficult to keep eternal purposes in mind because we do live in a *mean* time. Evil threatens on every side. We have valid reason to fear. Nuclear weapons are poised in our direction, and a mere knee-jerk reaction by an annoyed terrorist could blast us into oblivion. But it's not just the precarious condition of the world at large that bothers us. At times, evil has barreled into our own personal lives without a moment's notice, turning our days and even our lives upside down.

The day-to-day is no picnic, either. Worldly concerns pull at us: the job, the marriage, the family problems, and the tedious repetition of daily demands. It's no surprise we're distracted from God's kingdom concerns. How can we focus on eternal things with so many other issues pressing?

We can know one thing for sure: God wants believers to use this time called *life* preparing for an even greater work—ruling with Him in His future kingdom. In the verses preceding today's passage, God tells us to pursue good, never to return evil for evil, rejoice always, pray incessantly, and give thanks in every situation. The playing field upon which we develop these image-bearing, Christ-like traits is our world; filled with terrorists, tragedy, and a daily routine encumbered by worries and tedium.

Though we wouldn't choose the means God chose to train us for heavenly endeavors, God promises to preserve us "complete" until Christ's return. Further, we have a great cloud of witnesses—believers from every age and nation—cheering us on in our struggle until the day He will "sanctify [us] entirely."

Lord, I open my life to You to use any and all means to sanctify me so that I may be presented to You complete and without blame upon Your return. Amen.

# ❀ Double Light in the Darkness ❀

*God made two great lights—the greater light to govern the day and the lesser light to govern the night. He also made the stars* (Genesis 1:16).

In a single day, Job lost almost everything he had. A messenger reported that a band of thieves stole his oxen and donkeys and killed the servants attending them. While that messenger was still speaking, another came to inform him that fire burned his sheep and the servants attending them. A third messenger came to report that three bands of thieves stole his camels and killed the servants attending them. A final messenger told that a great wind struck the house of his oldest son, and all his children and servants were killed.

Job then contracted a disease that covered his body with painful boils. In spite of all, Job did not curse God, but rather lamented the day he was born. Job felt the light of his life had been snuffed out by the darkness of his misery.

A dear friend of mine, Teresa, recently experienced the death of her only child. For months we had anticipated her daughter giving birth. The day finally arrived. Complications arose. The baby lived, but her daughter died. The long awaited *due date* of the baby became the *death date* of Teresa's daughter. There are no words to express the darkness we experienced. For awhile, we seemed to live in perpetual darkness and night.

Recently Teresa asked, "Have you ever noticed that God gave only one light (the sun) for the day, but He gave two sources of light (the moon and stars) for the darkness of night?" God knew that in the darkness Job, Teresa, and all of mankind would need extra light.

God restored the light to Job. In the last chapter of the Book of Job, we find that God blessed Job with twice as much material wealth as before, plus seven more sons, and three more daughters. God is also restoring the light to Teresa. It happens each time she looks into the face of her grandson.

Dear God, thank You for giving double light in the darkness of night.
In Jesus's name, amen.

# ❀ Feeling Out of Your Mind ❀

*For God has not given us a spirit of fear, but of power and of love and of a sound mind* (2 Timothy 1:7 NKJV).

*Hurried, frazzled, overwhelmed,* and *scattered* aren't ideal words to describe a godly woman's state of mind, but what female hasn't occasionally felt swimmy with confusion? These unpleasant traits are somehow related to fear. *What will people say if I'm late again? Am I a bad mother if I don't chaperone this trip?* Fear can make your palms sweat and your stomachache, but fear is foremost a matter of the mind, based on what you think may happen if you don't perform to perfection. A sound mind rejects fear, because fearfulness is a product of Satan's lies.

You may feel like it's debatable some days, but if you're a Christian, God has given you the spirit of a wise, disciplined, sound mind to prepare you for spiritual warfare. It is *knowledge of God* that defeats Satan's arguments (2 Corinthians 10:4–5).

Satan tries to convince you to doubt the trustworthiness of God. His lies can be specific to your situation: *It's foolish to tithe when you don't know if you're going to lose your job,* or, *life is too short to waste energy trying to fix a broken marriage.* Perhaps he's trying to convince you that God's truths don't apply in your particular situation. His appeal to your intellect may be subtler, pitching the same argument to you he used on Eve: *"Has God indeed said…?"* (Genesis 3:1) Satan wants to convince you to do things your way, that you know better than God. And you can be sure of it, when you attempt to define your own destiny, with the limitations of your personal knowledge, you'll soon experience what Paul called a "spirit of fear."

The more you know of God and His ways, the more you recognize Satan's ploys. How can you grow in knowledge of God? Begin with Scripture.

Father, I long for a sound mind, strong and focused, filled with Your wisdom.
Help me to grow in knowledge of You. In the name of Jesus, amen.

# ❀ *Only One Way* ❀

*Salvation is found in no one else, for there is no other name under heaven given to men by which we must be saved* (Acts 4:12).

Aren't there many roads to heaven? A conversation with an acquaintance revealed that many believe so. When I asked what she believed it took to enter heaven, she said she believed in God and Jesus, as well as in teachings from other religions.

What does it mean to *believe*—in a saving sense? The New Testament word for "believe" means to trust in, to rely upon. Intellectual assent is not enough, for Scripture teaches that the demons believe there is one God (James 2:19) and recognize Jesus Christ's identity (Matthew 8:28–32). Yet, they do not *believe in* Him.

On what or whom do you rely to gain entrance into heaven? Good works? Church membership or baptism? In Matthew, chapter 7, Jesus said that in the end many will call Him, *"Lord, Lord,"* claiming they've done great works for Him, but He will respond, *"Depart from Me, I never knew You"* (v. 23).

The Bible asserts that faith in Jesus Christ provides the *only* access to heaven and to peace with God the Father (John 14:6; Acts 4:12). How can we know Christ personally through faith? We can acknowledge our sin to God: *"For all have sinned and fall short of the glory of God"* (Romans 3:23). We can accept the free gift of salvation offered by faith in Jesus Christ: *"The wages of sin is death, but the gift of God is eternal life in Christ Jesus our Lord"* (Romans 6:23). We can trust Jesus Christ and turn away from our sin—from living our lives our way: *"Repent therefore and be converted, that your sins may be wiped out"* (Acts 3:19).

Would you like to trust Jesus Christ as your Savior? Simply ask and He will give you salvation.

Lord, I'm a sinner and deserve death. I turn from my sin and by faith ask You to forgive my sins, and be my Savior. Amen.

# ❀ Make Me a Blessing ❀

*If you love those who love you, what reward will you get?*
(Matthew 5:46).

During the Sermon on the Mount, Jesus told His followers how to be an incredible blessing to others. He told them how to live in relationship with those who were their friends, but more importantly, with enemies.

Jesus began with the old rule, *"An eye for an eye"* (Matthew 5:38–39). He says instead of seeking revenge, if someone strikes you on the right cheek, turn the other cheek also. Second, He says if someone asks you to give him your tunic, give him your cloak as well (v. 40). Next He says if someone forces you to go with him one mile (a favorite demand of Roman soldiers), then go with him two miles, blessing him far beyond what he hoped (v. 41). Finally, He says give to anyone who wants to borrow from you (v. 42).

Jesus turned people around, teaching them to go in opposite directions. Where they were selfish, he taught overabundant unselfishness. Under the Roman occupation, legalistic rules demanded punishment, sometimes with unfair enforcement. Instead of chaffing under that servanthood, Jesus suggests His followers go overboard, returning more than expected! Filled with the Holy Spirit, Christians are able to build good will for our Lord.

It's not easy to turn the other cheek and to give to anyone who wants to borrow, but such unselfish gestures pay off. Our relationships with trusted friends—or even those on the outer edges of the community or church—can bring God joy.

Christians have four blessed looks:
1. Look back and thank God. (Remember the blessing of good past relationships.)
2. Look forward and trust God. (Encourage self and others in the future.)
3. Look around and serve God. (Find someone to help in Jesus's name.)
4. Look within and find your need for God. (Establish a personal relationship with God.)

Paul says *"Blessed be God the Father of our Lord Jesus Christ, who has blessed us with all spiritual blessings"* (Ephesians 1:3 NKJV). Praise Him. Then use relationships at work, at school, or at play to bless others.

Lord, thank You for Your blessings, physical and spiritual. Help us, Your people,
to bless others in Jesus's name, amen.

# ❋ Word Carriers ❋

*The centurion replied, "Lord, I do not deserve to have you come under
my roof. But just say the word, and my servant will be healed"*
(Matthew 8:8).

When I taught AP (Advanced Placement) English at Clinton (South
Carolina) High School, I helped prepare students to take the AP exam.
A good grade on the exam earned college credit so they could skip to
sophomore English.

One year a former AP student, who had failed the exam in high school,
came back to report an interesting turn of fortune. In her first college
essay, she used the word *aficionado*, a favorite of Ernest Hemingway—an
avid enthusiast of bullfighting. Her professor gave her an A+ saying, "I'm
going to recommend you skip freshman English. The word *aficionado* told
me you're more advanced than anyone in this class." She and I were both
flabbergasted. The use of one big word earned her a new status!

The centurion who came to Jesus also knew the power of Jesus's word.
His humility is evident when he says, *"Just say the word!"* Jesus did, and the
centurion's servant was healed.

Throughout the Bible, we read about *word power*. God created the world
through words, saying, *"Let there be"* and whatever He spoke appeared—
and it was good. The New Testament records Jesus Himself as the Word.
*"The Word was with God, and the Word was God. He was with God in the beginning"*
(John 1:1–2).

As a Christian, you're a Word Carrier. You study God's Word,
memorize it, and believe it. You accept the Living Word into your heart
as your Savior and Lord. Word Carriers are powerful influences in the
world, since God's Word is powerful. Think big. The world is waiting for
Word Carriers. Hurting, hungry people need your influence to heal their
hurt and feed their hunger. Depressed, grieving people need your influence to comfort them and restore their joy. What everyone in the world
needs is the Word. If you hold that Word, carry Him to others.

O God, help us read Your Word, remember Your Word, and share the Living
Word with people who are hurting, hungry, depressed, and grieving. Help us as
Word Carriers to think big, sharing Your Word with the whole world. Amen.

# ❀ One Body ❀

*The body is a unit, though it is made up of many parts; and though all
its parts are many, they form one body. So it is with Christ*
(1 Corinthians 12:12).

When I taught deaf preschoolers, I began by taking a concrete object—
a ball—and moving to the abstract concept of that object. After playing with various types of balls, I showed them pictures of balls, carefully
pointing out the printed word, *b-a-l-l*. I reinforced this by teaching them
the sign language for *ball* and how to fingerspell it. It was an exciting time
as I watched them capture the concept of words and their previously
nonexistent vocabulary grow.

Jesus, the Master Teacher, also uses concrete objects to teach us spiritual lessons. The analogy of the human body correlating to the church is a
perfect example.

The human body amazes scientists. They cannot explain it. After con-
ception, a human being begins as one cell, which is capable of becoming
a person. However, the cell begins duplicating itself, almost like making
photocopies of itself. After a time of exponential numerical growth, the cells
become a cell cluster, similar in shape to a raspberry. At that point, the cells,
each of which is capable of becoming a human being, begin to differentiate
and start joining other cells to form the various organs and systems.

This process completely baffles scientists. They cannot understand
how cells limit themselves to specialized activities and accomplish a greater
achievement for the good of the whole person.

Through the human body, God shows us the perfect example of the
Body of Christ. Believers have various spiritual gifts and diverse talents and
abilities. Any one of us could go our own way and accomplish much for the
kingdom of God. However, when we choose to work in one accord, more
is accomplished and we experience the blessing of unity and community.
Only then do we understand what it means to be a part of *one body*!

Dear Lord, thank You for giving us such a clear picture of what You want
from us. Just as our cells work together for the good of our bodies, let us work
together for the good of Your body. Amen.

# ❀ *Building a Legacy* ❀

*By faith Abel offered to God a more excellent sacrifice than Cain,*
*through which he obtained witness that he was righteous, God*
*testifying of his gifts; and through it he being dead still speaks*
(Hebrews 11:4 NKJV).

Legacy. Abraham Lincoln created a legacy of leadership in the face of adversity. Martin Luther King Jr. left a legacy of reconciliation. Abel is remembered for acceptable worship through sacrifice. In contrast, Pete Rose will forever be the famous baseball player who was caught gambling. Adolf Hitler desired to be remembered in history, but not as a crazed man who died in defeat. Though Cain surely had a few tender moments with his family and a history sprinkled with some finer moments of humanity, his legacy will forever be the jealous murderer of his brother.

Legacy is what you leave behind. The decisions and actions of your life build your legacy, and then whatever rises to the top in people's memories will be what you're forever known for in human history. Most people will be long forgotten just a decade or two after they pass into eternity, but the legacy they leave behind will have long-lasting ripple effects on future generations.

From the grave, Cain has no ability to alter his legacy; his day is gone. While you have life and breath today, you still have the opportunity—and the responsibility—to live in such a way that honors God and points people to Jesus Christ for generations to come. Through legacy, the Scripture teaches us that it's as if the dead still speak. What will your legacy tell the next generation about the faithfulness of God?

Heavenly Father, please teach me to have a larger perspective on the consequences of my actions. Give me a sense of the significance of my legacy for the people whose lives will be affected in the future by the decisions I make today. God, please guide me in paths of righteousness, and allow me to be a witness for Christ even to generations to come through my legacy. Amen.

# ❀ *Just Like Jesus* ❀

*For whom He foreknew, He also predestined to be conformed to the*
*image of His Son* (Romans 8:29 NKJV).

What does it mean to be conformed to the image of Jesus Christ? In bygone eras believers would have understood the phrase to mean that through obedience to Christ believers become more like Him in character. The Jewish people understood the concept perhaps better than we in postmodern western society. When a disciple followed a rabbi, he not only obeyed his teachings, but he also wanted to think and act as his rabbi did.

Today, however, some so-called biblical teachers recast this worthy and holy calling into a mantra promoting human divinity. We may become "little gods," that is, individually possess godness in our humanness, they assert.

But does this thinking line up with Scripture? In John 15:5 Jesus clearly stated *"without Me, you can do nothing"* (NKJV). How can we as contingent beings, that is, beings dependent on another Being for our very breath and existence, ever aspire to godness? Christ calls us to holiness, but it is a holiness derived not from our increasing self-determination, exaltation, and actualization but from our dying to our own sinful tendencies, desires, and aspirations. We can't become more like Him unless we are willing to become less like our natural selves. Our image-bearing potential completely depends on our focus of pleasing Him increasing while our focus on ourselves decreases.

How can one become a "little god" when God is anything but little? He is awesome, omniscient, omnipotent, and eternal. We are not. If we want to become conformed to Christ's image we must first relinquish, even banish any hope of accomplishng God's purposes by our own strength. Then we become "like Christ."

Lord Jesus, supreme God who came in the flesh for our sakes, may we never mistake Your call to holiness as an affirmation of our personal ability to accomplish this work except through our absolute dependency on Your power. In Jesus's name, amen.

# ❀ He Will Not Be Silenced ❀

*But the word of God is not chained* (2 Timothy 2:9 NKJV).

God is on the move. I read about the growth of the underground church movements in countries with oppressive governments, I receive emails from missionary friends who are praising the Lord for lives being transformed through Christ, and I witness people around me who are excited about living for God.

But oh, how distressing much of the news is today. I also get reports of outside pressure to suppress the name of Jesus in society. I read articles about Christians who are targeted in their workplaces. My stomach churns and my heart aches as I read commentaries from countless people filled with rage and confusion, lashing out at Christianity and righteousness. I'm not sure if the spiritual oppression has greatly heightened recently or if I've formerly been oblivious, but a war is being waged against Christianity, and I so often feel small and powerless to affect the situation.

But God has assured all of us: the battle is the Lord's. Though we may feel censored in society or oppressed in our faith, *the Word of God is not chained*. No matter how the world may deny its authority, the Bible is living and active and will continue to be the source of truth. No power under heaven will suppress God's holy, perfect, powerful Word.

The Word of God is not chained, but it is often neglected. Are we studying daily to allow God to mold and shape us? Our strength to stand for God's righteousness will be bolstered to new heights when we stand for the truth given in God's Word. The next time we read a disturbing commentary about the oppression of the Christian faith, we can go directly to the Bible and look for God's answers. God has spoken to us through the Scriptures, and His voice will not be silenced.

Mighty God, I am so small, and the powers of evil in this world are so great!
I turn to You for guidance. Your Word must go forth. I want to be a
better steward of the powerful Word of God. Praise You, Father,
that You will not be silenced. Amen.

# ❀ *Pray for Your* ❀ *Great-Great-Grandchildren?*

*I will pour out my Spirit on your offspring, and my blessing on your descendants* (Isaiah 44:3).

A young missionary told me, "I'm sure my children, grandchildren, great-grandchildren, and great-great-grandchildren will have good lives. They'll be nestled in God's hands."

"What did you mean about your great-great grandchildren having good lives? You seem so sure. How can that be?" I asked.

She smiled. "I pray every day for them."

I interrupted her. "How can you say that? You don't even know their names."

"I pray one of God's promises," she said calmly. "He tells us in Psalm 40:8 that His Word lasts forever. Since that's true, we can pray using His written promises in the Bible." She opened her Bible and flipped to Isaiah 44. Here God tells us He'll pour His Spirit on our "offspring"—our children, grandchildren, great-grandchildren, and other future generations. He promises to pour out blessings on all our descendants.

As Christians, we often find ourselves in a spiritual dry land, hungry and thirsty for God's Spirit. Once we are filled with His Spirit, our overflow pours out through our words and actions to those around us—such as neighbors, shut-ins, fellow church members, homeless people, and especially our own families. No generosity or kindness goes unnoticed by God. He honors our sharing with others, especially with children, who face the future. He holds the power to pour out to future generations an even greater sense of His Spirit than we could ever share ourselves. Since prayer transcends time and space, we can pray for future events, those we may never see physically. God honors His Word and honors our sincere prayers, as we lift up the next generations to Him.

I try to remember the advice of the missionary: pray for future children in the family, church, or community. God promises to keep His Word, and His Word promises He will pour out His blessings on descendants of the righteous.

Father of all, pour out Your blessings on our descendants.
May future generations experience the joy of knowing You as Your Spirit
indwells their hearts. In Jesus's name, amen.

# ❀ *In One Accord* ❀

*Then make my joy complete by being like-minded, having the same*
*love, being one in spirit ["in one accord," KJV] and purpose*
(Philippians 2:2).

For the past few weeks, the words *in one accord* kept coming to my mind. Pondering these words, I realized that God was teaching me anew the importance of unity. Miraculous occurrences in the Bible happened when people prayed and worked together *in one accord*.

While on earth, Jesus taught that the only way the world would know that He was "for real" was through the unity of His followers (John 17:21). That's a pretty sobering thought, isn't it?

Years ago I heard the story of a young girl who wandered into the massive wheat fields of a farm in the Midwest. She got lost in the acres of long stalks of grain. Search and rescue operations went on for days. Shift after shift of volunteers covered different areas of the farm. The nights were cold and the searchers wondered if one so young could withstand the combination of weather conditions and lack of food and water.

Finally, someone suggested that all the workers join hands and make a long human chain that would reach across the fields. Dozens of volunteers clasped hands and moved forward slowly across the farm looking for the little girl. A short distance into the fields they found her not far from where she had entered and gotten lost. It appeared she had walked in circles trying to find her way home. To their horror, she had not survived.

With tears streaming down their faces, they quietly stood looking at the lifeless body of the little girl. One of the volunteers broke the stunned silence with the words, "If only we had joined hands sooner."

We live in a world filled with people who are lost and can't find their way. *"The fields are white already to harvest"* (John 4:34). Let's continue to join hands *in one accord* and help bring them safely home!

Dear Lord, please help us to remain in one accord so we can find those who are
lost and bring them to You. Amen.

# ❊ *No Defense* ❊

*Pray that I may declare [the gospel] fearlessly, as I should*
(Ephesians 6:20).

I'll call her Dr. Daj. As a public health nurse in our rural community, I had become acquainted with Dr. Daj while caring for her homebound patients. Her dusky brown complexion revealed a homeland far removed from the little southern town, and she was Muslim, quite an oddity in the Bible belt at the time.

When we learned she had developed leukemia, the health professionals in our area were heartbroken. We held out hope she would conquer the dreaded disease. But, it was not to be. In a matter of months, she lay near death in a hospital bed.

Realizing I may have only one chance to tell her good-bye and pray with her, I drove to the hospital. She lay nearly motionless, attempting a meager smile. I made small talk then realized her energy was failing quickly.

"Dr. Daj," I started, "may I pray with you?"

"Oh, yes," she whispered her reply. "We all pray to the same God."

How should I respond? I knew in my heart that her *Allah* was not the same God I worshipped, for Muslims respected Jesus as a great prophet, but not as the living God. But, she was weak and I had only a few moments. I didn't want to upset her. What would be the point in giving a defense of Jesus as God with her in such frail condition? Besides, there was very little chance that anything I would say could change her beliefs.

I prayed aloud, not in the name of *Allah*, but to God the Father, and asked Him to bless this precious woman and give her strength. In my heart I prayed to the Lord whom I knew personally but never spoke the name of Jesus aloud. When finished, I patted her hand and left the room quietly. As far as I know, Dr. Daj entered eternity a few days later to meet Jesus as Judge, rather than as Savior.

What should I have done? If I had told her Jesus is more than a good prophet and could give her eternal life, would she have listened? I will never know. The fact that I didn't try leaves me unspeakably sad. The Lord has used my failure as the impetus for equipping me to respond more wisely than I did to Dr. Daj.

How about you? Would you like to give a stronger defense of your faith in Christ?

Lord Jesus, Savior and God, please burn upon our hearts
the urgency of preparing ourselves to speak Your name. Amen.

# ❁ *He Is with Us* ❁

*"Be strong and of good courage, and do it; do not fear nor be dismayed,*
*for the LORD God—my God—will be with you. He will not leave you*
*nor forsake you, until you have finished all the work for the service of*
*the house of the LORD"* (1 Chronicles 28:20 NKJV).

This Scripture reminds me of my friend Karen who forsook a well-paying job and said good-bye to her lifelong friends to live among an unbelieving people in Siberia. I never visited her flat, but I could envision her sitting at a small primitive table beneath a single light bulb, having fellowship with Jesus.

Then my mind goes to Panama, where a missionary couple has spent their lives ministering to Indian people dressed in colorfully dyed wraps. The aging couple's gait has slowed, but they haven't finished God's work in Panama. They intend to minister there until the end.

Then I think of my children. My little stair steps are at different stages, from the oldest who has just begun to dream of her future, to the littlest one who has just conquered walking. Each of my three children is different in personality and skills, designed specifically for what God has in store for his or her service to the Lord. I try to imagine my daughter walking the streets of Calcutta to minister to forgotten women in back alleys. I picture my son, all grown up and preaching the gospel on a grassy knoll overlooking the African plain. I envision my youngest son, playing soccer with the locals in washed-out, muddy streets in Central America, spreading the good news of Jesus to little boys in worn-out cleats. These are happy scenes of my children fulfilling God's purpose for their lives.

But what if God's plan lands my daughter under house arrest, or my sons in chains? These dark scenes cause my heart to ache. But I must adjust the scene, recalling there's another figure in that scene: Jesus. If my loved ones and I are called to suffer for Christ, I know *my* God will never leave us or forsake us. He will be our stay.

Precious Father, You are with me. Whatever I can do for the sake of the gospel,
I want to do it. Amen.

# ❀ Plan Your Work ❀ and Work Your Plan—Together

*Plans fail for lack of counsel, but with many advisers they succeed*
(Proverbs 15:22).

When my children were small, I confess I didn't teach them how to cook or clean house too often because it was easier to do it myself than to muster the patience to teach them. I could save time, energy, and frazzled nerves by ignoring their offers to help. However, today my children still remember the time I cared enough to teach them to make a peach salad with two clove-eyes and a pimento smile on each peach half. They also remember the time I asked them to help clean small throw rugs by shaking them out in the backyard. As an older adult, I reflect on those good times and wonder why I didn't ask for their help more often. The camaraderie was lasting.

If you've ever planned a dinner party, a missions trip, or a Bible study in your Sunday School class, you know it takes hours to accomplish. However, the writer of Proverbs tells us good leadership takes something else: consultation with others. If you feel overworked today in any area of your life, follow God's Word: get advice from others.

Ask the group for feedback and evaluate periodically to see if you are following the wishes of the majority, allowing for the minority viewpoint as well.

Good leaders keep in touch with others as they plan. Everyone is a part of the planning process. Leaders ask God to lead them, take time to get wide input from others, offer options, present several possible outcomes within God's will, and discuss prioritizing their resources for maximum benefit.

Spend a moment praying for group leaders you know, and then pray for yourself, that you will ask for help and involve others in all God leads you to do.

Lord, help me to remember that You are the Master planner.
May I always consult You as I also seek help from others.
Relieve me from self-righteousness, self-sufficiency, and burnout. Amen.

# ❀ Faith Unfurled ❀

*"I tell you the truth, if you have faith as small as a mustard seed, you can say to this mountain, 'Move from here to there' and it will move. Nothing will be impossible for you"* (Matthew 17:20).

During his first missionary journey to China, Hudson Taylor traveled on a sailing vessel. The wind became very still, and the boat drifted toward the shore of an island where a savage tribe of cannibals lived. The captain came to Mr. Taylor and asked him to pray for God's help. Mr. Taylor replied that he would pray only if the captain agreed to set the sails to catch the breeze.

The captain didn't want to appear foolish to his crew by unfurling the sails when there was no wind. Again Mr. Taylor declared that he would pray for the boat only if the captain prepared the sails. Reluctantly, the captain agreed. After some time, the captain came into Mr. Taylor's stateroom and politely asked him to stop praying. The crew could hardly manage the vessel in the high winds that had arisen.

Often we find ourselves in a dilemma similar to the captain's. Seemingly impossible circumstances come our way and reasoning lessens our faith. Jesus used the example of the mustard seed to teach a lesson in faith. He explained in Mark 4:30–34 that although the mustard seed is the tiniest vegetable seed of all in these lands, it grows to be the largest garden plant. It grows so large that birds can perch in its branches. Jesus compares this principle to the kingdom of God. Even a little faith goes a long way in helping us grow in holiness and obedience. It is simply a matter of trusting God.

Faith the size of a mustard seed is all it takes. However, we must unfurl those sails.

Dear God, I want to walk with You in total faith and obedience.
I pray to You the prayer found in Mark 9:24, *"help me overcome my unbelief."*
In Jesus's name I pray. Amen.

# ❀ A Perfect Fit ❀

*For the word of God is living and powerful, and sharper than any two-edged sword, piercing even to the division of soul and spirit, and of joints and marrow, and is a discerner of the thoughts and intents of the heart* (Hebrews 4:12 NKJV).

It was just like a yucky funk or a hazy cloud hovering about my head. I knew in my *mind* I needed to forgive; yet I knew in my *heart* I still clutched onto the bitterness I was harboring against a friend. For days, I had cried out to God to remove the bitterness, but my flesh seemed to block every notion of wisdom God was giving in response to my cries. I felt like the Apostle Paul, battling my flesh, but this time I was on the losing team. As desperately as I wanted the freedom to forgive, a seed of bitterness had burrowed itself in my heart, and the situation called for major surgery.

The Word of God is the Great Physician's scalpel, and we come under the knife when we open our Bibles and submit ourselves by laying on the Surgeon's table, that great place of surrender. In my time of weakness, God prompted a friend to send a passage of Scripture to me, a passage that didn't directly speak to forgiveness, but was a perfect fit to my need. Like a scalpel removing that evil seed from my heart, or a key undoing the lock on the chains of bitterness I carried, God's Words immediately gave me the power and the "want to" I needed to forgive my friend. Once again, peace dwelt in my heart.

Are you engaged in a spiritual battle with your flesh? Open the Word of God, ask God to lead you to His message for your situation, and find victory as you submit yourself to the surgical tools of the Great Physician.

Lord, Your Words are indeed powerful and sufficient for every need in my life. Show me Your wisdom in Your Word today, and heal my broken places. I submit myself to You. Amen.

# ❁ Personal-Preference Christianity ❁

*"Everyone who calls on the name of the Lord will be saved"*
(Romans 10:13).

What does it mean to be a Christian? I asked. "Well, to me it means I do good things because I love God," replied one woman. "Personally, I think it means I believe Jesus died on the Cross for my sins and I pray to Jesus," added another. "I think being a Christian means that we love others more than we love ourselves like Jesus did," said the third.

The conversation could go on for days, each woman sharing what Christianity means to her individually. But do we each get to define personally what we believe it takes to call oneself a Christian?

The apostle Paul responded to this line of thinking in Romans 10:1–13. Paul started by recognizing the sincerity of his Jewish brothers' belief in God. Paul understood sincere belief. In Acts 22, we see that before meeting Christ, Paul was a God-worshiping, Scripture-quoting, warrant-toting Jewish zealot. He was so sincere that he fought tooth and nail against those who opposed his understanding of God. If sincerity saved, then Paul would have won first place.

But he was lost, separated by a great chasm from the God he longed to please. That's why in Romans 10:2 Paul could say that the Jews were "zealous for God, but their zeal is not based on knowledge." He added that they did not submit to God's requirements of righteousness, rather, defining righteousness to suit themselves. He added in Romans 10:4 that righteousness comes only through faith in Jesus Christ.

Some argue he meant that people just needed to believe things *about* Jesus that are true, such as that He lived and was a great prophet. Or, maybe he meant they must agree that Jesus died for sin and they should follow His sacrificial example, to call themselves Christians.

But, no, Paul didn't let them off the hook so easily. He stated emphatically the only way of salvation in Romans 10:9–10: not to proclaim Caesar as Lord God, but to declare Jesus alone as Lord God—the only one worthy of worship. Moreover, one must believe that Jesus died to pay for our sins and arose to live today. There was no wiggle room in the saving faith definition, no room for personal preferences. Which brings us to a question: Are you a Christian as *God* defines the word?

Lord, You are clear about what it means to be a Christian. Examine my heart to see if I am a true believer according to Your definition. Amen.

# ❀ *Stop, Drop, and Roll* ❀

*As Jesus walked beside the Sea of Galilee, he saw Simon and his brother*
*Andrew casting a net into the lake, for they were fishermen. "Come,*
*follow me," Jesus said, "and I will make you fishers of men. At once they*
*left their nets and followed him"* (Mark 1:16–18).

When Jesus called Simon Peter and his brother Andrew to follow Him as disciples, they stopped fishing, dropped their nets, and followed Him. We see this instant obedience in the next passage: James and John "left their father Zebedee, in the boat with the hired men" and followed Jesus on the spur of the moment! (Mark 1:20). Imagine Zebedee's surprise when his sons left him and rolled along with Jesus!

I love teaching preschool children. They entertain me! Each child is quite animated as they learn new things. I wish you could have seen them the day I taught them to "stop, drop, and roll"! When I gave the clue words, they stopped everything they were doing, dropped paper, crayons, and books on the floor, and rolled across the room to an exit, where I led them out.

In our Christian walk, we often know the right words, but we find excuses not to give God instant allegiance. We sometimes say in our prayers, *"Lord, I'd like to go on that missions trip, but I have a big deadline at work that week,"* or *"I'd like to help that homeless man, but I'm on my way to church."*

We could learn a lot from the early disciples—and from preschoolers. First, we might become better listeners to God's commands. Tuning-in our spirits to the Holy Spirit is an art. Second, we might learn to drop everything: prioritize, putting Jesus first. Third, we might consider responding along with others, like the phrase made famous on 9/11: "Let's roll." When Jesus calls, He wants active participation, not lazy, slow response. Let's roll on out! May each of us join other present-day disciples as we work in tandem with all Christians to serve Him.

Just stop, drop, and roll!

Dear Lord, help us to stop what we're doing in our everyday world,
drop the things that don't matter, and serve You in an active way,
rolling in Your service. Amen.

# ❀ *Pick and Choose* ❀

*"I am the way, the truth, and the life. No one comes to the Father*
*except through Me"* (John 14:6 NKJV).

If you are a mother, you'll agree with the motto "pick and choose your battles." In the home, parents must decide which moral beliefs and behaviors require immediate intervention, and which matters can be left to address another day. In the world, Christians must decide which points of doctrine are necessary and foundational when sharing Christ with the world, and which matters are better left to address when discipling new believers. When sharing Christ, you may be approached with many different "religious" questions from lost people. *How do I know if God is hearing my prayers? What if I don't want to go to church all the time? Does God care about what beverage I have with my meal?* Trying to answer every question can be exhausting, and not every doctrinal question must be settled before a person can place her faith in Jesus Christ as Savior. But how will you respond to someone who is unsure that Christianity is the only true "religion"? What would you say to someone who asks, "Does it matter to Jesus whether we believe that He is the only way to heaven?"

In John 14:6, Jesus responded to Thomas's question about the way to enter heaven. He made a plainspoken claim to be the only way to have a right relationship with God the Father. Each individual must decide if he or she believes Jesus, or if they are willing to say that Jesus is only "a" way, not "the" way.

Many of His fellow Jews in Jesus's day were skeptical of Jesus's claims. He told them, *"I am from above. You are of this world; I am not of this world. Therefore I said to you that you will die in your sins; for if you do not believe that I am He, you will die in your sins"* (John 8:23–24 NKJV). Because Jesus didn't backpedal from the truth to gain more followers, we can have full confidence that we can reach the world for Christ without having to bow to popular opinion, but by standing on every word of the Way, the Truth, and the Life — Jesus.

Father, my full faith is in Jesus my Savior. Help me stand firm in my belief that Jesus is the only way to salvation. Teach me to express this truth in love. Amen.

# ❀ *The Language of His Eyes* ❀

*"The eye is the lamp of the body. If your eyes are good, your whole body will be full of light"* (Matthew 6:22).

Buddy Collins' eyes were full of light. Years before I met him, Buddy had experienced a stroke that left him unable to talk. However, we were able to communicate with each other. Perhaps from my years of working with the deaf, I looked into his eyes for messages he was trying to convey.

One day his daughter, Cathy, called and asked me to come quickly to the hospital. Upon arriving, I found that Buddy had experienced heart failure and was taken to ICU. The family did not know if he was alive.

I sought out the appropriate medical personnel for information. The nurse explained that they had resuscitated Buddy and were getting ready to notify the family. She asked if I would like to see him.

When I walked into the room, I could tell Buddy had experienced something profound. He tried to express what he had seen. I assured him that I knew it was extraordinary and that his family was on their way to see him.

Some time later, Buddy and his wife, Joyce, were both hospitalized at the same time. Cathy again called and asked me to come quickly. I found that Buddy had taken a turn for the worse and appeared to be dying. His family gathered around him pleading with him to stay with them longer. I could sense his struggle to stay alive for their sakes.

After awhile the family realized they needed to release him. They had a precious time of closure as they expressed to him how much they loved him. Then, Joyce turned to me and said, "He seems to respond to your voice. Will you walk him home?"

I read Scripture to him, sang to him, talked to him, and in a few moments he peacefully entered into the presence of the Lord. In his honor, I wrote a poem titled, "The Language of His Eyes was the Language of His Heart." Truly he laughed and loved with his eyes!

Dear Lord, help our eyes reflect Your light to others around us.
In Jesus's name, amen.

# ❀ Just an Average Joe ❀

*The word of the LORD came to Jonah son of Amittai: "Go to the great*
*city of Nineveh and preach against it" .... But Jonah ran away from*
*the LORD and headed for Tarshish* (Jonah 1:1–3).

"Hold my hand," I said to my almost-two-year-old, Sara, as we walked
down our concrete driveway. She had learned to walk long before, but her
little feet sometimes got tangled, and the concrete was hard and unforgiving.
She took hold as I had instructed, but in a moment pulled away, wanting
to do it on her own, and headed in a different direction. A moment later the
inevitable stumble crashed her on the pavement, scraping the palms of her
hands as she tried to break the fall. A wail followed and much consoling
was required before she was ready to try again, this time holding firmly to
my hand.

It's a familiar story. The details may vary, but the theme is always the
same. God commands His child to obey, offering His hand to hold. But the
called one wants to do things his own way, and off he heads to Tarshish
instead of Nineveh.

We sympathize with Jonah. Who could blame him for running the
other way when the Ninevites were known for their cruelty? Nevertheless,
God had commanded him to go and preach to Nineveh.

What has God called us to do? We hear Him clearly. But our hearts
may scream, "Run!" and our feet are inclined to follow. As we contemplate
our choice, consider that though Jonah was a reluctant messenger, he was
the first cross-cultural missionary identified in the Bible. If he had known
God's Word would record his story for billions of yet-to-be born people to
read as an example of how God uses the average Joe to bring people to
their senses and seek God, would he have run away? I don't think so.

Jonah's story is written. But yours is yet to be recorded. Will we run
away to Tarshish, or will we head for Nineveh, holding God's hand?

God Almighty, though my heart trembles at Your call, I won't run away.
Knowing You hold me tight, I will do all that You have asked. Amen.

# ❀ Email from God ❀

*"Watch and pray"* (Matthew 26:41 NKJV).

Email has revolutionized communication in the modern world, and it certainly has impacted my lifestyle. My loved ones and I are busy, making it sometimes difficult to stay in touch. But with email, it's so easy to sit down for a quick minute, send out a question to a friend, and then return to my computer at my convenience to read her response. A quick minute here, a brief moment there—communication is fast and convenient to my schedule.

When we pray, are we communicating with God like using email? Do we sit down when we have a quick minute, shoot God a question, then rush off to do other things? Then later in the day, when we have another moment to spare, we check back in with God to see if He's got an answer waiting in our inboxes? God's always with us and willing to hear our prayers as we offer them up to Him with clean hands and pure hearts; however, God's called us to seek Him with all our being. He's told us to be watchful in our prayers and to wait on the Lord.

Regardless of how quickly we send out a question or a request to God, He'll respond to our need according to His timing, not our convenience. And in the meantime, God will build our faith, strengthen our testimonies, and teach us how to communicate with Him as Father and Friend.

Incorporate a new facet to your prayertime: patient listening. Open your spirit to whatever God wants to say to you. He may have an answer to a question you haven't even thought about asking yet! Wait upon the Lord; He is exalted, so be patient and know that His whispers to your heart are worth the wait. Rather than approaching prayer like using email, enjoy an encounter with Almighty God who will hear you from heaven.

Father, I confess I sometimes neglect the "listening" portion of my time of communication with You in prayer. What do You want to bring before my heart today? I am watchful now as I pray. Amen.

# ❧ A God-Ready Woman ❧

*God sticks his head out of heaven. He looks around. He's looking for …*
*just one God-ready woman* (Psalm 14:2 *The Message*).

Are you God-ready? Since I'm a woman, I study the "God-ready woman" in the verse above as a personal ideal a Christian woman like me should follow. Here are the characteristics of a God-ready woman.

1. We give God our hearts, even if we don't understand all we should know about Him. Paul says, *"Live a life of love, just as Christ loved us and gave himself up for us as a fragrant offering and sacrifice to God"* (Ephesians 5:2). We don't worry about understanding all the concepts in the Scriptures. We'll never accomplish that. We just take the leap of faith, believing we're *"justified freely by his grace through the redemption that came by Christ Jesus"* (Romans 3:24). That's the only way we can live as God-ready women.

2. We give God our bodies, even if we're lazy or tired. If we're not motivated to give our total physical beings to God, Paul says, *"Therefore, I urge you, brothers, in view of God's mercy, to offer your bodies as living sacrifices, holy and pleasing to God—this is your spiritual act of worship"* (Romans 12:1). Notice three words in this passage that describe us: *holy, pleasing, worship [ful]*. How can any of us be holy, since only God Himself is holy? We accept Christ into our hearts, asking Him to *make us holy*, pleasing God at all times—not perfect ourselves, but depending on Jesus's perfection.

3. We give God our minds, even if they're cynical and petty. Paul explains: *"Do not conform any longer to the pattern of this world, but be transformed by the renewing of your mind. Then you will be able to test and approve what God's will is—his good, pleasing and perfect will"* (Romans 12:2). If we turn our backs on the secular world, asking God to transform us by renewing our minds, then we're God-ready women!

Dear God, help me love You with all my heart, serve You with all my body's strength, and praise You with a renewed mind, according to Your will. Amen.

# ❀ *Keeping Your Eyes on the Prize* ❀

*"I do not run like a man running aimlessly; I do not fight like a man
beating the air"* (1 Corinthians 9:26).

In the bottom of the ninth inning, the team was behind by one run. Bases were loaded and they had two outs. The fans and players considered Mark the ultimate chance for his team to win the championship.

A thunderous roar came from the stands as he came to bat. The crowd chanted, "Go Mark! Go Mark!" Fans held posters and signs throughout the stadium: "MARK's our man! We know he can!" "Get on your MARK! Get set! Win!" "We're #1! MARK it down!"

Tapping the bat on home plate a few times, he steadied his feet and crouched into his favorite batting stance. The sound of the ball cracking the wooden bat echoed through the ballpark. It was a foul to the left. "S-t-r-i-k-e one!"

With the second pitch, Mark slammed the ball, but it sped just behind first base. "S-t-r-i-k-e two!" Mark's hands began to sweat. The chanting of the crowd increased. The fans rose to their feet. All eyes and all hopes were on Mark. He took a deep breath and settled back into his batting stance.

The pitcher threw the ball and for one millisecond Mark's eyes veered to first base where he was preparing to run. He drew back the bat and swung as hard as he could. SWHOOSH! He had swung only at the air. Although it had been just one fraction of a second, Mark had taken his eyes off the ball.

Paul reminds us in today's Scripture that if we do not keep our eyes on the prize, we are like a man who is fighting but only beating the air. What is that prize? It is the heavenly crown promised to those who remain faithful to God throughout life. No reward on earth can even begin to compare to it!

Dear God, help me when I look at the circumstances around me and
take my eyes off the prize. Please help me stay focused daily on the prize
that will last forever. In Jesus's name I pray. Amen.

# ❋ *Sympathy Pains* ❋

*Neither fornicators, nor idolaters, nor adulterers, nor homosexuals,*
*nor sodomites, nor thieves, nor covetous, nor drunkards, nor revilers,*
*nor extortioners will inherit the kingdom of God. And such were some*
*of you. But you were washed, but you were sanctified, but you were*
*justified in the name of the Lord Jesus and by the Spirit of our God*
(1 Corinthians 6:9–11 NKJV).

Have you ever noticed how pregnancy tends to break out in a church and spread like wildfire? In the last "wave" of pregnancy to hit my church, I was shocked at how affected I was by the experience. I am now the mother of three robust and beautiful children, two by birth and one by adoption, but I battled infertility for several years before my first child was conceived.

When I recently began to hear friend after friend announcing her pregnancy, I was thrilled at everyone's good news, but feelings of loss and sadness washed over me. I hadn't felt the pain of infertility in years, but old emotions resurfaced, and I relived the hurt all over again. I quickly recomposed myself when my brain reminded my heart of my three children, but immediately I felt sorrow for my friends who still have an unfulfilled longing for a child. I was experiencing genuine sympathy.

We can better sympathize with hurting souls when we've walked that same path of pain they're traveling. As Paul explains that the unrighteous won't enter heaven, he follows with a startling statement that makes the redeemed sit up and take notice: *and such were some of you* (v. 11). Lest we forget we also were once dead in trespasses and sin, we do well to approach the lost with compassion and patience, and not with contempt and scorn. We can sympathize with the lost soul because we were once lost ourselves.

Your ministry to the lost will strengthen as your compassion deepens. All sin—no matter the category—separates us from God. As you interact with sinners in need of a Savior, take a loving approach, as one who can sympathize.

Lord, may I never lose sight of who I used to be apart from Your grace.
Give me compassion for the lost that springs out of gratefulness to You.
In Jesus's name, amen.

# ❁ *Ungodly Sorrow* ❁

*Godly sorrow brings repentance that leads to salvation and leaves no*
*regret, but worldly sorrow brings death* (2 Corinthians 7:10).

Peter and Judas. Have you ever thought about how much they were alike? Both had walked with the Lord for three years. Both ate with Him and sat at His feet daily to learn from Him. Both served the Lord and served *with* the Lord, at least externally. Both failed the Lord miserably; both regretted their failures.

So, how is it that Peter was restored and Judas's life ended so dismally? Their stories reveal the difference between godly sorrow and the sorrow that leads to death. Peter's life showed marks of godly sorrow not evident in Judas's life. For instance, Peter's declaration that Jesus was indeed the Messiah, the long-awaited One, revealed a regenerated heart of faith. As much as we fault him for his failure, we identify with Peter's inconsistencies. One moment he draws his sword, prepared to fight to the death for Jesus, yet moments later he panics when called, not to draw his sword, but simply to name himself as the Lord's disciple.

Judas, on the other hand, while serving beside the Lord for those three years, must never really have repented of his selfishness or trusted Jesus as Savior. The Scripture reveals that his betrayal was no momentary lapse of judgment. He wasn't just immature. He was unrepentant, greedy, and self-consumed. Some time before his betraying action, when the woman anointed Jesus with expensive perfume, Judas reprimanded the Lord for accepting the extravagant gift, not because he thought the perfume should have been sold to provide money for the poor but because he regularly pilfered from the treasury. His betrayal was the culminating action in a long line of betrayals that revealed his true heart.

Peter's and Judas's stories remind me that it is possible to be sorry without repenting. One sorrow leads to bitterness and death, the other to repentance and restoration. The question is which characterizes our own lives?

Father, like Peter and Judas, I have failed You. Reveal to me sin for which I have felt remorse but have not repented. Forgive and restore me. Amen.

# ❀ A Pillow for Jesus ❀

*Jesus replied, "Foxes have holes and birds of the air have nests, but the Son of Man has no place to lay his head"* (Matthew 8:20).

As a pre-teen I accepted Jesus into my heart and began the most exciting relationship in my life! His presence filled every part of me. I grew closer to Him daily, learning more about His dynamic Spirit in my life, His rollicking sense of humor, and His miraculous supernatural movement in my environment that left me breathless.

However, only in the last few years have I thought how much each Christian means to Him as a *friend*. Scriptures say He rejoices when we accept Him as Savior. We know we make Him happy when we obey Him and live in the Spirit, worthy of our calling. But have you ever considered how you, as a friend, could bring Jesus *comfort*?

Dietrich Bonhoeffer lived in Nazi Germany during World War II. His friends helped him escape twice, but he kept returning to the place of suffering, fully aware of the danger, because he wanted *to comfort Christ*, who was distressed by the abuse, torture, and deaths of the children of God.

Think about that phrase, *to comfort Christ*. Did you ever place a pillow under your parents' heads to make them comfortable when they were sick, or reach down tenderly where your children had fallen asleep and slip a pillow under their heads? Think of ways you could bring comfort to Jesus Himself. We know He shed tears over Jerusalem, such a lost city in His day. He must cry over many of our cities today. What can you do personally to bring joy to Him? How can you eliminate His tears today?

Determine ways you can provide a "pillow" for Jesus by drawing near Him or reaching out to others. Try the pillow of worship, the pillow of sacrifice, the pillow of joy, or the pillow of service. Show Him you mean it when you say you care about His comfort.

Dear Jesus, I want to provide a pillow for You today. Thank You for providing so many comfort pillows for me. Help me draw near Your heart and place my own version of a pillow beneath Your holy head. Amen.

# ❀ *Bygones* ❀

*"I have sinned against heaven and before you, and I am no longer*
*worthy to be called your son"* (Luke 15:18–19 NKJV).

A good friend recently apologized to me for something she did several years ago. I was astounded! I hadn't thought about the incident in years. There was not a trace of malice between us because of what had happened back then, but she felt compelled to offer an official apology. She had a peace and a sense of joy in her voice. I was greatly humbled and impressed with her high esteem of forgiveness and her love for our friendship. She made such an impression on me that I was sure I'd be quicker to apologize the next time I had wronged someone.

Do you have difficulty apologizing when you've hurt a friend? As you've matured in your Christian faith, perhaps you run swiftly into God's arms with repentant lips when you have sinned, but it's a different situation to approach another human to admit your shortcomings to her. Saying "I'm sorry" was not easy for the prodigal son either, for he'd shown wanton disrespect to his father and their family. He'd disappointed his father by his reckless actions, but he also had wounded his father's heart, making a selfish choice despite the consequences to their personal relationship. The prodigal must have been truly repentant and humble in spirit, though, because he didn't feel worthy for his father to restore their father-son relationship, asking to be only his father's servant. He admitted his wrongdoing, and he spoke with a genuine attitude of remorse, just as we must go before the Heavenly Father to confess our sins.

In like fashion, God is pleased when we confess our wrongdoings to one another. Not only does confession mend relationships, but also it strengthens the bond between brothers and sisters in Christ, we who above all should understand the power of forgiveness as it comes down from our Heavenly Father.

God, how can I ever thank You enough for the forgiveness You've given me for my sins through Jesus Christ? Whom have I wronged? Guide me to go humbly with a repentant heart to ask for forgiveness. May my willingness to apologize be an inspiration to others. Amen.

# ❀ New Thoughts on Old Hurts ❀

*Do not be grieved or angry with yourselves, because you sold me here,*
*for God sent me before you to preserve life* (Genesis 45:5 NASB).

We called them "sword drills" when I was a kid. During family devotionals, my sister, Lynna Rea, and I stood at attention, my parents called out a Scripture reference and said, "Go!" and then we raced to find the passage in our Bibles. The winner got to read the verse aloud. Sword drills are on my list of "affirming" childhood experiences. They helped set my course toward God that carried into adulthood. Other affirming experiences include my mother singing us to sleep with the Lord's Prayer and my dad praising my first efforts at preparing to teach a Sunday School lesson when I was in fifth grade.

Experiences during our growing-up years influence our thoughts, beliefs, and actions into adulthood. The affirming experiences are positive investments in our character development, giving us a sense of safety and a can-do attitude. Conversely, hurtful childhood experiences may have left us scarred, fearful, and unwilling to trust God.

Joseph could have identified with that feeling. Dumped in a pit and then sold to slave traders by his big brothers, he ended up in a foreign country. He must have been confused and terrified. Perhaps the first few years he cried himself to sleep many nights, homesick for his family. Perhaps he prayed his father would come find him and wondered why he had not. Over the years his fear easily could have crystallized into bitter hatred for his brothers who had abused him.

But when Joseph was finally reunited with his brothers, instead of seething with bitterness and revenge, he affirmed God's working in and through his life, even through the awful experience of being betrayed and kidnapped. Joseph teaches us that while fear and confusion are normal childhood responses to mistreatment and hurt, once we are adults, we are granted the wonderful gift of reviewing those experiences through the filter of God's love and divine purpose. When we forgive and determine to trust God, He can free us from bitterness and bring joy once again to our hearts.

Father, I choose to forgive those who've hurt me
and trust You as Joseph did. Amen.

# ❀ *Two Sides to Everything* ❀

*"We live by faith, not by sight"* (2 Corinthians 5:7).

God created everything with balance. We can see this principle in nature: the planets are balanced with perfect tension to hold them in place. Earth contains the precise balance of water and air to sustain life.

Even a small lima bean illustrates a tremendous truth of life: everything is complex, with at least two sides to balance it. If you plant and water a dried lima bean, (a *dicot* seed, from which we get the word *dichotomy*), it sprouts two equal leaves in the sunlight. Each leaf balances the other on the stem, which quickly grows sets of similar leaf-pairs that pull against each other to balance the plant as it shoots upward.

Most of life contains a tension between opposite forces: light versus dark, north versus south, evil versus good, and so forth. Sometimes we become confused when facing the juxtaposition of basic pulls in life. Paul says it's a spiritual dilemma: *"What I do is not the good I want to do; no, the evil I do not want to do—this I keep on doing.... when I want to do good, evil is right there with me. For in my inner being I delight in God's law; but I see another law at work in the members of my body, waging war against the law of my mind and making me a prisoner of the law of sin at work within my members"* (Romans 7:19–23).

God has a solution for this human dilemma. We have the Holy Spirit, Who indwells us. He helps us reject the bad, living for good. Paul says, *"So we fix our eyes not on what is seen but on what is unseen. For what is seen is temporary, but what is unseen is eternal"* (2 Corinthians 4: 18). We can walk in the Spirit, rejecting old habits of walking in the flesh, or sinfulness.

And here's the greatest dichotomy: we don't have to be perfect. God says, *"My grace is sufficient for you, for my power is made perfect in weakness"* (2 Corinthians 12:9).

Lord, thank You for creating balance in life. Help us live in the world but walk in the Spirit, by faith. Amen.

# ❀ *Making Distinctions* ❀

*Be of the same mind toward one another. Do not set your mind on high things, but associate with the humble* (Romans 12:16 NKJV).

Imagine you just moved into your community, and you're attending your church for the first time. In your mind's eye, see the people who attend your church as they make their way down the aisles and select their seats. Study each person's features, examine their outfits, and take note of the way they talk and how they act. If you were this newcomer in the crowd, to whom would you gravitate? With whom would you want to be friends, and why?

Every TV commercial and magazine ad emphasizes that who you are is determined by what you wear and what you own. Don't like yourself? The world encourages you to *buy* a new image. These false messages are so prevalent that you may start to believe the lies yourself.

Paul teaches not to set your mind on high things—bowing to status symbols or making life a popularity contest—but to associate with the humble. Paul isn't dictating you befriend only the people who don't own expensive things, but he's calling attention to the criterion you use to select your associations. Just as God offers His love to each person freely and equally, He's calling you to look beyond a person's physical appearance and possessions to connect with the person inside.

Now imagine you're walking down a crowded street, overwhelmed by the sights and sounds of an unfamiliar city. People are mingling in their crowds of distinction—the wealthy socialites, the clean-cut business crowd, the trendy coffee-drinkers, and the weary homeless. God urges your heart to share Christ with a stranger. Whom will you choose? Will you shy away from those wealthier than you, fearing their status? Will you avoid the homeless, fearing their neediness? The human eye sees individuals who are different on the surface, but the spiritual eye sees no differences among these souls, all equally lost, equally in need of the good news of a Savior who died for all.

Father, teach me not to allow social barriers to determine my willingness to share the love of Christ with the people You place in my path. Amen.

# ❀ *The Harvest* ❀

*Then he said to his disciples, "The harvest is plentiful
but the workers are few"* (Matthew 9:37).

This narrative occurred early in Jesus's ministry. He already knew
the heartache of not having enough disciples to meet the needs of the
multitudes that followed Him. God could have chosen to help the masses
in many different ways. However, He chose to reach the world, both then
and now, through His disciples. God's compassion for the world must be
lived through us.

My parents live in the rural area of my hometown. I love to visit them.
It seems that when I walk through their back door, every muscle in my
body relaxes. One of my favorite things to do while there is to help my
father pick ripe vegetables in his garden. After all his hard work of planting,
fertilizing, watering, and weeding, he allows me the fun of helping him reap
the harvest.

Last summer my father was in a serious car accident. Since internal
injuries kept him from being able to harvest his garden, the neighbors on
either side of my parents came daily to pick the vegetables for him. Without
those wonderful neighbors, my father would have lost his garden.

When I go to visit my parents, my father has already done all the hard
work. I simply enjoy harvesting the fruits (and vegetables) of his labor.
Similarly, when it comes to sharing the gospel, our heavenly Father has
done all the hard work. He allows us to join in the fun of helping with the
harvest!

One thing I've learned from my father's garden is that if the garden is
not picked when ripe, the harvest is lost. Jesus pleads for us to work while
souls are ripe so the harvest will not be lost.

Dear Lord, we pray as You taught us to do,
"Please send more laborers into the field." In Jesus's name, amen.

---

\* *My father died not long after I wrote this devotional. Only now does he realize the harvest of souls he helped bring
into God's kingdom.*

# ❀ What Would I Do? ❀

*But the end of all things is at hand* (1 Peter 4:7 KJV).

Do you ever not want to witness? I admit, sometimes I want to go to the movies, or eat in a restaurant, or visit with friends, or checkout at the grocery store, without the ever-present concern over the eternal destiny of each person I come across—whether neighbor, relative, or stranger. But just when I'm tempted to go home, close my garage door, and take the phone off the hook, I think of how short our time is, and how His return is one second sooner with every tick of the clock. As I pondered the countdown toward eternity and Christ's call to share Him, I wrote:

What would I do, if I knew, You were coming back today,
How would it change the way I think, what I do, and what I say,
Would my fear still choke the words, leave Your message yet unheard,
What would I do, if I knew, what would I do?

I wonder sometimes, Lord, if I believe You,
That Light is light, and dark is dark, and people die and go to hell,
That I may be the only chance for someone to receive You,
If I knew—I know, I know I'd tell....

What would I do, if I knew someone cried alone one night,
And in my hands I held the hope, a searing, holy, healing Light,
Would I hide it deep inside, leave the hurting one to die,
What would I do, if I knew, what would I do?

I wonder sometimes, Lord, if I believe You,
That Light is light, and dark is dark, and people die and go to hell,
That I may be the only chance for someone to receive You,
If I knew, what would I do, what would I do?

What would I do, if I knew, that when I failed to speak Your name,
Though the loss was great, Your precious blood could heal my shame,
That You'd grant me courage still, another chance to do Your will,
What would I do, if I knew, what would I do?

© Tricia Scribner, 1999

Father, keep my priorities eternal, my passion ignited, and my perseverance strong. In the name of Jesus, Faithful and True One, Amen.

# ❀ God's Perfect Timing ❀

*And he determined the time set for them and the exact places
where they should live. God did this so that men would seek him
and perhaps reach out for him and find him, though he is not far
from each one of us* (Acts 17:26–27).

Our church planned a missions trip to New Jersey. We stopped along the way to allow the participants to enjoy various tourist sites. We also stopped by Baltimore so I could visit my grandmother who was in a nursing home there.

My husband, Wayne, and I entered her room and found her unresponsive. She had become critically ill while we were en route. I immediately planned to stay there and not go on with the missions trip. However, her nurses encouraged me to go on, explaining she might remain in that condition for days or even weeks.

I called my mother in South Carolina to let her know of Granny's serious condition. Then, leaning over the bed, I held Granny in my arms as I expressed to her how much I loved her and what a wonderful grandmother she was. I thanked her for the weeks of summer vacations I spent with her and all the fun we had. Then I talked of spiritual things, and I asked Wayne to pray with her.

After the prayer, as I held my precious grandmother in my arms, she breathed her last breath. I looked at Wayne and asked, "Is she gone?"

He simply said, "I'll get the nurse."

The nurse asked us to leave the room. She came back out into the hall and found me crying. "Honey, please don't cry. Your grandmother is better off," she assured me.

I explained that I was crying because God is so good He allowed Wayne and me to be there with her. In God's perfect timing, He planned for us—on our way from South Carolina to New Jersey—to make the all-important stop in Baltimore.

Dear Lord, thank You for Your attention to every detail of our lives.
In Jesus's name, amen.

# ❀ Cheer on the Runners ❀

*And let us consider one another in order to stir up love and good works,
not forsaking the assembling of ourselves together, as is the manner of
some, but exhorting one another, and so much the more as you see the
Day approaching* (Hebrews 10:24–25 NKJV).

Jane is running in a big race. Some of her church family comes to her
privately, saying she's too out of shape to run. Others publicly discourage
her from running. Some people would never tell Jane to her face, but they
will be talking about her in the church parking lot, saying how foolish Jane
is to think she can compete in a race. Other church members won't know
about it, because they don't care enough about Jane to keep up with her
or anybody else in the church. They come only when it's convenient; they
don't take time to get involved in the lives of others.

But then there is a crowd that loves Jane, and they believe she's
capable of doing all things through Christ's strength. They want Jane to
succeed, but they're also thrilled at her willingness to try. They say, "I'm
praying for you," and mean it. Some will offer to train with Jane, others will
want to babysit for her during the race, or sponsor her with new running
shoes. On race day, this is the crowd who'll be there to cheer Jane along
the way. They'll offer her water along the path, and she'll see their faces on
the home stretch, when her muscles are tightening and her feet are getting
sore. They'll call out to Jane, "Run! Don't quit! We believe in you! You're
not alone!" These people are the champions of Hebrews 10:24– 25.

Christian encouragers regularly plan how they can support others to
do the very best they can for Christ. They play a vital role in the life of any
church. Rather than stirring up trouble, they stir up love and good works.
Are you a Christian encourager? Are you cheering on the runners?

Heavenly Father, I want to encourage my brothers and sisters in Christ.
Who needs encouragement today? Please guide me in a plan to lift her up.
Amen.

# ❀ Stop and Smell the Memories ❀

*Train a child in the way he should go, and when he is old he will not turn from it* (Proverbs 22:6).

I began the task of cleaning out my closet. As usual, I had four piles of clothes on the floor: those to pack away until next season; those to give away; those to throw away; and those to keep until I fit in them again.

Our two daughters, Meri Beth and Molly, came home from their college classes about an hour apart. To my amazement, they reacted the same way to an old calico dress from the 1970s, a floor-length "maxi-dress," that was in the throwaway pile. Both girls begged me keep it.

I laughingly pointed out to them the pitiful condition of the dress. They explained as they buried their faces in the old calico dress. "All we have to do is smell this and it takes us back to when we were little girls on Friday night."

Friday night at our house was "family night." I would wear the calico dress, Wayne would cook steaks on the grill, and I'd place TV trays in front of the television. We'd cuddle up, eat our steaks, and watch *The Dukes of Hazzard*.

I had no idea what those nights meant to them. I knew only how special they were to Wayne and me.

Five years ago we moved to a new pastorate and left the town where our precious daughters and their husbands live. I made each of them a teddy bear. My friend took the back out of the calico dress and made each bear a dress from the calico fabric. I recorded a message that is activated by pressing a paw on each of the bears. "If ever you are feeling blue, just cuddle this bear and know that my heart is with you." Now they can stop from time to time and smell the memories.

Dear Lord, thank You for helping us relive happy times in life
through precious memories. In Jesus's name, amen.

# ❀ The Season of Singing ❀

*Flowers appear on the earth; the season of singing has come, the cooing of doves is heard in our land* (Song of Songs 2:12).

The Song of Songs is more than an earthly love story. This truth can be seen through the meanings of many of the phrases in the Hebrew context. It foreshadows the love between God and His people.

One thing is seen clearly in this short book of the Bible. It beautifully paints with words the progression of love. In Song of Songs 2:1–12, "first love" is developing to a deeper level. It can be a picture of our maturing relationship with Christ.

In Israel, there are basically two seasons—winter and summer. In winter—late September to March—it rains frequently. Winter often is associated with bondage. Summer, on the other hand, is bright and sunny. This passage proclaims that the oppression of winter has passed and the beauty and freedom of summer have arrived.

Jesus, our Bridegroom, released us from the shackles of sin. For those who have accepted His love and chosen to become His bride, *"the season of singing has come, the cooing of doves is heard in our land"* (Song of Songs 2:12).

We would do well to take some lessons from birds. Life is not always easy for them. They have to face incredible hardships in their flights of life. Yet no matter what, they are faithful to sing. The Hebrew words that are used in this verse mean more than merely the singing of the birds. The language implies that it is a time for singing for all. This verse seems to express, "It is time for every living being to sing God's praises!"

Life has been described as a series of seasons. Which season are you in at this time? Have you responded to the love of the Bridegroom and passed from winter into summer, or are you still in the dreariness of winter? The birds are singing. Do you hear them? Even more importantly, are you singing with them? The time of the singing has come.

Dear Lord, like the birds, please let me sing of Your glory!
In Jesus's name, amen.

# ❀ No Pulling the "God Card" ❀

*Ezra had devoted himself to the study and observance of the Law of the
LORD, and to teaching its decrees and laws in Israel* (Ezra 7:10).

Do you ever feel panicked when a friend asks a question about Christianity
you can't answer? Most of us can identify with that feeling.

We tend to respond, "You just have to have faith in God." It's true that
believing is the key. But we shouldn't be surprised when the person with
whom we are talking responds,

"There you go, pulling the God card."

"What do you mean?" we might ask.

"Every time I ask a question about Christianity, you just say, 'You just
have to have faith that the God of Christianity is real.' That's no answer
at all."

After such a dialogue, we shut down, retreating into our cocoon of personal faith, assuring ourselves that lost people are just hostile and simply
cannot understand faith. Besides, we reason, most people already think that
Christians are pushy, hypocritical, narrow-minded and bigoted. There's no
sense in antagonizing them.

But, instead of retreating, we can rationally and lovingly respond to the
questions of unbelievers, breaking down walls and opening their minds to
the possibility that Christianity is true. How? By preparing ourselves.

If we as believers want to be able to respond intelligently and be used,
then we need to prepare. Ezra was an Old Testament prophet whom God
used to bring His people, the Israelites, back to their homeland out of
Babylonian captivity, paving the way for the Messiah to come later, as was
prophesied, out of the land of Israel.

It strikes me that Ezra, chapter 7, records twice in the first eight verses
that God's hand was upon Ezra because Ezra was devoted to the study of
God's Law. He was able to speak the truth and lead God's people because
he had determined to study what God said and live out God's truth.

Are you willing to study?

God, give me a passion for knowing You that will equip me to answer
the good questions people ask about Christianity. Amen.

# ❀ *Giving Thanks* ❀

*Give thanks in all circumstances, for this is God's will for you
in Christ Jesus* (1 Thessalonians 5:18).

I wasn't feeling well that week. I sat in my living room looking at family pictures: my late mother and husband, my children, my sisters, their husbands and children, grandchildren…. the list goes on. I began to pray, giving thanks to God for my relationships with each one. I remembered a precious moment here, a sad time there, and unforgettable joy over births of newborns in some of the extended family. I knew every favorite article of clothing, and many a relationship they had with the Lord—all a blessing in their own way. Then I thought of those I wished were different, thinking how I could change them.

Sometimes God gives us moments of recuperation so we'll pause to meditate on His ways. There's an old saying, "He puts you flat on your back so the only way you can look is up." That day, as I sat thinking about my family, I ran across the verse above: *"Give thanks in all circumstances,"* and I cried out, "But, Lord, I'm sick. How can I thank You for that?" I felt His presence in a special way that day, as if He were saying, "Be still, my child, and look up. All is well in *every* circumstance."

Suddenly a great truth rushed forth: in the worst moments, nothing had wiped me away. God had been there to see me through. Because of Him, family, and Christian friends, I made it! God had enriched me, made me stronger through every trial.

I read the second half of this verse, *"This is God's will for you."* If we grasp the certainty in this verse, we'll rejoice daily. God's will is for us not to try to change others, or worry, complain, or strain against His will. Our personal relationship with Him, the most important one, enables us to bend to His will and welcome every relationship with open arms, singing, praising Him, and helping others.

The last line in the verse comforted me: *"in Christ Jesus."* As long as I am in Him, all is well. I can give thanks for *everything*.

Lord, forgive us when we whine. Help us to thank You
for every relationship we have. Amen.

# ❀ One Size Doesn't Fit All ❀

*In him the whole building is joined ["fitly framed," KJV] together and
rises to become a holy temple in the Lord* (Ephesians 2:21).

A large woman stood in the plus-sizes section of a big department store.
"One size does *not* fit all!" she yelled in a loud voice. Embarrassed customers
scurried out of the area. Sales clerks were nowhere in sight.

The woman was right. One size doesn't fit all people, despite the tags'
claims. From nightgowns to sweat shirts, one size does not even fit the
people that usually wear that one size! Each of us is so different that a size
11 woman can wear a size 10, 12, or 13.

I have wide toes and a narrow heel. When I shop for shoes, if the toes
fit, the loose heel slips up and down. If the heel fits, the shoe pinches my
toes. Last week, as I tried on shoes, Ephesians 6:15 came to mind: *"And with
your feet fitted with the readiness that comes from the gospel of peace." At least my feet
are ready to go with the gospel*, I thought, as I tried on another pair of shoes with
tight toes.

The Bible is filled with examples of diversity, such as the incident of David
trying on King Saul's battle armor, which didn't fit (1 Samuel 17:38–39), or
the two different temperaments of sisters Mary and Martha, whose personalities didn't seem to fit into the same family.

At times when we become weary of adjusting to diversity in our
churches or neighborhoods, we can pause to reflect on God's wide arms
of acceptance. He accepts all humanity. In God's eyes, one size of love,
salvation, and inclusiveness fits all. Once saved by God to live in unity, the
church fits together and rises to the occasion: it's a holy sanctuary, a temple
for all people. While we adjust our witness to accommodate all cultures and
ethnicity (and all size 2s as well as size 2Xs), we also communicate with the
whole world through the same-size gospel: come on in! One size—in the
greatest sense—does fit all here!

Lord, whether our church fellowship is large or small, help us welcome all into
the sanctuary of God without excluding anyone. Amen.

# ❀ It'll Come Out in the Rinse ❀

*"Ask and it will be given to you; seek and you will find; knock and the door will be opened to you"* (Matthew 7:7).

I first met Peggy Means when a new student with multiple disabilities joined our deaf preschool class. Although Angela was almost five, she was small and could not walk or talk and was still in diapers. Peggy became her personal aide.

Peggy's Christian faith was strong. When the children took their naps, we prayed together and asked God to guide us in teaching them. Two weeks after Peggy started, Angela began walking. Within a month she was out of diapers.

Peggy worked diligently with Angela trying to help her recognize shapes and colors. However, Angela seemed to have a mental block. I also noticed that she could not release a ball. She stood and held it tightly, but it would not leave her hand.

I felt that the inability to release the ball correlated with the learning block. We asked God to show us a way to reach her.

Sitting on the floor, I repeatedly threw the ball to her. She got it but could not throw it back. Peggy attentively observed us the whole time. After awhile she said, "Brown, what don't come out in the wash will come out in the rinse." Those words encouraged me to keep believing that someday we would see the breakthrough.

Finally, I said, "Come on, Angela, one more time." I threw the ball and, without even thinking, made a sound, "bupp."

Angela, who had some residual hearing, got the ball. She looked at me, said "bupp," and threw it back to me. My heart raced, and Peggy rose from her chair. *Could it be that simple?* we both wondered.

I threw the ball again and said, "bupp." Angela did the same back to me. The sound clued her to release the ball.

Peggy and I rejoiced as we thanked Jesus. We asked Him and sought answers. He opened the door. Within days Angela could recognize colors and shapes. Indeed, our answer had "come out in the rinse."

Dear Lord, thank You for answering our prayers in Your timing and Your way. In Jesus's name, amen.

# ❧ Watch for Hidden Black Ice ❧

*"Leave your gift there in front of the altar. First go and be reconciled with your brother; then come and offer your gift"* (Matthew 5:24).

I was excited about giving my testimony in a nearby church on the upcoming Sunday morning. A bit of snow disappeared as the sun shone high in the azure-blue sky. It was beautiful! In my best dress, high heels, and new sunglasses—with my notes and Bible tucked under my arm—I sailed out the front door into the driveway. Slipping on a strip of hidden black ice, I fell, breaking my elbow. I was surprised when I couldn't get up off the slippery pavement. I had to scream for help and wait for a neighbor to rescue me.

Sometimes Christian leaders make the same mistake I made that morning: looking at the world through rose-colored glasses, believing all is well. They don't notice—or they choose to ignore—trouble brewing just under the surface. Instead of honest discussion, some leaders prefer to ignore unpleasant situations that need addressing, hoping hidden problems will melt away.

Consider Jesus's directions on giving alms at the temple in today's Scripture verse. Besides money, our gifts come in many varieties. Some are gifted in optimism, others in managing details for completing a project, others in hospitality, some in keeping the letter of the law—while others in flexibility. As each leader lays her leadership gift on the altar, she knows God accepts it, but do others appreciate her gift the way she does? If not, conflicts can build like hidden black ice, sometimes just under the surface.

One of the hardest things for Christian leaders is addressing, mediating, and resolving conflict. The leader must recognize controversy and reconcile with other leaders so the group can move on.

Good leadership includes this evaluation process. As we lay our leadership gifts on the altar before God, we include discussion in every planning time. We look for hidden black ice, dig it out, and make sure everyone is aware of hidden dangers. Then we use our gifts to lead on!

Lord, help us to evaluate to be sure we are on the right path,
clear hidden problems, and then use all our gifts to serve You. Amen.

# ❊ I Affirm ❊

*"But let your 'Yes' be 'Yes,' and your 'No,' 'No'"*
(Matthew 5:37 NKJV).

I recently had to complete some official forms, and the last line above my signature offered the option to check whether I would "swear" or "affirm" that the information I had given was accurate. How curious that a form of the United States government would take into consideration my preference of wording about my truthfulness. As I wrote my signature to complete the form, I couldn't help but be curious about what interesting story was behind those two options for me to check.

Regardless of whether or not we have to affirm officially the truth of what we're saying, our words can be completely reliable when we follow this simple principle of Jesus given above. In the context Jesus says these words, He forbids us to give an oath. When we require ourselves to speak only truth, there's no need to swear, as if the words *I swear* could make our words more believable.

To paraphrase Jesus, *mean what you say, and say what you mean.* Do you have a solid record of reliability? Telling the truth is difficult for some Christians who must fight the temptation to say what is convenient to avoid consequences for mistakes or to place the blame on someone else. Others of us feel tempted to embellish a story for entertainment, while some of us struggle to follow through and do what we have said we would do when we volunteered to help with a task. As you consider which of these temptations attacks you most often, realize that your commitment to being truthful matters not only to your relationships with friends and family, but also to your relationship with God. Weigh your words carefully, or refrain from saying anything at all, only let your "yes" be "yes" and your "no" be "no."

Heavenly Father, I want to be a reliable person in what I say.
Please place a guard over my mouth, and teach me to say only what is true,
no matter what the consequences to me. Teach me to think and pray before
I make a commitment that I cannot fulfill. In the name of Jesus I pray, amen.

# ❊ Rest and Refreshment ❊

*Blessed are the dead who die in the Lord from now on.*
*"Yes," says the Spirit, "they will rest from their labor,*
*for their deeds will follow them"* (Revelation 14:13).

We are all familiar with the sight of a tombstone engraved with the letters *R.I.P.* As a child I often wondered about the association of a tombstone with the word *rip*. Later, I learned that it was an abbreviation for *Rest in Peace*, which conjures frightening feelings for many people.

However, God's Word teaches that just the opposite should be true. Rest in Peace is a promise given to all who die in the Lord. To "die in the Lord" is to have "lived in the Lord" choosing to follow Jesus.

Those who die in the Lord are referred to as "blessed," the Greek word *makarios*, carrying overtones of "supremely blest, fortunate, well off, happy." This is certainly a far cry from the scary R.I.P. on a lonely tombstone.

The latter part of today's verse explains why those who die in the Lord are well off and happy. They are truly "at rest." They are not at rest in the sense of nothingness, but in the sense of "rest and refreshment." They rest from the trials, temptations, worries, and troubles with which they labored in this world. They are refreshed for the worship, acts of service, and the celestial fun they experience in heaven.

The earth is beautiful and is filled with many wonderful things to enjoy, but life here is only a tiny preview of what we'll experience in the future. *"No eye has seen, no ear has heard, no mind has conceived what God has prepared for those who love him"* (1 Corinthians 2:9).

God's Word points us to such hope so we can tell the world about heaven. It will be more wonderful than anything we ever have seen, heard, or imagined. No wonder we have to "rest and refresh" to enjoy it!

Dear God, thank You for the rest and refreshment You offer believers here and hereafter. In Jesus's name, amen.

# ❃ *What Blind Men Can't See* ❃

*God our Savior … desires all men to be saved and to come to the*
*knowledge of the truth* (1 Timothy 2:3–4 NKJV).

An ancient Hindu fable tells the story of six blind men who touch different parts of an elephant, each one leaving with a different perception. One touches the tail and thinks it's a rope. Another touches the side and thinks it's a wall. Another puts his hand on the elephant's leg and thinks it's a tree trunk.

The fable has been used by pluralists to illustrate that all religions are true. Truth is subjective, they say—what each person perceives it to be. Oprah Winfrey, like many other Hollywood icons, agrees. At the nationally televised post-9/11 New York prayer service in 2001 she asserted that we all pray to the same God.

If so, the Six Blind Men and the Elephant fable makes sense. But, the truth is, the blind men weren't touching a rope or a wall or a tree trunk. Sighted people know that their perceptions were wrong. They were touching an elephant. All truth is objective and narrow, excluding its opposite. This means that even the pluralistic claim that all religions are true is a narrow, exclusive claim, since it excludes the possibility that only one religion is true, as Christianity claims.

As Christians, we agree that many religions have some truth in them. But the world's major religions hold contradictory, mutually exclusive essential beliefs.

For instance, though Islam believe in one God, as does Christianity, Islam's God is not triune—one nature yet three Persons. Muslims believe Christianity's assertion that God is triune is blasphemous.

So, when someone tries to convince you that all religions can be true, tell them the fable of "The Six Blind Men and the Elephant." Explain that no matter how sincerely one of the blind men believed the tail was a rope, it wasn't. It was an elephant. Truth is like that. And we as believers can take courage and tell people about truth.

After all, what blind men can't see *can* hurt them.

Father, help me be someone's eyes to help them see truth. Amen.

# ❀ *Fly Balls* ❀

*"'Take what is yours and go your way. I wish to give to this last man*
*the same as to you. Is it not lawful for me to do what I wish with my*
*own things? Or is your eye evil because I am good?'"*
(Matthew 20:14–15 NKJV).

At the bottom of the seventh inning, with two outs and the game on the line, the batter hit the ball to where I stood as first baseman. It meant so much to me as the ball descended into my glove and I caught the final out for my team to become high school state champions in softball.

I enjoyed playing softball, but holding a starting position on the team was a serious challenge to my limited abilities. I stretched myself to become a better hitter and fielder, but my hitting was usually less than stellar. I was the first baseman during the championship game, but another player batted in my place. When the final out of the game landed in my glove, I had been able to contribute to the win, even though I hadn't scored a run.

Every person on our team received a championship medal, from the greatest superstars to the mediocre players like me. My medal wasn't a different color because I hadn't batted during the game, nor was anyone else's fancier than mine. In the eyes of our coach, we were all champions. I was on the winning team.

In the parable of the workers in the vineyard (Matthew 20:1–16), Jesus illustrated God's divine goodness to give heaven graciously to all believers, including the woman who labors in the Lord's fields most of her life as well as the man who receives Christ only moments before death. No one earns salvation. It's God's gift, and He lovingly grants salvation based upon His grace and mercy.

Have you been looking in the Lord's harvest fields lately, feeling subpar beside Christians you esteem as more worthy than you, or conversely, feeling disdain for laborers who seem less worthy than you? Let go of comparisons and rest in God's goodness. Rejoice in His blessings in others' lives.

God, I rejoice at the gifts You freely give me! Give me a desire to celebrate every blessing I see You pouring into others' lives as well. In Jesus's name, amen.

# ❀ It Only Takes a Spark ❀

*And you will be my witnesses in Jerusalem, and in all Judea and*
*Samaria, and to the ends of the earth* (Acts 1:8).

The popular song, "Pass It On," says, "It only takes a spark to get a fire going. And soon all those around, will warm up in its glowing." These words came alive when I taught in the high school at the South Carolina School for the Deaf and Blind.

I taught there only one year because Wayne and I married and I joined him at seminary. However, of any year in the history of the school, I'm thankful I taught there that year—the year of the great awakening on campus.

It began with the co-captains of the football team, Pete and David. David invited Pete to his parents' home one weekend to attend a revival service that was interpreted for the deaf. They both accepted Christ.

When they returned to the boys' dormitory after the weekend, they went from room to room witnessing. Many students accepted Christ and they began to share their experience with others.

The boys talked with the girls during their free time and the same thing happened in the girls' dormitory. Students came to me during recess and after school seeking to know more about Jesus. Sometimes I would stop teaching to answer their faith questions because they had so much they wanted to learn about their new Savior. I invited ministers to meet with them after school and I interpreted for them.

As far as I could tell, all but one girl in the high school had accepted Christ by the end of the year. Thirty years later in another town at a revival for the deaf I saw her. She is now a Christian and happily serves the Lord.

David's invitation for Pete to come to his home was the spark that started the fires of awakening on campus. Through those two young men, the students at our school received and accepted the greatest invitation of all!

Dear Lord, help us recognize the far-reaching effects of the witnessing we do in
Your name. In Jesus's name, amen.

# ❀ Revive the Joy ❀

*This is what the high and lofty One says…he whose name is holy:*
*"I live in a high and holy place, but also with him who is contrite and*
*lowly in spirit, to revive the spirit of the lowly"* (Isaiah 57:15).

Mom, I love this green dish detergent," Patsy said. "The smell reminds me of my childhood. Good times and good smells go together."

I remember Patsy's childhood in a different way. Those days without a dishwasher were drudgery. I labored under never-ending chores: washing dishes, making beds, cooking, washing clothes…. Jack, Patsy's older brother, was in the first grade learning to read. I remember the nights of listening to his reading: "He were happy."

"*Was*, not *were*," I said. "*He was happy.* Look again."

"He were happy."

After he learned to read, Patsy began, with similar mistakes, which we read over and over. I was bored to tears. At the end of a hard day, with greasy pans left in the sink, it was hard to muster enthusiasm for the nightly readings—what felt like the worst times of my life.

Imagine my surprise that my children have great memories of fun in those days! They often reminisce about making mud pies, running races down the neighborhood hill, or rolling with several friends under the pews during adult choir practice. God encouraged them, even during my lowest days.

Boring places and humdrum hours fill the world, but God brings joy on the worst day. When daily chores get us down, we can always remember that God loves us, blessing us in spite of discouragement. Isaiah says the lofty One living in a high place revives the spirits of the ones in a low place.

The best cure for the doldrums is helping others. Call someone today who needs your encouragement. Invite her to a movie, to dinner, or just a walk with you. Take her some green liquid detergent and help her wash dishes! The two of you can make good memories, like the ones Patsy remembers.

O, God, help me find every day exciting as I serve You.
Revive my spirit and show me how to share Your love with others. Amen.

# ❀ Hustling and Bustling ❀

*Only let your conduct be worthy of the gospel of Christ, so that whether*
*I come and see you or am absent, I may hear of your affairs, that you*
*stand fast in one spirit, with one mind striving together for the faith of*
*the gospel* (Philippians 1:27 NKJV).

Leaves were falling in dancing wisps across the street, and I was perfectly content as I waited at the traffic light. Christmas music played on my radio, and excitement was in the air. On the Saturday after Thanksgiving, I was Christmas shopping with the masses, and I felt positively giddy. Suddenly I felt a kinship to everyone in the stopped cars surrounding me at the light; I had grandiose visions that we were all hustling and bustling from store to store and house to house with Christmas cheer.

It was mere fantasy, but it was a wonderful wistful feeling that I refused to let go of at Christmas. Wouldn't it be marvelous if that sense of unity were real, not just imagined? How almost dreamlike it would be if everyone we met was interacting with a common heart and for a common goal: Jesus. That must be what heaven will be like. We'll have a spring in our steps as we hustle and bustle about the streets of gold without worries, questions, or the weight of sin. I thoroughly look forward to an eternity with the saints in glory as we joyfully work in the kingdom of heaven.

But until then, Paul called us to stand fast in unity, cooperating with one another for the sake of the gospel, even when we don't agree. He instructed us to be of "one mind." If we are to be unified, we cannot expect others to think like us, nor can others demand that we think like them; instead, we must all agree to take on the mind of Christ, unifying ourselves under His authority.

Father, I desire to be an agent of unity in the body of Christ. Teach me to have
the mind of Christ. Help me to lovingly encourage others to join me to seek
Your glory, and not my own agenda. Amen.

# ❀ Lord, Restore My Joy! ❀

*Restore to me the joy of Your salvation, and uphold me by Your generous Spirit. Then I will teach transgressors Your ways, and sinners shall be converted to You* (Psalm 51:12–13 NKJV).

Robbers are after a precious jewel—your joy. They know their thievery will blur your focus on serving the Lord; they know that Christians who aren't joyful are ineffective. Guard your heart against these enemies of joy.

**The Blahs.** Are you in a spiritual rut? Are you excited about what new thing God will bring to your life, or are you expecting nothing more than business as usual? *"Look with your eyes and hear with your ears, and fix your mind on everything I show you; for you were brought here so that I might show them to you"* (Ezekiel 40:4 NKJV).

**Self-absorption.** Whether it's a painful loss, an emotionally-trying relationship, or even something as wonderful as redecorating the living room, we sometimes fall into the trap of turning our focus inward instead of looking outward for the needs of others. *"Let nothing be done through selfish ambition or conceit, but in lowliness of mind let each esteem others better than himself. Let each of you look out not only for his own interests, but also for the interests of others"* (Philippians 2:3–4 NKJV).

**Anger.** Anger and joy repel one another. When anger enters your heart, joy finds the nearest exit. *"Cease from anger, and forsake wrath; do not fret—it only causes harm"* (Psalm 37:8 NKJV).

**A Critical Spirit.** Have you assumed the role of Chief Critic in your church, home, or workplace? Those who are looking for flaws in others are usually able to find what they're looking for, all at the expense of a light heart and joyful spirit. *"Every way of a man is right in his own eyes, but the Lord weighs the hearts"* (Proverbs 21:2 NKJV).

Let this be a day when you overflow with the joy of your salvation. Your spiritual joy will nourish your soul until you cannot help but tell others about the wonderful Savior, leading people to Jesus Christ. Let's get excited about the salvation of the Lord!

Father, truly there is great joy in walking daily with You.
May I be a joyful traveling companion today. Amen.

# ❀ Did Jesus Claim to Be God? ❀

*And some of the scribes were sitting there and reasoning in their hearts,*
*"Why does this Man speak blasphemies like this? Who can forgive sins*
*but God alone?"* (Mark 2:6–7 NKJV)

If Jesus never claimed to be God and the honorific title was simply foisted on Him many years after He died, then there's no need to argue that He *is* God. But the New Testament reveals many instances when Jesus claimed to be God.

When speaking to resistant Jewish leaders, Jesus claimed to be the same "I Am" who spoke to Moses in the Old Testament (John 8:58–59, Exodus 3:14). In John 10:30–33, He claimed to be one in divine nature with the Father. This was no mere claim to be one in purpose with the Father, as Jehovah's Witnesses assert, or else the Jews would not have tried to stone Him.

Another incident shows Jesus's claimed to forgive sins only as God does. When Jesus entered the town of Capernaum one day, throngs of people came, hoping to witness a miracle. They were not disappointed. Four men carrying their paralyzed friend on a mat plowed through the crowd and up to the roof, where they broke through, letting the sick one down in front of Jesus. Jesus immediately pronounced him forgiven. The man stood, gathered his mat, and walked. Jesus claimed to forgive the sin of someone whom He had never met! We would never presume to forgive sins of someone who had never wronged us. Yet, Jesus did just that.

Finally, in John 20:28 the Apostle Thomas fell down and declared, *"My Lord and my God!"* when Jesus showed Him the scars as evidence of His death and resurrection.

Sometimes people wonder why Jesus was not more explicit in His claim to deity. One reason was that Christ determined to die according to the Father's perfect timing in order that all prophecy might be fulfilled. Knowing the religious leaders sought to kill Him, He avoided inciting them to murder prematurely.

Numerous Scriptures illustrate that Jesus will not settle for our admiration of Him as a good prophet or a self-giving person whose example we should follow. He desires that we worship Him as God.

Seal in my mind, Lord, these passages that affirm Your claim to be God. Amen.

# ❀ A Place to Call Home ❀

*Jesus replied, "Foxes have holes and birds of the air have nests, but the
Son of Man has no place to lay his head" (Matthew 8:20).*

As an itinerant rabbi, Jesus must have felt He had no place to call home.
He traveled many miles teaching about the truth of His Father's kingdom.
We read that He stayed in the home of friends such as Mary, Martha, and
Lazarus and returned to His family's home in Nazareth. However, there is
no mention of His having a home of His own.

Perhaps the reason Jesus did not feel He had a place to call home was
that He recognized this world as His temporary address. In that sense, we
all should be "homeless" people. We are in this world to prepare for the
wonderful place that is really our home. As the old gospel song says, "This
world is not my home. I'm only passing through."

Hebrews 11:8–10 records that Abraham felt the same way. He lived his
life on earth looking forward to a city whose architect and builder is God.
He could enjoy the beauty of this world, as well as endure its hardships,
because he understood that he was "homeless" here while preparing for
there.

This same realization allowed Jesus to stand before Pontius Pilate and
proclaim, *"My kingdom is not of this world"* (John 18:36).

We once lived beside the church building where my husband served
as pastor in the downtown section of our city. Very often homeless people
came to our door for help. Truly, many of them had no place to lay their
heads.

As we offered them physical help, we also shared how to have a relationship with Jesus Christ. Several of them responded by opening their
hearts to the Savior.

It fills my heart with great joy to realize that though they are homeless,
they are now also "homeless." Even though they have no place to lay their
heads here, they will one day have a heavenly home as their real home!

Dear Lord, thank You for the beautiful home You are preparing for us.
Help us to live with eternity in mind. In Jesus's name, amen.

# ❀ To the Jew First ❀

*He came to His own, and His own did not receive Him. But as many*
*as received Him, to them He gave the right to become children of God,*
*to those who believe in His name* (John 1:11–12 NKJV).

Giddy excitement fueled every greeting between believers on Jerusalem's streets. The Savior had risen; more than 500 had seen Him. Some had witnessed His ascension into heaven. A few days later, Peter preached on the Jewish holy day of Pentecost, and the Holy Spirit descended in a stunning display of tongues, enabling the gospel to spread like wildfire. More than 3,000 responded in faith.

Then, one day Peter and John entered the temple to pray. Meeting a lame man, they healed him in the name of Jesus. Word spread quickly, and a crowd flocked to see an encore. Like any good preacher, Peter seized the opportunity. He began: the resurrected Jesus Christ deserved credit for the lame man's healing. *An audacious claim,* thought one listener.

Moreover, the God of Abraham, Isaac, and Jacob—the God whom the Jewish people claimed as their own—had sent Jesus Christ. *Could that be true?* Remember, said Peter, how God promised through Moses to raise up a prophet from among the Jews from the Seed of Abraham? *Yes, of course.* Jesus was that Promised One! *So, it was true. The One prophesied, the One risen—He was Messiah.*

But they had committed a terrible sin, Peter added, killing God's Messiah—the "Holy and Righteous One." *We killed the One for whom we so long waited? Oh, God, let the rocks fall upon us. We are doomed.*

Peter looked into the faces of his own countrymen. He recalled the Lord's words to him: *"Feed my sheep."* Tenderly, he began again. "Brethren, I know that you acted in ignorance…." And then, the lifeline: "Repent therefore and return that your sins may be wiped away, in order that…He may send Jesus, the Christ appointed for you." *Appointed for us. O praise God!* Many Jews trusted Jesus as Savior that day.

Lord God, You call us to share with the Jewish people that Jesus Christ,
the One sent for them and through them, lives for their hope,
as well as the hope of all people. Amen.

# Child, Get Out of That Box

*She had a sister called Mary, who sat at the Lord's feet listening to what he said. But Martha was distracted by all the preparations that had to be made* (Luke 10:39–40).

Isn't it a blessing to know God's design made each of us totally different? His Word gives these examples:

- Farmer Cain—bad attitude; Shepherd Abel—good attitude;
- Ruth—strong arms, eager learner; Naomi—little strength, eager teacher;
- Mary—quiet listener; Martha—bustling worker.

Throughout the Bible, God gives us lots of contrasts between personalities.

You may have noticed that siblings are different. I served both of my children the same food, but Jack grew tall. Call it DNA or lifestyle, we can see God's hand in designing each unique person. I saw this uniqueness when Jack and Patsy were preschoolers. Jack enjoyed going outside to run around the backyard. Patsy enjoyed staying inside, climbing into a cardboard box in our kitchen, snuggling up there for hours with a coloring book or a doll.

I compare my struggle with getting her out of the box to the struggle God has getting Christians out of our boxes. So often we settle into a comfortable corner at home or at church, and we just don't want to get out of familiar boxes. We pray the same words and minister in the same old areas; we don't want to try anything new. Sometimes the greatest blessing of our lives may be waiting around the corner, if only we would answer God's call to come out of the box.

Let's try an exercise of listening with our devotions today. Sit in a quiet nook at your house, or box yourself in a serene corner—safe from all the noise of the day. Listen. Is God calling, "Child of God, get out of that box"?

Heavenly Father, whatever my niche, when You call me, I'll step out of the box in faith. In Jesus's name, amen.

# ❀ Listening to Your Dreams ❀

*In a dream, in a vision of the night, when deep sleep falls on men as*
*they slumber in their beds, he may speak in their ears*
(Job 33:15–16).

My prayer partner, Vicki, was on a missions trip to the Ukraine. I prayed for her safety and God's power and anointing on her work, but I longed to know how to pray for specific needs.

Two nights before her return I had a vivid dream. In my dream I saw Vicki sitting in a chair with baby on her lap and a young girl standing beside her. She looked at me and said, "The child's name is Bogoda."

I turned to our mutual friend, Dee Dee, and said, "*Bogoda* means 'the world.'" Then, the dream ended.

When Vicki returned, she called to let me know she was home. I asked if she had made a strong attachment to some children she didn't want to leave.

She seemed astonished. "How did you know?" She told me about the 12-year-old orphan who had become pregnant through a sexual assault. The girl did not want to let her baby go because he was the only family member she had.

The missions team connected her to the missionaries. Then, the team left to work in other villages. All week long, Vicki kept thinking about the young girl and the baby and did not want to leave them there.

On their last weekend in the Ukraine, she went back to that first village. When she walked into the church, Vicki saw the young mother and her baby, clean and nicely dressed. The missionaries had taken her under their wing and obtained the help she needed to raise her baby.

Vicki said, "Had we not gone back to the village and seen the change, I don't think I could have left Bogdonna."

When she said her name, I gasped. I explained about the dream and how close I came to actually knowing the mother's name.

I thank God that He spoke through the dream. It showed me the importance of listening for His voice—even while we are sleeping!

Dear Lord, we pray Your continued blessings upon Bogdonna and her baby.
Thank You for revealing Yourself in so many ways. In Jesus's name, amen.

# ❀ The First Ride ❀

*Anxiety in the heart of man causes depression,*
*but a good word makes it glad* (Proverbs 12:25 NKJV).

Have you ever been to a theme park with someone who won't ride the amusement rides? It's almost unbearable for someone like me who loves a good adventure. You try earnestly to convince him of the safety of the machinery. You remind him that you both paid big bucks to enter the park, and you can't imagine the price was worth it if all you're going to do is sit and watch others have a good time. You nudge and encourage the best you can, reasoning that if you can get him on just one ride, you'll win him over to ride for the rest of the day. But the trick is that first ride.

Do you know anyone sitting on a park bench, seeming content to watch other Christians enjoy the adventure of a life surrendered to Christ? It's frustrating to survey all of the unfilled gaps in the ministries of your church or community, knowing that many Christians seem glued to their seats, unwilling to serve. However, what may appear to you as apathy or selfishness may actually be anxiety and fear, holding that person to the bench.

You can help a fellow believer get off the bench and take her first "ride" in ministering to others. Let go of your personal judgments and opinions about why she isn't serving, and go alongside her with encouraging words. Rather than assuming she's uninterested, try to find out about the interests God has stirred within her, and help her find a good match between her interests and the ministry needs around her. You may have to be patient and persistent, but hold fast in your determination to help her get off the bench. Your good words can help bring *gladness to her heart.*

Dear God, I want to be loving, patient, and encouraging to believers around me who have not yet gotten up the courage to engage fully in serving You. I confess my judgmental attitudes against them, and I ask You to help me speak good words to them as a means of encouraging them to start serving You in new and exciting ways. Amen.

# ❀ Need an Attitude Adjustment? ❀

*Now godliness with contentment is great gain* (1 Timothy 6:6 NKJV).

Give my daughter a sticker, and she'll follow you anywhere. Offer my son a cracker, and you're his new best friend. What does it take to entice you? Satan knows as well as you do, and he is successfully luring many Christians into the trap of dissatisfaction by dangling their "wants" before their eyes.

Christ offers the key to satisfaction through a personal relationship with Him. Do your peers see within you a contented heart that would compel them to desire Christ, or a distracted heart that always wants more? Your choice to live in godliness with a spirit of contentment will not only yield great gain in your life, but will also grant you a powerful credibility in your witness as others see how Jesus truly satisfies the soul. How can you adopt a spirit of contentment?

As a Christian, you can be content, knowing God will supply what you need (James 1:17). The key is to *acknowledge* this sufficiency, and therefore, not require or demand any more than your current status.

Hebrews 13:5–6 sends a clear message about contentment: *"Let your conduct be without covetousness; be content with such things as you have. For He himself has said, 'I will never leave you nor forsake you.' So we may boldly say: 'The Lord is my helper; I will not fear. What can man do to me?'"* (NKJV). Have you considered how discontentment might be a result of fear? Fear of being taken advantage of, of missing out on a privilege you "deserve," of being disappointed with your life…all these fears can sabotage your witness if you're distracted and choose to act on these fears instead of boldly trusting in Jesus.

Carefully evaluate the messages you send to the world about the sufficiency of Christ. Count your blessings. Thank God for providing far beyond what you need or deserve. Then say it with conviction and live like you mean it: "I have enough."

Lord, thank You for the abundance I have in Christ. Teach me to reflect the extravagant blessings I've received through Your Son, drawing others to the fulfilling life available through Christ. Amen.

# ❀ *What It's All About* ❀

*Every day they continued to meet together ["with one accord," KJV]
in the temple courts. They broke bread in their homes and ate together
with glad and sincere hearts* (Acts 2:46).

If you live in a place where it snows often, chances are your car has gotten stuck in a mound of snow. If so, you know to the all-too-familiar sound of your tires spinning and your car engine racing. Before long, you are in a rut, and the situation may require extra assistance to get you out.

Being stuck in a rut of snow is one thing. Being stuck in a rut as a Christian (or, as a church) is another. If we're not careful, we will find ourselves spinning our wheels and racing our engines without going anywhere. We can become stuck in a mound of ceaseless activity and busyness.

So, what is the answer? How do we find "what it's all about"? God's Word (Acts 2:42–47) presents a succinct summary of the Christian life:
- Devotion to God's Word (v. 42)
- Fellowship and Communion (vv. 42, 46)
- Prayer (v. 42)
- Meeting the needs of others (vv. 44–45)
- Regular worship and praise (vv. 46–47).

When the early Christians grasped the meaning of "what it's all about," people were saved and the church grew exponentially.

Once our family traveled out of town where one of our daughters was to model in a fashion show. A surprise blizzard hit the area bringing almost a foot of snow. Our destination—the hotel—was in sight, yet our car was stuck in a rut.

Finally, my husband devised a plan. One daughter got behind the steering wheel, the other daughter and I sat on the hood of the car to weigh it down, and my husband got behind the car and pushed. We made it up the hill to the entrance of the hotel, laughing and singing the theme song from *Rocky*. We had grasped "what it's all about"—working in one accord doing the *right* things.

Dear Lord, please pull us out of the ruts so we can move forward
toward our final destination! Amen.

# ❀ While Standing in Line ❀

*In lowliness of mind let each esteem others better than himself*
(Philippians 2:3 NKJV).

"Ugh, is this the line?"

As I stood as person number four in the return line at the customer service department, it seemed to me the answer to the woman's abrupt question was rather obvious. We were standing single file, aligning ourselves with the cash register, but I obliged her question with a friendly, "Yes, ma'am." After all, it was Christmas time, and I felt cheery!

"Well! I've got chicken in my cart!" I felt sorry for the chicken in her cart, but I had a babysitter at home waiting for me to finish my errands, so I said nothing. Moments later, the woman who was now customer five in line blurted out, "Go, woman! That's so ridiculous, these people and their cell phones." She was referring to the customer in front of us, who had failed to move immediately as the line inched forward. Customer five then remarked, "Oh, look at me. I'm special. I'm talking on my cell phone!"

I wondered what had happened in this woman's life to fill her heart with bitterness. She was so livid at having to stand in line that she could hardly withstand the wait. How could she be so self-important? Then my mind traveled back about 15 hours earlier, when I stood beside my unadorned Christmas tree and threw a tantrum because my husband wasn't help me quickly enough. I was being self-important. As I realized how unattractive that attitude looked on the woman behind me in line, I thought about what my poor husband had endured the night before, simply because I was frustrated with a Christmas tree.

The it's-about-me attitude is pervasive in our society, but Jesus sends a very different message: it's about God first and others second. How damaging when we as Christians exhibit the it's-about-me attitude before people in the world who need to know about Jesus. The next time you feel a self-important attitude welling up in your spirit, fight the urge to indulge! Remember—Christ first, then others.

Father, if I am tempted to be self-centered today, remind me to put others before myself for Your glory. Amen.

# ❁ Thinking Vertically ❁

*"I have become all things to all men,*
*so that I may by all means save some"* (1 Corinthians 9:22 NASB).

I sat in the car with one of my teen daughters not long ago when a popular song came on. "Turn it up," she said, "I love this song."

I recognized the remake of a 70s song I knew well. "I loved it too, when I was a teen," I said.

"No way, Mom. This song just came out."

I started singing the words, and my daughter stared at me with a flat-pan expression, then said, "Wow, Mom. You're a fast learner!"

The story didn't happen just like that, but it's close. I'm subjected to daily doses of déjà vu. You know what I mean if you're over 40. Old is new. Retro is in. I see my teen-self in hip-hugger bell-bottoms and clogs, only now with a cell phone stuck to my ear. Canvas tennis-shoe high-tops, lava lamps, and Care Bears have all made a comeback. Today's teens even talk like us boomers. I actually heard a young Christian musician in concert recently say *right on* and *cool.* It's not fair, really. The boomer generation invented all the good stuff, and the new generation steals our thunder. Of course, as soon as I complained to my mom while showing her my new Capri pants, she reminded me that *her* generation called them pedal-pushers.

We live in an amazing time and place. Because of our increased life expectancy, we face the challenge of having five generations of women living at one time! To missions- and ministry-minded women the implications are far-reaching. Our witness must be as relevant to the 20-year-old woman as to the 90-year-old woman. Our challenge is no less real than that of a missionary who moves to a foreign country and seeks to assimilate into the local culture, crossing barriers presented by a new language, new food, and new social customs. If we want to reach them, we must reach vertically across generations with the same passion as we reach horizontally across the nations.

Lord, teach me to reach forward and backward to younger and older generations with the same zeal I reach into cultures of other lands. Amen.

# ❁ *The Sense God Gave a Billy Goat* ❁

*"Do not worry beforehand about what to say. Just say whatever*
*is given you at the time, for it is not you speaking, but the Holy Spirit"*
(Mark 13:11).

Imagine two college freshmen: one young man, Ahman, lives 3,500 miles away from his home. His assigned roommate, John, lives 80 miles away from his home. Ahman's parents send letters (and money orders!), but John's mother sends homemade candy, cookies, and other treats, which he shares with Ahman. When packages arrive, all the dorm friends attack the home-baked sweets. John promises he'll always share with Ahman before anyone else.

One day John confesses: "I haven't shared one special gift I've received. I've hidden it from you." Ahman becomes angry. "Why withhold treats from *me*? I can't believe you're so selfish."

"I *have* been selfish, Ahman, but this gift wasn't from my mother."

"Who was it from?"

"From God. Let me explain...." John explains the gift of salvation He's received. Ahman accepts Jesus into His heart, and—on their knees—they celebrate the greatest gift in the world together!

As the Spirit of Christ indwells us, who knows where He may allow us to share His love? Jesus said, *"On account of me you will stand before governors and kings as witnesses to them"* (Mark 13:9).

Only one question remains. How will we know what to say? Today's verse answers that question: Trust God. *"Say whatever is given."*

As a teenager, I asked a friend, "What will I say when I witness?"

She answered, "Just use the sense God gave a billy goat!"

"What?"

"God's given every Christian an innate sense of what to say. You're no genius. Just use the good sense you have. Relax! Rely on God. He'll tell you what to say."

Her words are true. Even though most Christians seek training in how to tell others God's plan of salvation, we don't have to depend on a set form. Every witness is different, and God always leads.

Lord, help us use the common sense You gave us and the power of the Holy
Spirit within us to lead others to accept Jesus as their Savior. Amen.

# ❀ *And a Child Shall Lead Them* ❀

*I am not ashamed of the gospel, because it is the power of God for the
salvation of everyone who believes* (Romans 1:16).

Meri Beth and Wayne had a wonderful father-daughter afternoon as they
traveled to visit the graves of his parents. They turned to drive up the hill to
the cemetery when she saw two men on the porch of the home beside the
road. She asked to stop to talk with them.

Wayne noticed their brown bags and, wanting to protect our young
daughter, said maybe they could stop by later. At the cemetery, they had a
special time recalling memories of Nanny and Granddaddy and moments
they both treasure.

On the way back down the hill, Wayne was relieved to see that the men
were gone. However, Meri Beth asked again to stop. "I just wanted to tell
them that Jesus loves them."

Wayne immediately turned to go back to the house. A very inebriated
man answered the door. Wayne explained that Meri Beth had something
to say.

The man invited them in and called his brother. "This little girl has
something she wants to tell us."

He and his brother leaned down to Meri Beth and asked, "What do
you want to say, little girl?"

Meri Beth simply said, "Jesus loves you, and so do we."

The room became silent and both men began to cry. "Thank you, little
girl," they responded.

Years later Wayne shared this story at a revival in his home church.
After the service, a woman told him "the rest of the story."

The two men were her uncles. Something happened that made them
suddenly start attending the church near their home. They both became
believers and active members of the church. Now both are deceased.

Wayne and I can't help but believe that "the rest of the story" is due in
part to a beautiful, blue-eyed, eight-year old girl who cared enough to stop
and tell two inebriated men, "Jesus loves you and so do we."

Dear Lord, help us to have the faith of a child and the courage of one
who is not ashamed of Your gospel. In Jesus's name, amen.

# ❀ Learning One Thing at a Time ❀

*So the warden put Joseph in charge of all those held in the prison, and he was made responsible for all that was done there* (Genesis 39:22).

The young man sat in a damp waterhole. He screamed. He cried. He struggled to climb out, but fell again and again. Imagine the emotions of Jacob's favorite son, Joseph, as he sat in the worst predicament of his life. He probably prayed for help. Not long afterward, his brothers sold him into slavery; caravan traders took him to Egypt for a life of hardships. Falsely accused of attacking his master's wife, Joseph found himself again in a predicament: an Egyptian jail. But he'd learned a lot on his journey through slavery. He didn't scream, cry, or struggle. He tried hard to become a model prisoner, and the warden put him in charge of other prisoners and activities. At full adulthood, Joseph became second in command next to Pharaoh, and eventually he was given charge of certain activities in the whole Egyptian Empire!

Some say Joseph was a born leader, but his life displays his *acquired skills*. He had learned keys to leadership that today's Christians still use.

Several women I know have found themselves, like Joseph, in a hard or boring place where they struggled, marking time—getting nowhere. Once they prayed, they felt God leading them to move to a higher calling. One woman felt a burden for single parents. She went to college, got a degree in social work, and made a difference helping single parents achieve their goals. She introduced many of them to Christ. Another woman heard about ministries with hearing-impaired learners, and listening to God's whisper, signed up for night classes to help the hearing impaired. Another one started to college at 55. "It's never too late," she said. "I'm just learning one thing at a time."

Like Joseph, these women weren't born leaders, but they took the initiative under poor circumstances and attained their leadership goals. May God inspire you to learn one thing at a time. We can aim high, as He helps us attain *unbelievable* leadership goals.

Lord, help us step out in leadership, doing one thing at a time,
until we've completed the lofty kingdom plans You have for us. Amen.

# ❀ Gather Up Your Pots ❀

*Then (Elisha) said, "Go, borrow vessels from everywhere, from all your*
*neighbors—empty vessels; do not gather just a few.... Then pour it*
*into all those vessels, and set aside the full ones." Now it came to pass,*
*when the vessels were full, that she said to her son, "Bring me another*
*vessel." And he said to her, "There is not another vessel."*
*So the oil ceased* (2 Kings 4:3–4, 6 NKJV).

The widow had a problem, and God had a solution. Creditors would soon enslave her sons because of debts she couldn't pay. In her hour of greatest need, having nothing but a jar of oil, Elisha sent her to gather vessels.

Can you imagine being in such a bleak predicament and spending your time gathering pots? Perhaps the neighbors knew her situation and thought she had lost her mind. Regardless, God rewarded her obedience.

Imagine the scene. She and her sons have a room filled with all sorts of vessels, and they shut the door. The widow fixes her eyes on the first empty pot. She raises the bottle of oil to eye level and thinks for a brief moment that she's about to pour her only possession into another man's container. She loosens the cap and begins to pour. The vessel fills, yet the original oil container hasn't emptied. "Bring me another vessel." Eyes wide, she pours the oil into another pot, and then another, then another, as her sons scurry to bring vessel after vessel, not sure when the miraculous abundance might suddenly cease, when she says yet again, "I need another container." The sons reply, "That's it—no more pots." And when they ran out of vessels, the miraculous flow of oil ended.

What an object lesson: the number of vessels they collected was an indicator of their measure of obedience and faith, and God's blessings flowed abundantly to the extent they had prepared for that blessing. In this instance, the measure of blessings was equal to their measure of faith.

God has made promises of blessings to every believer. Have you prepared yourself in faith to receive God's blessings?

Father, I'm open to Your blessings.
What steps of preparation do You want me to take? Amen.

# ❀ Where's Your Crown? ❀

*And being found in appearance as a man, he humbled himself and
became obedient to death—even death on a cross!* (Philippians 2:8).

God prepared a beautiful, wonderful world and then placed humans in it.
Humankind's mission was to show the world God's glory. (See Isaiah 43:7.)

Both Psalm 8:1–9 and Hebrews 2:6–9 state that God made us a little
lower than the angels. Both passages confirm that man was crowned with
honor and glory.

Then humans chose to sin and symbolically the crown fell from his
head to the dust. God provided only one way humankind could regain his
crown of honor and glory.

In Hebrews 2:9, God tells us how He accomplished this: *"But we see
Jesus, who was made a little lower than the angels,…crowned with glory and honor,
that He by the grace of God might taste death for everyone."*

At a climactic point in history God Himself came to earth through
Jesus, the physical manifestation of the Godhead. *The Creator took on the
form of the created.* In an unprecedented act of mercy and grace, Jesus came
to earth for the purpose of suffering death for us.

Can we even fathom what the incarnation really means? At His death,
it is as if Jesus took the crown of glory and honor from the dust and offered
to place it on the head of everyone (Hebrews 2:9) who would accept it.
Scripture tells us that those who choose to accept His gift will one day judge
the angels (1 Corinthians 6:3, 4).

I often wish I had something of great value to give to God for all He has
done for me. One day a thought filled my heart with joy. I pictured myself
kneeling in His presence and lovingly placing my crown at His feet. Then
I realized something profound. If it were not for Him I would not even have
a crown to present. It really belongs to Him anyway.

Dear Lord, thank You for tasting death on my behalf and for lifting the crown
from the dust and placing it on my head. In Jesus's name, amen.

# ❀ In My Generation ❀

*I am sending to you Timothy, my son whom I love,
who is faithful in the Lord* (1 Corinthians 4:17).

When it comes to communicating with a different generation from our own, we are foreigners to each other in many ways. We speak different languages. While the younger is talking in text-message language, some older ones are trying to master email. And because churches tend to segregate women according to age, we can go through life cloistered away in our own little generational comfort zones.

Paul and Timothy provide a beautiful picture of how cross-generational relationships can be used by God to reach the world for Christ. Paul loved Timothy, entrusted him with responsibility, and challenged him to grow in faithfulness in ministry. Timothy, Paul's protégé, humbled himself as a learner so that he could pass on the gospel treasure after Paul was gone. He also ministered to Paul's physical needs.

Read the following verses to learn how Paul and Timothy used their generational differences to become a dynamic ministry duo.

1. Acts 16:1—Paul harbored no prejudices that would keep him from being able to see Timothy's value to God's work. *What prejudices limit your openness to working with women of other generations?*

2. Acts 16:2—Timothy's integrity among the brethren opened the door to working with and learning from Paul. *Does your integrity cause younger or older women to desire working with you?*

3. Acts 16:3—Timothy humbled himself to the customs of the culture among whom he and Paul would witness. *Are you willing to humble yourself and adapt to the cultural characteristics of women from other generations?*

4. Acts 16:4–5—Timothy and Paul worked side by side, witnessing and teaching in many cities. They worked synergistically, each contributing his own gifts and unique generational insights. They were unified in the one hope of Christ. As a result, many converted and were strengthened in the faith. *What could God do if you were willing to work with any woman of any generation of God's choosing in order to accomplish His mission and ministry?*

Lord, cleanse me of prejudices that hinder me from connecting with women
of other generations. Enable me to see others' uniqueness
as an asset for colaboring. Amen.

# ❀ Cheap Gas ❀

*"Let your light so shine before men, that they may see your good works
and glorify your Father in heaven"* (Matthew 5:16 NKJV).

I've seen thousands of gas station signs over the years, but none ever caused me to do a double take until a recent trip. I had grown accustomed to seeing gas prices of up to $4.00 per gallon, but a station on the highway I was traveling advertised its cheapest gas at $1.09. Wow! I was feeling excited for about 2.4 seconds until I realized the station had gone out of business, and judging by the advertised gas prices, they had closed down several years ago.

I wonder how many travelers have discussed the cost of gas after passing by that station and its bargain pricing. Sometimes it's not just seeing how bad something is, but seeing how much better something could be, that makes us realize we want things to change. I had started to accept the gas price of $4.00 per gallon until that sign reminded me of the good old days, when gas tanks were filled with a lot less money, and suddenly I was dissatisfied with status quo.

Jesus knew that sometimes people can better realize how miserable life is apart from the Lord if they first see how wonderful life can be for a Christian. When your light shines, it highlights for the lost person the way things are and the way things could be in his life. Just as the old gas prices made me long for the time when cheap gas could be had, the lost person sees the inner peace and the light in the life of a Christian, and he begins to believe that knowing God in an intimate way is possible.

Let your light shine brightly today. The Holy Spirit can stir up conversations among the lost in your path as they see in your life a reason to be dissatisfied with empty living and a reason to begin believing in the potential for an abundant life through Christ.

Father, thank You for Your light shining forth in my life.
Help me to draw attention to You. May the lost be compelled
by the beautiful manner in which You bring satisfaction into my life.
In Jesus's name, amen.

# ❀ All I Want for Christmas Is Jesus ❀

*She gave birth to her firstborn, a son…and placed him in a manger*
(Luke 2:7).

One day while skipping through department stores, selecting Christmas gifts for teachers and grandparents, my exuberant children suddenly dropped everything, running to a large crèche with a plastic Mary and Joseph. Peering over Patsy, who quietly kneeled, I saw the ugliest Baby Jesus I've ever seen: with a large, disfigured nose and eyes painted off center. Jack stood reverently, as if it really were the Christ Child. "Mother, we've just got to get Mary and Joseph." Looking into the manger, he whispered: "And Baby Jesus."

I peered at the hideous plastic baby with swaddling clothes that didn't completely swaddle, a crooked mouth, and hepatitis-yellow plastic skin. Jack showed me lights to illuminate them. "Let's put them in front of the porch! The neighbors will love them." *Our neighbors would believe we lost our minds to put a cheap eyesore like this plastic-trio blight in the neighborhood.*

"Take the money for my toys and get these," Jack said.

"Me, too," said Patsy. "All I want for Christmas is Baby Jesus. It's His birthday."

If all our children wanted for Christmas was Jesus, how could I refuse? That afternoon we set up the scene in front of our porch. I looked at our neighbors' tasteful decorations, and then at our plastic Christ Child, which looked like a comedian I'd seen on television.

*Oh*….tears flowed as I realized why I hated the plastic Christ Child. He looked so different.

*I'm not prejudiced against Jews. I don't even know one in this town*, I thought.

God whispered in my ear: "You *are* prejudiced, Edna. You think everyone unlike you is ugly."

I learned a lot that Christmas: to love others—regardless of how they looked—and not to be concerned about the neighbors—regardless of how *they* looked at us. Patsy and Jack cherished the manger scene until they moved to homes of their own. As a family tradition, we displayed the Christ Child proudly: a symbol of unprejudiced, unconditional love.

Lord, help me love all people—especially those who aren't like me. Take my prejudice away as I share Jesus's love with everyone I meet. Amen.

# ❊ *Standing in the Gap* ❊

*Carry each other's burdens, and in this way you will fulfill
the law of Christ* (Galatians 6:2).

I woke up one cold Saturday morning in January with a burden on my heart. I believed that God had called me to become a writer and speaker. This new calling involved a significant amount of travel and I was a "homebody." I began to feel very inadequate and insecure with my new role in life.

I stood in my morning shower praying. Finally, I voiced to God, *"I can't do this alone. I need help."*

God assured me that He did not intend for me to do anything alone. I was to surround myself with prayer warriors who would intercede for me and the new ministry. I asked Him to show me the person or persons I should ask.

A few hours later, a longtime friend phoned. She explained that God had called her to a new ministry. She knew she was supposed to partner with me. However, she had wrestled for hours about making the call, fearing I would think she had, in her words, "gone off the deep end."

I inquired about the nature of her new ministry and she quietly answered, "Intercessory prayer. Do you need me and the prayer team to pray about anything specific for you?"

With a trembling voice, I assured her I did. I could hardly believe what was happening. Once again God had gone ahead of me by providing the answer to my needs.

In the years since that experience, God has used Vicki and the prayer team to bless my life immeasurably. Our relationship has deepened as we moved from "friends" to "co-laborers for Christ."

The Bible says in Ezekiel 22:30 that God seeks people to *stand in the gap* between Him and His people. How I praise God for my precious friend who willingly and consistently stands in the gap for me and for countless others.

Dear Lord, thank You for those who stand in the gap between heaven and earth.
In Jesus's name, amen.

# ❀ Getting Weaker, Getting Stronger ❀

*And there shall be no more curse, but...they shall see His face*
(Revelation 22:3–4 NKJV).

I bought my first pair of reading glasses. I'm under the impression I look snazzy in them because they're red and rectangular. My husband said I look *cool*, but since he chose that particular word, that probably means we're both getting old since no one under 30 says *cool* anymore, except to describe the weather.

I won't be wearing my red readers next week when I go to my hair appointment to get my roots dyed. However, I'll likely be wearing some comfortable clothes that won't constrict the middle section of my body, which lately is losing elasticity.

My vision is dimming, my hair is graying, my mid-section is getting padded, and I've been to the doctor more in the last 12 months than probably I've been in the last five years. Yes, I'm right on target. As promised in God's Word, my body is slowly expiring.

However, as my physical self grows weaker, my inner person is becoming stronger as the Holy Spirit teaches me things I've never known. I'm picking up the pace as I run the race of life. I'm determined that with God's strength I will not slacken my speed. One day I'll round the track of life for the last time as I see the finish line finally before me.

On the day I enter heaven, I wonder, will all of us have gray hair because God has determined that it's the ideal hair color, and we'll all approve because we will have the mind of Christ? Will I be thrilled that all of us in heaven have the same sized midsection for all of eternity, or will I rejoice at God's creativity that we're in different shapes and sizes? One thing I am sure of—when I look with my eyes that have never before experienced eyesight perfection, not dimmed by the effects of this fallen world, these eyes will see Jesus. Until that day, my focus won't be that which is passing away, but that which is eternal.

> Dear Lord, I look forward to seeing You with perfected eyes.
> As my body weakens, strengthen my spirit. Give me resolve
> to run swiftly for the sake of the gospel! Amen.

# ❊ Hare Today, Gone Tomorrow ❊

*Now may our Lord Jesus Christ Himself, and our God and Father,*
*who has loved us and given us everlasting consolation and good hope*
*by grace, comfort your hearts and establish you in every good word and*
*work* (2 Thessalonians 2:16–17 NKJV).

After six years of marriage, Kevin and I decided to take a major step in our relationship: we adopted a bunny. I remember feeling nervous as we tried to give Pudding Pop her first bath in the kitchen sink.

Over the next four days, Kevin and I enjoyed getting to know our little bundle of joy, yet I felt anxiety about giving her proper care. I wished I could call my mother for advice, but mother had no tips on bunny care.

On our fifth day, I awoke to find Pudding Pop lying motionless. Was she asleep, resting, or worse?

I called my husband on my way to work. "Kevin, please go home soon and check on Pudding Pop. She doesn't look well, and I'm scared." Kevin agreed to check on her.

Later, the phone rang at my desk. Kevin said, "I'm sorry to tell you this, but Pudding Pop is dead." My world collapsed at the finish of one sentence.

After a few days, I began to reflect on the reason behind my extreme reaction to her death. Though I would miss Pudding Pop, my devastation was fueled by the shame and guilt that I couldn't properly care for this helpless little one. I felt like a failure. I had been a "mother" for less than a week, and I had royally failed the test.

We all experience failure. If we focus on the losses of life, they consume our attention and drain us of our zeal to press onward for Jesus. When the circumstances remain bleak or the failure is permanent, a godly perspective can renew our hearts. Our hope cannot rest in job security, friendships, financial statements, or bunny rabbits; our hope is in the Lord who made heaven and earth! We can't control the circumstances of our lives, nor can we completely avoid making mistakes, but we can experience joy by resting in the hope we have in Him.

Lord, establish my heart to rest my hope in You and You alone. Amen.

# ❀ The Glorious Mystery ❀ of the Resurrection

*All flesh is not the same: Men have one kind of flesh, animals have another, birds another and fish another* (1 Corinthians 15:39).

The church at Corinth raised some of the same questions we ponder today. How can the dead be resurrected? What kind of body will a resurrected person have? Paul's strong reply is found in 1 Corinthians 15:35–58. The Corinthians could find these answers by observing the nature around them.

First, seeds are examples. A seed cannot produce new life until it first dies. A seed is different from the new plant that springs forth with life. God is the One who gives each seed its own body and causes a plant to rise from the seed's death.

Next, animals are examples. Just as God gave each animal its own body (flesh), He surely is able to change a person's body from physical into the awaited heavenly form.

Finally, the heavenly bodies are examples. God made the heavenly bodies different from earthly bodies, and different from each other. He gave each of them their own glory. God also will give each believer a resurrected body with its own glory.

Paul continues with an explanation of differences between our future resurrected bodies and our present earthly ones. Our resurrected bodies will be incorruptible and will never deteriorate. They will not be dishonorable, but glorious and full of perfect light. They will not be weak, but strong and powerful. Although they will retain the qualities that make us recognizable, they will somehow be changed into a different composition prepared for a different dimension—heaven.

Thank you, Paul, for answering those questions and giving such powerful insights to the church at Corinth and to us, more than 2,000 years later.

Dear God, I want to thank You in advance for the resurrected body I will have one day! In Jesus's name, amen.

# ❊ A Negative Times a Negative ❊ Equals a Positive

*"And we know that in all things God works for the good of those who love him, who have been called according to his purpose"*
(Romans 8:28).

I learned in algebra that multiplying a negative number times a negative number yields a positive number. This formula has become my favorite, although math was not my favorite subject. I remember well those days in math class, working with positive and negative signed numbers:

positive x negative = negative;
positive x positive = positive;
negative x negative = positive.

Until last year I had forgotten most of my algebraic rules. Just a few months ago I had to have a biopsy of a thyroid cyst. The doctor startled me, saying he wanted to be sure it wasn't malignant. I was shaky as I lay on the operating table. I prayed over the instruments lying on a table. I prayed for my doctor, nurse, and the others working on me, that He would touch them with His divine finger. Then I drifted into unconsciousness.

I recovered quickly, and a few days later, when I got the test back, it showed no malignancy. That day was a Praise-the-Lord time!

Then a few weeks ago during my routine monthly breast exam, I discovered a small lump. My regular primary physician said it could be an inflamed duct. The lump was easy to find, just under a mole, and it did not diminish with treatment. An ultrasound report came back negative. I sought the opinion of a vascular specialist, who examined me, looked at my ultrasounds and x-rays, and found nothing out of the ordinary, but said if it bothered me, he would remove it.

In less than a month I felt pressure and pain, so he removed it. After the surgery, the biopsy also came back negative. As I thanked God and contemplated my two negative tests, I remembered my math work from years ago.

The worldview of most Christians is one of optimism and faith. We know for sure that God brings blessings out of negative situations. At least in the past year, true to the algebra formula, two negative situations have turned out to bring positive things for me!

Dear Lord, Thank You for healing me. Thank You for taking my negatives and turning them into positives. Amen.

# ❀ Not Just a Dream ❀

*"Being justified as a gift by His grace through the redemption which is in Christ Jesus"* (Romans 3:24 NASB).

It was a precious Christmas. Daddy had arrived home on furlough after his first six months of a year-long isolated tour assignment at Greenland's Sondrestrom Air Force Base.

We stuffed a lifetime's worth of memories into those few days. My year-younger sister and I regaled him with our piano skills, playing on our little 21-key electric chord organ. The snaggle-toothed renditions were punctuated by blips of silence as our fingers reached for imaginary notes that were printed on the page but not provided on our abbreviated keyboard. Still, Daddy acted suitably impressed.

I dreamed of a real piano, but it was out of the question on my dad's Air Force salary. It was just as well; where would we put a piano in our 10-by-55-foot trailer?

The days of furlough wound down quickly. We soon found ourselves packing Daddy's suitcase so he could leave the next day for another six months.

As usual, my sister and I bickered incessantly. Finally, Mom said, "Girls, go to my bedroom." My sister and I plodded to the bedroom and sheepishly awaited the reprimand. "Girls, this is your daddy's last day home. Please, don't make it miserable by arguing."

*What was that bumping noise?*

She went on, "You two have been at each other..."

*There it went again.*

"So, I want you both to work hard...." My sister and I couldn't bear it. We bolted into the living room.

It was the most beautiful piano I had ever seen with a full complement of 88 keys. I stood mute. Maybe it was a dream. Tears crept into my eyes. With trembling fingers, I reached out and touched the keys. It was real. And it was ours.

Today, when I think of that piano, I am reminded of the sacrifice Jesus made for my eternal life. Just as with the piano, there are times I wonder if the salvation gift is just a dream.

Then, I remember the moment when by faith I received the gift of salvation from Jesus. Tears crept into my eyes. With trembling heart, I reached out and touched it. It was real. And it was mine.

Thank You, Lord Jesus, for Your sacrifice. I am unspeakably grateful. Amen.

# ❀ A Chicken with Its Head Cut Off ❀

*Then Moses cried out to the Lord, "What am I to do*
*with these people?"* (Exodus 17:4).

God miraculously released the Israelites from Egyptian bondage—freed slaves on their way to *the Promised Land!* However, they continually complained. Moses cried out to God, asking for help.

Forty years they wandered; instead of working together, ministering to one another's needs, their slave mentality kept surfacing. They expected Moses to provide their basic needs. He prayed often for God to forgive their immature behavior (Exodus 32:9–14).

I once faced a mob of rioting people with a similar mind-set. Before that, I had enjoyed helping feed over 300 flood victims. One day the Red Cross delivered large boxes of tortillas and 50 cans of peaches. "Let's serve peach tortilla-cobbler for lunch," our "White Hat" leader said. "They'll love it!"

At lunch, one man named Jesus [hey-soose] spoke angrily, demanding plain tortillas, salsa, and chilis. I found salsa and chilis, but they still grumbled about the rolls.

Later the group approached angrily. I ran to tell the White Hat. He called police, who saw the crowd with large sticks and left! I watched from the safe kitchen as the White Hat met the loud crowd. Speaking their language, he danced around, flapping his arms.

"What did you say?" I asked.

Red-faced from the happy dance, he said: "I told Jesus about *my Jesus*, how He'd led me to come feed them. I was running around like a chicken with its head cut off, changing donated ingredients into decent meals. I was sorry the food didn't suit them, but I hadn't seen my own family in weeks because I was serving *them!* When I said 'like a chicken with its head cut off,' Jesus giggled. The others laughed, too. They understand now."

Have you ever seen a chicken with its head cut off? As a child, I watched my grandfather prepare a hen for dinner from scratch—not a pretty sight! Usually running around like a chicken with its head cut off—a mindless solution—doesn't help. What's your method of communication with others who don't understand? Mindless activity? Serving with a smile? Running away? Reflect today on appropriate communication to share Jesus's love.

O God, lead us to do whatever it takes to communicate Your love to others.
Amen.

# ❀ Cheerful Giving ❀

*Each man should give what he has decided in his heart to give, not*
*reluctantly or under compulsion, for God loves a cheerful giver*
(2 Corinthians 9:7).

As I walked into the classroom after recess, I noticed that Ginger looked sad. I asked what was bothering her. She explained her concern about the children who would not get much for Christmas and her desire to help them.

I asked Ginger to share her concerns with the other class members when they arrived, and she agreed. The students immediately related to Ginger's desire to help. I told them I would contact the Department of Social Services (DSS) to get the information we needed to help a family. They could begin collecting items to share.

On my way home, I stopped by the grocery store to get an empty box. The next day we decorated it and placed it in the back of the room. I was not prepared for what happened next.

My students lived at the school for the deaf and most did not have extra money to spend beyond their basic needs. However, within a few days our Christmas box was filled to overflowing.

I got another box and placed it at the back of the room. The same thing happened.

This continued until the entire back of the room was filled with items. We had to clear a path so we could get to the pencil sharpener on the back wall.

You might be wondering how students who had so little could share so much. The answer touches my heart. The girls gave items (broken jewelry boxes, etc.) that needed repairing to the boys, and the boys fixed them and painted or polished them. The boys gave clothes that needed mending to the girls, and they fixed them then washed and pressed them. The whole dormitory got involved and the school with abuzz with the Christmas spirit.

When we delivered the items, DSS told them that their gifts would help several families. The students rejoiced that they could help so many. I rejoiced that I had such wonderful, caring students!

Dear Lord, increase our desire to be cheerful givers. In Jesus's name, amen.

# ❀ *Excuses* ❀

*Then said I: "Ah, Lord GOD! Behold, I cannot speak, for I am a*
*youth." But the LORD said to me: "Do not say, 'I am a youth,' for you*
*shall go to all to whom I send you, and whatever I command you,*
*you shall speak"* (Jeremiah 1:6–7 NKJV).

Jeremiah was grappling with the calling of God on his life. Jeremiah didn't
*deny* the call, nor did he *refuse* the call, but instead he wanted to *postpone* the
call because of what he perceived to be a limitation—his age. Jeremiah
was hardly more than a teenager at the time of this conversation with God,
and he felt compelled to remind God of this fact. Have you and I ever been
guilty of informing God of your limitations? Listen to our excuses:

"I'm too old to take on that project. Let young folks do that."

"I'm not educated. I can't stand up and talk to those people; I could
never teach."

"I don't have the money to quit my job and go back to school."

"I'm a woman; no one will listen to me."

Jeremiah wasn't the only one in Scripture making excuses. Can you
hear the excuses of Moses ringing in your ears? He was a man who eventually led an entire nation of people out of bondage, stood with a rod in hand
as God parted the Red Sea, and brought the Ten Commandments down off
of the mountain. Jeremiah and Moses weren't flawless men, but the Lord
used them to accomplish great things for the kingdom of God.

The same God who creates planets, solar systems, little babies, and
delicate flowers isn't challenged by what you and I see as our limitations.
Fix your eyes on the God of the universe, and think on His trustworthiness.
God isn't asking you to have faith in yourself; He's asking you to have faith
in Him.

Heavenly Father, I am greatly aware of my shortcomings. I'm sure I fall short
in more areas than I realize. I'm not worthy to serve You, but my heart greatly
desires to do Your will. I bring all of my weaknesses to You, and I lift them into
Your capable hands. Do Your will in my life. I will trust You. Amen.

# ❀ *Sight Unseen* ❀

*"See, I have this day set you over the nations and over the kingdoms,*
*to root out and to pull down, to destroy and to throw down,*
*to build and to plant"* (Jeremiah 1:10 NKJV).

God clearly had a particular purpose in mind for Jeremiah's calling; God was specific with Jeremiah about what he would be doing in his ministry as a prophet, but God certainly left out a lot of details as well, didn't He? Jeremiah had no idea of the full magnitude his ministry would have on the people of God.

We have the benefit of hindsight over Jeremiah, because we can look at the history of Jeremiah's ministry as a prophet and see where God used him to root out wickedness, pull down evil strongholds, destroy sinfulness, and then build and plant again. However, when Jeremiah first heard the Lord speaking these words to him, God offered him only a sketch of his life's portrait, with only the broad and sweeping strokes in place. No details were given, but God made a promise to Jeremiah that assured him his life would be significant. God was calling Jeremiah to surrender completely to the commission, sight unseen.

God also has a particular purpose in mind for your life, but that specific purpose may not yet be clear to you. It's not uncommon to want to know the who, what, where, when, why, and how of your future before taking a big step in a new direction, but God isn't known for giving those kinds of details to His servants. Do you feel that you need to know your purpose before you can move forward? Continue praying for God to reveal that purpose, but also keep pressing forward as you sense God prompting you to move. You may not be able to see at the initial moment of surrender what great and mighty things God will do through you, but rest assured that God has a specific purpose in mind.

Dear God, I'm sure You have a plan for my life, but it's not easy to step forward without the details. You are trustworthy. I want to trust the details into Your capable hands. Thank You for giving Your attention to my life. Amen.

# ❁ *Eternal in the Everyday* ❁

*Boaz begot Obed by Ruth, Obed begot Jesse, and Jesse begot
David the king* (Matthew 1:5–6 NKJV).

The Book of Judges describes a bleak period in ancient Israel when God raised up judges, or deliverers, to guide His people. The book closes with a sad epitaph: *"In those days there was no king in Israel; everyone did what was right in his own eyes"* (Judges 21:25 NASB). But in the midst of that dark time shone a glimmer of light.

The story begins with a Jewish man in Israel, Elimelech, who moves his wife Naomi and their two sons to nearby Moab to escape famine. Then Elimelech dies. Both of his and Naomi's sons marry Moabite women, and then the sons die as well, leaving three widows to fend for themselves. When Naomi decides to return to Israel, one daughter-in-law, Ruth, goes with her.

Life was especially tough for widows in those days. To avoid starvation, Ruth searches for a field where she can follow reapers and retrieve leftover grain for food. God's hand providentially guides Ruth to a field owned by one of Elimelech's relatives, Boaz.

Naomi tells Ruth about a Jewish custom in which a man marries his relative's widow and father's a child to carry on the dead man's name and inheritance rights. Ruth risks her reputation and approaches Boaz one night to request such a marriage. Boaz, a godly man, is honored that she, a young woman, would choose him. But there's another relative closer than he, who has first rights to marry Ruth and buy her family land. Fortunately, the other relative declines so Boaz and Ruth marry, providing safety and hope for Naomi and Ruth. The story closes with Naomi cuddling a grandson in her lap and the community women rejoicing at her blessing.

We might dismiss this account as a sweet fairy tale if it were not for the rest of the story. Matthew 1:5 includes Ruth in the ancestral line of Jesus Christ. This woman, a Gentile, whose life was banally simple, brought deliverance in ways the judges never could have. Her obedience opened the doors of heaven's grace that ushered in Messiah through the line of David.

> Lord, Ruth reminds me that by doing things Your way,
> I can be used also to impact the world for You. Amen.

# ❀ *Sleepers, Awake!* ❀

*"Are you still sleeping and resting? Look, the hour is near, and the Son of Man is betrayed into the hands of sinners"* (Matthew 26:45).

Today's Scripture, to me, is one of the saddest in the entire Bible. Jesus observed the Passover meal with His disciples, and then they went to the Garden of Gethsemane. He took Peter, James, and John apart from the others to support Him and intercede for Him.

Jesus confessed to them that *"My soul is overwhelmed with sorrow to the point of death"* (Matthew 26:38). Our blessed Savior struggled because He did not want to drink "the cup" that was before Him.

What was "the cup" that so grieved the Son of God? He who had never known sin would take on the sins of all people for all time—past, present, and future—and thus would incur God's wrath poured out on evil (Revelation 14:10; 16:19). The holy, innocent, sinless One would atone for murder, abortion, hatred, war, violence, genocide, torture, robbery, child molestation, incest, rape, adultery, homosexual behavior, pornography, robbery, drug abuse, gluttony, lies, deceit, extortion, crime, filthiness, cursing, envy, pride, and every imaginable abomination to God. On the Cross, Jesus accepted the judgment for our sins and covered them with His precious blood, freeing us from sin's curse forever.

All He asked from Peter, James, and John was that they pray for Him as He agonized over "the cup." He needed them. He needed their prayers on His behalf. Three times He returned to them and found them sleeping. Finally, He lamented, *"Look, the hour is near, and the Son of Man is betrayed"* (Matthew 26:45).

The Savior needed them as never before. They could have helped Him more in that one hour than in the entire three years they followed Him, but they missed their golden opportunity. Why? They were simply too tired.

The reality of this passage haunts me. I want to guard against letting myself get too tired to do what the Lord prompts me to do!

Dear Lord, show us when and how to best receive Your gift of rest so we can "be there" for You. In Jesus's name, amen.

# ❦ It's Not a Dream ❦

*"Let him know that he who turns a sinner from the error of his way*
*will save a soul from death and cover a multitude of sins"*
(James 5:20 NKJV).

I had the craziest dream last night that my husband and I had moved to a new neighborhood. I decided to take a walk and got terribly lost. I first went to a helpdesk window for assistance, but the employees made fun of my problem and sent me away embarrassed and still lost. I happened upon people gathered to listen to their minister. They listened to my tearful explanation about my lostness, but they only referred me to their minister. By this time, I was panicked and begging for help. The minister talked with me, but nothing he said was helping me find my way home. I stood to go, and he offered me clothing. What I needed wasn't a handout; I needed to get home. Finally, I found my husband. He wasn't at our house, but he was with a group of people who were rescuers. He was so impressed with them that he, too, wanted to be a rescuer. We weren't back in our house, but in the midst of these dynamic, focused individuals, he and I felt at home.

I woke eager to talk to God, who started building the analogies. Can you relate to my character, weary and desperate to find your way home? If that's not you, please realize that most people in the world play that role. They're lost and looking for answers. They want to find a place of peace.

Perhaps you relate to the other characters. As Christians, we can lead the lost to Jesus, but are we? The helpdesk workers despised my ridiculous situation and offered no help; are we disgusted with the choices people make, critical, and keep the answers to ourselves? Are we like the church group who only wanted their minister to offer solutions, or the minister more interested in giving a handout? What about the rescue team? Their enthusiasm for saving lives compelled my husband and me to join them, and we were instantly a part of their family, feeling at home in their midst.

Friend, it's not a dream; lost people are tucked into every nook and corner of this world, searching to find their way home, the way to God. Join the rescue team! Be that enthusiastic, contagious life of light and hope that guides people safely home, into the arms of the Heavenly Father.

God, make me a vibrant, excited, contagious soul-winner
every day of my life. Amen.

# ❀ *Painful Procrastination* ❀

*"As has just been said: 'Today, if you hear his voice, do not harden your
hearts as you did in the rebellion'"* (Hebrews 3:15).

During most of my high school years, my friends and I walked to and from
school together. We met along the way and by the time we got to school we
had a crowd.

After school I often stopped to talk with an elderly man, Mr. A., in
the neighborhood. He stood in his yard and we talked across the fence.
These daily conversations had become an expected, and enjoyable, part of
my day.

One day I felt burdened to ask Mr. A. about his relationship with the
Lord. I was not quite sure how to approach it since he was a senior adult
and I was a teenager. With a lump in my throat I eked out the words, "Mr.
A., are you a Christian?"

He stopped talking and stared at me without responding. After a long
silence, he completely changed the subject.

That night I planned to ask my pastor to visit him. I waited to speak
with the pastor, but he was busy talking with a long line of people. Sunday
services and the next week's prayer meeting came and went. I still did not
mention Mr. A. to my pastor.

Thursday afternoon as I was walking home, horror gripped my soul
when I got to Mr. A.'s house. A white wreath hung on his front door. He
had died that day.

Even though that happened more than 40 years ago, the pain of my
procrastination still stings. According to the obituary, Mr. A. was a member
of a local church. However, I don't know about his true relationship with
the Lord.

From that experience I learned that when God leads us to witness to
someone, we cannot depend on another person to do it. In my case,
I expected my pastor to do what God was leading me to do. As today's verse
indicates, when we hear God's voice we cannot harden our hearts. Otherwise, our procrastination can be painful.

Dear Lord, please forgive us when we expect others to fulfill the role You have
prepared for us. In Jesus's name, Amen.

# ❀ Be Strong and Do the Work ❀

*David also said to Solomon his son, "Be strong and courageous,*
*and do the work" (1 Chronicles 28:20).*

The Bible contains hundreds of illustrations of people working hard. Ruth gleaned barley every day "until evening" and then late at night she threshed the grain she had gleaned (Ruth 2:17). Proverbs tells us the wife of noble character got up while it was still dark (Proverbs 31:15), provided food for the family from distant places (vv. 14–15), bought and sold fields (v. 16), spun and wove clothes (v. 19), and sold them in the marketplace (v. 24). She worked so hard her arms looked muscular (v. 17), and she was never idle (v. 27). Martha of Bethany was a great hostess, busy in the kitchen, and often tired (Luke 10:40), even interrupting Jesus, instructing Him to make her sister help her in the kitchen!

In the focal verse above, David instructs his son Solomon in the virtue of work. As David believed, work is usually hard, and it takes courage to work well. Sometimes workers today take the coward's way out, sit down on the job, take a long lunch hour, or find some way to cheat the employer out of time and money. In recent years, worldwide businesses have come to ruin because of dishonesty. Courts and churches alike are calling us to integrity and better business ethics. As Christians, we bear responsibility to have the courage to be strong and do the work God has called us to do.

A woman nowadays may not even believe in working hard; she feels entitled to a life of leisure. Some parents have reinforced lax work ethics, encouraging children to *get something for nothing*, refusing a lifestyle of moderation. You may know someone who feels honest hard work is old-fashioned, only for dull-witted people.

A Christian's work is to do ministry for the God's kingdom. Have you looked around lately to see what temples God wants you to build, or what servant leadership He needs? As David taught his son, are we teaching our children to work hard in ministry and sacrifice materialistic luxuries so God can be glorified?

Lord, help us return to honest values and hard work for You.
May we be worthy workers in Your missions fields, we pray. Amen.

# ❀ *Serving When It Hurts* ❀

*He got up from the meal...and began to wash his disciples' feet*
(John 13:4–5).

Thirteen men gathered in an upstairs room to eat their last meal together. Jesus looked around the room and saw not only Peter and His other dearest friends, but also the one who was out to get him.

Imagine how you would respond if you had been Christ. I would have shouted, "Unfair! " Maybe I would've thought, *I'm God; I don't have to take this!* and would have commanded a battalion of angels to give him what he deserved.

Jesus didn't choose any of these options. He quietly got up from the table, put on a towel, and began washing the disciples' feet. How did He garner the strength to serve in that moment?

The secret lies tucked away in two simple words, *"Jesus knew"* (John 13:3). What did Jesus know that empowered Him to serve in His final moments?

Jesus knew the time had come for Him to die. He had one more opportunity to show the disciples the meaning of love through an act of service. Jesus knew also that all power was His. He understood that just beyond the microcosm of an upstairs room, where 13 men ate their supper and Satan premeditated murder, God reigned supreme.

Jesus saw the big picture. Just as He had come from God, He also would return to God. The outcome was sure—His future secure. He obeyed in the moment knowing God would bring about His purposes however bleak the situation appeared at the moment.

Perhaps you've been serving but see little fruit. You're tired. You're disillusioned. But just as Jesus knew His call, you know God has called you. You know that Christ has given you power to please Him in every situation. Further, you know that beyond the microcosm of your ministry troubles, God reigns supreme. And you know how it will eventually end since God has assured the ultimate victory. So, don't give up. Kneel and wash those dirty feet.

Lord, help me keep my eyes focused on You as I serve. Amen.

# ❊ Get Your Head in the Clouds ❊

*Have you not known? Have you not heard? The everlasting God, the*
*LORD, the Creator of the ends of the earth, neither faints nor is weary.*
*His understanding is unsearchable* (Isaiah 40:28 NKJV).

Clouds amaze me. How do they stay suspended in air? What dictates the shape of a cloud? Why do clouds come in millions of shades of white? And how can the wind move a cloud so rapidly and it still retain its form? I'm sure someone knows the answers to those questions, but I'd rather not know. I enjoy the more direct line of logic: it's God.

We humans are getting smart, aren't we? We have found the cure for many diseases, and strides in travel and communication are being made every day at a pace we can scarcely keep up with in society. Yet, with all our intellectual prowess, we have yet to learn how to make rain clouds that will burst forth a downpour on command. And with the impressive knowledge of the mind, we have yet to figure out how to cure the evil of the human heart. We need God.

Do you find yourself mentally laboring over a situation? Do you pour over every detail in your mind, trying to figure out how to get the results you want? Attempting to solve all of your problems on your own is exhausting and futile at best. However, everlasting God is never exhausted or over-whelmed with your problems, or my problems, or the problems of every living creature on the planet. His understanding of every layer of your per-sonal problem is beyond what you could even begin to give Him credit for, best described as "unsearchable." With this in mind, it begs the question: can you trust God with your problems today? Look to the clouds for your answer.

Father, what a relief to realize You are never stumped with my problems.
How worthy of honor and praise is Your name! Now I must learn to trust You.
In my limited understanding of how marvelous You truly are,
help me to grow in my faith every day. Amen.

# ❀ Bull's-Eye! ❀

*Now He said to them, "These are My words which I spoke to you while*
*I was still with you, that all things which are written about Me in the*
*Law of Moses and the Prophets and the Psalms must be fulfilled"*
(Luke 24:44 NASB).

During my teenage years my family had a darts game set up in our carport.
Woe be to the person who dared walk between the players and the target.
None of us teens was particularly good at the game, as the nicks in the brick
wall proved. But we kept at it because that center circle taunted us from
afar. On the rare occasion when one of us hit the bull's-eye, we earned brag-
ging rights for weeks.

Now, imagine a target in which the bull's-eye represents one person
and we must discover this person's identity. Descriptions given throughout
a book provide clues about him, clues that are more general in the earlier
chapters and become progressively more specific, until only one person
qualifies as the subject—that's the bull's-eye.

Now, let's apply this to identifying Messiah-God who the
Old Testament promised would come. In the first Book of Genesis God
promised Abraham that all nations would be blessed through him and
his descendants (Genesis 12:3). Later, God said that out of the 12 tribes
of Israel, Messiah-God would come specifically from the tribe of Judah
(Genesis 49:10). Next, He revealed that out of all Jesse's sons, Messiah
would be a descendant of Jesse's son David (2 Samuel 7:12). Later, God
promised Messiah would be born of a virgin (Isaiah 7:14) and would be
both God and human (Isaiah 9:6). Of all the birthplaces that God could
have chosen, Bethlehem was the one city forecasted as Messiah's birthplace
(Micah 5:2). According to prophets, this God-man would perform many
miracles (Isaiah 35:5–6). Ultimately, He would be rejected by the Jews
and executed (Isaiah 53:3). His side, hands, feet, would be pierced (Psalm
22:16, Zachariah 12:10), and He would die with criminals (Isaiah 53:12).

These and many more Old Testament prophecies recorded hundreds
of years before the first century A.D. point to only one person: Jesus Christ
of Nazareth, a descendant of David, born in Bethlehem of a virgin named
Mary, known as a wonder worker, and crucified as a criminal under Pontius
Pilate after being rejected by His own people. This one, this Jesus, is the
one who hits the bull's-eye.

Lord Jesus, thank You for marking the way so we could recognize You and
receive salvation through faith in Your name. Amen.

# ❀ Tell Me One More Thing ❀

*He took her by the hand and said to her, "Talitha koum!" (which*
*means, "Little girl, I say to you, get up!"). Immediately the girl stood up*
*and walked around* (Mark 5:41–42).

On our previous visit with her, Mary asked if my husband, Wayne, and I would come back and stay up all night and talk about "things." We knew she meant spiritual things.

"We'll have a pajama party," I assured her.

"But this time we'll let the guys come," she laughingly replied.

A week later, her husband, Bill, phoned to say she was getting weaker daily and also asking daily about the "pajama party." We immediately made plans to go.

What a precious memory! We laughed, we talked, we sang, we prayed, we watched television, but most of all, we discussed spiritual matters. She asked many questions about death and dying. She reaffirmed her faith, and we talked about heaven and the glorious things that were awaiting her. We assured each other of our love and appreciation for the friendship we shared.

The next day, I went back into her room one last time. It was then she made a poignant request.

"Tell me one more thing that will make me feel better," her weak voice pleaded.

I pondered what that "one more thing" should be, realizing it might be the last thing I would ever say to her.

"Mary, did you know that your spirit will not die?" I asked.

Her face lit up, and she seemed surprised. "Really?"

"Imagine that you are in your foyer and you are going to a wonderful party in the most beautiful dining room you've ever seen. Many people you love are there, and you want to see them. However, to get there you must walk down a little hallway. Mary, death is that hallway. It's how you get to the place you want to be."

She smiled and settled back on her pillow. A few days later we received the call that she had walked down that hallway. If she could tell us "one more thing" today, I wonder what glorious thing it would be?

Dear Lord, help us to tell others the "one more thing"
that can change their lives forever. In Jesus's name, amen.

# ❀ *Where's Your Compassion?* ❀

*But the LORD said, "You have been concerned about this vine.... It*
*sprang up overnight and died overnight. But Nineveh has more than a*
*hundred and twenty thousand people who cannot tell their right hand*
*from their left.... Should I not be concerned about that great city?"*
(Jonah 4: 10–11).

Looking out the window today, God shows me young and old walking by. "Lord," I whisper, "Show me people to share your love with." My cell phone rings.

"Almost there. I'll be right over to pick you up." My sister is driving me to my other sister's house to have a good time. I jump up, put on my coat, and stand by the door, looking for her car.

Usually, as you and I look out, we see our world through God's eyes. Sometimes I'm just curious. I think one is a friend, but she turns and I see she's a stranger. I wish I had a relationship with some of them, but I'm too busy today to chat. Tomorrow I've planned a day with my children, and Wednesday I'm learning that computer program. Someday I'll get to know these people who walk by. There's one who looks sad. I wonder if she needs a helping hand.

God gives us people nearby to notice, but usually we refuse to accept the call to relationship.

Jonah, an Old Testament prophet, didn't want to minister to people in Nineveh. They weren't likable; he thought they didn't deserve God's love and care. Because God saved them from destruction, having *"compassion on them"* (Jonah 3:10), Jonah pouted. He sat under the shade of a vine, which died after a worm ate it the next morning. God reminded Jonah he should love the Ninevites as much as he did the vine that had sheltered him—like a friend.

What kind of relationships are you forming? Do you care about people who need God's love? His words for Jonah apply to us today. Do we care about things—computers, soap operas, or gadgets—better than our neighbors' needs? We have the secret to hope and eternal life. Let's share it today.

> Dear Lord, show me people who need Your love.
> Help me share with them. Amen.

# ❀ Pool-Table Prayer ❀

*Always be prepared to give an answer to everyone who asks you to give
the reason for the hope that you have.* (1 Peter 3:15).

My husband, Wayne, stopped to get gas after an out-of-state bereavement
visit, but neither of us had a credit card or any cash. We each thought the
other had it. We did have a checkbook, but no one accepted an out-of-state
check. Wayne finally said, "Let's just drive as far as we can and see what
happens." This time, our daughters were asleep. Wayne and I watched the
gas needle and prayed we would not get stranded on the side of the road
with our daughters.

Finally, we passed a pool hall/bar with two lone gas tanks in the gravel
parking lot. Wayne stopped and said, "It's our only hope. I wonder if they
will take a check?"

"Please be careful," I cautioned, as the place looked dangerous to me.

Wayne did not return for a long time, so I quietly slipped out of the car
and cupped my hands against the dirty glass to veer through the window.
The sight I saw makes me smile even today.

Wayne genuinely loves people and is truly an agent of God's love in
a hurting world. He also is a mighty man of prayer. I saw the patrons and
workers in the establishment gathered in a circle around the pool table,
holding hands, as Wayne prayed for them.

As I eased back into the car, a woman came out to talk with me. We
prayed for God's intervention in certain areas of need in her life. More
people came out to the car to meet me, and I talked with them.

We were there about an hour ministering to the people. Then, Wayne
filled the car with gas (yes, they did take a check) and we drove home. All
the while I reflected on the pool table prayer and how God works in mysterious ways, even using an empty gas tank.

Dear Lord, thank You for Your divine appointments. In Jesus's name, amen.

# ❀ *The Unexpected Gift* ❀

*"Do not judge, or you too will be judged"* (Matthew 7:1).

We did not realize we were moving into a high-crime neighborhood. A church member allowed us to rent a house without a lease so we could look for a home to buy. Molly was a baby, and Meri Beth was four years old.

Once we settled into the house, we began to meet the neighbors. In our little neighborhood we learned of a house of prostitution, a drug ring, and a neighbor who was imprisoned for sexual assault shortly after we moved there.

Almost daily I drove around looking for a house. I was anxious to move our daughters to a safer place.

Finally, we realized we were there for a reason. We began Bible clubs and other activities for the neighborhood children.

For the adults and families, we asked our youth to do a musical they had presented at the church. We delivered flyers to all the homes, inviting our neighbors to bring their lawn chairs or blankets to our front yard for a time of musical entertainment and fellowship. We called it a "Sing-Along-on-the-Lawn."

The day of the sing-along I was busy preparing refreshments for that evening. Late in the afternoon someone knocked at the door. When I opened it, the madam of the brothel was standing on our porch with a freshly baked cake.

"I will not be here tonight for obvious reasons, though I believe in what you are trying to do. I wanted to make a contribution toward the refreshments."

I was almost speechless. I thanked her and reached out to hug her.

That evening remains a beautiful memory in our hearts. Our yard was filled with neighbors, many who met each other for the first time. We shared food, fun, and fellowship. Most importantly, we shared Jesus Christ with people from all walks of life. However, I specifically remember the kindness of the madam who was an important part of the evening—even though she was not there.

Dear Lord, help us to look beyond the faults of others to their needs,
just as You do. In Jesus's name, amen.

# ❀ *Eyes Wide Open* ❀

*And Elisha prayed, and said, "LORD, I pray, open his eyes that he may
see." Then the LORD opened the eyes of the young man, and he saw
(2 Kings 6:17 NKJV).*

When God called me to do missions work in Niger, I made a request. *God,
please help me know who to ask to go with me, and please tell them, too, that You're
sending them to Niger.*

A few weeks later, I stood worshipping in the sanctuary, when I looked
on the platform at a woman who was leading in singing. God gave me
clear directive: *Ask her to go.* I soon emailed her about the missions trip. She
scanned my email, quickly rejected the idea of going to Niger, and then
within the hour began to sense strong words from God that He was calling
her to Africa. God answered my prayer.

A short time later, I boarded a plane with a team to fulfill a missions trip
in Jamaica. One of the women leaned across the aisle and said, "Kimberly,
I heard you're going to Niger." I quietly affirmed what she said, and then
changed the subject; I didn't want to "advertise" the trip in order to see
clearly the hand of God move.

A few days into the Jamaican trip, I sensed God whispered to me to
invite this same woman to go to Niger. When I talked with her the next
week, she told me she had already sensed God sending her there, and she
had been waiting patiently for me to invite her. God once again was faithful,
having opened her eyes to the call.

Elisha's young servant was filled with fear by the Syrian army
surrounding them, but Elisha was a wise leader. Rather than shaming the
young servant for his lack of faith or trying to convince the servant with
mere words, Elisha asked God to intervene. God opened the young man's
eyes, bolstering his faith—not in Elisha, but in God.

Perhaps you know Christians who need to see God at work in their
midst. Like Elisha, pray!

God, open my eyes to see where You're working all around me. Surround me
with godly people who have their eyes opened, that we might boldly move
forward according to Your will. Amen.

# ❀ *Sacrifice* ❀

*When… you reap its harvest, bring to the priest a sheaf of the first*
*grain you harvest. He is to wave the sheaf before the LORD so it will be*
*accepted on your behalf… On the day you wave the sheaf, you must*
*sacrifice… to the LORD* (Leviticus 23:10–12).

Our Scripture reading for today explains the origin of the annual biblical feast of Firstfruits. The Israelites presented a sheaf (a bundle of grain held together by a cord) of the first harvested grain crop to God. The priest waved it before God as a sacrifice. It was considered a sacrifice because they were not to eat the crop, or even make bread from it, until they had presented this bundle of grain to God.

Paul says that believers have the firstfruits of the Spirit (Romans 8:23). Pentecost (Acts 2) marks the Spirit's coming, 50 days after Passover. In response to God's wonderful gift, we are to offer our lives as a sacrifice to Him. Paul admonishes us to "offer our bodies as living sacrifices, holy and pleasing to God" (Romans 12:1). Amazingly, when we make lifestyle choices beneficial to our health we are actually offering a sacrifice to God.

However, the most wonderful example of firstfruits in the Bible is the resurrection of our Lord and Savior, Jesus Christ. He became the firstfruits of the dead (1 Corinthians 15:20).

Several years ago an airplane crashed in frigid waters near Washington's National Airport. A friend of mine saw the wreckage shortly after it happened. A rescue helicopter pulled survivors onto the lift ladder. Suddenly, a man dived into the water, hoisted five people onto the ladder then disappeared beneath the waves. None of the five people knew the man. He gave his life for people he did not know.

Jesus gave His life for us, yet He knew us with all our sins and faults. Let us offer a sacrifice to Him of the best harvest of our lives, not merely what is leftover.

Dear God, I praise You for providing Your Son as the ultimate sacrifice. May I live for You as fully as You died for me. In Jesus's name I pray. Amen.

# ❀ Jesus Said It Was True ❀

*Jesus answered, "It is written"* (Luke 4:4).

As Christians we should believe what Jesus believed. So, what did Jesus believe about the Bible? Through Jesus's own declarations recorded in the New Testament, we can learn a great deal about how He viewed the Hebrew Scriptures, which we know as the Old Testament, the Bible that He and His apostles studied.

After His baptism, even before He started His public ministry, during the wilderness temptation Jesus resisted Satan by quoting Old Testament truths from Scripture, introducing each one with the solemn declaration, *"It is written"* (Matthew 4:4). While many people today believe that the story of Jonah ending up inside a great fish is just a fairy tale, in Matthew 12:40 Christ treated the story of Jonah as an historical reality. In Matthew 24:37–38, the Lord affirmed also the reality of Noah and the flood. He even described the setting, saying that people were going about their everyday lives, eating and drinking and marrying, when Noah built the ark and was saved by entering the ark when the floods came and wiped out the human race. Jesus even made an assertion about the origin of humans on earth, saying that God Himself created Adam and Eve (Matthew 19:4).

Most importantly, after His resurrection, Jesus Christ made an audacious claim about His personal fulfillment of the Old Testament prophecies. He claimed that the three sections of the Old Testament — the books of law, of the prophets, and of the writings such as Psalms, all were written about Him (Luke 24:44).

Jesus Himself claimed that the Old Testament was not only true but also that He was the central figure forecasted throughout the Old Testament writings. We can choose to believe Him or call Him a liar, but we cannot deny that Jesus viewed the Bible as true, authoritative, and sufficient even to help those tempted to overcome.

Lord Jesus, I believe what You believe. The Scripture is true and
God has spoken in His Word. May I take seriously its truths,
be strengthened by its promises, and find genuine help in times
of temptation so that I may not sin against You. Amen.

# ❀ *Self Central* ❀

*There will be terrible times in the last days.*
*People will be lovers of themselves* (2 Timothy 3:1–2).

Read through these statements, marking each as true or false.

1. Humans are essentially good-hearted.
2. We should accept all religious beliefs as equally valid.
3. I deserve to be happy.
4. I need to love myself more.
5. We can trust our hearts always to tell us the truth.
6. Most women need to learn how to assert their rights more often.
7. Since God is loving; He will not send to hell people who have never heard about Jesus.
8. Most of my problems result from the tough situations life has dealt me.
9. The Scriptures teach I must first love myself before I can love others.
10. When I've sinned, I must forgive myself.
11. Our goal in helping others is to encourage them to reach their highest potential—self-actualization.
12. To find answers to our problems, we need only look within ourselves.
13. Humans are the most highly-developed creatures in the animal kingdom.
14. Most women suffer from poor self-esteem.
15. When tragedy occurs, I must forgive God.
16. In the end, as long as a person is sincere in whatever he believes, that person will go to heaven.
17. We need to learn how to be more self-reliant.
18. Many of my issues today can be traced back to my childhood.
19. Only I can judge what I need.
20. It's good to let your anger out; otherwise, you're likely to explode.

How many did you mark as true? All 20 statements reflect a human-centered mind-set. The fact that most Christians would label some statements as true illustrates the subtle invasion of self-centered thinking into the Christian mind-set.

Even many Christian ministries have embraced the cause of "self," promoting self-esteem, self-forgiveness, and self-love, all with the unholy focus on *strengthening self*, instead of glorifying God wholeheartedly. Should we advocate self-loathing? Of course not. But whether we love ourselves too much or hate ourselves, "self" dominates center stage.

The center stage of our lives is designed for God alone. When we consume ourselves with bringing Him glory, doing His will, and building His kingdom, the need to build up ourselves diminishes.

Jesus, teach me to focus on You, trusting that as I die to self,
I will find You give life abundantly. Amen.

# ❦ *Patterns* ❦

*In all things showing yourself to be a pattern of good works*
(Titus 2:7 NKJV).

When I was a math teacher, my friends would often turn to me when it was time to crunch numbers. Talk about pressure to perform! That's why I knew exactly how the makeup saleslady felt the other day when she and I met for the first time. I had caught her off guard, and she apologized profusely for not wearing any eye makeup. I was in no way offended by her lack of eyeliner, but she was embarrassed because she felt she wasn't setting a good example for me. She felt she hadn't met my expectations.

People turn to teachers for facts and figures, makeup sales people for facial beauty, and Christians for strong moral behavior. Though unbelievers may not have a solid grasp of who God is, they have a strong opinion about what godly behavior should look like, and they're carefully scrutinizing the lifestyles of Christians to detect hypocrisy. As believers, you and I don't have to feel guilty and defeated if we can't measure up to those expectations, because we have freedom in Christ. We have victory over sin through the blood of Jesus, even though we have to wrestle with our sinful flesh. We can choose daily to live for Christ and submit ourselves to the Holy Spirit to bear out His fruit in our lives. We can't be perfect, but we can establish a pattern of good works.

When a pattern is in place, others can look at the pattern and know what to expect to see next. As Paul wrote to Titus, he was encouraging Titus and the other young men to consistently and faithfully follow godly principles of living, doing good works as a standard practice in their lifestyles. By establishing this pattern of good works, they would bring glory to God and set an example to the outside world of what it means to be a follower of Christ.

What do your established patterns of behavior say to unbelievers? Do they see Christ in you?

Heavenly Father, I want to have patterns of good works in my life
as a witness to the world. May I be consistently pointing others to Jesus
through my daily actions. Amen.

# ❀ From Plea to Praise ❀

*I will praise you, O Lord my God, with all my heart;*
*I will glorify your name forever* (Psalm 86:12).

Lizzie was a thin girl with fuzzy pigtails who failed the second grade—
again—the year I went from first grade to second. I didn't understand
why she was so tall, why her dresses were thin, or why she seldom said
anything. In the second grade, all students think about is survival; they
seldom think of reaching out to others because they're preoccupied with
hoping someone will reach out to *them!*

It was social suicide to stand by Lizzie. No second grader had the nerve
to do it. We ran from her and played elsewhere. I didn't think much about
Lizzie one way or the other. Most of us accepted Lizzie as we did the wall-
paper: she was just *there.*

At the end of Christmas break, Lizzie didn't come back to school. I was
sorry I hadn't been a friend and wished I had another chance. Four years
later, when I became a Christian, I searched for Lizzie in crowds, hoping to
see her and tell her about Jesus. I never got that opportunity.

Reflecting on my childhood perspective of the "other" world—those
who were poor, abused, or shunned—I realize the importance of teaching
children to glorify God at an early age. I'll never have the chance I had
with Lizzie in the second grade. My heart was too busy pleading with God,
"Gimmie, gimmie"; Lizzie never heard me show His overflowing love.

In Psalm 82, the psalmist changes from a prayer of *pleas* to one of *praise*.
He begins with requests. *"Answer me, for I am poor and needy"* (Psalm 86:1).
*"Guard my life"* v. 2). *"Have mercy on me"* (v. 3). *"Listen to my cry"* (v. 6). However, he changes his pleas to praise: *"Among the gods there is none like you,*
*O Lord; no deeds can compare with yours"* (v. 8). *"But you, O Lord, are a compas-*
*sionate and gracious God…abounding in love and faithfulness"* (v. 15). *"You…have*
*helped me and comforted me"* (v. 17).

May each of us learn to praise God early and late.

Lord, may we proclaim Your words to all the Lizzies of the world. Amen.

# ❀ *All Things to All People* ❀

*I have become all things to all men so that by all possible means I might save some* (1 Corinthians 9:22).

We once lived less than an hour from New York City, so we spent a good deal of time there. God gave us numerous opportunities to minister to people in the entertainment industry—actors, models, and producers. They invited us to attend parties in the city. We saw these invitations as golden doors of ministry opportunities.

When we walked through the door, Wayne and I laughingly said "good-bye" to each other knowing that in a short while we would each be in a different corner of the room talking with people, and listening to their hurts, and praying with them.

One night a very distinguished woman walked up to me and handed me an envelope saying, "I'd really like for you to come to this."

As she walked away, one of the guests asked if I recognized the woman. When I told her I did not, she explained the woman was on the New York Social Registry. I opened the envelope to find an invitation to "the event" of the year.

As we were leaving a party one night, the butler asked us to wait a moment. He hurried to the kitchen and brought back some warm quiche in a container. "The caterer just took these out of the oven," he explained. "Take them back to your daughters in New Jersey."

We walked out of the beautiful Park Avenue apartment onto the street and found a homeless woman crouched by the door. We gave her some quiche and prayed with her. As we drove away, we looked back at the lights of the beautiful apartment where the party was still in progress and the homeless woman sitting by the door eating the quiche. We realized anew that whether "down and out" or "up and out," people need the Lord.

Dear Lord, please help us recognize that everyone—regardless of his or her situation in life—needs You. In Jesus's name, amen.

# ❁ *Spiritual SAC* ❁

*Be diligent to present yourself approved to God, a worker who does not
need to be ashamed, rightly dividing the word of truth*
(2 Timothy 2:15 NKJV).

During my elementary school years when my dad was in the Air Force
working with Strategic Air Command (SAC), we had to be in a constant
state of preparedness. Our family schedule revolved around making certain
my dad could get to his job site in the number of minutes allotted if a state
of emergency was declared.

Most Christian believers want to be used by God. We may even want
to lead others. But do we meet the job requirements of readiness? Second
Timothy 2:1–26 teaches us that preparedness at any given moment requires
intensive preparation during all previous moments. First, Paul's admonishes us to remember the source of our strength and to continuously submit
ourselves to Jesus Christ as we talk with Him throughout the day. Second,
he says that one mark of readiness is willingness and readiness to suffer. In
fact, willingness to suffer is a crucial part of our job description.

Third, Paul urges believers to study hard the Word so that we can correctly interpret it and thus, avoid being ashamed. Diligent study helps us
know Him and His way of thinking so we are able to make wise decisions
and wisely counsel others.

Fourth, as we learn and mature, we are responsible for passing on what
we've learned to those coming behind us. Effective leaders always multiply
themselves so they don't monopolize the corner on knowledge, truth, or
skills.

Finally, we need to practice humility and forgiveness, so that when
during our teaching we must correct or challenge skewed thinking, we
do so in a way that the person can hear and respond to the truth without
feeling attacked. It helps us to remember how we want to be corrected
when we think wrongly.

Being ready to be used by God requires intensive preparation. But
then, serving as a soldier has always demanded discipline and sacrifice.

Lord, I want to be prepared at all times to know and teach Your truth. Show me
the steps to take, and I will obey. Amen.

# ❄ A Time to Be Brokenhearted ❄

*Now I rejoice, not that you were made sorry, but that your sorrow
led to repentance. For you were made sorry in a godly manner,
that you might suffer loss from us in nothing. For godly sorrow
produces repentance leading to salvation, not to be regretted*
(2 Corinthians 7:9–10 NKJV).

A mother once again finds herself in the peacemaking role between her two quarreling children. After much discussion and a firm lecture, she turns to the older child and commands, "Tell your sister you're sorry."

The boy turns to his sister and says with a defiant scowl, "I'm sorry!"

The mother sees right through her son's feeble attempt at reconciliation and refuses to accept his open dishonesty. "No, you must say it like you mean it." The son repeats his words, still half-heartedly, but with a tinge of sincerity.

Why wasn't the mother satisfied with her son's words of apology? Because words spoken without sincerity are worthless! A wise mother can detect insincerity in one of her children. How much more easily can our Heavenly Father recognize emptiness in our requests for His forgiveness? The Lord spoke in 1 Samuel 16:7, *"For the LORD does not see as man sees; for man looks at the outward appearance, but the LORD looks at the heart"* (NKJV). While a mother may have to settle for an apology that at least *sounds* sincere, God looks past how sincere we *sound* to determine how sincere we truly *are* in our hearts. He desires us to come to Him with a contrite spirit, brokenhearted over our disobedience, and desiring to walk righteously before Him.

God isn't pleased when we gloss over our sin or make excuses for our shortcomings, nor is He honored when we confess with our lips but have no repentance in our hearts. Repentance is turning away from sin with determination to no longer walk in that direction of wrongdoing. We will continue to fall and displease Him, but God is always faithful to forgive us when we're earnest in our repentance.

Dear God, as I confess my sins to You today, may I be sincere in my heart.
Help me not to take Your forgiveness lightly, as it is a precious gift
of Your grace and mercy. Amen.

# ❀ How Far Would He Go? ❀

*The Lord is… not willing that any should perish but that all should come to repentance* (2 Peter 3:9 NKJV).

It was Christmas Eve and our then six-year-old Sara longed for a specific doll that wore a pink ballerina costume. Her dad looked at every store in town, but ended up having to drive to a store several hours away. A dad will go a long way to get his little girl a doll because he loves her.

God loves humans, and the story of Cornelius and Peter in Acts 10 proves just how far He will go to demonstrate that love. A high-ranking Roman soldier, Cornelius was a sincere worshipper of God but had not yet received the gospel message. God heard his prayers, prayers that revealed a heart open to the truth.

In Joppa, more than a day's walk away, Peter was praying. Peter was a Jewish Christian man. But Jews, Christian or not, were expected to keep themselves ritually clean, which to their thinking required them to avoid Gentiles. So how was God going to bring them together?

First, God sent an angel to tell Cornelius to contact Peter who would explain what to do next. To prepare Peter, God gave a vision of a sheet filled with creatures, both "clean" and "unclean," descending from heaven. Peter was hungry, so when the Lord spoke and told him to eat, no one would blame him for grabbing the nearest ham hock. But even with his stomach growling, Peter resisted the temptation to eat unclean food.

God then explained the vision was less about animals but more about His plan to bring the Gentiles into God's kingdom. Peter went straight to Cornelius, shared the gospel, and rejoiced when God confirmed that Gentiles who believed would be joint heirs in Christ.

What strikes me is the lengths to which God would go to make sure that a person whose heart was open would hear the gospel. He sent an angel to Cornelius and a vision to prepare Peter. Peter traveled more than a day's journey on already-weary feet, just to share with Cornelius the gospel. With a God who is willing to go to this much trouble, we don't need to worry about a lost person slipping unnoticed by Him through the cracks.

God, thank You for showing through the story of Cornelius
that You will make sure every ready heart hears the gospel. Amen.

# ❀ Born Again ❀

*I tell you the truth, no one can enter the kingdom of God unless he is
born of water and the Spirit* (John 3:5).

Nicodemus said the religious leaders (indicated by the *we* in John 3:2) knew
Jesus had come from God or He could not perform His many miracles.
Jesus the master Teacher responded by employing an important educa-
tional strategy. He piqued the student's curiosity.

Jesus told Nicodemus that unless a man is born again he cannot see
the kingdom of God (John 3:3). Nicodemus thought Jesus meant that to
see God's kingdom, a person would have to crawl back into his mother's
womb to be born a second time. The strategy had worked. The student was
hooked!

Jesus then proceeded with the lesson by explaining that a person must
be born of water and of the Spirit or he cannot enter the kingdom of God.
"Seeing" the kingdom was important to Nicodemus, but "entering" was
even more important.

Being a religious leader, Nicodemus was familiar with the water. The
Jews had numerous rites of ceremonial washing and baptisms to purify
themselves. One was also born of water when the sac of amniotic fluid
broke during childbirth. But what did it mean to be born of the Spirit?
Nicodemus wondered.

Jesus then presented the heart of the lesson. The way to be born again is to
be born of the Spirit. The way to be born of the Spirit is to believe in God's
only begotten Son as the atonement for sin. Jesus's words in John 3:16
explained it all.

*Believe* is much more than head knowledge. It is heart knowledge. The
actual Greek word used is *pisteuo*, meaning "to have faith in, to trust, to
commit." Jesus taught Nicodemus that he must be born again spiritually.

From John 7:50–52 we discover that Nicodemus defended Jesus
before the chief priests and Pharisees and from John 19:39 that Nicodemus
brought spices to anoint Jesus's body for burial after the Crucifixion.
Evidence confirms that the student learned the lesson!

Dear God, Help me to share with others the way to be born again. In Jesus's
name I pray. Amen.

# ❀ Pull Up a Couch ❀

*God is faithful, by whom you were called into the fellowship of His*
*Son, Jesus Christ our Lord* (1 Corinthians 1:9 NKJV).

My neighbor's daughter Kate accepted Jesus as her Savior during Vacation Bible School. She said, "Mommy, I feel like Jesus has moved a couch into my heart." What a wonderful image of the Christian life: Jesus moves into our lives, and we invite Him to make Himself at home in our hearts! We can enjoy intimate fellowship with Almighty God.

God has created us as social creatures; we were made for fellowship. Unfortunately, loneliness plagues many people. A single friend once took me to a nursing home to do ministry and said, "Just be yourself, and be sure to hug each resident. For many of them, that may be the only hug they'll get all week, and I know just what that feels like." Do you know any lonely people?

You have two things to offer a lonely person. First, you can invite her to connect with your life. As you open your heart to share it with her, you're widening the boundaries of your sphere of influence for Jesus Christ. Your friendship could have a significant effect on her life as you model before her the authentic Christian life. Second, you can offer a lonely person the opportunity to meet the best friend she could ever hope for, Jesus the Savior. She needs to know that God is calling her into fellowship with Him, and you can be the one to introduce her to your best friend: Jesus!

As you look for opportunities each day to share your faith in Jesus Christ, think about the people you know who may be searching for a meaningful relationship. Tell them about Jesus our Lord, Jesus our Savior, and Jesus our Friend. The fellowship that Jesus offers is a wonderful benefit of Christianity, and we need to spread the word to the empty-hearted—Jesus wants to pull up a couch!

Heavenly Father, thank You for calling me into fellowship with Your Son.
What a privilege to draw near to Jesus as He draws near to me.
Help me be a friend to the lonely, and allow me to tell others
about the fellowship available through Jesus. Amen.

# ❀ Lost and Found ❀

*"Rejoice with me; I have found my lost sheep"* (Luke 15:6).

Probably every speaker lives with the nagging fear that he or she will forget a date or a place for a speaking engagement. In the midst of heavy traffic I received a call asking me to speak again at a church where I recently had been.

In the mountains where we lived at the time, many communities derive their names from the type of trees that grow there. I often confused the locations by forgetting the name of the trees indigenous to that area.

The church that called was Oak Grove Baptist Church. Since I was in heavy traffic I made a mental note of the date but did not write down the name of the church.

When the night arrived, I drove to Poplar Grove Baptist Church's empty parking lot. With horror I realized I was at the wrong "Grove" and should be walking in the door of Oak Grove about that time. Even though I had spoken there only a few weeks earlier, I could not remember how I got there.

I stopped at a convenience store and explained my dilemma. A customer overheard the conversation and offered to lead me to the right place. When we arrived at the church, I invited her to the service.

She had not been to church in years but decided that she needed to attend. We entered to a room filled with loving people loudly singing hymns of praise. They said they knew I would come, and they decided to sing until I got there.

I explained the situation and introduced them to the woman who led me to the right place. The message that night was on the Cross. She sat and listened in rapt attention.

As we walked out to our cars after the service, she shared some of her life's story. It was an amazing journey of joys and sorrows, victories and defeats. However, she realized it was time for a new start. We both realized I was lost, but she had been found!

Dear Lord, thank You for bringing one of Your precious lambs
back into the fold. In Jesus's name, amen.

# ❀ *When Little Is Much* ❀

*All these people gave their gifts out of their wealth; but she out of her
poverty put in all she had to live on* (Luke 21:4).

Often a mystique seems to surround the words *missions* and *ministry*. People
feel that involvement in missions and ministry requires large amounts of
time, financial resources, and/or many difficult sacrifices. Sometimes this
is true.

However, more often than not, the mission and ministry to which God
calls us involve performing small acts of love in our everyday world.

Many times, I see God use the simple gift of a cake to bless lives. In
churches where my husband, Wayne, has served, we've encountered many
wonderful bakers. Their cakes are their signature creations, and a person
can recognize the baker by looking at the cake. These cakes always seem to
appear during times of celebration as well as times of grief and sorrow.

Mrs. Henry is a legend in our region. She had a genuine love and compassion for prisoners, and regularly visited the jails and detention centers.
During her visits, Mrs. Henry discerned that many of the prisoners came
from homes where their birthdays had not been celebrated. Most had never
had a party or even a birthday cake.

Mobilizing people in area churches, Mrs. Henry kept a supply of cakes
baked by the participating congregations. She froze them. Then, when
prisoners had birthdays, they were presented with their very own birthday
cakes. Many women in our congregation were not comfortable visiting the
prisons. However, they joyfully baked cakes for the prisoners. Both the
ones who baked the cakes and the ones who delivered them were involved
in missions and ministry.

Wayne preaches a sermon entitled, "Little Is Much When God Is in
It." Even baking a cake can be a part of advancing God's kingdom here on
earth—missions and ministry. That's when little is much!

Dear Lord, thank You for accepting our small acts of love
as acts of missions and ministry. In Jesus's name, amen.

# ❀ *When the Eggs Explode* ❀

*Therefore, whether you eat or drink, or whatever you do, do all to the glory of God* (1 Corinthians 10:31 NKJV).

I should explain that I left the eggs to boil for three hours due to extenuating circumstances. In a hurry to get to church, I donned my pantyhose only to find a hole in them. Knowing the culprit was my 15-year-old daughter, who must have borrowed them, I insisted she give me her hole-less pair, now already on her legs. After the frantic switch, I ran out the door, completely forgetting about the steaming eggs.

On leaving church three hours later, I found a note on my windshield, written by my husband, Randy, who had gone home earlier to change clothes for work. It said, "The eggs are done."

Once home I found another note: "I let out most of the smoke and cleaned up what I could. I will finish the kitchen ceiling if you can finish the walls and floor." His drawing showed how far the exploding eggs had traveled—from the kitchen, over an archway, through the living room and dining area, splattering on the back door.

My husband could've fussed, or in his best parental tone, lectured me about the danger of fire. But he didn't. He cleaned up what he could and brought a little humor into the situation.

As a servant of God, you know that sometimes things won't go as planned. The ministry you spent hours planning fizzles out. Family needs conflict with service commitments. You argue with your spouse. In short, the eggs explode.

When you get discouraged and your servant's heart is about to give out, remember you're not alone there, scraping egg goo off the back door. Jesus knows. And He's not lecturing or asking you why you can't get your act together. With His help, clean up what you can, and find someone who will laugh with you about the oddities of life and the joys of serving.

Lord Jesus, when I'm alone on my knees scraping up egg goo, thank You for joining me there and helping me see things from Your eternal perspective. Amen.

*"The Egg Goo" first appeared in* Woman to Woman: Preparing Yourself to Mentor *by Edna Ellison and Tricia Scribner (New Hope Publishers, 2005).*

# ❧ Throw It Down ❧

*The Lord said, "Throw it on the ground." Moses threw it on the
ground and it became a snake, and he ran from it* (Exodus 4:3).

Moses was a shepherd for 40 years in the wilderness of Midian. His
shepherd's rod was an important part of his own protection, as well as the
protection of his flock. The shepherd's rod gave him a sense of security.

Therefore, God had Moses throw his "security" to the ground. God
was teaching early on that He, not a piece of wood, would be Moses's security. God required Moses to rid himself of it quickly in a deliberate act of
obedience.

When Moses obeyed, God revealed the true nature of Moses's dependence on the rod. The shepherd's rod became a serpent, the biblical picture
of Satan (Revelations 20:2).

Nothing was inherently wrong with the rod itself for it was only a
piece of wood. However, God knew that anyone or anything that usurped
Moses's dependence upon Him was wrong.

The very thing that Moses once clung to was now the thing from which
he ran. The object that kept him from fear now brought him fear. Ironically,
he now runs for protection from what once was his protection.

God then told Moses to pick up the serpent. In another deliberate act
of faithful obedience he did as God asked, and the serpent transformed
back into a shepherd's rod. It was no longer the rod of Moses. It was now
the rod of God. This rod was used to confound Pharaoh's magicians, to part
the Red Sea, and to lead hundreds of thousands of Israelites through the
wilderness.

One of the most powerful songs I've ever heard is "Moses" by Ken
Medema. The closing lines express the following:

> What do you hold in your hand today?
> To what or to whom are you bound?
> Are you willing to give it to God right now?
> Give it up, let it go, throw it down!

Dear Lord, please show me anything that hinders my dependence on You.
Help me to throw it down, and if it is Your will that I pick it back up,
help me do so under Your authority. In Jesus's name, amen.

# ❀ Who's Taking the Lead? ❀

*Now it came to pass, when the time had come for Him to be received up, that He steadfastly set His face to go to Jerusalem*
(Luke 9:51 NKJV).

There's a warrant for Jesus's arrest in Jerusalem. You and several other disciples are trying to keep pace with Him. When He turns to speak, you notice His countenance looks foreign, preoccupied. His gaze never leaves the road as He speaks of horrors awaiting Him up the hill in the city. He will be betrayed to political and religious leaders who will put Him on trial and condemn Him to death. They will mock Him and spit on Him and beat Him. And kill Him? Impossible. Surely He hasn't forgotten His promise to restore the kingdom and free Israel from the tyranny of foreign oppression.

How could God expect Him to suffer and die? Wouldn't that thwart God's plan? Perhaps the Lord misunderstands His destiny.

Like the disciples, we often forget that our interpretation of God's promises may be colored by our own selfish desires. The prophet Isaiah had explained the necessity of Messiah's suffering as integral to His ultimate victory as Redeemer.

*"Yet it pleased the LORD to bruise Him; He has put Him to grief. When You make His soul an offering for sin, He shall see His seed, He shall prolong His days, And the pleasure of the LORD shall prosper in His hand. He shall see the labor of His soul, and be satisfied. By His knowledge My righteous Servant shall justify many, For He shall bear their iniquities. Therefore I will divide Him a portion with the great, And He shall divide the spoil with the strong, Because He poured out His soul unto death, And He was numbered with the transgressors, And He bore the sin of many, And made intercession for the transgressors" (Isaiah 53:10–12 NKJV).*

Without Christ's suffering and death, there would be no kingdom and no freedom. May we as His disciples joyfully accept the Lord's means of accomplishing His goals and join Him.

Lord, I often read into Your promises my own purposes and means.
Forgive me, and teach me to follow rather than trying to lead You. Amen.

# ❀ *Dear Allah?* ❀

*For God was pleased to have all his fullness dwell in him*
(Colossians 1:19).

I was speaking with a ministry team to high school students about evidence for the truth of Christianity. Afterward, a student asked, "If someone prays to Allah, is he praying to the same God as the Christian God?"

If we were to look in an Arabic Bible, we would see the word *Allah* for God. What we call God, though, is more than a question of *name*. What we have to discern is whether the name of the God being discussed matches the *character* of the true God. The true God is three persons—the Triune God—and He sent His Son, who was God in the flesh, to die for man's sins. If the Allah we worship has all the essential character traits of the Bible's God, then it is the same God of Christianity.

But suppose the Allah worshipped is not a trinity (three persons yet one substance). Suppose He did not come in the flesh to redeem mankind from sin. And suppose He does not offer salvation by grace through faith alone and instead determines eligibility to enter heaven solely on whether one's good works outweigh the bad. That Allah is not the true God.

Imagine you knew me personally. You would know that I am just over five feet tall with brown hair and freckles. One day a friend of yours said, "Oh, yeah, I know Tricia Scribner. Now, that's one tall lady. And she's got a tan like nobody's business!" Since you know me, you would undoubtedly know that your friend was *not* talking about the same Tricia Scribner. I will never have a tan unless all my freckles run together. (One can always dream.)

You would point out to her that she may know someone by the same *name*, but it is not the same *person*. So it is with God. He possesses essential character traits. People call their supreme object of worship *Yahweh*, *God*, or *Allah*, depending on the nationality of the worshipper. But the true God's character is forever the same.

O God of Abraham, Isaac, and Jacob, who sent God the Son in the flesh
to redeem us from our sin, thank You that we can recognize
You by Your eternally unchangeable character. Amen.

# ❀ *Sacrificially* ❀

*"I will not take what is yours for the LORD, nor offer burnt offerings*
*with that which costs me nothing"* (1 Chronicles 21:24 NKJV).

What does it cost to serve the Lord? Your first thought might be the expense
to your pocketbook, offering your tithes and giving to missions. Next, you
might reflect on your time, and the personal investments you make to serve
in the church or community. Consider the sum of what you're currently
offering to the Lord; does your giving come at no real expense to you, or are
you sacrificially giving of yourself to honor the Lord?

I recently talked with a woman whose life offered a new perspective
on sacrificial giving. She is living with a bad-tempered husband in a difficult marriage. Her husband doesn't know Jesus as His Savior, nor do her
children. However, she has great hope that God is at work in their lives.
She desires for her children to have their father in their home, and she
doesn't want to do anything that would hinder her husband from receiving the Lord. Most of all, she wants to honor God in her marriage vows,
so she stays in a marriage filled with dark days, offering up her very life as
a moment-by-moment sacrifice to the Lord. It's costing her something, but
she is trusting God to intervene in her family according to His perfect timing. Instead of dwelling on "what my life could be like if…", she is choosing
to dwell on God's trustworthiness. She is making a daily decision to die to
self and to be a living sacrifice.

Do you long to live whole-heartedly for God? Seek God's face as you
come before Him today to offer up your praise and commit the day to Him.
With a cheerful heart, ask God to show you what He would have you sacrifice today to honor Him. Rejoice that you have a heart to give God an
offering that costs you something.

Heavenly Father, I want to offer my life to You to such depths
that it costs me something. Please reveal to me what I can give sacrificially
to You that will honor Your holy name. Amen.

# ❀ *Recognizing Answered Prayer* ❀

*Before they call I will answer; while they are still speaking I will hear*
(Isaiah 65:24).

Our little mission-type church hosted the annual, spring Girl's Auxiliary (GA) meeting for the entire association. We confirmed on several occasions that our only responsibilities were to provide the location and refreshments.

The morning of the all-day meeting, I received a call from one of the associational leaders saying we had been given wrong information. We were responsible for the program as well.

Panic-mode set in with me as I conveyed the message to my husband. We immediately began drawing from our many years of youth work to try to plan a day that would be meaningful and fun.

Suddenly, in the midst of my panic, I realized the golden opportunity God provided through this situation. I knelt and prayed that God would bless the girls and that someone would receive salvation that day. In my mind I pictured a sea of little girls' faces as I prayed.

GAs from New York and parts of Connecticut and New Jersey arrived, and we had a wonderful time. God truly blessed the day. However, as far as we knew, no one accepted Christ.

Afterwards I was cleaning the church kitchen when a teenage boy walked in looking for one of his friends. I explained that his friend left after finishing the yard work.

As we continued talking I asked if he had ever accepted Christ. His eyes lit up as he said, "No, I haven't, and I've always known I needed to. Can you tell me how?"

I explained how the Cross is our bridge to holiness. "I'm ready to walk across that bridge right now," he said excitedly. We prayed, and he confessed his faith in Jesus.

When I asked the Lord for someone to experience salvation that day, I assumed it would be a GA girl. However, God's answer was a fine young man who eagerly walked across the bridge into His kingdom.

Dear Lord, help us learn to recognize Your answers to our prayers even when they do not look like we envision. In Jesus's name, amen.

# ❀ Young Man on a Yellow Line ❀

*Just as Christ was raised from the dead through the glory of the Father,*
*we too may live a new life* (Romans 6:4).

Driving through town one night, my husband and I found a young man lying on the yellow center-line in the middle of a highway. Snow got out, picked the guy up, and talked with him. The young man (I'll call him John) was high on drugs, almost incoherent. He wore only a pair of jeans—no shirt, underwear, or shoes—his long hair matted together in clumps. Snow, who worked at city hall, gave him a bed in the city jail. The next morning Snow gave him clean clothes and found a place for him to live. Several other city employees got involved in helping John.

Two weeks later, Snow and I went to a Bible study, where I saw a clean-cut young man across the room. *Why couldn't John live like this young man? What a difference in their behaviors and lifestyles! If only John could meet him …*

After the Bible study, Snow and I walked over to him. "Remember John?" Snow asked.

"Yes, I…" I realized this clean-cut young man *was* John. What a change! His clothes were clean; his hair was cut, combed, and styled.

John continued to be a faithful member of that Bible study, joined a support group, and became a member of a Christian church, where he accepted Jesus as His Savior! Within a year, he was reunited with his parents, who had kicked him out of their home and family. Today he walks *"in newness of life"* (Romans 6:4 KJV).

John is typical of thousands of people who wander, looking for answers to their problems. Christian ministers—all of us who are *on mission* to introduce lost, wandering people to Jesus—have the answers. As we share Jesus with them, we can be the gatekeepers to new life.

Lord, help us find lost, wandering people who need You. Enable us to reach out to show them new life in You. Amen.

# ❀ *Your Turn* ❀

*Freely you have received, freely give* (Matthew 10:8).

I've been the receiver of so many blessings through my mentor, Edna. She spent hours upon hours teaching me how to write in a way that would minister, bringing hope and healing. She served as my listening ear when I lived far away from extended family, prayed for me, and opened doors for me I had only dreamed about.

I feel unspeakably grateful to her. Because of Edna's impact on my life, I want to pass on to others what she has given me.

A few years ago I met a younger woman who wanted a mentor. Stephanie was pregnant at the time. A few weeks after her baby was born, Steph wanted to have her hair done. I realized that the best way I could minister to her would be to accompany her to the salon. I took care of the baby while she got her hair cut and styled.

Perhaps you've been blessed by a friendship with a woman farther along in her walk with the Lord. How about passing on the gift you've been given? Countless women long for a mature Christian friend to lean on; perhaps you are that woman. Before you push aside the thought and get back to your busy day, remember what you've appreciated most about a farther-along-friend in your life: probably not her perfect halo or the fact that she always gave perfect advice or that she had her relationship with God in perfect order. What you appreciated was that she loved you just as you were and stood by you through thick and thin. You always knew she was praying for you and that she loved Jesus. She didn't try to hide all her imperfections. She looked to Jesus, who is perfect!

With these attributes in mind, recognize that in Christ you are more than able to give what you have received!

Father, thank You for bringing someone to come alongside and strengthen me. Lord, help me be that friend to someone else. Amen.

*Stephanie's story first appeared in* Seeking Wisdom: Preparing Yourself to Be Mentored *by Edna Ellison and Tricia Scribner (New Hope Publishers, 2001).*

# ❀ Joy in the Mourning ❀

*Weeping may remain for a night, but rejoicing comes in the morning*
(Psalm 30:5).

We've all been there at one time or another. Our hearts are broken. We disappoint someone; we are disappointed by someone; or we disappoint ourselves. We feel as if the fist of sorrow has such a hold around our hearts that it will squeeze the very life from what is left of the bruised tissue. We cry so hard and long we feel that no salty liquid could be left in our bodies. The darkness of the night magnifies the darkness of our souls.

David knew the depth of such pain. Sadly, he lost sight not only of who he was, but also who God is. He allowed lust to lead to adultery, deceit, and eventually murder. He, who had been a man after God's own heart (1 Samuel 13:14), had become an enemy of the very nature of God.

Oscar Wilde once stated, "Where there is sorrow, there is holy ground" (from *Profundis*). Truly, God seeks to restore and renew broken hearts. David confessed his sin with godly sorrow. He repented of it. He sought restoration with God. He praised God for His loving forgiveness. He declared in Psalm 30:11, *"You turned my wailing into dancing; you removed my sackcloth and clothed me with joy."*

As the colorful strokes of dawn brush the morning sky, we are reminded that it is indeed a new day. It is a day that never has been lived. It is time for the restoration of light and the restoration of life. Truly, weeping may remain for a night, but it is not night forever. Joy can and will come in the morning and "in the mourning!"

Step forward onto holy ground, and allow God to meet you. He is already there waiting for you.

Dear God, please give us the courage to face the things in our lives that bring the darkness of sorrow. Help us to claim the joy that will come in the morning! In Jesus's name, amen.

# ❀ *Whose House?* ❀

*And He entered the temple and began to drive out those who were buy-
ing and selling in the temple, and overturned the tables of the money
changers.... And He began to teach and say to them, "Is it not written,
'MY HOUSE SHALL BE CALLED A HOUSE OF PRAYER FOR
ALL THE NATIONS'?* (Mark 11:15–17 NASB).

Imagine you are running late for a flight and skip lunch in order to board
the airplane on time. You plunk down in your seat just as the flight attendants close the hatch. As soon as the plane is airborne, you push the flight
attendant call button, thinking you will ask for a little snack to tide you over
until supper. Thirty minutes pass and still no sign of the flight attendant.
The guy sitting next to you says he's hungry, too. He pushes the flight attendant call-button. Nothing.

A movie comes on, and you both try to distract yourselves. When the
movie is over, the pilot comes on the intercom to say that the flight will soon
be landing. Still, no snack. Finally, you turn around to see if you can spy
the flight attendant. You do. She's in the back, standing by the snack cart,
scarfing down peanuts as fast as she can rip open the bags. To top it off,
she's washing it down with the soda—your soda. You wave.

She arrives at your seat, at which point the guy sitting next to you says,
"What do you think you are doing? Those aren't your peanuts!"

Irritated, she replies, "So what? Who do you think you are?"

He replies, "I am the owner of the airline."

Scripture describes an incident that reveals Christ's authority as God.
In the temple's Court of the Gentiles, merchants sold sacrificial animals.
Amid the flying feathers and animal dung, Gentiles worshiped in the only
section allotted to them. The Lord's righteous wrath was provoked by the
blatant disregard for God's house as a house of prayer for all nations.

For *all* nations. Isaiah had prophesied that God's house would be a
house of prayer not only for the Jews, but also for all the world's peoples
(56:7). The merchants acted as though the temple belonged to them. But it
belonged to God alone, and as God, Jesus Christ had authority over His
house.

> Lord Jesus, may we remember that Your church is to be
> a place of worship for all people. Amen.

# ❀ *Eyes that Cannot See* ❀

*"Though seeing, they do not see"* (Matthew 13:13).

The human eye. Darwin believed the eye evolved, in little baby steps, over billions of years into the amazingly complex organ we know today. Many scientists now recognize flaws in Darwin's claim, and one fact in particular puts the idea of the evolutionary process in jeopardy: the eye requires all its parts—its micro-systems—to be present, fully functioning, *and* interacting in sync in order for the eye to work at all. This characteristic is called *irreducible complexity*.

Think of a flashlight. For a flashlight to work, all parts—themselves comprised of smaller parts, such as the bulb, the batteries, the switch—must be present and positioned correctly within the casing before the flashlight can be turned on. Thus, the "anatomy" of the flashlight must be exactly right.

Even then the flashlight is useless unless each part interacts with all others correctly *and* simultaneously (try putting a battery in backwards). So the "physiology"—how the parts function together as a unit—must also be exactly right.

It is the same with the human eye. All the parts must be in place and all the sub-systems must work together simultaneously to produce vision. Moreover, for vision to occur, other systems such as the brain must function collaboratively with the eye organ. Given these requirements, we reasonably conclude that it is more rational to believe the design of the eye calls for a Designer—a personal Creator who weaved together its intricacies.

Why do many scientists cling to the notion that evolutionary processes produced the human eye? Not because of the scientific evidence. Many scientists hold a worldview called naturalism, which asserts that the world is all that exists. Their prior commitment to naturalism prohibits the possibility of supernatural causes.

Jesus described people who were given truth but ignored it as seeing, but not understanding. Because of their worldview, they refused to accept the truth staring them in the face.

Lord, give me the opportunity to share these truths with someone who is blinded by a commitment to a way of thinking that excludes You. Amen.

# ❀ Silence from the Grave ❀

*Be kindly affectionate to one another with brotherly love*
(Romans 12:10 NKJV).

My buddy Mark, and Jan from school, were driving into the city to pick up their paychecks. I wanted to join them, but I stayed home to finish a school project. Mark promised to stop by later to eat dinner with me.

The heavy rains were distracting. Shouldn't Mark have arrived already? Suddenly the phone rang. Mark and Jan had been in a serious automobile accident. Mark had sustained serious injuries, but was stable. However, Jan died.

Jan was the kind of girl who didn't quite fit in with the rest. She was friendly and bright, but she had a theatrical flair about her. The day after Jan's death, sorrow loomed in our school's hallways. Most students grieved over their own sick feelings, realizing that a girl they had openly rejected and ridiculed was now gone. No apologies accepted for unkind words or rude rejections; only silence from the grave.

I kept thinking about Jan. I had never been mean to Jan, but had I ever been really nice to her? Had I included her in activities, cared about how she felt when I saw her sitting alone, yet walked by empty seats to sit somewhere else? My indifference made me guilty.

But she had shown me kindness. We both had a class that required us to leave campus. I didn't have a car, but Jan offered to drive me. She filled the car each day with good-natured chatter. Then my mind raced to the accident. Mark and I were best friends; if I had joined them, I would've been in the front seat passenger's side. The silence from the grave would have been from me.

At the request of Jan's parents, their minister read portions of Jan's diary at the funeral. What was read aloud only confirmed what we already knew: Jan realized that few people understood her, yet she had made peace with God and with herself about it. And now, because of her relationship with Christ so beautifully expressed in her diary's secrets, we knew Jan had left this earth to enter into the presence of God. I knew I wanted to leave the funeral a changed person. Kindness would have cost me little, but it would've been a priceless treasure to Jan. In the stillness of the moment, I asked God to change my heart.

Who needs your friendship today? Look carefully.

Father, help me to willingly show kindness to a lonely person today,
demonstrating Your love. Amen.

# ❦ *Who Cares?* ❦

*I looked on my right hand, and beheld, but there was no man that
would know me: refuge failed me; no man cared for my soul*
(Psalm 142:4 KJV).

Invitations to family reunions are some of the perks of being a pastor's
family. We've met wonderful people and enjoyed delicious meals through
them. The Holloman family invited us to their annual celebration.

There we met Uncle Pete, a distinguished elderly gentleman from
Virginia. He captivated us with tales of his life's experiences.

The next day I was busy with household chores when Uncle Pete came
to mind. My heart began to pound, and I knew God was leading me to
share the message of salvation with him.

Excuses immediately filled my mind. The longer I procrastinated,
the more excuses I rationalized. Finally, the burden was so great I had to
act on it.

As I drove to the Holloman home, I rehearsed what I would say.
I knew I needed to speak with Uncle Pete alone, and I practiced ways to
ask the family for some privacy. I walked onto the porch and knocked on
the door.

Uncle Pete answered the door! In his gracious Southern manner, he
seemed delighted to see me and motioned for me to enter. Not knowing
how long it would be until someone else entered the room, I went straight to
the heart of the matter as I asked him about his relationship with the Lord.

Uncle Pete sat and stared at me for awhile. He then told me about his
conversion as a young person but confessed that he was not as close to the
Lord as he had been in the past.

Then, Uncle Pete said, "I've lived my whole life and no one has ever
seemed to care for my soul."

David expressed the same sentiment in today's verse. Will you ask God
to reveal someone who needs you to show concern for his or her soul?

Dear Lord, thank You for the many ways You show that You care for all souls in
the world. In Jesus's name, amen.

# ❀ A Gift from ❀ the Other Side of the World

*So in everything, do to others what you would have them do to you, for this sums up the Law and the Prophets* (Matthew 7:12).

We were in Russia for almost two weeks with one main mission—to get God's Word into the hands of the people. We distributed approximately 50,000 Bibles and thousands of gospel tracts. Our church members had attached candy or gum to the tracts as an enticement for people to accept them.

We walked for miles passing out tracts. As we handed them to the Russians, we said *puzhalsta*, the Russian word for "please." In doing so we asked them to accept the gifts we offered.

One afternoon, I handed a tract to a woman who seemed thrilled with the gift. We smiled at each other and went on our way in opposite directions.

A short time later, I heard someone behind me shouting to get my attention. I turned and saw the same woman hurrying toward me. I walked back toward her. As we approached each other, she handed me a gift in exchange for the tract. It was a simple plastic bag—the ones we get in stores that become a nuisance to us as they build up inside our cabinets. In Russia, stores didn't give bags when people bought things; their items were simply wrapped in paper.

I don't know where this precious woman had gotten a plastic bag, but it obviously was a treasure to her. She gave the cherished gift to me as a thank-you for a simple tract with candy.

I stood and cried as I accepted her gift. It represented friendship, graciousness, and a loving, giving heart.

She lives on the other side of the world. I may never see her again. However, that day she gave me a gift I will never forget—*a plastic bag*.

Dear Lord, please help us realize that true love, simply shown,
is the greatest gift of all. In Jesus's name, amen.

# ❀ *Bless Her Heart* ❀

*There are different kinds of service, but the same Lord*
(1 Corinthians 12:5).

You'll hear one phrase often if you live in the southern portion of the United States: *Bless her heart*. It's used in this way: "She's just goofy, bless her heart"; "She's obese, bless her heart"; "Her husband left her, bless her heart"; "She failed two grades in high school, bless her heart." People soften all sorts of accusations and gossip with these three words.

Another word we use in Christian circles is *different*. We use it this way: "She's not obnoxious; she's…different" (This means she's obnoxious). "I'm not saying she's ignorant; she's just…different" (she's ignorant). "She's not mean-spirited, she's sometimes…uh, different" (she's mean).

Leadership is a delicate balance between kindness and decisiveness, between honesty and tact. Often leaders must tackle complicated issues, blurred by inexact language, and they flounder over small points of friction. Sometimes leaders fear upsetting others, so they fall silent, whisper rumors to gather a group on their side, or talk about others behind their backs. People who use passive-aggressive tactics to communicate with others can complicate the way good leadership should work.

While we seek good leaders who are decisive and bold, we also adjust to various personalities in leadership and encourage cooperation. For example, if a person gifted in administration has reserved days on a church calendar for training or ministry opportunities, she's apt to be disappointed if another leader plans something on top of that event. Working together demands patience and unselfishness.

Paul tells the fledgling church in Corinth that each Christian can do different kinds of service to which they are called, and still serve the same Lord, Jesus Christ. If you have a leadership position this year, may God give you insight into the personalities of other leaders as you serve as a unified group. Praying together beforehand can help ensure success. With great patience and kindness, you can please traditional planners and yet remain flexible and innovative.

May God bless you as a leader who is "different." Bless your heart!

O God, lead us to be strong but kind leaders. Help us to love all the different leaders in our church and appreciate their uniqueness as they serve You. Amen.

# ❀ We're Recognized by Our Fruit ❀

*Thus, by their fruit you will recognize them*
(Matthew 7:20).

Galatians 5:16–26 paints a graphic portrait of the two contrasts in life. Either God's Spirit or our sinful bent controls each person. In this letter to the church in the region called Galatia, Paul calls the attitudes and actions of the sinful person "acts of the sinful nature." In contrast, he calls the attitudes and actions of the redeemed person the "fruit of the Spirit."

*"The fruit of the Spirit is love, joy, peace, patience, kindness, goodness, faithfulness, gentleness, and self-control"* (Galatians 5:22). The manifestation of such fruit is the way to recognize whether or not a person is one of God's (Matthew 7:20).

The fruit of the Spirit can be divided into three groups, each with a different emphasis. The attributes in the first group—love, joy, peace—concern our relationship with God. Those in the second group—patience, kindness, and gentleness—affect our relationships with other people. The attributes in the third group—faithfulness, goodness, and self-control—regulate the conduct of our personal Christian lives. Paul refers to all these attributes in the singular rather than the plural, by calling them "fruit" instead of "fruits."

We can take a lesson from the giant redwood trees in California that rise as high as 300 feet above the ground. Unlike other trees, redwoods do not take in water and nutrients through the root system to reach the leaves and branches, but the gravitational pull from above the trees draws in water and nutrients. Likewise, may our nourishment for the fruit of the Spirit come from above!

Dear Lord, I ask You to reveal to me anything in my life that could be blocking the flow of Your Holy Spirit. In Jesus's name, amen.

# ❀ Hoping to Meet a Friend ❀

*For the Son of Man came to seek and to save what was lost*
*(Luke 19:10).*

One morning, I inexplicably felt a strong leading to go to the Christian bookstore in our small southern town. I was not quite sure why I was there, but then I saw a bearded man. I did not know him, but somehow I knew he was the reason I was there. However, each time I tried to speak to him, he was talking with someone else. Then he left while I was looking at a book.

On Monday morning, I went back to the bookstore and accidently drove up on the curb in front of the bookstore. A man from India jumped back from the curb onto the sidewalk. We both laughed about my poor parking skills. Then he said, "I am a stranger in your country, and I came to town today hoping to meet a friend."

After we talked awhile, I invited him into the bookstore with me. He said that he was a Buddhist but would be happy to go into the store with me.

I silently shared my excitement with the Lord, "Jesus, You've got a Buddhist in Your bookstore!"

When we entered, I thought I saw the mystery man from Friday. However, he no longer had a beard. I approached him and said, "Pardon me, sir. Were you in here on Friday?"

"Yes," he answered curiously.

"Did you have a beard on Friday?" I asked.

Looking even more curious, he replied, "Yes, I did."

Then I didn't know what to say next. Suddenly I remembered my guest from India. I introduced the two of them. The mystery man said he was studying Bible prophecy concerning India. The Indian man, who had been a captain in the army, said he could teach much about his country.

The two of them made plans to study the Bible together. I stood in amazement. I was not supposed to speak to the mystery man on Friday. I was only supposed to recognize him on Monday to introduce him to a seeker who was "hoping to meet a friend."

Dear Lord, thank You for all the ways You work to accomplish
Your purposes. In Jesus's name, amen.

# ❧ *Walking Them to the Gospel* ❧

*So when the Samaritans came to him, they urged him to stay with them, and he stayed two days. And because of his words many more became believers* (John 4:40–41).

When we share with people who don't believe the Bible is true, we can meet them where they are and then walk them back to the gospel. First, we can show that truth exists and is knowable. If there is no such thing as truth, then what we believe doesn't matter. We can point out the inconsistency in saying truth does not exist, since the speaker believes that comment is *absolutely* true!

Next, we can share evidence from the world that one, personal, Creator God exists: evidence that the world had a beginning and Beginner, that the tiniest amoeba demonstrates complex design by a super-intelligent Being, and that the universal sense of right and wrong demonstrates the existence of a Supreme, Moral Being.

We can then show that miracles are possible—important since the truth of Christianity hinges on the miracle that Jesus actually arose from the dead. We can explain that if God exists, He can suspend His self-designed laws of nature in order to confirm the truth of a message or messenger who claimed to speak or act on His behalf.

Next, we can show that the Bible is a trustworthy document. More than 5,700 ancient handwritten Greek copies of the New Testament—fragments and whole books exist—far more than that of any other ancient document, such as Homer's writings. By comparing the thousands of New Testament copies, scholars can confirm with confidence what the originals said. At this point, the believer has earned the right to open the Bible and share the claims of Christ in the New Testament.

Admittedly, starting with truth and moving forward requires study and time. But John's account of Jesus's sharing with the Samaritan woman reveals that Jesus not only took time to respond to her questions, but He also went back to her town and spent two days teaching others. Many believed in Him because He was willing to explain and spend time with them. We can do no less.

Lord Jesus, prepare me to walk someone to the gospel. Amen.

# ❀ *Mysterious Oneness* ❀

*"I do not pray for these alone, but also for those who will believe in Me*
*through their word; that they all may be one, as You, Father, are in*
*Me, and I in You; that they also may be one in Us, that the world may*
*believe that You sent Me"* (John 17:20–21 NKJV).

I recently talked with a nine-year-old girl who felt the Lord tugging at her heart, but she still had a question. She wanted me to explain the Trinity.

Most Christian leaders will confess the difficulty of trying to explain the Trinity. Our ability to put it into simple words is impaired by the limitations of our finite brains. However big the challenge to explain it, we still cling to the doctrine of the Trinity as crucial to our beliefs. God has affirmed the Trinity to us in His Word, and we know that God is the Omnipotent One who could never be fully explained or defined by the humans He created. God has revealed Himself to us, yet the totality of who He is remains somewhat of a mystery to us.

As Jesus prayed to the Father in the garden, He prayed specifically for you and me. We are the ones who would believe in Jesus through the words of His disciples, and what a precious gift to be able to read about the life of Christ as we study the Bible. Jesus prayed that we believers would be one, just as He and the Father experience oneness. The mysterious and beautiful Trinity is the bar set for us as believers to experience unity.

Many days you may find it a strain to get along with a brother or sister in Christ, much less experience true unity. However, it must be our aim, for Jesus said in His prayer that our oneness in the Lord—this mysterious bond that is sometimes just about as hard to imagine as the Trinity is to explain in plain words—would be a witness to the world of the validity of Christ.

Father, I want my relationships in the body of believers to point others to You.
I submit to Your authority today. In the name of Jesus I pray, amen.

# ❧ Hands-On Ministry ❧

*I have become all things to all men, that I might by all means*
*save some. Now this I do for the gospel's sake*
(1 Corinthians 9:22–23 NKJV).

*Yuk! That was somebody's gum. Ugh, it's so sticky. Gross, gross. Oh, this is nasty!*
These were my thoughts as I fumbled around in the dark at the movie
theater, feeling the ground for my daughter's ring that had just dropped
from her petite finger. "Found it!" she cried, much to my relief.

As I settled back into my seat, wishing I had a mega-sized bottle of hand
sanitizer, I had disparaging thoughts about that little ring. My daughter's
prized jewelry was worth 25 cents, yet I had just massaged the disgusting
floor where drinks had spilled and gum goes to die. I would've gladly given
a quarter not to have to touch such filth. How did I talk myself into doing
it? My daughter treasured the ring. I did it because it mattered to her. By
stooping down to help get her ring, I expressed love and concern to her.
I was a tad queasy from my hands-on ministry, but my heart was thrilled
that my daughter was relieved.

It's curious how everyone has such different priorities and interests.
Sometimes others' concerns are nowhere near our radar screens. Does it
really matter that we share their concerns? You may loathe baseball, but
imagine how God might bless a relationship you build with an unsaved
single mom as you join her to watch her children's games. Or ponder the
possibilities if you were to listen longer to your neighbor describe her herb
garden's woes; you may prefer your basil from a plastic shaker, but taking
an interest might be the best way to say *love* to your neighbor.

Being all things to all people for the sake of the gospel may include
delving into a hobby, conversation, or project that renders no personal
satisfaction to you. Are you willing to sacrifice your interests—or touch a
sticky, gummy theater floor—to build a bridge for the gospel?

Precious Lord, am I missing out on an opportunity to witness to someone
because I haven't been willing to show interest about what matters to her? Teach
me patience and self-sacrifice for the sake of the gospel. In Jesus's name, amen.

# ❀ The Power of ❀ Praying God's Word

*"My word… will not return to me empty"* (Isaiah 55:11).

Lois Moore and I co-led the singles group at our church. We had several members stationed at the air force base in our town. Nine of our members were deployed to Saudi Arabia during Operation Desert Storm.

Collective grief gripped our singles group. We did not know what would happen to them or if we would ever see them again. Stories of Iraqi weapons of mass destruction and biological warfare abounded. Psalm 91 was our prayer for them.

One Sunday, a member excitedly shared a letter she received from one of the young men. He explained that at noon there had been a cloud burst and flash flood in tent city where they lived. Many of the tents were flooded. However, he had checked with the military members of our class and no one's tent was damaged. He went on to write that they could not explain it. The water had rolled up to the entrance of one member's tent and stopped. None of his things got wet.

We remembered our prayer from Psalm 91, particularly, *Thou shalt not be afraid…the destruction that wasteth at noonday* (vv. 5-6 KJV) and *no disaster will come near your tent* (v. 10).

We later found out that a scud missile was fired at the troops. A patriot missile tried to intercept it. However, the patriot missile misfired and rapidly sped backwards toward the weapons' arsenal on the edge of tent city. It could have wiped out the entire complex.

Suddenly, and inexplicably, the missile lifted up, traveled above the arsenal, and landed in the desert. The troops began praising God for His protective care in sparing their lives. We in the class praised God for the answer to our prayer from Scripture, *"You will not fear the terror of night, nor the arrow that flies by day"* (Psalm 91:5). God showed us anew the power of praying His Word.

Dear Lord, teach us to pray in faith using Your Word as the foundation.
In Jesus's name, amen.

# ❀ Why the Wilderness? ❀

*Then Jesus was led up by the Spirit into the wilderness to be tempted by the devil* (Matthew 4:1 NASB).

Throngs of people stand upon the Jordan River's banks watching Jesus's inauguration into public ministry. As He arises from the baptismal waters, with the droplets still glistening on His face, those few insightful souls who perceived Him to be the Messiah may have wondered: *What will be His first public miracle? Will He raise someone from the dead? Turn water into wine? Maybe He'll feed thousands with a handful of bread and fish.*

But no—where is He going—to the wilderness? But there's nothing in the wilderness but, well, *wilderness.* There's no food, no water, just sun beating down all day and wild beasts howling all night. Considering that His entire public ministry spanned only about three years, why would He waste 40 days of it in the wilderness?

Before He descended to earth, Jesus basked in the adoration of heavenly angels. Easy enough for the Father's Son to exude glory where He was adored. But how would heaven's fair Son keep Himself holy once clothed in man's flesh? How would He respond to temptation when dehydration fogged His thinking and vultures circled overhead? Only the wilderness would tell.

Forty days: 960 hours—57,600 minutes—3,456,000 seconds. A long time to hunger. A long time to thirst. An unbearably long time to survive, only to face the tempter's taunts. But the wilderness was necessary, for if He failed in the wilderness, nothing else mattered. If Jesus Christ would serve as the holy, perfect, and only acceptable sacrifice for man's sin, He must also endure *without sin* the temptations common to humans.

Praise God, Jesus did endure. We now have in heaven a High Priest to intercede for us, a Priest who was tempted in all points as we are, *yet without sin.* This is the hope we share with every soul caught in sin's stronghold. This Savior qualified Himself as our perfect sacrifice. We know—because of the wilderness.

O Savior, thank You for persevering in the wilderness.
Thank You that because You did, I can trust You to strengthen me
to endure in the wilderness, as well. Amen.

# ❀ *WOW!* ❀

*"I have loved you with an everlasting love, therefore with
lovingkindness I have drawn you"* (Jeremiah 31:3 NKJV).

The mild temperature on this winter's night offers a hint that spring is on
its way. Tonight I sat on the porch to enjoy the balmy air. A beautiful, full
"Carolina Moon" shone brightly in the dark slate sky between the silhou-
ettes of two leafless trees. Each star seemed to outshine the one that previously appeared. In the distance I heard the sound of ocean waves rolling
on the shore.

"*Wow*," I thought as I observed that everything around me glorified my
Savior.

Then, I wondered how often God looks at His creation and also thinks,
*Wow*. I realized anew that the same God who created all this beauty created
me. I determined that I want to live life as the "wow woman" He intended
me to be.

First, I want to be a **woman of** worship. In today's world it seems that
true worship has been replaced by ritualism, tradition, fads, and trends.
I want to be a woman whose heart beats purely to praise the one, true,
living God.

I also want to be a **woman of** the Word. On a missions trip to Russia,
we distributed Bibles in the Russian language. Many recipients held their
new Bibles close to their hearts and swayed back and forth with their eyes
closed as if embracing a rare treasure. I never want to lose my reverence for
God's Word.

I want to be a **woman of works**. I desire to make a difference in
the world. I long to be so filled with God's love that wherever I go the
people I encounter will experience God's love. Love is the greatest gift
(1 Corinthians 13:13), and I want to share that gift with a hurting world.

Yes, I want to be a woman of worship, Word, and works—a "wow
woman." Won't you join me in my quest?

Dear Lord, as I reflect on who You are, all I can do is say, "Wow!"
In Jesus's name, amen.

# ❀ *Wait on the Lord* ❀

*Wait on the LORD: be of good courage, and he shall strengthen thine heart: wait, I say, on the LORD* (Psalm 27:14 KJV).

Life is hard when things are popping with growing children, a busy church life, and rigorous work hours. After long days, your back hurts, your stomach is hungry, your adrenaline is still pumping, and you have a list of things to do. Yet the worst times are not the too-busy times, but those when you can't do anything but wait.

Many Bible characters—Moses, Jacob, Jonah, Noah, Job, to name a few—found waiting difficult. They jumped into many things before they knew God's direction. They sought their will and not God's, but then God showed them how to wait.

Learning how to wait is useful. You'll find opportunities to wait in the Lord in the checkout line for groceries, in a ball game or movie ticket line, and at home with others getting ready after you are ready. However, the most time we wait comes after our plan fails and we're waiting on God to give new directions.

I remember the word *wait* from an acrostic I learned as a child.

W—Watch to see where God is leading you. Put your Bible first. This is the first step to a successful waiting period.

A—Ask God to show you clearly what your possibilities are. Ask Him to use you in missions ministries or other tasks specifically for you. Be open to new possibilities.

I— Identify possibilities for the future. What are your assets and liabilities, positives and negatives that He wants you to use as you wait? Identify your present challenges. Read Scripture verses you memorized as a child—or some you just found yesterday—to give you a clue for the future. Pray over these passages, asking God to relate them to the present wait for marching orders.

T—Turn. Are you walking down the wrong path? As you read your Bible and wait, ask God to show you things you need to release. Leave them, and follow His new path.

Once you watch, ask, identify, and turn, you are near the end of your wait. Have patience in the wait.

Lord, help me be patient as I wait on You. In Jesus's name, amen.

# ❁ The Importance of a Name ❁

*He determines the number of the stars and calls them each by name*
(Psalm 147:4).

Imagine the super-intelligence of God. Not only did He determine how many stars the universe would have, but also He created them. Then, He assigned a name to each of them.

The concept of a "name" was very important in Bible times. A name did more than identify a person or an object. It also expressed the essence, the character, or the reputation of the person or thing. Therefore, when the Psalmist exclaims that God calls each star by name, we know that He assigned its name for a special purpose.

If God took the tender care to give each star a significant name, imagine how special His loving thoughts are toward His most treasured creation — us! David says in Psalm 139:17–18 (TLB):

> *"How precious it is, Lord, to realize that You are thinking about me constantly! I can't even count how many times a day Your thoughts turn towards me. And when I waken in the morning, You are still thinking about me!"*

I remember the time and care we took with naming our two daughters. Our first-born, Meri Beth, was three days old before we finally confirmed her name. After much deliberation, we named her in honor of her two grand-mothers, and changed the spelling so that her name conveys, "happy house of God." She certainly is that!

We knew we wanted to name our second daughter Molly. However, the deliberation came in choosing a middle name to accompany it. Again, after researching the meanings of many different names, we chose Melinda, which means "mild, gentle one." She certainly is that!

I cannot imagine the task of naming each star in the universe. The next time you look into a starry sky, take a moment to consider God's wonder. As you reflect on His tender care for each star, try to imagine how special you are to Him!

Dear God, thank You for my name. Please help me to live my life
in such a way that my name will be synonymous with a godly reputation.
In Jesus's name, amen.

# ❊ One Dark and Stormy Night ❊

*For great is your love toward me; you have delivered me from the depths
of the grave* (Psalm 86:13).

I lay on the camp cot watching the clouds rolling in; I began to hear thunder
in the distance, then closer.

"*God,*" I prayed, "*please take away this storm. I'm afraid to walk down that hill
to check on the girls. My metal umbrella is like a lightning rod.*"

As I ended with an *Amen*, the bright flashes and rumbling thunder
began to diminish. "*Thank You, Lord,*" I whispered.

"Sounds like the storm's turning," Gail, another camp leader, said in the
dark.

"Yes, I was praying it would go away."

Her next words surprised me: "You Christians are all alike. You pray,
expecting God to jump at your command. What if there's a farmer on this
mountain praying for rain?" She paused.

"And what about the virgin birth? Explain that if you can!"

"Uh…"

"And what about a poor pygmy in Africa tonight?"

"What?"

"You think he's going to burn in hell, don't you? Because he never
heard about Jesus…"

I tried to answer, but she interrupted: "My mother died this year and
was not a Christian." I couldn't see Gail, but heard her sobbing. "You're not
going to tell me …my mother's …in hell …tonight."

A child knocked. Was I happy to leave! I took her back to her cabin,
tucking her in. On the way back, I prayed. "*Lord, I tried to explain Your love
to Gail, but I've bumbled it. Please let her be asleep. Her pastor could talk with her on
Sunday.*"

I tiptoed in.

Then I heard Gail: "God spoke to me while you were gone." She paused.
"He said, 'Don't worry, Gail. Your mother would want *you* to become a
Christian …because she loved you. My grace is sufficient for you.'"

I knew Gail was ready. I knelt down beside her cot and we prayed.
That night she asked Jesus to come into her heart, and He took away all
fear and worry.

Lord, help us tell others about You.
Thank You for Your love that delivers us from fear. Amen.

# ❀ Signs of Life ❀

*And you He made alive, who were dead in trespasses and sins*
*(Ephesians 2:1 NKJV).*

After a few days of summer vacation, I returned to find the plants in my two hanging baskets browned and withered, cooked by the summer heat. For the sake of nostalgia and a small twinge of hope, I watered them anyway while I gave my other plants on the screened porch a drink. A few days later, 90 percent of each plant in the hanging baskets was still just as brown and toasty as ever, but a few strong sprigs of green had emerged from the dirt in each basket, and beautiful pink blooms were trumpeting new life.

When all hope appears to be lost for a person whose life is dry and withered, keep watering. Until that day when the Lord brings a life to an end on this side of eternity, with God there is always hope. Love consistently. Encourage consistently. Pour the living water of Christ into that person's life with consistency. It may appear to you that the Living Water just runs off the surface, but only God knows if small droplets are penetrating the hardened soil.

I noticed something curious about those few fresh sprigs in my hanging baskets. The new life was springing forth on the outer edges of the baskets in the portion closest to the screen, and the green stems were extending themselves to be in the sunlight. Jesus is the Light of the world John 8:12). As believers, Jesus says that we also are the light of the world (Matthew 5:14). His light shines in and through you. Ask God to help you be a strong source of His light as you interact with the lost, and pray that they find the light of Christ so compelling that they find themselves longing to draw near to the Savior.

Persevere with joy as you reach out to the most evidently lifeless of souls, because the Giver of life is always at work in unseen ways in His harvest field.

Giver of life, no soul is beyond Your reach. Please pour out Your Living Water
upon the hardened hearts of the lost. Please allow me to shine Your light
brightly into this dark world. Amen.

# ❀ Not My Child ❀

*That we should be called children of God! And that is what we are!*
(1 John 3:1).

When our dog had a litter of puppies, she rejected one. The little brown fuzzy dog became thinner, more confused daily. Our family began feeding him, after trying to help her accept him. We felt sorry for this little runt of the litter; it reminded us that sometimes we also reject others. It may be a church member, a person of another race, a sibling, or an obnoxious person.

Have you ever wanted to reject a family member? If you're a parent, you would be less than honest if you said you love children unconditionally every day. Our children disappoint us, maybe making a snark—a snide remark—that makes us think: *I know I just didn't hear my child say that! That's not my child.* On the other end of the spectrum is the deep hurt from children denying Christ and godly childhood training. Children may even break the law, needing special help getting their lives together. Loving our children unconditionally takes patience.

When my children were little, we said, "We don't talk (or behave) like that." We had basic rules and expected our *little darlings* to stick to them. In the same way, God has written moral rules for His children, saying: *"Get rid of all bitterness, rage and anger, brawling and slander, along with every form of malice. Be kind and compassionate to one another, forgiving each other, just as in Christ God forgave you"* (Ephesians 4:31–32).

Do you ever wonder if God sometimes says, "Surely that's not my child! Not mine." Notice the last clause in Ephesians 4:32. We are to forgive others just as God forgave us when He sent His Son to die for our sins. We can consider all people God's children. He loves all people, no matter what, just as He loves Christians unconditionally. May we grow more like Him as we love others with patience.

Lord, help us love our children and grandchildren unconditionally as we guide them in Your direction. Help us reach out to all God's children, no matter what age they are, claiming them as ours and leading them to claim that they are Yours. Amen.

# ❀ *Within the Limits* ❀

*Bondservants, be obedient to those who are your masters according to the flesh, with fear and trembling, in sincerity of heart, as to Christ; not with eyeservice, as men-pleasers, but as bondservants of Christ, doing the will of God from the heart, with goodwill doing service, as to the Lord, and not to men* (Ephesians 6:5–7 NKJV).

"Lord, You know I've got to get home quickly. Please help me drive safely." Moments after that prayer, a police car drove up behind my car. God must've felt I needed some visible incentive to watch my speed!

Obedience motivated by threat of punishment is better than disobedience any day, but the sweetest obedience is fueled by a deep love and gratitude for the Savior. What does Ephesians 6:5–7 teach us about obedience to those in authority?

**We're biblically called to submit to earthly authority figures.** "You're not the boss of me!" has probably rolled off the tongue of every child on the playground, and that same drive to be in control of our decisions doesn't lessen with age. Unless our leaders ask us to sin or do something questionable, we're to submit to authority.

**Our record should be consistent.** When no one's looking and the threat of punishment is removed, our integrity is revealed: do we work hard and obey guidelines only to stay out of trouble, or do we maintain a strong work ethic because we want to honor our all-knowing God?

**Obedience flows from the heart.** Our sincere efforts to obey and work hard can bless co-workers and employers. A cheerful attitude and prayerful spirit will entice others to hear what keeps us whistling while we work, and our quick response enhances the gospel.

**We ultimately serve Christ in all we do.** When the boss is cranky and demanding, or our husbands don't seem to be making wise decisions, we can rest in the authority of Christ. Look above the figureheads of earthly leadership and see the Savior—loving and kind, full of wisdom, and in ultimate authority. As we submit as unto Christ, He will honor our obedience as a direct act of obedience to His Lordship.

God, convict my heart when I begin to drift into eyeservice.
I desire to honor You in all things. Amen.

# ❀ The Seven Cs ❀

*In his love and mercy he redeemed them; he lifted them up and carried them all the days of old* (Isaiah 63:9).

Some of us feel we don't have good backgrounds in missions and ministries. Consider these seven Cs as preparation for open spirits.

1. **We're Crafted.** God crafted us as complicated humans, formed in God's image (Genesis 1:27). The psalmist said, *"I praise you because I am fearfully and wonderfully made"* (Psalm 139:14. [See also vv. 13–16.]). When we don't attempt big things, we deny His perfect creation. He crafted us exactly as we are, forming His perfect will for our lives.

2. **We're Carried.** We acknowledge Isaiah 63:9 above, knowing He still carries us today. While His steady steps strengthen us, we hope for the future.

3. **We're Caring.** As Moses did, we sometimes protest God's call to serve. (See Exodus 4:1, 10, 13.) Focusing only on *our* frailties, we can't follow *His* will. Like Moses, once we forget ourselves and care about God's people, we lead in a visionary manner we couldn't have imagined.

4. **We're Compassionate.** God gives everyone preferences. One likes music, one carpentry; another cooking, or prayer. Isaiah says, *"'This is the one I esteem: he who is humble and…trembles at my word'"* (Isaiah 66:1–2). Trembling before God, we use our passion and our compassion for others.

5. **We're Captivated by God.** To serve God, we must surrender *absolutely everything.* The woman with the alabaster jar threw caution to the wind and gave generously, pouring all her oil on Jesus's head. Jesus said, *"She did what she could"* (Mark 14:8). Allowing God's will to dominate ours, we experience the joy of His captivation.

6. **We're Confident.** Paul said, *"I can do everything through him who gives me strength"* (Philippians 4:13). *"Being confident of this, that he who began a good work in you will carry it on to completion"* (Philippians 1:6).

7. **We're Content.** Recognizing these seven truths, we can say with Paul, *"I have learned the secret of being content in…every situation"* (Philippians 4:12), and we can rest our spirits in the Lord with every ministry (Isaiah 28:12).

Lord, prepare our spirits with confidence, compassion,
and a caring heart to serve You. Amen.

*Adapted from* Stronger Still *by Edna Ellison (New Hope Publishers, 2007).*

# ❀ *Knowledge Pertaining to Life* ❀

*Grace and peace be multiplied to you in the knowledge of God and
of Jesus our Lord, as His divine power has given to us all things that
pertain to life and godliness, through the knowledge of Him who called
us by glory and virtue* (2 Peter 1:2–3 NKJV).

Have you ever curiously thumbed through the little page-turner books about life lessons from a cat, or wisdom gleaned from kindergartners? We can all be thankful that there's a greater source of knowledge than our friendly felines! Through His power, God has revealed all we need to know about obtaining a godly life through Jesus. As we grow in knowledge of God, we cultivate a deeper understanding of how to navigate life with success.

Your intentional exposure to the Word of God is critical for increasing your knowledge of God. Learn the Bible. Reading the Word of God is no quick-read to be digested in one sitting, but after all, God has promised that He has given us *"all things that pertain to life and godliness"* (v. 3)! Ask God to give you a ferocious appetite for Scripture. Study the Bible one book at a time. Consider using a helpful resource to see how that book fits into the timeline of the Bible. Another approach to Bible study is to study a topic thoroughly, such as joy or fasting. You can also benefit from examining how God interacted with a character from Scripture. Meditate on verses and passages and ask God questions as you study. Memorize verses that speak to your heart.

As you search for knowledge of God through Scripture study, look to Jesus. As God's Son, He reveals the nature and character of God. Jesus said, *"If you had known Me, you would have known My Father also; and from now on you know Him and have seen Him…. He who has seen Me has seen the Father"* (John 14:7, 9 NKJV).

What a worthy pursuit—what a great investment of your time and efforts—to go deeper in your knowledge of God. To know God brings eternal reward.

Father, there is no one I would rather know than You. Learning more about You is my great privilege. Reveal Yourself to me on every page of Scripture. Amen.

# ❀ *What a Day* ❀

*So the sun stood still, and the moon stopped, till the nation avenged*
*itself on its enemies, as it is written in the Book of Jasher*
(Joshua 10:13).

The moon inspires awe and mystery. As a child I gazed at the moon, imagining there was a man inside who watched everything I did. As a teenager I stared at the moon on a romantic summer's evening. As an adult I heard the immortal words of a tearful newscaster, "Ladies and gentlemen, man has landed on the moon."

Even as I write these words today, a total lunar eclipse is scheduled to occur tonight close to midnight. Excitement is in the air as Americans plan to arrange their bedtimes around this event.

Of all the mystique and wonder that surrounds the moon, perhaps none is more remarkable than the account in today's Scripture. The Book of Jasher is a collection of historical events put to music. In his songs, Jasher noted that Joshua prayed and asked that the sun and moon stand still. The nation of Israel needed extra light to avenge their wicked enemies. God answered Joshua's prayer and the Israelites defeated the Amorites while it was still day.

With today's scientific knowledge of the universe, we understand that the sun does not move but rather the earth revolves around the sun. However, we should not allow the terminology to diminish the importance of the miracle. We use similar terms even today when we talk about the sun rising and setting.

In whatever way God accomplished the miracle, the significance remains that God answered Joshua's prayer and somehow provided a longer period of light for the army of Israel. Jasher's song declares, *"There has never been a day like it before or since, a day when the LORD listened to a man. Surely the LORD was fighting for Israel!"* (Joshua 10:14).

God is always in control, and He is always on the side of right. He accomplishes His purposes however He chooses, for He has the power to make them come to pass!

Dear God, just as the moon reflects the light of the sun, help us live in such a way that our lives reflect the light of the Son. In Jesus's name, amen.

# ❀ *Hope in the Future* ❀

*I am the resurrection and the life* (John 11:25).

"Hurry! It's 7:30!" said my cousin, Doris. Her daughter Debra, a beauty-contest winner and college student at a nearby university, bounded into the kitchen, looking as beautiful as ever. She rubbed her brother's hair, ate a bite of breakfast, and swung her book bag over her shoulder. Debra and Robbie jumped into the car, waving good-bye to Doris. Less than an hour later, a policeman came to the door. After Debra had delivered Robbie to school, she slid on a slick spot and died as her car smashed against a cliff of rocks.

A few days later, I visited Doris. She said, "Debra was a Christian and went straight to heaven. I just wish I had had some last good-bye, a sign she's happy there now." I prayed with Doris; we asked for comfort during the coming days.

One day Doris called. "I got it!" she said. "God gave me a sign—a last good-bye."
"What happened?" I said.

As Doris had driven by the site of the wreck that day, she'd seen a crocus popping up between a crack in the rock and the hard ground. "It was bright yellow—" she said, "a sign from God that my precious Debra still lives."

Two days later, I got another call from Doris. "Edna, you won't believe this. I prayed all day yesterday: *'O, God, I know Debra lives. Thank You for the sign. Though I know a crocus can't live long in that crack, You sent it to me briefly, to show me life and resurrection from a little bulb squeezed into that desolate rock. It was a lonely place to die. I'm just a mama that needed assurance Debra's with You. Thank You, Lord.'"*

Doris paused. "This morning I had to go that way again. Beside the yellow crocus stood another crocus, very close. God is showing me that any solitary place is not lonely, if you have Jesus by your side. Debra is safe in His arms!"

Lord, thank You that Your Word is trustworthy. Thank You for bringing
resurrection into our hard places. You give us life everywhere there is death,
hope where there is fear, and comfort where there is loneliness. Amen.

# ❀ In an Uncertain Economy ❀

*"When your herds and your flocks multiply, and your silver and your gold are multiplied, and all that you have is multiplied; when your heart is lifted up, and you forget the LORD your God who brought you out of the land of Egypt, from the house of bondage"*
(Deuteronomy 8:13–14 NKJV).

Economic woes can be a spiritual blessing if we'll soften our hearts toward the Lord. Wealth comes with a deception that we don't need God. When wealth is taken away, we face the reality that we aren't powerful enough to be the masters of our lives; we're completely dependent on God. Could it be that economic recession can create the spiritual climate our nation needs to prepare us for a great revival?

Christians are not immune to layoffs and plunging stock market trends. However, our response to the economic trends must be distinctly different from that of the world. What are the flesh responses that we must resist?

**1. Dwelling on finances.** Because you belong to God and know He will meet your needs, you don't have to obsess on your finances. Paul taught, *the mind controlled by the Spirit is life and peace* (Romans 8:6 NKJV). Your peaceful heart will be a great testimony to God's faithfulness, opening doors for you to share Christ with people around you who are fretting over finances.

**2. Hoarding money.** Hoarding is a fearful reaction to uncertainty. All that you own—whether in good times or bad—has been given to you to use for the glory of God and the advancement of the kingdom. Christ's parable of the talents (Matthew 25:14–30) and also His teaching, *"Do not lay up for yourself treasures on earth, where moth and rust destroy and where thieves break in and steal"* (Matthew 6:19 NKJV) are specific instructions against hoarding.

As God's people, may we develop a deeper appreciation for the privilege of being children of God, not partakers of the world's goods. His goodness is certain, indeed!

Father, please give me opportunities to invest in Your kingdom more than I ever have before. Lord, may the people of this nation realize their need for a certain future through Jesus Christ. Amen.

# ❁ Celebration with Ice and Water ❁

*For whenever you eat this bread and drink this cup, you proclaim the*
*Lord's death until he comes* (1 Corinthians 11:26).

Lillian was physically beautiful with her long, silver hair. She was fun and funny. You always knew where you stood with Lillian and that made her even more special. She went with us to the Holy Land. We were told not take any food from Jordan into Israel.

When we arrived at the border, an armed soldier boarded our bus checking passports and seriously observing each passenger. From the back of the bus I heard Lillian calling to him asking what she should do with her leftover cookie.

I tried to shush her and get the cookie from her when the soldier walked back to her and stared. Finally, he turned and walked away, shrugging his shoulders. I laughed and thought that even the border guard didn't know what to do with Lillian.

Several years later, Lillian became very ill. While my husband, who was her pastor, visited her in the hospital, she pleaded with him to partake of communion.

He asked the nurse if he could give her some bread and juice, and the nurse said she could not have anything. Wayne returned to Lillian's room and explained the situation to her. She looked forlorn as she so desperately wanted to partake of communion one last time.

Then Wayne noticed the pitcher of ice and water on her bedside table. He placed a small piece of ice in a spoon, offering it to Lillian. "This is the body of Jesus that was broken for you."

He then gave her some water in the spoon and said, "This is the blood of Jesus that was shed for you."

Lillian took his hand crying and smiling simultaneously. With ice and water she was *proclaiming the Lord's death until He comes.*

He came for Lillian a short time later. My husband considers that communion one of the most meaningful of his life. I can't help but believe it was for Lillian as well.

Dear Lord, forgive us when communion becomes ritualistic.
Help us to realize that it is a way we proclaim Your death until You come again.
In Jesus's name, amen.

# ❀ *Desire the Greater Gifts* ❀

*Now you are the body of Christ, and each one of you is a part of it....*
*But eagerly desire the greater gifts* (1 Corinthians 12:27, 31).

I had asked our neighbors to come to church with us at least 12 times, but they never came. I told them about our warm, small-group fellowship and the good Bible study we experienced as we gained ethical and spiritual principles for life. No response.

One Saturday my best friend casually mentioned they needed to visit our church. They came the next morning!

My best friend was a born leader and such an influence on her world that I wondered why God had not given *me* that gift of leadership. I tried much harder than she did. I looked in the mirror to see what was wrong with me. Was I so scary that people ran from me? (I did see flaws in the mirror, especially since I'd replaced my smile with a hesitant, worried look.)

I questioned God. *Why did I ask the neighbors and get no response, and she just barely mentioned it, and they responded immediately?* For the next few years, that inferiority complex grew to paranoia; I shrank back from trying to influence anyone. I felt I was a failure at visitation, so I quit going on Thursday nights to the homes of those who had shown interest in our church.

Finally the pastor asked me to be a greeter at our side door, where many new members were coming in. I found a good place of service where I was successful, and forgot about my best friend's gifts of service. Looking back, I realize my foolishness kept me from helpful service to God.

May God encourage us to be patient and seek the leadership gifts He has reserved for us.

> Lord, forgive us when we're jealous and self-centered.
> Help us to serve You as humble leaders, grateful to be
> Your servant leaders. Amen.

# ❀ Get in the Water ❀

*Now faith is the substance of things hoped for,*
*the evidence of things not seen* (Hebrews 11:1 NKJV).

I learned to swim as a child, and I've spent plenty of time in the deep end of the pool. I have rafted some of the most adventurous whitewater rivers in the United States, and I've never been overwhelmed by fear from the rushing rapids. But I cannot make myself dive off a diving board. I stand on the edge, toes curled and leaning forward in the proper position. I hold my breath, bend my knees—and then I chicken out!

Lack of faith prohibits us from diving into those deep waters of Christian living, where God's waves of joy flow all about us. We see others placing their lives fully into the hands of the Lord, and it seems like such a rewarding way to live, but we cannot manage to make that first plunge for fear of the unknown. We want the "evidence of things not seen," forcing us to sit on the sidelines of God's work because we allow our fears to paralyze us.

What have we to gain from placing our faith in God? Consider the moon. It moves the oceans of the globe. Much of the moon's effects take place while we sleep, without our watchful eye on the matter. We have no effect on this process, and our level of faith in the process is of no consequence to the changing of the tides. Likewise, God is God and His plan for the work of the kingdom of God is in motion regardless of our level of faith in God's ability to sustain His children. There is power in trusting the reliability of the moon. If we choose to have faith in the reliability of the tides, we can play in the ocean, watch the beauty of the movement of the shoreline, and place our boats upon the water and sail. Likewise, if we choose to have faith in the reliability of God, He will bring us such pleasures in serving Him that our minds could not conceive.

Our faith is evidence to the world that we believe God can and will keep His promises for today and for all our tomorrows. Go on, get in the water!

Dear God, please help me to grow in my faith.
I know You love me beyond what words can express. Amen.

*Adapted from Kimberly Sowell's* Journey to Confidence: Becoming Women Who Witness *(New Hope Publishers, 1999).*

---

# ❀ *Hope in a Stovepipe* ❀

*"So shall My word be that goes forth from My mouth; it shall not
return to Me void, but it shall accomplish what I please"*
(Isaiah 55:11 NKJV).

I wrote the date in my Bible: October 10, 1982. A Russian man named
Nikolai shared in our church that many years before in Russia, commu-
nism came and crushed his country. With nationalism snuffed out, citizens
could not say, "I am Russian." Instead, they had to say, "I am a citizen of the
Soviet Socialist Republic." When World War II started, church buildings
were confiscated, leaving only a handful open for tourists. Youth were
forced to scour homes for religious materials, especially Bibles, which they
burned while dancing and singing communist songs.

Later, Nikolai was captured and sent to a POW camp. In his own
mind, his future was hopeless because even if he were released from the
camp, he could not return home since he would be viewed as a traitor for
surrendering himself to his captors rather than killing himself when faced
with capture, as they were expected to do.

When, in 1945, Americans finally liberated the camp, Nikolai migrated
to a refugee camp in Germany. One day, he found himself in a small room
trying to start a fire in a wood stove. When it wouldn't work, he checked
the pipe, and found it clogged with a tract, on which was written Matthew
11:28: *"Come to me, all who are weary and heavy-laden, and I will give you rest"*
(NASB). He said that for the first time in his life he cried. Nikolai surrendered his life to God, and went to Munich, Germany, where he searched
for a Bible. The two churches he visited did not have one. Finally, after
encountering a friend from the POW camp who had become a Christian,
Nikolai was taken to a church where he heard the gospel of Jesus and was
saved.

Nikolai's story confirms that God's Word will accomplish His purposes.
Our job is to make sure that the truth is proclaimed, trusting that God can
even use a gospel tract stuffed in stovepipe to bring someone to Him.

Thank You, Lord, that You will use even extraordinary means to get Your Word
into the hands and hearts of those who need to hear about Jesus. Amen.

# ❀ You're the Apple of God's Eye ❀

*Keep me as the apple of your eye* (Psalm 17:8).

The Sunday before Thanksgiving our church's flower committee prepared a beautiful holiday arrangement for the communion table. The cornucopia, surrounded by autumn leaves, was filled with colorful fruit. After the conclusion of the worship service our young daughters and I waited for my husband to counsel some parishioners. As a pastor's family, we are used to waiting, but this session was unusually long.

Our daughters had been patient, but it was past time for lunch. Reluctantly, I reached into the beautiful display on the table to get a piece of fruit for each of them vowing that I would replace it before the evening service. That satisfied *them*, but *I* kept looking at the fruit. The desire for the large red apple in the middle overcame me. As I reached for the apple and took a big bite, my husband walked into the sanctuary. I had been caught!

We got into the car and I continued munching on my "stolen delight." My husband's car window appeared to be open, so I decided to toss it out his window. (I only "littered" with the apple core because I knew it would decompose quickly and return to nature.) Just as I hurled it, he turned to look at me, and I threw the core right into his eye. Thankfully, it only stunned him without injuring him.

Later I recounted the story to a friend who is known for her humor. Her immediate response was, "I know you want to be the apple of his eye, but that is not how to do it."

A study of the phrase, "apple of the eye," reveals that many years ago people thought that the pupil of the eye was solid and responsible for vision. They named it the "apple." Due to the importance of vision, the phrase came to refer to anything of value.

God refers to His children as the apple of His eye. Do you realize how important you are to God?

Dear God, thank You for treasuring me and placing great value on my life!
In Jesus's name, amen.

# ❀ What a Waste ❀

*Because of laziness the building decays, and through idleness of hands
the house leaks.* (Ecclesiastes 10:18 NKJV).

A little white house sits empty in the cove of the lake near my community. The home is dirty and rundown, with weeds and vines in the yard and a heavy film on the exterior cinder blocks. The house was likely a quaint beauty in its heyday, but after years of sheer neglect, I cringe to think what the inside of the home has digressed to, not to mention what creatures may have made their home in the vacant house so near to the water's edge. What a waste of potential beauty, an eyesore to neighbors, and a great loss of hours of fun for some family because no one has tended to the lake house over the years. Through extended neglect, the house is probably now in disrepair.

Many a healthy marriage has fallen apart due to sheer neglect. Countless friendships have slowly disbanded from a pile-up of days of no effort to stay connected. Ministries that were once thriving are slowly dying because the leadership has lost its passion for the work of serving others. And Christians who once walked in the fullness of Christ now find themselves feeling empty and without direction because they have ceased pouring their energies into reading and studying the Word of God. Is laziness the culprit—seeing signs that the situation is growing worse, but failing to have enough concern to do something about it?

Just as a lake house requires a dedication to maintain its beauty and use, relationships also require maintenance to remain healthy and vibrant. But what a pleasure to have a home by the lake, and what joy to have strong relationships with those who enrich your life! Examine the connections in your life. Think about your relationships at home, work, church, and with God. Ask God to help you assess whether you're fully committed to building those relationships, or if you've slackened your hand and allowed breakdowns to creep into your relationships. Ask God to renew your resolve to be a contributing member in the relationships of your life.

Father, help me to see what I can do to strengthen
the relationships in my life, starting with my relationship with You. Amen.

# ❀ *Words of Joy* ❀

*The tongue has the power of life and death* (Proverbs 18:21).

When God called me into Christian writing and speaking, I chose Words of Joy as the ministry name. It's not only a play on words with my own name (Joy), but also it conveys the purpose of my writing and speaking.

Have you ever watched the chain reaction that transforms a place when someone speaks a few genuine words of encouragement? One beautiful autumn day, I stopped in a restaurant to eat. The server was rude from the moment she seated me. Then I observed how she treated the other customers. She was equally rude to them.

When she came to the table to take my order, I told her I had noticed how busy she was. I assured her that our two daughters have been in the service industry and I know the work is tiring.

On her next trip to my table, I told her that I love to pray for people and asked if she had any prayer requests. She had none.

A few moments later she came back to my table and told about her beloved aunt's illness. She pulled out a chair and sat on the edge. I asked her aunt's name then inquired if she wanted me to pray privately or with her.

She said, "Let's pray together."

I led in a prayer and when I looked up she was crying. She thanked me and went around to the other tables to see what they needed.

Her demeanor was different as she approached them. She smiled and even teased with them. In turn, they responded positively to her. The entire room was transformed because her attitude was transformed.

We never know what burdens those around us carry. The power of life and death lies in our tongues. A huge responsibility accompanies that realization. We only get one chance to live each day. Someone's day—maybe even our own—can be transformed by the words we say.

> Dear Lord, just as You spoke the world into existence,
> we can speak joy or sorrow in the world by our words.
> Please help us to choose wisely. In Jesus's name, amen.

# ❀ One of Life's Lessons ❀

*Whatever you did for one of the least of these brothers of mine,*
*you did for me* (Matthew 25:40).

The planners of the North American Mission Study did a wonderful job. They decorated rooms throughout the church and had actors from the congregation portraying various scenarios of social issues. The participants moved from station to station, getting an inside view of the difficulties many Americans face daily.

My group walked into the room titled "Homelessness." The actors in that room began presenting a mini-drama about homelessness. Then Richard entered and silence gripped the room.

Richard was a homeless man who occasionally attended our church. Our family knew him as a lovable character because he frequently came to the parsonage asking for food. However, most people in the church, including the ones in the study, did not even know his name.

I could sense the uncomfortable emotions in the room. So, after the presentation, I turned to Richard and said, "We've had a drama about homelessness, but, Richard, I know you experience it firsthand. What would you like to share with us about what it's really like?"

Richard came alive as he realized he had something of value to share. People stood enthralled as they listened to him. They asked him numerous questions about the difficulties of homelessness. Richard went from station to station with our group, and we gave him a chance to address the issues that affected him. He offered suggestions about what we could do as a church to help.

After that night, Richard was no longer a nameless, homeless man. He became a person of worth and value as he had taught important truths to people who, in many cases, had been in church all their lives.

The church responded by developing a large ministry to the homeless that continues today. It is no coincidence that Richard came to church that night. Through him we learned one of life's greatest lessons.

Dear Lord, help us to do for others, and thus, to bless You!
In Jesus's name, amen.

# ❃ *Leadership of One* ❃

*If you confess with your mouth, "Jesus is Lord," and believe in your heart that God raised him from the dead, you will be saved* (Romans 10:9).

When I was a young mother in Clinton, South Carolina, our church observed a week of renewal. On the last night, my husband had to work, so I went by myself, left our two children in childcare, and sat down in the sanctuary. The evangelist quoted Romans 10:9 above. Then he read verse 8: *"The word is near you; it is in your mouth and in your heart, that is, the word of faith we are proclaiming."*

I knew I was saved, with Jesus's Spirit in my heart, but suddenly I heard *proclaim,* and *confess.* I had always been laid back—never a volunteer unless someone called on me. The evangelist said, "I want everyone to stand up and say aloud, 'Jesus is Lord. Jesus is MY Lord.' If you know it, proclaim it."

I scrunched down in my pew. Maybe nobody would see me. I looked down at my dress, with a baby spit-up spot on the front, and a small tear under the arm. *I couldn't possibly stand up and let anybody see this dress.*

No one stood up. The silence was uncomfortable. *I could stand and confess Jesus, but I'm ashamed of this dress....* The evangelist read, *"Anyone who trusts in him will never be put to shame"* (v. 11). I squirmed.

Then I noticed a woman rising on the fourth row. It was my former teacher from the third grade, Miz M., a good church leader. She spoke clearly: "Jesus is Lord. Jesus is MY Lord!" No doubt Miz M. believed every word.

That did it. I stood, spit-up, torn dress, and all. "Jesus is Lord. Jesus is MY Lord." The sound of my own voice startled me, but I knew I'd never again be ashamed to confess Him aloud.

All over the room people began to stand, shouting the words "Jesus is MY Lord!" Miz M. had demonstrated a Leadership of One. I wanted to be just like her.

Lord, thank You for exemplary leaders. May we never be ashamed of You, but take a leadership stance, proclaiming You as our personal Lord. Amen.

# ❦ From Rags to Riches ❦

*In love he predestined us to be adopted as his sons through Jesus Christ,*
*in accordance with his pleasure and will* (Ephesians 1:4–5).

As a college student, I searched for what seemed to be the illusive "will of God." I read books on the subject and sought wise counsel from my parents and ministers. My quest to find God's led me to work at one of our denomination's conference centers for the summer in Ridgecrest, North Carolina.

While there I attended worship services, talked with missionaries, and spent much time in prayer and Bible study. At that age in life, I thought that "God's will" meant finding the right mate and choosing a career.

Within a few short years, I married the person whom I consider to be the most wonderful man in the world and had a fulfilling career as a teacher of the deaf. With those major decisions settled, I still sought to discover "the will of God." After expecting and not encountering a Damascus Road experience, I realized that "the will of God" is really quite simple. God's will is that we are adopted as His children and submit to our Father's authority. "A Child of the King" (which was my earthly father's favorite song) is more than a song. It's the will of God!

The comic strip "Annie" tells the story of a wealthy man, Daddy Warbucks, adopting an orphan girl. This "rags to riches" story of a poor girl, adopted by a wealthy man to live as his child in a beautiful mansion captivates the imaginations of millions of people.

In reality we are all "Annies." This world is one huge orphanage, and our wealthy, powerful Heavenly Father desires to adopt us so we can live holy lives as His children. One day believers will live in His home, a beautiful place especially prepared for us. This is not a comic strip or a movie. This is the will of God.

Dear God, how we thank You for making it possible that each of us
can live as a child of the King! In Jesus's name, amen.

# ❀ *Uniquely Me* ❀

*And even the very hairs of your head are all numbered*
(Matthew 10:30).

I felt I was losing my identity. Has there ever been a time in your life that you felt left out of the loop? From the time I told Charles Alston I would marry him, our two families took over the big event. No one thought to tell me what was up.

Of course, I wanted to be united with Charles's family. As we planned the wedding ceremony, we wanted it to be a worshipful experience, uniting our families into one. We chose phrases from the Bible as our theme. We wanted the uniting into one heart, faith, and family—in one accord. I soon learned this ideal was going to be a feat, for it was not happening. I felt like a woman walking around in the dark.

However, I knew Jesus said He was the light of the world. I tried to walk confidently in the Light. I read again Paul's words: *"I have been crucified with Christ and I no longer live, but Christ lives in me. The life I live in the body, I live by faith in the Son of God, who loved me and gave himself for me"* (Galatians 2:20–21).

My pre-wedding "cold feet" period was over. I recognized that no two fingerprints are alike. Every footprint and ear print of every one of us is unique. Even if my personality did meld with Charles's family, if I lost my identity as a single adult, I would still be unique. I was happy to become known as Charles's wife.

As I approached the ring ceremony, I thought of God's Word: *"'I will make you like my signet ring, for I have chosen you,' declares the LORD Almighty"* (Haggai 2:23). I knew God had chosen me, as I looked to the future as Mrs. Charles Alston.

Many times after I married Charles, I have changed identities. As I moved into new ministries, I became "Jennifer's mom," "Emanuel's mom," "the preacher's wife," or "Miz Alston, the schoolteacher"—but I never lost my Christian identity. I've shared these verses many times with brides and others who felt that they had also lost identities. Each one is unique. You are uniquely you. I am uniquely me. God's Word says I can see myself through the eyes of God who knows each hair on my head.

Dear God, thank You for making me uniquely me. May all Christians
have confidence in who we are and who You are, able to share
Your words with others who seem to have lost their identities. Amen.

# ❀ The Joy of the Lord ❀

*"This day is sacred to our Lord. Do not grieve, for the joy of the Lord is your strength"* (Nehemiah 8:10).

*Strength* has become a household word. "Strength training" exercise equipment, "extra strength" detergents and cleansers, and "maximum strength" pain relievers flood the consumer market. However, the Bible clearly gives the formula for strength that is both infallible and eternal—the joy of the Lord (Nehemiah 8:10).

After a split, the nation of Israel divided into two kingdoms—Israel in the north and Judah in the south. Through various prophets, God warned them to repent or judgment would come. Continued disobedience resulted in Israel's exile into Assyria, and Judah's exile into Babylon.

After 70 years of displacement in Babylon, the Jewish captives who desired to return to their beloved homeland were allowed to leave in order to rebuild the temple at Jerusalem. After rebuilding the temple and the city walls, a scribe named Ezra held a public reading of God's law, and Nehemiah and the Levites helped explain its meaning.

The people became so remorseful that they began to weep. The leaders instructed them not to cry but to rejoice, for the joy of the Lord would be their strength.

God's Word quickens our hearts to mournful repentance, but it also gladdens our hearts by depicting God's mercy and forgiveness. The joy of the Lord comes from a reconciled relationship with God.

Satan tries with all his might to rob us of our joy, for he knows that therein is our strength. One tactic he uses is to get us so focused on our wretchedness as sinners that we miss the joy of regeneration. Today's verse is a perfect example, but thankfully we can learn from the people of Judah. Their remorse turned into rejoicing as they observed the Feast of Tabernacles for the first time in many years, affirmed their covenant with God, and denounced their sins: *"The sound of rejoicing in Jerusalem could be heard far away"* (Nehemiah 12:43). They regained their joy and with it their strength.

Dear Lord, help us to focus on Your truths rather than Satan's deceptions.
Help us accept Your forgiveness and walk in joy throughout life.
In Jesus's name, amen.

# ❀ *In My Shoes* ❀

*Do not judge, or you too will be judged* (Matthew 7:1).

When I was a home health nurse, I visited Donna, a single mom, who cared for a bedridden relative—a recent stroke victim—along with her own three children. The house was cramped, with no air-conditioning in the humid, 90-degree heat. I examined Marcie, who lay in her bed with limbs contorted from the stroke. The room reeked of urine mingled with Marcie's pungent body odor.

As I straightened the sheets I asked Donna how she cared for Marcie. The more questions I asked, the terser Donna's answers became. Finally, she left the room. I followed and asked what was wrong.

"It seems like you don't think I'm doing a very good job," she said.

I realized I had assumed that Donna was negligent in her care for Marcie. In reality, Donna had taken Marcie into her home out of love and juggled the responsibilities of a single mom with the demands of providing 24-hour care to a bedridden stroke victim.

At that moment, the Lord touched my heart with His grief at my judgmental attitude.

I said, "It must be hard to be a single mom, take care of your three children, and take care of all of Marcie's needs, too. I can't imagine how you do all this—making beds, giving medicine, playing with the children, preparing meals, feeding Marcie as well as your kids...." Tears slipped down her cheeks. From that day on, we were close friends because she knew I respected her.

Sometimes we harshly judge because we assume people could do better if they tried. Whether that is true or not, we are not to look down on them. We do not know the hearts of people as God does. Nor have we walked in their shoes. When we critically appraise others according to our personal standards, we ourselves fall under accountability to God.

Precious Savior, You literally walked in my shoes all the way to Calvary....
Remind me to show that compassion to others. Amen.

*Donna's story first appeared in* Woman to Woman: Preparing Yourself to Mentor *by Edna Ellison and Tricia Scribner (New Hope Publishers, 2005).*

# ❀ Peace When You Don't ❀ Know the Way

*"Along unfamiliar paths I will guide them; I will turn the darkness into light before them and make the rough places smooth"*
(Isaiah 42:16).

Judy Williams told me the story of a dear friend's teenaged daughter, who had run away from home with another teenager. Judy visited her friend to comfort her. The friend calmly told about the police tracking the teenagers, falling just one step behind the runaways at each place. Judy's friend assured her that she trusted God, who was capable of taking care of her daughter. Judy admired her friend's faith.

The police called; they had found the girls. God made this mother's rough places smooth.

I, too, admire this mother's firm faith. Even Christians sometimes show fear of the unknown. We worry, fretting over the unexpected, fearing fear loss of any kind. However, I know one group who give up their original homes, extended families, and familiar surroundings to serve God: missionaries.

Some missionaries I've known have served in war zones, yet they feel deep peace about their situations. Sometimes they face possible death—of themselves and their families—but they maintain a calm attitude, trusting God moment by moment. Like Abraham, who received God's call to go, they take a leap of faith. Abraham immediately left home, moved his family, including livestock, hundreds of miles to Canaan (Genesis 12).

Missionaries are ordinary people, called by God to do the extraordinary. Listening to God intently, they answer confidently, knowing what it means to become people of the Lord, centered in His will. With that worldview, they follow Him anywhere!

How about you? Has He given special Spirit-nudges, an awareness of Him in your life? Are circumstances falling into place so you can serve Him better? Spend time today praying you'll have courage to follow His will. Ask Him to give you enough confidence that you'd consider moving, getting more education or training, and—yes—facing the unknown in your future. He'll guide you along unfamiliar paths, and He'll make *your* rough places smooth.

Holy Leader, I now take the leap of faith to follow You anywhere. Thank You, Lord, for turning darkness into light before me and making my rough places smooth as I take the first step. Amen.

# ❀ Songs Can Minister Too ❀

*O my Strength, I sing praise to you; you, O God, are my fortress,*
*my loving God* (Psalm 59:17).

One of the most memorable days of my life happened in Moulton, England, in a gray stone church where an Anglican congregation first sang
John Newton's hymn, "Amazing Grace." A hardened former slave trader,
God's grace overwhelmed Newton when he realized God's amazing grace
to forgive him. He confessed his faith in Jesus and later set out to make
amends for all his sins in buying and selling human beings and transporting
them in inhumane conditions. His wonderful song, arranged in an English
folk tune, caught on, and Christians around the world still sing his rousing
words about grace.

More than 200 years later, as a group of Americans researching the
lives of early Baptists in England, we stood in a circle in the quiet of the par-
ish church on the edge of the village of Moulton. Someone spontaneously
began singing "Amazing Grace." As we joined in the song, bright sunlight
came from behind a cloud and beamed through multicolored stained-glass
windows on our heads inside the church sanctuary as we sang reverently
with colors dancing like halos.

Several of us remarked how that song had ministered to us over the
years. God took the brokenness of a slave trader and transformed his heart
into an unbelievable mind-set of words that still minister to the world today.
Praise God today that we can minister to others through song as well as
deeds.

Lord, minister to our hearts today as You did in John Newton's day. Help us to
sing Your praises to others as we minister through word and deed. Whether we
sing or serve, help us bless others as we minister in Jesus's name, amen.

# ❀ See, I Have Made You a Witness ❀

*See, I have made him a witness to the peoples, a leader and commander of the peoples. Surely you will summon nations you know not and nations that do not know you will hasten to you because of the LORD your God, the Holy One of Israel, for he has endowed you with splendor*
(Isaiah 55:4–5).

God encouraged David as seen through many words we have recorded in the Psalms; David, a poor shepherd boy anointed by God to be the king of Israel, God's chosen nation to lead other nations to know the Living God.

David, like many of us today, needed to be endowed with the strength and splendor of God before he could be a good witness.

For your devotional time today, think how God has given you experiences to be a witness to others. If you are only willing to share the experiences He has given you, you have a wonderful testimony to God's love. God has prepared you as a leader by giving you these experiences.

Maybe God is telling you through today's Bible verse, "See, I have made you a witness, a leader, a commander." Sometimes it may be hard for us to realize God is making leaders out of us. It must have been hard for David too. God has shown through David's story that He has power to make a leader out of any of us if it's His will.

It is true that all the nations of the world have come to us. No matter what country you live in, you will find those of other nationalities and customs. Think about the opportunity. Is God asking you to lead these others to know Him better? Ask God for His strength and splendor that is more amazing than we can imagine. May each of us bow to His will and obey Him totally.

Dear Lord, give us strength and unbelievable splendor from Your heart.
We worship You and bow down before You. Make us servant leaders, Lord,
so we can tell everyone about You.

# ❀ Render unto Caesar ❀

*We have different gifts, according to the grace given us. If a man's*
*gift is…contributing to the needs of others, let him give generously*
(Romans 12:6, 8).

One year my husband and I wondered how we would pay our annual county taxes. I was a homemaker who didn't work outside the home, both our children had been in the hospital that year, and we had depleted our extra funds. We asked for a tax extension from December 31 to January 31. Waiting until the last day, Snow paid the taxes in person.

Coming home, he said, "Hey! We made it. I got just the right amount of money and went straight to the courthouse. Here's the receipt." When he pulled it out of the envelope, the check he'd given the county clerk fell out!

"I'll take it back on Monday," he said. She just slipped it into the envelope by mistake.

"Wait a minute," I said. "We have the receipt to show we've paid the taxes."

"Yes, but we didn't pay. Here's our check."

I'm ashamed of my next words. "But maybe this is God's way of rewarding us. We've had lots of medical bills lately. Maybe He's making it up to us…."

Snow shook his head. Marking the envelope "Pay on Monday," he thumb-tacked it on our bulletin board.

Snow had to work that weekend, so I went to church with the children on Sunday, praying that God would show him it was all right to keep the check. After all, I thought we deserved it.

After leading the children to their rooms, I walked into my Sunday School class in time to hear the teacher say, *"Give to Caesar what is Caesar's, and to God what is God's"* (Mark 12:17).

Have you ever experienced someone's words that you knew were really God's, aimed straight at your heart? God's Spirit pierced my heart that day. I knew what I had to do. We paid the taxes again, cheerfully, the next day.

Lord, thank You for enabling us, first to give cheerfully to You,
and honestly to the authorities You have in place over us., Thank You that we
can trust You to meet our spiritual and our physical needs. Amen.

# ❀ *The Cornerstone* ❀

*Consequently, you are no longer foreigners and aliens, but fellow
citizens with God's people and members of God's household, built on
the foundation of the apostles and prophets, with Christ Jesus himself as
the chief cornerstone. In him the whole building is joined together and
rises to become a holy temple in the Lord. And in him you too are being
built together to become a dwelling in which God lives by his Spirit*
(Ephesians 2:19–22).

The boulders were stacked in two separate heaps like lumpy pyramids. The
good stones, naturally smooth and oblong, required minimal preparation before
being set into the building wall. Other stones weren't worth the work it took to
make them usable for walls. The crew would later toss them in the ravine.

The astute master builder noticed one oddly-shaped rock in the dis-
card pile. He saw in it what others had missed—the perfect cornerstone.
In his book, *Manners and Customs of Bible Lands*, Fred Wight says that the
cornerstone, a unique large square-shaped stone instead of the usual oblong
shape, was laid in the foundation as the base where two walls met.

The Jews knew the significance of the cornerstone in constructing a
sound building. They also understood the spiritual significance, for Isaiah
the prophet had proclaimed that God said He had laid in Zion a cornerstone
to provide a stable foundation (28:16). Jesus became that cornerstone. He
had come to His own people, and they had tossed Him into the rubbish pile,
oblivious that the One they rejected was God in the flesh.

We can choose to build our lives upon many foundations. We can
know what our foundation is by evaluating what absorbs most of our mental energy. A mother, for example, may be consumed with meeting children's needs, but if her foundation is Jesus Christ, she will direct her mental
energy toward meeting those needs in Christ's way and in His strength.
Conversely, a mom whose foundation is merely her children will consider
meeting her children's needs as her priority and may trust only in herself to
accomplish her goals, not giving them the kinds of godly lessons they need.

Paul reminds us in 1 Corinthians 3:11 that Jesus Christ is the only true
foundation, and throughout Scripture He is portrayed specifically as the
cornerstone, the key stone in the foundation. We can ask ourselves whether
we have put the Cornerstone in the proper place in our lives or have we
rejected Him, as did the unbelieving Jews.

Lord Jesus, Cornerstone of the Church and of my life, may I stand on You,
not on my own strength each day. Amen.

*"If anyone would come after me, he must deny himself and take up his cross daily and follow me"* (Luke 9:23).

Jesus had miraculously fed more than 5,000 people who dogged His steps in hopes of hearing Him preach and seeing Him heal. After feeding the multitude, He pulled His disciples aside to pray. Peter declared that he recognized Jesus was God's Anointed Messiah for whom the Jewish people had so long waited. But Jesus would not mold Himself to the vision of those who believed Messiah would free them from Roman rule. He had a different mission. He put the choice to them clearly, *"If anyone would come after me."*

One of the most crucial aspects of this passage is one little word— *if*. This may be the biggest little word in the English language. *If* teaches us that following Christ is a choice. In one sense it teaches us that we don't grow gradually or automatically into salvation or relationship with Christ. We aren't Christian because our parents were; or because we were baptized, sprinkled, christened, or circumcised. We aren't Christians because our husbands are deacons, because we teach Bible study class, or because we try to follow Christ's teachings. We aren't Christians because we're Americans or because we believe that "one nation under God" should be left in the Pledge of Allegiance. We are Christians *if* we choose to believe in Him.

*If* teaches us that the gospel message is simple, but not easy. Christ never said, "If you want to be my disciple, you can live as you wish; I won't disrupt the day-to-day too much." *If* leaves the option open as Almighty God requests that which He could mandate—that we follow and obey Him. He lays out the demands. He calls us as Christians to deny ourselves, take up our cross of self-death each day, and live with our eyes fixed on Jesus alone for the rest of our lives. Then He will breathe into us His life in exchange for our death. But, only *if*....

Lord, with all my heart I want to follow You. I trust You now
to enable me to do all that You ask of me. Amen.

# ❀ *Glory and Praise* ❀

*Give thanks to the LORD, call on his name.... Sing to him, sing praise to him; tell of all his wonderful acts. Glory in his holy name; let the hearts of those who seek the LORD rejoice* (Psalm 105:1–3).

I grew up in a large family with many sisters. We enjoyed each other and had a close life together. One thing I'm sure of. I can thank God for each member of my family. As I grew up, I was taught to spend time in praise. I learned to sing early in life, and enjoyed belonging to the New Directions, which blended cultures and races to praise the Lord with our music.

Let's make today a wonderful time with God by praising Him and thanking Him for all His goodness to us. As His children, we can find fresh reasons for thanking Him every day. I am thankful for the companionship of sisters. I am also thankful for each of my four children. They are precious to God in separate ways. I could thank Him for hours for the particular qualities of each of them. As a sister, mother, or other family member, let your prayertime today be filled with praise for the relationships in your family.

The verses above tell us to give thanks and call on God's name. How many of the names of God can you recall? I like to praise Him by calling every word I see in the Bible that describes Him. The verse says *"Glory in his holy name."* Can you proclaim His name aloud and feel the glory in His name? Call His name and thank Him for who He is. Whether you can sing or not, make a joyful noise in His ears as you sing praise to Him.

The verse also says: *"tell of all his wonderful acts."* Name all the things He's done for you, and praise Him!

Dear Lord, may the hearts of each of us "who seek the Lord rejoice." You have blessed us; help us to bless You as we give thanks today. Amen.

# ❀ *I Love a Parade* ❀

*But thanks be to God, who always leads us in triumphal procession
in Christ and through us spreads everywhere the fragrance of the
knowledge of him* (2 Corinthians 2:14).

Do you love parades? In my hometown the Christmas parade was always
the hit of the year. Large groups gathered, lining the streets. A police escort
led the parade, then a convertible with the parade's master of ceremonies,
the hometown high school marching band, visiting bands from nearby
cities, brightly-decorated floats from churches and businesses, and Santa
Claus in a large sled-on-wheels at the end. Immediately after Santa passed,
the Christmas lights on every electric pole in town burst into dazzling colors and a giant Christmas tree bathed the town square in twinkling lights.
Occasionally costumed people on a civic-club float or a fire truck tossed
candy, perfume samples, or small plastic toys to the crowd.

What is a "triumphal procession"? Paul refers to the Roman soldiers
who came home from wars to an awaiting crowd! Sometimes they brought
back loot or slaves to display before fellow citizens. In figurative language,
Paul says God will lead the parade, and we will follow as victorious people,
as He uses us to spread the "fragrance" of the knowledge of Christ.

Fragrance is expensive — unless we receive it as a gift. If we're wearing
it, others notice and are usually impressed with its pleasant aroma. However, allergic people turn their backs, or step away.

If we possess the fragrance of Christ, we allow Him to lead us in the procession to share our fragrance with others. We know it's not cheap, because it
cost Christ dearly, though we can give it away freely because it's a gift from
God. We can be confident and triumphant, but we are careful not just to
toss the fragrance out to the crowd like fragrance samples at a Christmas
parade. We cherish the fragrance of Christ as we carefully share it.

O God, may each of us be aware of Your sweet fragrance in us.
May we cherish it and share it with everyone we know. Amen.

# ❀ The Reason for Ministry ❀

*When Jesus had called the Twelve together, he gave them power and
authority to drive out all demons and to cure diseases, and he sent them
out to preach the kingdom of God and to heal the sick* (Luke 9:1–2).

When the disciples were sent out, Jesus gave them a two-fold mission:
preach the Word and heal the sick (Luke 9:2). They followed His directions: *"So they set out and went from village to village, preaching the gospel and
healing people everywhere"* (v. 6).

Evangelism and ministry go hand in hand today just as they did with
the disciples in the New Testament. You can minister in Jesus's name:
encouraging patients in a hospital or nursing home, bringing a Bible study
into a prison, teaching English to nonchurched internationals from other
countries, providing meals during tragedy, water on a hot day, or shelter
after a disaster. The list goes on and on.

The ministry of presence—just being there—may be the best ministry
of all. Every kindhearted person wants to help get rid of human suffering
and have mercy on others, but Christians don't want merely to show compassion and kindness to others. They have a greater call. Every Christian
ministry has a valid purpose and focus: leading the recipients of ministry
to Jesus. The greatest need anyone has is the need for the Savior. Spiritual healing is more important than all physical, psychological, and mental
needs combined.

Like the disciples, we want to focus on our witnessing to the power of
Jesus Christ, who brings salvation and eternal life to all of us. Though we
want to be on mission for God by ministering to a hurting world, remember
our focus: leading them to Jesus.

Through ministry, we move to an intimate relationship with them that
leads them to the intimate relationship with the Lord Jesus.

Dear Lord, in our ministry to others, help us focus on the best purpose
for ministry: meeting the spiritual needs and sharing Jesus's love. Amen.

# ❀ *Kindness* ❀

*Clothe yourself with compassion, kindness, humility, gentleness and
patience... And over all these virtues, put on love, which binds them all
together in perfect unity* (Colossians 3:12, 14).

A little girl asked her mother for butter on her biscuit. The mother placed a
small sliver of butter, which promptly melted. The child held out her hand
again. "Mama, I *really* like butter." The mother placed another sliver of butter, and then she opened a jar of strawberry jam and spread a generous
amount of the fresh, delicious jam on the biscuit.

"Why did you give me so much?" she said.

"Baby, I love you so much. If I gave you that butter, I would show you
*kindness*, but if I gave you butter and jam, then I show you *lovingkindness*!"

Many strong leaders think they must always be decisive, always in
control, as they lead. However, experience shows most leaders that simple
kindness is a primary aspect of leadership. Have you ever had a leader (perhaps a supervisor or teacher) who was unkind? Any spirit of cooperation
you formerly had may have melted away like butter if the leader treated you
unkindly. Unkindness breeds a spirit of contention and rebellion.

You and I can take the advice of Paul, who explained to the fledgling church at Colosse that compassion, kindness, humility, gentleness, and
patience were the best virtues for a leader. Then he tells them to clothe
themselves with these virtues—and then put on, like an overcoat—the
virtue of love, which binds all the other virtues together. Notice that the
perfect solution for disunity in a group is for the leader to cover the entire
group with love. Add *love* on top of kindness, and a leader creates *lovingkindness*, which brings "perfect unity."

Father, like a parent to all of us, You have fed us and clothed us with abundant
lovingkindness, compassion, and patience. As we use these virtues to lead others,
we pray in King David's words, "O *continue thy lovingkindness unto them that know thee*"
(Psalm 36:10 KJV). Amen.

# ❀ First Love ❀

*You have persevered and have endured hardships for my name, and*
*have not grown weary. Yet I hold this against you: You have forsaken*
*your first love. Remember the height from which you have fallen!*
*Repent and do the things you did at first* (Revelation 2:3–5).

Do you recall when you first fell in love? You spent hours getting ready to meet your bough. Every hair had to be in place. The moment you and your love were separated you both started planning how to meet again. Over time, though, the intensity waned. Little annoyances disrupted the intimacy you once shared.

So it was with the church at Ephesus and her relationship with the Savior. The church possessed many laudable attributes. Her members had persevered through trial, practiced good deeds, and stood against false doctrine. Yet, they had left their "first love."

Where had the church gone wrong? Perhaps they made a dramatic shift in attitude. More likely though, just as in marriage, they took each other for granted, busied themselves with life's daily demands, and then one day seemed to worship a God they hardly knew.

The Lord Jesus beckoned them to return to Him and to show their change of heart by three actions. First, they were to remember the heights from which they had fallen. Second, they needed to repent. Remembering what it had been like at first was a start, but they also needed to turn around and pursue the right, a much harder task than simply reflecting upon how life could be different. Finally, the Lord told them to do the deeds they had done at first.

Like the church at Ephesus, we can't will ourselves to do "the first works" out of grudging obligation. The only way we can really love as we first did is by remembering Him, the lover of our souls, by repenting from our self-centered attitudes and lifestyles, and by repeating the loving actions we once did with fervor. This is the best antidote for believers like us whose hearts have grown cold.

> Lord, I recall my early years with You when my passion was strong
> for You and Your Word. I've gotten distracted by lesser things.
> Guide me back to Your heart. Amen.

# ❀ My Yardstick ❀

*But they, measuring themselves by themselves, and comparing them-*
*selves among themselves, are not wise* (2 Corinthians 10:12 NKJV).

Self-esteem and self-expression have taken on increasing prominence in our society. In fact, finding out who I am has become the ideal by which I should plan my life. Once self is discovered (by self), the ultimate goal becomes expressing that identity. A popular children's television network, for instance, repeats the slogan, "Express yourself," while presenting vignettes of teen stars sharing what they like about themselves.

Instead of being taught to focus on glorifying God with their lives, children are encouraged by secular media, educators, and parents to "follow their hearts." Vested with intrinsic authority over their lives, young people are also urged not to have sex "until they are ready," which presupposes that children know when that is. Instead of teaching honor, respect, and esteeming others above one's self, contemporary culture asserts that parents should view as their greatest responsibility building their child's self-esteem, so he grows up feeling good about himself.

The individual holds himself accountable only to *himself*, owing no one else an explanation of his behavior. Hurtful acts toward others are not remedied by confession, repentance, and restitution, but by the perpetrator learning to love, trust, and accept himself.

Paul says that we can use the wrong yardstick by which to measure ourselves. He points out that a person who uses himself and others as a standard by which to measure himself is unwise.

In contrast, Scripture says that a person's heart is deceitful and wicked, and that God alone can discern the heart's motives (Jeremiah 17:9). Measuring ourselves using God's measuring stick, Jesus Christ, we fall hopelessly short. Recognizing that we've used the wrong yardstick is the first step in seeing ourselves as we really are: dirty and destitute, with a heart stain so ingrained that we cannot wash ourselves clean. Then we are ready to approach Christ with the humility necessary to receive His gift of salvation by faith, a faith that is totally dependent on God's grace, not our goodness, for salvation.

Lord Jesus, I confess that often I put my self-absorption above You. Point my
thoughts toward esteeming You highest instead. Amen.

# ❀ Hurry Up and Wait ❀

*But those who wait on the LORD shall renew their strength; they shall mount up with wings like eagle, they shall run and not be weary, they shall walk and not faint* (Isaiah 40:31 NKJV).

My father-in-law amused us with his funny witticisms. One of them was, "It seems like all people ever do any more is hurry up and wait."

We live in a world where we don't want to wait for anything. We have fast foods, fast cars, and fast computers; and we push our children to grow up too fast. We get impatient waiting for stoplights, checkout lines, appointments, and the end of worship services.

Yet in the midst of all this hurrying, aided by conveniences that are designed to save us time, we seem more tired and stressed than ever.

These beautiful verses from Isaiah offer hope. God promises that if we wait on Him, we will soar on wings like eagles.

Eagles are noted for their power and strength. They also are known for their ability to mount up and soar. In fact, their long, broad wings were designed for soaring. The wingspan of an eagle is between 72 to 90 inches. For eagles, soaring requires very little wing flapping.

Eagles have about 7,000 feathers that are lightweight, but very strong. The hollow, yet flexible, feathers consist of layers that are interlocked in an astonishing design of nature. The tips of the feathers at the ends of the wings are tapered, which helps reduce turbulence as air currents pass over the end of the wings. All these attributes combined ensure a smooth ride. Through Isaiah God gave a beautiful analogy about the kind of flight we can expect if we wait on Him. Even in turbulent times, if we wait on God to accomplish His purposes through them, we can still enjoy a smooth ride. As my father-in-law would say, it is time for us to "hurry up and wait!"

Dear Lord, please help me quiet myself long enough to hear from You, even if it requires a little wait. In Jesus's name, amen.

# ❀ Culture Shock ❀

*The righteous will flourish like a palm tree, they will grow like a cedar of Lebanon; planted in the house of the LORD* (Psalm 92:12).

"Root shock; that's what it is," said the nursery man, who planted new tomato slips in our garden to replace several that died.

After talking with him, I learned if plants get air around the roots, they go into shock. Gardeners must stamp on the soil around a freshly-planted slip to push all the air out of the soil. They also pour *too much* water on the new plant, so any air bubble in the soil will rise to the surface.

"Why did you place those matches beneath the roots?" I asked.

"Nothing better than a bit of sulfur to get the root system up and running in its new place," he said. "Using one match out of a book of matches is the best treatment for successful plants."

"Looks like a dose of sulfur would shock the roots."

"Nope, root air is the worst shock. Gotta get that air out!"

Plants and humans have trouble with culture shock when transplanted. When I moved from South Carolina to Alabama and then to California, I learned a new culture in each place. I joined churches in the same denomination, but each relationship was a little different.

Probably the greatest culture shock happens when newborn Christians join a church. If they've never attended a church before, they may not know unspoken rules some members have about acceptable clothing or language. They may have heard religious talk in the media that is poor theology. They must also change their daily routines to accommodate Bible study and prayer. We often expect them to know the unspoken requirements for godly behavior, yet they've had little training in such things.

Several new Christians have laughed with me about their embarrassment when they lit a cigarette inside a church hallway or were reprimanded for wearing a miniskirt, when they sincerely didn't know they'd done anything offensive.

As we form relationships with new Christians, may we welcome them, helping them grow and flourish in our churches.

Lord, help us minimize culture shock for new Christians. May we tenderly enable them to put down roots and bloom where they are planted in our churches. Amen.

# ❀ Smellin' Mighty Good in Here! ❀

*For we are to God the aroma of Christ among those who are being
saved and those who are perishing* (2 Corinthians 2:15).

One of our favorite family jokes is a line my mother said throughout the
years. Whenever she walked into the kitchen during a meal, she said,
"Smellin' mighty *good* in here!" and began looking for food on the stove.
Not many families consider such an old-fashioned saying funny, but it's
special to us. When we gather at one of our homes for lunch or dinner, family members come in, shouting that sentence as an announcement of their
arrival. Immediately everyone stops cooking or eating, laughs, and hugs
the others!

Mother, a strong Christian who knew the verse above, hung out in
places where people were "being saved and…perishing." She faithfully
attended church and other evangelistic meetings. Every Thursday she
went with a friend, Nell, to visit shut-ins or those who had questions about
becoming a Christian. Mother usually made friends with people they visited,
welcoming them into her Sunday School class or missions group later.

With tears Mother tried to witness to others. I watched her rehearse for
hours her testimony about how much Jesus meant to her. She was basically
a shy person, but she attempted a verbal witness when she could—though
she never remembered exactly what to say. She shed tears when she told a
loved one about Jesus, but her tears and her fumbling words were a witness in themselves. My cousin once told me, "I knew she was sincere. She
knows God." Always soft-spoken, humble, forgiving, and kind, she *was* the
aroma of Christ.

Like my mother, does a godly person in your life possess a spiritual
aura that you have perceived? Sometimes words can't describe the spiritual
aroma of Christ, the sense of His presence in a spiritual mother you know,
which follows her wherever she goes.

May we follow the lead of those Christians: becoming to God *"the aroma
of Christ among those who are being saved and those who are perishing."*

Lord, may we be the aroma of Christ, our Savior, who sacrificed His life on our
behalf. Thank You for godly examples that lead us closer to You. Amen.

# ❀ *Here Comes the Bride* ❀

*Let nothing be done through selfish ambition or conceit,*
*but in lowliness of mind let each esteem others better than himself.*
*Let each of you look out not only for his own interests, but also for the*
*interests of others* (Philippians 2:3–4 NKJV).

Wedding ceremonies are designed to draw attention to the bride. The bridal party strolls down the aisle first, building anticipation. As the bride enters, her gait is slow, allowing the guests seated in even the worst seats to catch a glimpse of every sequin adorning her train. All eyes are on the bride.

It's a wondrous blessing to be the bride of Christ. We don't get to parade around in our white satin gowns and netted veils (but wouldn't that be fun, at least for a week or two?), but we can be radiant nonetheless, because the light of Christ shining through us creates a lovely glow. It's not sequins but the fruit of the Spirit that will catch the attention of the crowd, compelling them to look more closely.

Knowing God has ordained for His Bride to be the display of His glory, we deflect all praise to our Savior. However, in a world that constantly sends the false message that we should heap up glory for ourselves, sometimes we get swept away in the madness. I remember that as I made preparations for my wedding day, I received the advice, "It's *your* special day. It's OK to think about yourself first." I so wanted to believe that I was entitled to be selfish on my wedding day, but I discovered quickly I couldn't be a radiant bride who honored her parents and family if I was going to insist on pleasing myself first. Likewise, we sometimes wish we could justify pleasing ourselves, but we realize we can't be the radiant bride of Christ who honors her Father and blesses the Bridegroom if we're consumed with thoughts of gratifying our personal desires.

All eyes are on the bride—the bride of Christ. May we possess humble servants' hearts that daily compel other believers around us to honor the Bridegroom, Jesus Christ.

Father, give me a heart to refuse selfishness and embrace servanthood for
Your glory. Thank You for the privilege of being Your bride. Amen.

# ❀ One, Two, Three ❀

*Brothers, choose seven men from among you who are known to be full*
*of the Spirit and wisdom. We will turn this responsibility over to them*
*and will give our attention to prayer and the ministry of the word*
(Acts 6:3–4).

Mary Frances was a good leader. She was quiet and unassuming, yet she kept our missions group active and busy. I asked her about her secret to leadership.

"It's as easy as one, two three," she said.

Since she saw I was confused, she continued: "Don't do anything yourself." She smiled her usual shy grin.

I watched Mary Frances as she involved everyone in the group process. Ann emailed or telephoned all the group members to remind them of the meeting. Kathryn managed the publicity. Sara brought sodas and tea. Jill brought napkins, paper plates, and cups. Lawana prepared finger food: fruit and vegetable sticks. Suzie brought nuts or chips and dips. Lynn baked cookies. Barbara set up the church meeting room. Heather cleaned up afterward. Billie led in prayer. Kari presented a short Bible study. Marcy led missions projects. Everyone had a responsibility and felt an integral part of the group, which bonded quickly.

The New Testament church also diversified their leadership skills. Some of them waited on tables (Acts 6:2). Others were in charge of fellowship and distributing food. The original leaders gave their attention to prayer and the ministry of the word (v. 4).

Today I'm using Mary Frances' simple leadership instructions, which are remarkably similar to those in the first-century church: Establish a small group. Then give everyone some responsibility. As group members get involved, they take ownership, adjusting and matching skills-to-gifts-to-tasks, increasing their satisfaction with responsibilities, and become experienced leaders. A good leader works herself out of a job. Leadership operates just as Mary Frances said: "Don't do anything yourself." Involve one, two, three…everyone!

Lord, help us develop leadership skills as we share the responsibility with others. May we not do everything ourselves, but spotlight the leadership of others. In Jesus's name, amen.

# ❀ *Mary's Savior* ❀

*And Mary said: "My soul glorifies the Lord and my spirit rejoices in*
*God my Savior, for he has been mindful of the humble state of his*
*servant. From now on all generations will call me blessed"*
(Luke 1:46–48).

Mary, the mother of Jesus, was clearly a godly young woman, a woman "highly favored" by God. Imagine being told you would become pregnant and bear a child by God's power, without physical relations with a man. Imagine trying to tell friends how your pregnancy occurred. Most folks would just laugh and say, "Yeah, right." You would become the object of scorn and mocking, especially if you lived in first-century Israel.

Mary's purity, trust, and obedient heart made her the ideal candidate to bear the Savior of the world, God in the flesh. Still, Mary was a sinner. She needed a Savior, just like everyone else.

In today's passage we read Mary's famous prayer, recorded in Luke chapter one. She has just visited her cousin Elizabeth, who is pregnant with John the Baptist, and who recognizes the miracle that would come through Mary. In adoration of God, Mary proclaims two truths that reveal her belief that she, too, was merely human and in need of a Savior. She recognized her "humble state" and also declared God as her Savior.

Like all moms, Mary would sometimes fail as a woman, as a wife, as a parent. She would make sinful choices and misunderstand Jesus's actions and purposes. Like all other sinners, Mary also bore the stain of original sin in her life brought on by Adam.

As Mary prophesied, even in this generation some 2,000 years later we call her blessed, for she was faithful to serve the Lord as His chosen handmaiden to bear the Savior of the world—and to bear her own Savior, as well.

Precious Lord, if Mary needed a Savior, then so do I. I recognize that
You alone are perfect and holy. You alone are worthy of worship and
You alone always intercede for me at the Father's throne. Amen.

# ❀ Hope Floats ❀

*My word… will accomplish what I desire and achieve the purpose*
*for which I sent it* (Isaiah 55:11).

I met Anne when she sat across the table from us at a banquet. One of the things we have in common is that we both experienced Hugo, the devastating hurricane that hit the South Carolina coast in 1989.

However, Anne lived further south at the time in a little seacoast town named McClellanville. Their town experienced terrible loss and ruin and were the recipients of much of the aid that came into the area.

Anne related that the storm hit a few days before her son's ninth birthday. Her house was completely flooded and they sustained great loss. However, an amazing thing happened. As most of their belongings submerged beneath the rising water, all of the Bibles in her house floated!

I kept rethinking that remarkable event. This morning as I woke up pondering her story again, I realized one of the messages God conveyed through it.

No matter what happens, God's Word always prevails. It cannot be destroyed. It remarkably withstands the storms of life. It also helps us withstand life's storms.

I well remember how our church became the receiving center for relief supplies after Hugo. Our family-life building was transformed into a massive relief operation. One day we sent two vans of supplies to McClellanville. The drivers found that another shipment had just arrived. They were not sure where to take their supplies so they drove south toward another devastated area.

Suddenly they spotted some men removing a large tree that had fallen across a small road. They stopped and asked if they knew of anyone who might need their supplies. The men rejoiced and took them to the church at the end of that road. It was filled with people who took shelter there during the storm. Their food and water were gone, and they just had finished a prayer meeting asking God to send help.

God's Word and God's will always prevail. That's why, as a movie title expresses, *Hope Floats*, even during a storm.

Dear God, help us remain hopeful people in a turbulent world.
In Jesus's name, amen.

# ❀ *Consider the Climate* ❀

*"But the one who received the seed that fell on good soil is the man who
hears the word and understands it"* (Matthew 13:23).

Jesus often used stories from daily life to illustrate what the kingdom of
God was like and how to bring people into the kingdom. Jesus's parable of
the sower teaches us that the condition of the soil in which the seed is sown
is critical to a successful harvest. Just as the farmer considers the climate
as he plants, tills, and reaps, so must we consider the cultural climate as we
discern people's readiness to receive the seed of the gospel message.

Relativism, the belief that no absolute truth exists, represents the current cultural climate. Christianity and belief in the Bible are viewed as
archaic and narrow-minded. Yet, for all their bravado, people who claim
truth is relative *live* as though absolute truth exists.

For example, not one person who claims to believe truth is relative
(that it depends upon the person or situation) would accept the comment,
"Well, it's *my* truth!" from a bank teller who had just told him his account
was overdrawn, when he knew, in fact, that he had plenty of money in his
account. Nor would a mom accept an automaker's assertion that "the seat
belt seemed safe to us" as an acceptable explanation from a company whose
seat belt malfunctioned in a car accident, causing her daughter's death. And
when a witness testifies in court, no juror would accept a person's testimony
as valid who claimed, "Well, even if it isn't true for you, it's true for me." The
testimony is either true or false.

So, we should consider the climate in which we live. The climate
informs us of how people are currently thinking. But, we don't need to be
intimidated by a climate that defiantly claims truth is relative since in all
important aspects of daily life people live as though absolute truth exists,
and we can share this with confidence.

Lord, give me courage to share the evidence for truth. Amen

# ❀ Do Not Weep for Me ❀

*But Jesus, turning to them, said, "Daughters of Jerusalem, do not weep*
*for Me, but weep for yourselves and for your children"*
(Luke 23:28 NKJV).

Today may be your day to mourn, but perhaps tomorrow will be when tragedy visits my home. Death strikes every family, relationships break apart, and every twisted form of tragedy is like a weapon of Satan that he hurls at his next victim. What should we do with our moments of loss? We needn't be surprised by them, because Jesus said we would have trouble (John 16:33), but we're rarely able to anticipate our moments of sorrow. We can draw encouragement from the friendship of others who will weep with us as we weep (Romans 12:15). Yet in Christ, we learn of another response, one that demands incredible passion for the kingdom of God if we are to attain to the mind of Christ in the midst of sorrow.

As Jesus struggled to drag His broken and bleeding body down the path that would lead to Golgotha, the Son of Man must have surely felt the pain of His mangled flesh, the agony of betrayal, and the bitter sting of rejection. Women who were near Him were crying, moved with compassion for the battered frame of the man before them. Jesus knew His pain was only temporary, but the desperate spiritual lostness of the people would have eternal consequences. He instructed the women to direct their brokenheartedness toward the greatest tragedy of all—the terrible plight of those who do not know Christ as Savior.

Are you a woman of sorrows today? God cares about your every need. He takes no joy in your pain, and He's wrapping His arms around you. Share your grief with a friend. But resolve to keep this perspective offered by our Savior on the road to Calvary—our sorrows on earth are temporary, but the loss of a person's soul is an eternal tragedy. As God heals your pain, seek a deeper compassion for the lost.

Precious Lord, I am hurting today. I know You care about my sorrows. As You
heal my heart, teach me to be brokenhearted for the great sorrows that are
ahead for those who do not know You. In Jesus's name I pray, amen.

# ❀ Not in Rivertown ❀

*"If I ascend up into heaven, thou art there: if I make my bed in hell,
behold, thou art there.... Even there shall thy hand lead me, and thy
right hand shall hold me"* (Psalm 139:8, 10 KJV).

"Would you help me lead a Backyard Bible Club across town?" asked
Helen, my pastor's wife. A true missions-minded woman, she often suggested
ways our church women could love people as Christ did.

"Sure. Where?" I asked.

My husband came across the churchyard, putting his arm around me.

"There's a good spot in Rivertown (name changed by author)" Helen
said, turning to smile at him.

"Rivertown?" he said. "That's a hot spot...gangs, drugs, break-ins....What
were you two talking about?"

"We're thinking of hosting a children's Bible club there," Helen said.

"Not in Rivertown!"

She nodded. Snow turned to me. "Honey, that neighborhood's a dangerous
place. Helen, what time would it be?"

"In the mornings...nine to twelve."

"I don't know. They call Rivertown a pit of hell at night." He looked at
me. "Will our children go over there?"

"I thought so, but if it's dangerous, maybe not."

"It's probably safe in the mornings," he said. "Let's pray about it."

The next day we both felt better about serving God in Rivertown. Later
our churchwomen led a Bible club there. My children joined in the activities,
but I kept a wary eye out for lurking gang members and drug dealers.
We saw none.

I found people in Rivertown to be friendly...and, yes, *nice*. Why was
I so surprised? Mothers looked after their children the way I did. They
seemed excited to hear about Jesus, just as I was. I had misjudged them
even before we met.

I'll never forget Sue, a thin girl with stringy blond hair. Her eyes sparkled
when she heard about Jesus. We had changed her life. I reminded
myself that she had changed me too.

Lord, forgive us when we are judgmental. Help us live out the incarnation of
Christ in the world. Send us without self-righteousness to bless others,
and to recognize their blessings to us. Amen.

# ❀ A Roaring Blaze ❀

*Therefore, since we are receiving a kingdom which cannot be shaken,*
*let us have grace, by which we may serve God acceptably with reverence*
*and godly fear. For our God is a consuming fire*
(Hebrews 12:28–29 NKJV).

On the coldest day of the year, I cozied up to the fireplace and enjoyed the blaze. The flames danced, each to its own rhythm, while the pop, pop, pop and crackling sounds created a lovely music like a lullaby. The fire had such a calming effect, and I felt at ease in the warmth of the flames. How odd, I thought, that I could find pleasure in watching something like fire, something that has great destructive power to bring death and devastation. But this fire was contained in my fireplace. It was under control, and I had taken measures to be the one controlling it. Knowing I was able to have just enough flame and no more kept me feeling peaceful about my fire.

The writer of Hebrews likens God to a consuming fire. He's no tiny flame to be controlled by mankind. Truly God brings peace into our lives, but the peace does not come from a false sense of being in control. We do not keep God at bay, contained in a small compartment in our lives where we want Him. He is the mighty God to be served in all reverence and godly fear.

Examine your approach to serving the Lord. Are you freely allowing God to possess your life and direct you as He desires? A view of God that reduces Him to the simple flame of a fireplace is nothing more than a false image of the one true God. Ask God to give you a renewed understanding of His power and might, that your approach to serving Him might be founded on the respect and reverence due His name.

Lord, forgive me for the times I have made You too small in my mind,
because I wanted to be in control. You are the mighty and holy God!
You are a consuming fire! I want my will to yield to Your Spirit
as I serve You every day of my life. In Jesus's name, amen.

# ❀ Get On Task ❀

*For the weapons of our warfare are not carnal but mighty in God for*
*pulling down strongholds, casting down arguments and every high*
*thing that exalts itself against the knowledge of God, bringing every*
*thought into captivity to the obedience of Christ*
(2 Corinthians 10:4–5 NKJV).

Followers of Jesus are severely outnumbered against an enemy rising in anger and bold fierceness. Every believer must be on task for the cause of Christ. The enemy is attacking, attempting to distract you. With Holy Spirit help, what can you do?

\* Remove strongholds.

What are those temptations that seem to snare you with guilt and shame? The Holy Spirit's power can destroy that which seeks to demolish your focus and effectiveness in serving with a pure heart.

\* Expose falsehoods.

Satan wants to convince you that you know better than God does about what is best for your life; he tempts you to exalt your will over the knowledge of God. Being on task to serve your *own* life agenda, based on what *you* think will make your life satisfying, will land you in a heap of ashes—defeated, broken, and ashamed. However, exalting the knowledge of God above your own perceptions will guide you into God's perfect truth.

\* Love God with your mind.

You can sit on your hands, bind your feet, bite your tongue, and cover your eyes, but have you ever tried turning off your mind? It's impossible! Imagine wayward thoughts trying to escape your control to overcome your mind with evil intent; through the Holy Spirit's weaponry, you can take captive those thoughts and turn them over to the authority of Christ. To be an on task believer, your challenge is to battle those thoughts that are not from God, and to submit your attitudes, motivations, ideas, decisions, and even your daydreams to the God of this universe. When your thoughts are of God, your actions will likely follow.

*"No weapon formed against you shall prosper"* (Isaiah 54:17). Get on task with God's purposes for your life!

Father, I want to be fully on task for Your glory! Thank You for equipping me
with weapons that are mighty in Your strength! Amen.

# ❀ Never Subnormal Again ❀

*Be filled with the Spirit* (Ephesians 5:18).

At salvation, the Holy Spirit indwells the believer. However, through our choices, the Bible tells us that we can *quench* the work of the Holy Spirit in our lives (see 1 Thessalonians 5:19.)

I accepted Christ at age eight and was on fire for the Lord. I wanted to be in church every chance I could, including weekly outreach visitation with the adults. I even walked up to people during the altar call and asked if they would like for me to walk down the aisle with them. I laugh now as I think about what a nuisance I must have been to the older people in our church.

After awhile, I noticed that my abundant enthusiasm seemed somewhat abnormal. So, with time, I became a more "normal" Christian.

In my twenties, I longed to regain the passion I once had. In my desperate search, I became aware of the importance of the Holy Spirit's work in the believer's life. I realized I had allowed sin, mostly in the form of unforgiveness, to quench the Holy Spirit's work in my life. Upon realizing this, I prayed to release the offenses (or perceived offenses) and the accompanying unforgiveness that God brought to my mind. The more I freed others from their "offenses," the more freedom I experienced. Floods of peace and joy filled my soul. My whole world seemed new.

The Bible became alive as God revealed new truths from His Word. My prayer life was meaningful and purposeful. I stood in church and cried as I sang the words to the same hymns I had sung for years. I now had a new desire and power to witness.

The Holy Spirit's presence had been with me all along. However, I had quenched His work and awareness by holding on to unforgiveness. The famous evangelist, Vance Havner, once said, "The church is so subnormal that if it ever got back to the New Testament normal it would seem to people to be abnormal."

Dear Lord, help me never to be subnormal again! In Jesus's name, amen.

*Joy's testimony also is in* Chosen and Cherished: Becoming the Bride of Christ *by Edna Ellison, Joy Brown, and Kimberly Sowell (New Hope Publishers, 2009).*

# ❀ *It's a Plan* ❀

*For you know that it was not with perishable things such as silver or
gold that you were redeemed from the empty way of life handed down
to you from your forefathers, but with the precious blood of Christ, a
lamb without blemish or defect. He was chosen before the creation of
the world, but was revealed in these last times for your sake*
(1 Peter 1:18–20).

It was Tuesday night visitation and the family we had hoped to visit was not
home. Not wanting to waste our trip, we walked next door, hoping someone
would answer the door. When a woman answered, we asked her a couple of
questions about what she believed. When we asked if she believed that prayer
worked, she said sadly, "I'm not sure I believe in God anymore since 9/11.
I can't understand how a loving God could let something so horrible happen."

I replied, "God understands our suffering. He sent His own Son to
suffer and die for our sins."

"Then He must be a very cruel God to kill His own Son," she continued.

This precious woman misunderstood Christ's identity and purpose in
coming to earth. She saw Him as a victim of unfair circumstances, abused
by an uncaring Father. She failed to understand what Scripture taught
about the necessity of Christ's suffering and death. Nor did she realize that
everything that happened *to* Him was orchestrated *by* Him before He ever
came to earth.

Today's passage explains that the Son's role as the Redeemer on earth
was determined from eternity because God in His great mercy made provision for our sin problem even before we existed! In John 17:24, Jesus also
clarified that we believers have been given to Christ and the provision for
our salvation grew from the fullness of love within the Godhead: *"Father,
I want those you have given me to be with me where I am, and to see my glory, the glory
you have given me because you loved me before the creation of the world."*

So when we read that the soldiers beat Him and then nailed Him to a
cross, we should not think that the soldiers or anyone else held Jesus's fate
in their hands. They simply enacted the itinerary Christ had scripted from
eternity in order to accomplish His one purpose on earth: to satisfy God's
righteous demand for justice by providing the remedy to our sin problem—
a problem He alone could cure.

Precious Savior, we adore You and Your plan and provision for our salvation. Amen.

*Based on Prayer Patterns devotionals* in Missions Mosaic (Woman's Missionary Union), *January 2005.*

# ❀ *Dangerous Prayer* ❀

*He will cover you with his feathers, and under his wings you will find*
*refuge.... For he will command his angels concerning you to guard you*
*in all your ways* (Psalm 91:4, 11).

My friend, I will call him Ron, an evangelist, answered the phone. Silently, he put down the phone and told his wife, Jo, to take the children to her mother's for an hour or so. He said, I just need to talk with several of the drug dealers I witnessed to last week." Jo and Ron had agreed long ago that their focus on Christ for the world would overshadow any fear.

A bit reluctantly, Jo agreed. Before she left, she affirmed her faith and promised to pray for him at her mom's. As soon as Jo left, Ron knelt in prayer. *"Lord, I'm praying David's prayer again today. Please command Your angels to guard me in all my ways. Cover me with Your feathers; help me find refuge in You. Show Your power. Lord. Show Your awesome power."*

Ron heard a knock. He rose, slowly and calmly walking unarmed to the door. Four muscular young men stood outside, their fists tight. "Won't you come in?" Ron asked.

"Uh, yeah" One responded.

Another pulled off his stocking cap and smoothed his hair as he entered.

"Gentlemen," Ron said, "I'm glad to see you. What's up?"

The word *gentlemen* stopped one of them cold. He dropped his fists, mumbling, "Jus' hangin' out."

"Have you thought about what I said last week?"

"That's what we're doing here. You were rough on us last week. Why'd you stick your neck out in that joint?"

"Don't you think God has a right to come into a place like that? He loves everyone in that place."

They snickered. "Nah. You wrong, Man. He'd never do that."

Ron looked them in the eye, one by one, telling each young man how much God loved him—that nothing he could ever do would make God stop loving him.

"Is there any reason why you couldn't make peace with God right now, right here?" Ron asked.

The unthinkable happened. The tough-looking men knelt by Ron's sofa and in a few words confessed they believed in Jesus as their Savior.

Lord, thank You for giving Ron the mind and courage to face those under the power of evil. May we dare think the impossible; that the most unlikely people we know would confess You as Lord. In Jesus's name, amen.

# ❀ Refined in Relationships ❀

*Give me understanding to learn your commands* (Psalm 119:73).

Randy and I have now been married more than 30 years. Three months before Randy and I met, his father suddenly dropped dead of a heart attack. He had no prior history of heart problems. With the family looking on in horror, Randy attempted CPR to no avail. A less determined teenaged boy would have crumbled. Instead, Randy got up the next morning and went to work as usual in the family business, this time as breadwinner. A week after the funeral, he stood before his high school graduating class to give the valedictory speech.

Randy wasn't worried about his dad's eternal destiny. He knew his father was in heaven. A few years earlier, Randy had become the first Christian in his family. His mom followed, and then younger siblings. Finally, shortly before his death, Randy's father accepted Christ.

Though Randy had peace about his father's presence with the Lord, his dad's death had left a big, empty hole in Randy's heart. As he got ready for work each morning, wondering what would happen to his family, he asked the Lord to fill that empty hole.

Three months later we met. I was attracted to his great smile, a smile that never betrayed the tragedy he had endured.

Many times in our 30+ years of marriage, our human love has faltered due to selfishness, unforgiveness, and lust for control. At those times, I tend to forget God's purpose in bringing us into the marriage relationship. Then, almost imperceptibly, God reminds me how He brought us together and how His strong cord of grace has sustained us. I'm also learning that marriage is the Lord's most effective tool for refining me, for it is within relationship that I learn how to live out in reality the truths I have learned in my heart. It is within relationship that I become more like Jesus.

Lord, it is in the most intimate of life's relationships that I must practice what You are teaching me. Help me to be a willing and humble learner. Amen.

# ❀ Framed Hacienda ❀

*The house of the righteous contains great treasure* (Proverbs 15:6).

One afternoon, dropping by Foster Park Elementary School in Union, South Carolina, I found my daughter, Patsy, and Nannette Jenkins, a fellow teacher, leading an after-school art class.

"Come on in, Mom," Patsy said. "We can use your help."

We diluted water-color paint, each student forming a rainbow of colors on his or her paper palette. As instructed, they began painting an imaginary landscape on their fresh art paper. Nannette, Patsy, and I also chose a clean piece of art paper. I remembered a grapevine growing next to the door of an adobe house I once saw in Panama and began sketching it.

Was I messy! The watercolors dripped, splattering in places I hadn't planned. My hacienda was lopsided with bright colors in the shade and dark spots on the sunny side of the house. The deep-purple grapes looked great against the yellow-orange house, but the windows leaned helter-skelter and the entrance looked more like a ladder than steps. As the class ended, when I was about to throw my lopsided hacienda in the trash can, Patsy asked for all the work—good and bad.

Weeks later I visited her school, and to my surprise, the hacienda was framed, sitting on a table near her desk.

"How do you like the painting?" she said, beaming. I mumbled a few negative words.

Ignoring me, she said, "You know what I love about art?" she said. "Every work is different because every painter is different. I love this house so much, Mom. It reminds me of you."

Standing at a distance from the painting in her beautiful mahogany frame, I had to admit the old hacienda looked good—maybe not great, but good. What I considered a disaster with many flaws seemed a unique treasure now.

I imagine God cherishes us in the same way. None of us is perfect, but we're uniquely *us*, and God sees good in us—cracks and all, lopsided and spotted—and He loves us just the way we are.

O God, thank You for loving us just the way we are. Help us to respect others as Your unique works-in-progress, as You frame and treasure each one. Amen.

# ❀ I Wonder Who's Singing ❀ with Them Now

*For we are God's workmanship, created in Christ Jesus to do good works, which God prepared in advance for us to do* (Ephesians 2:10).

At our house we all call our younger daughter, Molly, an angel. She quietly goes about her days looking for people to bless. Her sister, Meri Beth, always teased that when Molly had a baby, he or she would be born with wings. We could hardly believe our eyes when the first ultrasound of her daughter, Mazi Grace (from "Amazing Grace") revealed what looked like a little halo above her head!

When Molly was in elementary school and middle school, we served a mission-type church in New Jersey. One day her teacher called to inquire about her since she had been out with a flu virus. The teacher said they missed her and her desk had notes all over it.

She went on to explain that whenever students were absent, Molly put a note on their desks telling them how much they were missed. She often left a piece of candy or some other surprise with the note. During Molly's absence, the students had covered her desk with I-miss-you notes. My heart was touched to hear the teacher's story.

Four years later we moved to Myrtle Beach, South Carolina. One evening, Molly and I took a walk on the beach. I could tell something was on her mind as she was somewhat silent. Then she asked, "Mama, I wonder who's singing with them now?"

When I questioned her about what she meant, she explained how burdened she was for her friends in New Jersey who did not know Jesus. She decided that if she could get them to sing about Him, they would at least think about Him during the song. When the homeroom teacher did his paperwork, Molly led the class in choruses. She wondered who would share Jesus with them now.

God prepared good works in advance for us to do. If we don't do them—if we don't sing with them—who will?

Dear Lord, help us to do the works You have prepared in advance for us to do while we are on earth. In Jesus's name, amen.

# ❀ Help for the Helpers ❀

*Praise be to the Lord, to God our Savior, who daily bears our burdens*
(Psalm 68:19).

Does the thought of leadership terrify you? Many people automatically put up defenses when asked to assume a leadership role. They assume they are inadequate or ill-equipped for the task.

It may comfort you to learn that most biblical leaders experienced the same thing. Moses, one of the greatest leaders of all times, felt so inadequate that he tried to convince God to choose someone else to free the children of Israel (Exodus 4:13).

God confirmed His call to Moses. However, God sent Moses's brother, Aaron, to help him. If you carefully read the account of the plagues, you will see that Aaron first spoke to Pharaoh and raised the staff to evoke God's judgment. It wasn't until sometime later that Moses was able to speak and act on his own.

I find great comfort in knowing that when God calls us to leadership, He provides the help and support we need to accomplish His purposes. For example, King David had the mighty men of valor to help him assume the throne (1 Samuel 22:1–2; 2 Samuel 23:8–38). Throughout the Book of Acts we find that Barnabas, John Mark, Silas, Luke, and others served as Paul's colaborers.

Of course, Jesus was the greatest leader of all times. Yet even He had helpers to aid with the work that He came to do. He could have called 12 legions of angels (Matthew 26:53), but He chose to accomplish much of His work through human helpers, most of whom did not consider themselves leaders.

Today's verse reveals the greatest help any leader can have. God daily bears our burdens. When He calls us, He carries us!

Several years ago, my husband, Wayne, was chosen to chair a county-wide evangelistic crusade. Even though he felt led to accept, the task ahead seemed overwhelming. However, at the first organizational meeting, a group of women who are known for being prayer warriors filed into the room. He knew everything would be fine. God indeed had provided help for the helper. He does so every day.

Dear Lord, thank You for giving us the support we need to lead.
In Jesus's name, amen.

# ❀ *Lord, Rescue Me* ❀

*But you, O Lord, be not far off; O my Strength,*
*come quickly to help me* (Psalm 22:19).

I lay drifting off to sleep in a Christian camp in Honduras, where women had walked miles for a nationwide women's prayer retreat. We had ridden in a missionary's jeep on a bouncy ride up the mountain. After dinner, we had watched a Christian clown perform, laughing until our sides ached. We also had listened to beautiful hymns, sung in Spanish and English. Several of us gave testimonies of God's love.

Tired after a long-but-wonderful day, in a twilight zone before sleeping, I turned toward the wall. For a second, I thought I saw something move. *I am really tired*, I thought, looking at three large knotholes in the gray wood close to my face. *Those flat knotholes couldn't possibly move.* Then all three moved in tandem, as if one thing. I jumped flat-footed to the floor.

"What is it?" my roommate asked.

"I'm not sure. I thought I saw those three knotholes—as big as my hand—move!"

They moved again and I screamed.

Immediately several missionaries entered our room, flipping on the light. Others followed, carrying brooms. Chaos ensued. Women in pajamas ran everywhere, swatting spiders. Shouting, *"Mu-erto! Mu-erto."* After the chaos was over, one missionary lingered to help move my bed away from the wall.

"What were they shouting?" I asked. "Does *mu-erto* mean *dead*…spiders are dead?"

"No," she said. "They said you were blessed to survive. One bite, and *you would have been dead.*"

Soberly I lay down, thanking God for His goodness in watching over me. I thanked Him that I saw the spider twitching just before it attacked me, and I thanked Him for new friends with dead aim who were good at spider-hunting. I fell asleep remembering Psalm 17:15. *"And I—in righteousness I will see your face; when I awake, I will be satisfied with seeing your likeness.'"* *And nothing but Your likeness. Just Your holy face, Lord. No spiders, please!* I whispered, as I drifted off to sleep.

Father, help us to remember that You are ever near, to love,
save, and rescue us. Amen.

# ❀ *Straight to Her Heart* ❀

*For the word of God is living and active. Sharper than any double-edged sword, it penetrates even to dividing soul and spirit, joints and marrow; it judges the thoughts and attitudes of the heart*
(Hebrews 4:12).

The retreat planners asked me to teach my book, *The Creation Diet: God's Pattern for Health, Happiness, and Holiness*. Part way through the third session, the Holy Spirit led me to stop what I was teaching and switch to another subject. As I stood at the podium continuing to address the items on the listening guide, I inwardly rationalized all the reasons why it made no sense. Finally, I knew that I would disobey God if I didn't heed His leading.

I closed my Bible and moved away from the podium, explaining to the attendees what was happening. I transitioned into a teaching on how the major milestones in the gestation of a baby in the womb correspond to the biblical feasts in Leviticus 23. When I finished, the room was completely silent as the presence of the Holy Spirit filled the auditorium.

After the final service and a time of farewell, I packed my things to load the car. A woman came into the empty auditorium and asked to speak with me. She explained how after the first two sessions she wrote in her journal that she did not agree with my teaching. She felt I took the Bible too literally. However, when I taught about the correlation between the gestation of a baby and the feasts, she was overwhelmed with emotion. She had studied in depth the development of babies and affirmed what I had taught.

She said, "I now know the Bible is true. I can hardly wait to get home and study to see what else is in there."

I didn't understand why God led me to stop teaching and switch to another subject. However, God knew the exact part of His Word that would go straight to her heart. And it did!

Dear Lord, help us to obey even when we don't understand
what You are doing. In Jesus's name, amen.

# ❀ Transition ❀

*And if I go and prepare a place for you, I will come back and take you
to be with me that you also may be where I am* (John 14:3).

I rarely read obituary columns in newspapers. However, I realize that many
people read these columns each day as if they want to digest each person's
biographical sketch.

Recently, my husband, Wayne, noticed an unusual phrase in one of the
memorial tributes and read it aloud to me. Someone died following a brief
illness and the article stated, "She made her transition on...."

We have read phrases such as "died," "passed away," or "went to be
with the Lord," but never had we heard "making a transition." Isn't that
a beautiful way to express the fact the person has now gone to the place
promised to each believer by our loving Lord and Savior, Jesus Christ?

Jesus assured one of the thieves from the Cross, as recorded in
Luke 23:43, *"Today you will be with me in paradise."* The thief could not
descend from his own cross to be baptized or to do any good works.
This thief's simple statement of his own faith professed that he clearly
believed Jesus was the Son of God, the Savior: *"Lord, remember me when
you come into your kingdom"* (Luke 23:42). Jesus promised that because of
his faith, the thief would be with Him that very day.

The thief made his transition from the Cross into the glorious presence
of Jesus in Paradise. We can do the same through simple faith in our Savior.

David proclaimed in Psalm 23:4, *"Though I walk through the valley of the
shadow of death, I will fear no evil, for you are with me."* With the same confident
assurance of David, the thief on the Cross, and others who have walked
before us, we can make our transition in perfect peace and security.

Dear Lord, thank You for life and for Your promise of eternal life with You. May
I trust You however You lead me to make my transition into Your glorious
presence. In Jesus's name, amen.

# ❀ Avoiding the Tangled Mess ❀

*Pursue peace with all people, and holiness, without which no one will see the Lord* (Hebrews 12:14 NKJV).

Christmas is over, and it's time to undo the tree. You dread the task of removing and storing those frustrating strings of lights. As you wrestle with the scrambled mess, you decide to lay the frustration aside to take a break. Days pass, and you continue to step over the tangled pile. Finally in desperation, you throw the jumble of lights in a box, expecting to feel more inclined to untangle the mess next Christmas when it's time to trim the tree.

Next December rolls around. As you open the box and relive the frustration, you decide it's easier to throw the lights away and start fresh this year. An hour later, you're standing at the checkout counter pulling money out of your wallet for a large container of stringed lights, not tangled — yet.

Sometimes a relationship becomes a wearisome mess of tangles and knots. It's no fun to stay the course and patiently work on restoring the relationship, one twist and turn at a time. However, if you lay the problems aside out of frustration, don't be surprised if days or weeks later nothing has improved.

Should you ignore the mess, burying your problems and expecting to address them later? When those problems resurface, you may very well feel that it would be much easier simply to toss the relationship aside and start fresh with someone new. However, unlike a cheap string of lights, a relationship has value that cannot be replaced. The relationship a believer builds with another believer is a blessing from God to strengthen and encourage each other. Relationships with nonbelievers create a chord of communication through which the gospel can be shared with those who need Christ. Relationships are too valuable to toss aside when problems arise.

Relationships will have their frustrating moments, but God has given us the instruction to be active and diligent in maintaining harmony in our relationships: pursue peace. Following God's instruction swiftly and prayerfully, we can keep a small tangle in a relationship from becoming an unmanageable knot.

Dear Father, am I giving up on a relationship too easily?
I want to pursue peace with others. Amen.

# ❦ Hershey Bar in the Sky ❦

*The heavens declare the glory of God;*
*the skies proclaim the work of his hands* (Psalm 19:1).

One night my father drove our family outside the city to a field in the country. Far away from the street lights, we were amazed at the bright stars. I've never forgotten that night—the beginning of my awareness of the universe. Daddy named every constellation. Then he showed us a hazy spot in the sky, with millions of stars clustered in a giant band above us. "That's the Milky Way," he said proudly, "like the candy bar."

Today we know the Milky Way is our galaxy, where Earth hangs in space, but that magic night, we seemed far away from a vast universe of miraculous wonder.

Weeks later, my Aunt Alice and I were talking in the backyard one night. "I know what that clump of stars is," I said proudly. "It's the Hershey bar!" She burst out laughing.

Needless to say, my mistake was the joke of the family for years—every time we went outside at night. "There's the Hershey bar!" (followed by giggles) always added levity to any occasion.

Sometimes we just get it wrong, don't we? We don't understand the majesty of God's creation. We can't even use the right words to describe it! We don't understand what a great part of God's plan we are, how He intends us to be the incarnation of His love for the whole universe (or at least, for the Milky Way, our own galaxy. Or if we can't get a handle on that—at least, for this planet).

Take time today to look into the sky. Do you see the heavens declaring the glory of God? Can you honestly say you get it? As the skies proclaim the work of His hands, do we—who also are the work of His hands—proclaim Him? Do others see us declaring His glory and proclaiming the work of His hands?

Lord, forgive us when we feel inadequate to display Your love before others.
May our hands and feet become Yours as we serve others. May our love become
Yours as we care for others. Amen.

# ❀ An Amazing View ❀

*"Call to Me, and I will answer you, and show you great and mighty things, which you do not know"* (Jeremiah 33:3 NKJV).

Consider a pair of binoculars. There's nothing especially impressive about their shape or appearance. They are generally very dull to look at; nothing about them compels you to find them interesting or of any worth at all. Unless, that is, you know what the binoculars are able to do. Once you realize they strengthen your sight, it's hard not to pick up a pair when you have them in arm's reach. Once you've used the binoculars to your satisfaction, you can appreciate their worth and look forward to another time of delighting yourself with a long view.

It's one thing to be interested in the binoculars. A step further is to appreciate their abilities. But it's quite a different thing to give them personal value, at the moment of a deep need to see beyond what's possible with only your limited vision, and you pick up the binoculars with sincere gratitude. That's the funny thing about binoculars.

As followers of Christ, we know we need God. We have become familiar with His wonderful attributes, His power, and His might. We find Him compelling. We have lived under God's leadership and enjoyed His presence in our lives. We've experienced memorable "God moments" that enriched our life journey, and we look forward to the next opportunity to accomplish something wonderful for the kingdom of God with His guidance and help. However, it is when we begin to long for something more—when we desire to attain something beautiful and spiritual and lofty, something beyond the normal that extends to the extraordinary, when we aspire to see what we've never seen and we realize we must fully rely on the power of God to move us beyond the periphery to go to incredible heights of servanthood for Jesus Christ—that we begin to deeply sense the value of holy God. How magnificent it is to rely upon the Lord fully.

Father, You are an amazing God. I am in awe of You. I long to completely rely upon You for every aspect of my ministry for the kingdom of God.
Take me deeper, Lord, I pray. Amen.

# ❀ Ready for Change ❀

*And do not be conformed to this world, but be transformed by the renewing of your mind, that you may prove what is that good and acceptable and perfect will of God* (Romans 12:2 NKJV).

*Something's got to change.* Have you ever whispered those words? I've made that resolution many times, sometimes with the hopefulness of wide open spaces I had recently cleared to make room for God to move, and I've said those words in desperation as I sobbed over a sink filled with dirty dishes with two toddlers climbing my skirt. Your life can change, and the change begins in you.

Notice I didn't say the change begins *with* you, but *from God*. We are flawed creatures made of dust,. However, God is able and willing to make incredible transformations in your life. Not us staring at life's challenges and wishing something would change, but having courageous tenacity that jumps in with God's power and confidence in Christ. You reject that which leads you down a path of spiritual dullness—conformity to the world—and embrace that which places you on God's pottery wheel as wet clay ready to be molded and shaped—submitting your mind to the Holy Spirit to make new your thoughts toward God.

Change is not always good merely for the sake of change. Don't run down the first open path you see. You want only to be transformed by God's power, not to be molded by your own will, fears, fleshly desires, or the temptations of the world. You want to live out God's perfect will for you. Anything less is robbing yourself and cheating the kingdom of God.

God welcomes you to enter His presence to say, "Lord, something's got to change." Your challenge is to allow God to be sovereign in your life, determining when the change will occur, and what is going to change. Perhaps your circumstances will change, or maybe your scenery, but don't be surprised if the greatest change occurs within you! Welcome the transformational power of the Holy Spirit.

Heavenly Father, I need Your transformational power in my life.
I don't want to be conformed to any image of the world.
I submit my life for renewal by Your Spirit. Amen.

# ❀ Coming Home ❀

*But while he was still a long way off, his father saw him* (Luke 15:20).

Jesus shared a story in Luke 15 about a son who demanded his inheritance from his father, then left to party hearty in a far-away country. After the money was long gone, he found himself in the pigs' mess hall, elbowing porkers for a bowl of slop.

At that point "he came to his senses" and remembered his father's house, not with disdain, but with the clear hindsight of a man whose foolishness had left him friendless, famished, and fearful. All of his father's blessings awaited him back home. No groveling with swine; his father's table was always filled with food. No cold, miserable nights in a street alley; all the beds in his father's house sported down comforters. No more loneliness; in his father's house there were perpetual celebrations with friends.

What the son missed most, though, was not the sweet wine or the all-day buffet, or even the comfortable warm bed. All the goodies his father provided could fill his stomach and warm his feet, but they could not satisfy his soul. More than anything, the wayward child missed his father.

The son remembered his father's smell when as a small boy the son had snuggled against his dad's chest and fallen asleep against the deep rumble of his laughter. He remembered how his father's arms flung open wide to catch him, when as a toddler he had jumped like superman from the front porch step. Never once did he worry whether his father would drop him; his father could be trusted.

In the end, it was his father's love that gave him courage to climb out of the pig-pen, shake the mud from his sandals, and with head hung low and swine stench preceding him, walk the long road home. How did the father respond? *"His father saw him and was filled with compassion for him; he ran to his son, threw his arms around him and kissed him"* (Luke 15:20).

Wherever you are, dear child, the Father sees you. Whatever you've done, the Father still eagerly looks for you. Get up; turn your face toward home. The Father is waiting.

Father, I have failed badly. But I want to come home.
Thank You for loving me through it all. Amen.

# ❀ *Yep!—Nope!* ❀

*"Simply let your 'Yes' be 'Yes,' and your 'No,' 'No'; anything beyond this comes from the evil one"* (Matthew 5:37).

An Arabian proverb states, "Four things come not back: the spoken word, the sped arrow, the past life, the neglected opportunity." Who among us has not been stung by the words of others or have regretted words we said which hurt others?

I imagine we all know someone who is considered to be "a man (or woman) of few words." Their responses, when asked a question, usually are one-word replies like *Yep, nope* or *yes, no*! They generally do not elaborate or share many details in their conversations, and their answers are clear with no verbiage that requires interpretation.

My husband, Wayne, is quite a conversationalist. He is very open and friendly and is the epitome of an extrovert. He truly enjoys people.

As a certified personality trainer (through CLASS), I describe Wayne as an off-the-charts sanguine personality. While grading one of Wayne's responses to a question in a particular class, a college professor once wrote, "Do you have to be so verbose?" I often remind my dear husband that the person with a sanguine personality needs to share about one-half of what comes to mind. Wayne is learning this and tries to reel himself in if he finds his verbosity gaining ground.

The person who finds conversation difficult may not be as enjoyable to be around as the outgoing gabber, but in reality he or she is right on target with simple responses. According to the Lord Jesus, clear responses leave no room for misunderstanding or misinterpretation. And, according to Scripture, a simple response with no exaggeration definitely assures that you are not led by the evil one whose influence may confuse and cause conflict and hurt.

Lord, please guard my lips and help me simply say yes to the right and no to the wrong, as You help me to know the difference. In Jesus's love, amen.

# ❧ Leaving a Legacy ❧

*Only be careful, and watch yourselves closely so that you do not forget*
*the things your eyes have seen or let them slip from your heart as long*
*as you live. Teach them to your children and their children after them*
(Deuteronomy 4:9).

My son Joshua came into the house one day and said, "Mom, I really miss Dad." He paused as we thought of his father who had died a year before. Then he smiled. "At least Dad could cook!" What a legacy I'm leaving my children: the mom who didn't cook! Oh, I do cook sometimes, but Joshua remembered special meals his father had cooked for him.

What about our legacy? God told the Israelites to be sure to remember the things they saw. They had seen Moses able to talk to Pharaoh about their leaving Egypt. They had seen their firstborn sons spared after they painted their doorposts with lamb's blood, before they hurriedly ate flatbread, ready to escape. They had seen God destroy the mighty Egyptians after the Israelites had crossed the Red Sea on dry land. They watched miracle after miracle in the desert as God provided food, water, and directions on their way toward the Promised Land. They knew firsthand who God was. He had even given them His Word in writing.

The Israelites were God's chosen people. Since His promise to their forefather Abraham, they had a destiny: being a blessing to all nations. They had a different worldview from any other in the world at that time. They were a people of faith—not in idols—but in the one invisible God.

What a legacy they left us: a record in Holy Scriptures of their history and God's commandments for "the good life." They had hope for relationship with the eternal God. At God's command, they remembered the things their eyes had seen. Obediently, they taught their children God's principles.

Are we leaving a legacy grounded in such a legacy? Teaching our children how to be good Christians, godly parents, how to be great tithers? Do they know how to love because we taught them? Do they know how to become great prayer warriors because they've seen us on our knees?

May each of us be careful to remember the things our eyes have seen. May our worldview always reflect a God-view! May we remember to teach God's ways to our children so they can teach others down through the generations!

Dear Lord, thank You for the legacy You have for us. Help us to share our God-centered worldview and leave a godly legacy. Amen.

# ❀ On the Doorstep ❀ with Love in Hand

*Beloved, let us love one another; for love is of God; and every one that loveth is born of God, and knoweth God* (1 John 4:7 KJV).

When Joan answered the doorbell, she found her friend Sarah, face beaming, holding a wrapped gift.

"Merry Christmas! I've brought you a present."

"Thanks," said Joan. "It's so big! I can't wait to open it."

Sarah's smile suddenly turned into a look of uneasiness as she shuffled her feet on Joan's doormat.

"Sarah, is something wrong?"

Sarah paused for a moment, then began, "Well, I thought you had a gift for me, too. Joe saw you in a store yesterday, and he said it looked like you were shopping for me. So, I went and bought something for you."

Joan's heart sank to her stomach and her faced turned red. "Sarah, I'm sorry. I was picking out a gift for my sister."

Sarah took the present from Joan's hands and headed for her car. "That's OK. I'll just exchange this for something for me." Joan stood at the doorway, empty-handed and confused at her friend's concept of giving.

What if we decided to give presents only to people who also have something for us? The message in this sort of gift-giving would not be love, but selfishness. God loved the world so much that He sent Jesus to save us, even before we were willing to love Him in return (Romans 5:8). Jesus shed His blood out of love for all people, even those who choose to reject Him.

Jesus stood at your heart's door with the gift of eternal life in His hands, and you opened that door empty-handed when you welcomed Jesus in to be your Savior. God's love is your example. The Lord has called you to love. You can express that love by showing up on the world's doorstep with your gift of love in hand, knowing that the lost around you who open the door may not be able to love you in return.

Dear God, because I know You and have experienced Your love, I want to reach out in love to others without expecting anything in return. May Your love flowing through me make a difference in a hurting soul today. Amen.

# ❁ The Shadow of the Cross ❁

*And she gave birth to her firstborn, a son.*
*She wrapped him in cloths and placed him in a manger,*
*because there was no room for them in the inn* (Luke 2:7).

I wonder when Mary realized how each element surrounding Jesus's birth (Luke 2:1–20) also foreshadowed His death, burial, and resurrection. He was wrapped in strips of linen at His birth and at His death. (John 19:40) He was born in a borrowed stable and was buried in a borrowed tomb (Matthew 27:60).

In addition, an angel announced Jesus's birth, and an angel announced His resurrection. (Matthew 28:5) Shepherds were the first recorded visitors to behold *"the Lamb of God, who takes away the sin of the world!"* (John 1:29). Even the gift of myrrh brought by the wise men (Matthew 2:11) was a spice used for preparation of the dead (John 19:39).

Whatever season you read this poem I wrote many years ago, I pray it inspires you to praise the Christ of Christmas, the Savior of the world!

The shadow of the Cross was upon the manger there
As Mary held her baby close, and wonder filled the air.
A night of joy, a night of peace, now gone were all her fears.
But did she know as she held Him close, her joys would turn to tears?

Shepherds gazing, angels singing, gold, frankincense, and myrrh,
All of these must have been very strange to her.
How could she know as she pondered them and kept them in her heart
That each one would, at the end of His life, come to play a part?

Shepherds watching over sheep—He would be God's own Lamb.
Costly gifts of burial spices accompanied Him to His tomb.
Angels singing, "He's not here; He's risen from the dead!"
Could she have known that all of these were as the prophets said?

Gentle Mary, meek and mild, chosen for joy and for sorrow,
Enjoy tonight, hold memories tight, don't worry about tomorrow.
Just hold your baby close to you, tonight you gave birth to the Christ.
But, the shadow of the Cross is there and will be all His life.

Dear Lord, I can only say, "Thank You!" In Jesus's name, amen.

# ❀ Day Runner ❀

*So teach us to number our days, that we may gain a heart of wisdom*
(Psalm 90:12 NKJV).

I look at my personal calendar several times a day. Occasionally I find relief as I look at my daily square in the mornings and find very little or nothing written down that I must do, but most days that little square is filled with what promises to be a very busy day. No wonder the calendar company named this model of calendar a "day runner."

The psalmist prayed that we human beings would live wisely because we have grasped the brevity of life. Misuse of time can fall into more than one category. Are you a loafer? The lazy person says, "I'll put this ministry task off another day. There's still time to do it later." Procrastination is taking a gamble that the following day will have a free block of time to complete yesterday's work. Today will never be lived out again. Today has its own opportunities for accomplishments for the kingdom of God, and they may very well expire with the setting of the sun.

Perhaps you have no luxury to loaf even if you wanted to—you spend each day in a taxing sprint. The busy person is equally in need of a wise approach to time management. Busyness can become an addiction, and feeding the addiction takes a terrible toll on the body as well as the mind. The woman in motion will find great fulfillment when she has yielded her calendar, hour by hour, to the Holy Spirit. Unnecessary frustrations and internal conflicts can be avoided for the busy gal when she is where God wants her, when God wants her, doing the ministry God has called her to do. Because she has learned to number her days, she realizes she has a specific calling to positively affect the world for Christ, so she focuses her attention where God has perfectly suited her to serve.

Do you long for wisdom? Ask God to help you rethink your view of personal time.

> Father, only You know my number of days, but I desire for each day
> to count for Your glory. Teach me to treasure each day and
> submit each moment to Your authority. Amen.

# ❊ Lead Me Home, Lord ❊

*May the God of peace… equip you with everything good for doing his*
*will, and may he work in us what is pleasing to him*
(Hebrews 13:20–21).

A missionary took me through an inner city in South America, where traffic was madness. At several four-way stops, cars swerved near other speeding vehicles, re-forming multiple lanes in each direction! I watched several cars sideswipe others, ignoring responsibility for damage.

On the way home, we came to an impassable intersection. Vehicles lined up like bumper cars, with pairs in opposite directions immobilized hood to hood, horns honking, arms waving, and drivers shouting expletives. An SUV charged—shoving us aside, gouging a large dent in the missionary's door. To my surprise, she jumped out, running after the perpetrator and ordering a bicycler to find a policeman. Since the SUV was stuck in traffic in the next block, the missionary reached him, hammering on his door with her fists. She left me alone in the middle of the intersection, trapped in the standoff. I listened to all the insults, horns, and crashing noises as cars used force to push others aside.

Then she returned, her skirts swishing as she plowed through the intersection. She thanked the boy on the bicycle, who had brought a policeman to catch the culprit and settle the matter.

"We do this often," she said nonchalantly, jumping into the car and wheeling out of the intersection. "It's every man for himself here."

"I see," I said, but clearly I didn't understand South American ways.

At the seminary, I faced other culture shocks. Puzzled when a professor gave me two large bottles of water "for teaching," I began teaching mentoring principles with a melting marker. Warm bodies hung out the windows in the steamy night with mosquitoes swarming. In damp clothes, I finished both bottles of water. Listeners interrupted several times to ask whether a mentor should use beatings or harsh words to punish a mentee, or *merea*\*. I recommended mercy.

Later, I thanked God for His mercy, allowing us to lead others in His ways, in spite of our shortcomings.

Lord, help us cross barriers of misunderstanding when we lead. Amen.

---

*\*Hebrew word for the friend being mentored. For information on mentoring with a merea, read* Woman to Woman: Preparing Yourself to Mentor *(www.newhopepublishers.com or 1-800-968-7301).*

# ❀ The Front Seat ❀

*In all your ways acknowledge him, and he will make your paths
straight* (Proverbs 3:6).

The summer before college my mom, dad, sister, and I visited a church in a rural Louisiana town where my dad preached "in view of a call," meaning the church was considering asking him to become their pastor. My year-younger sister, Lynna Rea, and I sat near the front with our mom. Behind the pulpit facing the congregation the choir sat stoically, except for two teen guys wearing Cheshire-cat grins and staring. I wasn't interested. I wanted to go home.

While I pondered the unfairness of life, the guys strategized a way to divvy up the prey. During my dad's sermon they pondered which guy would take which girl. Finally, they decided the younger guy would take the younger sister, and, as older guy, Randy would take the older sister.

At the end of the service, Smiley One and Two invited us to go to the root beer stand. The foursome transition into couples was seamless. I was shorter and obviously younger, so Randy's younger friend made a beeline to my side and graciously opened the car door to the back seat, while Randy and my sister took the front seat.

Right away something felt off kilter. We engaged in light chitchat, which yielded the information that I was older than my sister. Silence fell. Clearly, the guys recognized this as a crisis.

"You gotta move to the front," said the guy beside me.

"Why?" I asked.

"'Cause he's older, and he's supposed to take the older girl."

"You're kidding, right?"

Both guys climbed out of the car to escort us to our proper positions. My sister and I complied, thinking we'd stumbled onto a couple of nuts. But I had to admit, once the change was made, the universe righted itself.

Now that Randy and I have been married for three decades, I sometimes think about how God used a seemingly insignificant event to orchestrate my life's course. I shouldn't be surprised. The Lord promised that if I consider His will as I go along, He will direct my path. But who could have guessed that He would even orchestrate my sitting in the front seat of a car?

Lord, You promise to guide us if we seek You in all our ways,
even in the small things. Looking back, I can see You are faithful
to Your promise. Thank You. Amen.

# ❀ When My Heart ❀ Came Home Again

*For what I received I passed on to you as of first importance, that Christ died for our sins according to the Scriptures, that he was buried, that he was raised on the third day according to the Scriptures*
(1 Corinthians 15:3–4).

My college years brought with them a faith crisis. Even though I was raised in a loving home and accepted Christ at a young age, I became confused and uncertain about my beliefs.

Existentialism, basically the belief that the world is meaningless and absurd, was the philosophy of the day. Many professors of that day espoused this theory.

The more I heard teachings that challenged my beliefs, the more confused I became about what I believed and why I believed it. As dark as that period was, I am grateful I experienced it. I emerged stronger in my faith and more certain of why I feel Christianity is true and Jesus is the one, true God.

Recently I met a professor from South Korea who is a new believer. I asked how she had come to faith in Christ. She explained that as she explored various religions, she realized that Confucius, Mohammed, Buddha, Hindu philosophers, and Taoist philosophers all were searching for truth. When she read that Jesus said, *"I am the truth,"* her search ended. She had found the way of truth.

Much like this young professor, when I confirmed that my faith was true, I felt that my heart had come home again. The simple truths I'd learned as a child really are the core of Christianity and of life.

If you are going through a period of doubt, please recognize that you're in good company. Many of the biblical heroes of the faith went through times of doubt. However, once they recognized who God is and who they were in relationship to Him their faith was renewed and restored.

Is it time for your heart to come home again? You'll never find complete happiness and fulfillment until it does.

Dear Lord, thank You for allowing us to question so we can grow in our faith. Thank You even more for giving us answers through Your truth. In Jesus's name, amen.

# ❃ *Precious in His Sight* ❃

*"Ask and it will be given to you; seek and you will find; knock and the door will be opened to you"* (Matthew 7:7).

My favorite movie is *Cinderella*. In the story, the main character's mother is deceased. Her father loves and adores her, but he soon meets and marries a widow with two daughters close to Cinderella's age. However, the father doesn't know his new wife is unkind to Cinderella when he's away. When the father dies, Cinderella's stepmother's true colors come out. She makes Cinderella do all the household chores and wear rags, while doting on the two well-dressed stepsisters, who don't do any work. Poor Cinderella works morning, noon, and night.

Not having time to make other friends, Cinderella befriends animals around the house: a dog, horse, mice, and birds. They love Cinderella because she has a gentle spirit about her.

Sometimes in life we may feel like Cinderella. We perceive we've been mistreated and our inheritance taken from us. We feel like slaves to the world—our families, our employers, even our communities or churches. When we spiritually "sit in the cinders," remember, we can have hope from Christ. Just as Cinderella had everything restored to her in the end, we can know, also, that our inheritance is safe. God will never mistreat us or violate our trust. He'll never leave us, or forsake us. He alone cares enough to lift us from the cinders of life and grant eternal life with joy. Jesus said, *"For the Son of Man came to seek and to save what was lost"* (Luke 19:10). When we ask, He gives; when we seek, we find, and when we knock, He opens the door and comes into our hearts.

Like Cinderella, we can believe in restoration—not through a fairy godmother who poofs pumpkins into carriages and rags into dazzling ball gowns—but through the one-and-only Christ who restores broken dreams. He restores a Christian worldview: all God's creatures are precious in His sight and can be redeemed. All of us children, born in His image, can be saved through His wonderful, sacrificial love.

Dear Lord, thank You for finding me and restoring all that was lost. May I show others they're valued by God, worthy of restoration. In Jesus's name, amen.

# ❀ *Arise and Shine* ❀

*"Arise, shine, for your light has come, and the glory of the LORD rises upon you"* (Isaiah 60:1).

Can't you imagine Isaiah's face aglow as he declares the magnificent truth of the glory of God's light? George Frideric Handel majestically set this verse to music. While composing "The Messiah," Handel felt God's presence by his side. Later someone told him that everyone admired his work. Handel responded that his desire was not that his listeners admire his work. Rather, he hoped his music would make them better people.

The glory of God's light can only make us better people. Faye Burgess Abbas, a vision-impaired singer, inspires thousands of people through her music. I first met Faye when she was a 15-year-old student at the school for the deaf and blind where I taught. She was led onto the stage during a concert to sing one song. That one song impacted my life in such a way that even now tears fill my eyes when I think of it.

She stood there in a flowing yellow gown with her high soprano voice pleading, "Savior, Like a Shepherd Lead Us." Faye is beautiful, and the song is beautiful. However, that is not what impacted my life in such a way. It was her sincerity that made the song such a memorable experience.

It was apparent through the way she sang that Faye knew the Shepherd personally. He indeed had led her from her physical darkness to His spiritual light.

Since then our family has enjoyed many wonderful times of ministry with Faye. The longer I know her, the more I realize how remarkable she really is. And, I see that still the glory of the Lord rises upon her!

Dear Lord, I truly want my life to be so filled with Your glory that it shines on those around me. Please help me live that way. In Jesus's name, amen.

# ❀ She Walked in Beauty ❀

*The sun has one kind of splendor, the moon another and the stars*
*another; and star differs from star in splendor* (1 Corinthians 15:41).

Like the heroine in a Lord Byron poem, Vera "walked in beauty like the night of…starry skies." Her husband, a retired minister, had a twinkle in his eye when he described her.

"She's always out, doing good," he said. "Tonight she's going to visit another man, Mr. G. I think she's in love with him."

"What?" I glanced at Vera.

He smiled. "She cooks meals for him, takes him magazines, mails his bill payments—even told me she loved Mr. G. with all her heart."

*Oh, no. Surely this couple isn't divorcing after all these years together*! I thought they were happy.

Her husband stopped smiling. "She never misses seeing him. Nobody loves him like Vera. Tomorrow she's giving him a birthday present— expensive, too!" I was already thinking about how they'd sell their house after the divorce.

Then they both laughed. Vera did have a man she visited, usually at night, since she often came home from work late: a 90-year-old shut-in with no relatives to care for him. (He had outlived his children and grand-children!) Her husband understood, but couldn't explain her deep fond-ness for Mr. G.; he just didn't have Vera's gift of mercy.

Vera loved unconditionally. Her husband laughed at the unexpected visitors she'd brought home from time to time: a kitchen full dinner guests— or maybe a box full of kittens.

God intended Christians to walk in beauty like a breathtaking night filled with stars. In fact, they are stars in God's eyes. Other people notice their special traits of mercy, administration, hospitality, teaching, or other spiritual gifts. God wired them in certain ways to build up the body of the Church and share His love with a world of people.

Mr. G. died a few years later, and a few years after him, Vera.

The stars seem a little brighter at night.

Creator God, thank You for Vera—an example of Your agape love. Like Vera, may we shine like bright stars in a dark world. Just as You made each star to *"differ in splendor,"* help us use our differences to glorify You. Amen.

# ❀ The Everything Party ❀

*Praise our God, O peoples, let the sound of his praise be heard: he has preserved our lives and kept our feet from slipping* (Psalm 66:8-9).

Nine people from the Sunday School class I taught were deployed to Saudi Arabia during Desert Storm. (Another devotional in this book provides more details.) They left in August and did not return until the following spring.

We decided as a class that upon their return we would celebrate all the holidays they missed while overseas. We called it "The Everything Party."

The artificial Christmas tree in our living room remained up from December until they returned home. On the day of the party, some class members came over to our home and decorated the rooms representing different holidays.

When the party began, we met at the church. We gave our military friends bags and invited them to come to the parsonage across the street to "Trick or Treat."

Then we enjoyed a Thanksgiving meal of turkey and dressing and all the trimmings. Afterwards we went into the living room and opened their Christmas gifts. Even though it was May, we also went around the neighborhood Christmas caroling. Our neighbors were such good sports they stood on their porches singing with us and waving good-bye as we walked away singing, "We wish you a Merry Christmas."

We moved on to Valentine's Day, St. Patrick's Day, and even celebrated with an Easter egg hunt.

Last, we went over to the church to celebrate our traditional New Year's Eve worship service. We timed it in such a way that we lit candles and walked out of the sanctuary of the church onto the porch at midnight wishing each other a Happy New Year. Everyone agreed that "The Everything Party" was the best celebration ever.

We were celebrating much more than holidays. We celebrated a loving God who had protected our friends and brought them safely home!

Dear Lord, thank You for rejoicing with us in times of happiness
and crying with us in times of sadness. In Jesus's name, amen.

# ❀ Take Down the Tree ❀

*And in this I give advice: It is to your advantage not only to be doing*
*what you began and were desiring to do a year ago; but now you also*
*must complete the doing of it* (2 Corinthians 8:10–11 NKJV).

Every Christmas, it's the same scenario. I enjoy decorating each room with reminders of the coming of our Savior. Then on New Year's Day, I turn into a robotic maniac, a woman with a cause; I channel my energy to do nothing but get my house back in order. Wreaths, stockings, and reindeer don't stand a chance against my driven fury to pack away all that is red and green.

I save the dismantling of our artificial trees for last. Finally, the end of the work is in sight! I carefully remove each ornament and secure it in protective wrapping, pull off the strings of lights, and then…and then…my husband and I procrastinate for several days before taking down each tree itself. It's such a scratchy, bothersome chore. Night after night as I rest on the couch, synthetic pine branches seem to taunt me: it's not over until it's over!

Serving in leadership positions brings many opportunities to do fulfilling work to honor the Lord. Starting a new ministry is exciting, and there's nothing like seeing the pieces fall into place. But eventually in any ministry, you reach a point when the work isn't so much fun anymore, or you have a hiccup because of a personal issue, or you're so in love with the process that you hate to finish it for having to say good-bye. Heed Paul's words from 2 Corinthians 8:10–11. It's to your advantage to finish what you've started. Just as the Christmas trees interfered with my rest on the couch, unfinished business (especially for the Lord) can weigh you down and leave you feeling defeated. As you bring one ministry task to completion, you'll find your hands free to pick up a new endeavor for the Lord, and your mind will be refreshed and ready to focus on a new beginning for the glory of God.

Heavenly Father, have I grown slack concerning anything
You've called me to do? I ask You now to give me the "want to" to complete
what I've started for Your glory. Amen.

# ❀ Our Amazing Savior, God ❀

*For by him all things were created: things in heaven and on earth, visible and invisible, whether thrones or powers or rulers or authorities; all things were created by him and for him. He is before all things, and in him all things hold together* (Colossians 1:16–17).

God has done an amazing thing for us. He delivered us out from under the authority and power of darkness. He changed our identity and transferred our destiny from that of children of darkness to children of His Son's kingdom. He loves His Son dearly, above all things, and it is all because of Him that we have been bought out of slavery to sin and have forgiveness for all our sins.

This Jesus, God's own beloved Son, is the perfect and complete manifestation of the invisible God. John the beloved assures us, *"For in Christ all the fullness of the Deity lives in bodily form, and you have been given fullness in Christ, who is the head over every power and authority"* (Colossians 2:9–10). He is above all creation. In fact, He was the agent through and by which all things were created: all things including the heavens, everything in and on earth, everything we see and everything invisible to the human eye—all levels of rulers, powers, and authorities in the spiritual realm.

Moreover, all things were created specifically for His good pleasure and purposes. He preceded and transcended all created things. Notice also that Christ not only created all things in the beginning, but also by His choice alone holds together and keeps all created things going in their present dynamic state moment-by-moment.

He is also the head of His body, the church. As the first to be raised from the dead, Christ opened the way for each of us who trusts Him to be raised from the dead, as well. What hope we have in Jesus Christ our Savior and Lord!

Lord Jesus, our Savior, You have created all things and sustain all things by the power of Your might. Thank You for sustaining believers each day of our lives.

# ✿ A Prayer from the Authors ✿

As you close the pages of this devotional book, we hope you will continue to reflect on the seven areas of missional living you have found within its covers, as you have sought to live in the passion and purpose of the Spirit and follow God's will for your life. We pray these daily times with Christ have enriched your life, led you closer to your Lord, and overflowed into your world.

In remembrance of our Savior's sacrifice, may almighty God empower you and His Holy Spirit use you daily in an abundant life of passion with purpose.


Kimberly Sowell, Edna Ellison, Joy Brown,

Tricia Scribner, and Marie Alston,

— Your will alone. We adore You, O Lord, our God!

New Hope® Publishers is a division of WMU®, an international organization that challenges Christian believers to understand and be radically involved in God's mission. For more information about WMU, go to www.wmu.com. More information about New Hope books may be found at www.newhopepublishers.com. New Hope books may be purchased at your local bookstore.

If you've been blessed by this book, we would like to hear your story. The publisher and authors welcome your comments and suggestions at: newhopereader@wmu.org

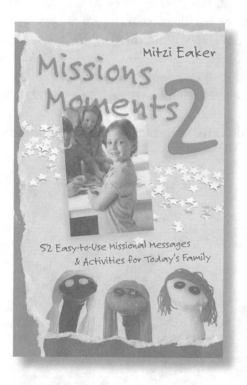